# Soldiers
## to the Last Day

# Soldiers to the Last Day

## THE RHINELAND-WESTPHALIAN 6TH INFANTRY DIVISION, 1935-1945

DENIS HAVEL

FONTHILL

*Den velassenen Söhnen—DMH*

Fonthill Media Language Policy

Fonthill Media publishes in the international English language market. One language edition is published worldwide. As there are minor differences in spelling and presentation, especially with regard to American English and British English, a policy is necessary to define which form of English to use. The Fonthill Policy is to use the form of English native to the author. Denis Havill was born and educated in the United States; therefore American English has been adopted in this publication.

Fonthill Media Limited
Fonthill Media LLC
www.fonthillmedia.com
office@fonthillmedia.com

First published in the United Kingdom and the United States of America 2019

British Library Cataloguing in Publication Data:
A catalogue record for this book is available from the British Library



ISBN 978-1-78155-744-0



Typeset in 10.5pt on 13pt MinionPro
Printed and bound in England

# Acknowledgments

I must first express my deep gratitude to Juanita Havill, who patiently and painstakingly prepared and formatted my manuscript. My thanks go also to Whitney Stewart, who over the past years has both located and made available to me critical source materials. Lastly, I extend my appreciation to my good friend Naomi Cox, who yet again gave me leave to dwell among the grey-clad ghosts of the past—and give them voice.

Denis Havel
May 2018, Mt. Carmel, IL

# CONTENTS

# Author's Note

In consideration that this work presents the German point of view, German words will not be italicized. German nouns with no distinctive plural or where context is lacking shall be provided the English plural. German nouns that do have a distinctive plural but are judged to be familiar to the military reader shall, likewise, employ the English plural, e.g. "Panzerfausts" instead of "Panzerfäuste." As for place names, those well-known will use the generally accepted English spelling; those lesser known, the German. For ease of reading, civilian time will be used in most instances and Arabic numbers employed for battalion designation instead of Roman numerals. The Soviet term "Front" refers to an army group ("Kalinin Front," "1st Ukrainian Front," "Central Front," etc.). The terms "Soviet" and "Russian" shall be used interchangeably.

## Dienstgrade (Ranks)

| | |
|---|---|
| Schütze | Private |
| Oberschütze | Private 1st Class |
| Gefreiter | Lance-Corporal |
| Obergefreiter | Corporal |
| Unteroffizier | Sergeant |
| Feldwebel | Company Sergeant Major |
| Oberfeldwebel | Battalion Sergeant Major |
| Hauptfeldwebel | Regimental Sergeant Major |
| Fähnrich | Ensign |
| Leutnant | Second Lieutenant |
| Oberleutnant | First Lieutenant |
| Hauptmann | Captain |

| | |
|---|---|
| Major | Major |
| Oberstleutnant | Lieutenant Colonel |
| Oberst | Colonel |
| Generalmajor | Major General |
| Generalleutnant | Lieutenant General |
| General der Infantry | General |
| Generaloberst | General |
| Generalfeldmarschall | Field Marshal |
| | |
| Kommandeur | Courtesy title for battalion and regimental commanders |

## Titles of Nobility

| | |
|---|---|
| Ritter | Knight |
| Freiherr | Baron |
| Graf | Count |
| Herzog | Duke |
| Prinz | Prince |
| König | King |
| Kaiser | Emperor |

# Introduction

Over the decades following World War II, the volume of literature devoted to the Wehrmacht surpasses that of nearly every other category of military studies in both the specialist and general markets. Surprisingly enough, this holds true even in those countries that were once Germany's most bitter enemies. Now, more than half a century after the war ended, the interest has not lessened; if anything, it has increased, greatly aided by the internet allowing quick access to records and sources, and the overall rapid dissemination of information.

During the war, a body of information concerning the German military was compiled by the intelligence services of the Allied nations, but hurried by necessity, much of this work was at best incomplete and at times erroneous. In the months following the collapse of the Third Reich, considerably more information was gathered from captured records and the interrogation of high-ranking prisoners. However, in time, this information was handed over to lawyers for prosecutorial purposes or to military clerks to be filed away, with a yawn, deep in the basement of military archives. The war was over, the world moving on, and besides, what of any value could possibly be learned from a defeated army?

The world did indeed move on, but not in the expected direction. The Western Allies fell out with their former Soviet ally to the extent that they were forced to admit that they had defeated one enemy only to be faced with a far more threatening opponent. As the Cold War settled in and the realization took hold that at any moment it could go hot, interest in the former German Wehrmacht revived; after all, its legions had almost brought the Soviet Union to its knees and had battled the Red Army for four long years. Perhaps there was something to be learned from the German campaigns in the East.

By the mid-1950s, with Germany having been restored to nationhood and becoming a member of the NATO Alliance, former members of the Wehrmacht were now willing to write of their experiences to a more receptive audience. Written by senior officers, these accounts of campaigns and battles could at times be self-serving and self-excusing, but in the main were objective analyses that contributed greatly to the understanding of the Wehrmacht's operations both in the East and West. These works were soon followed by the personal accounts of individual soldiers that, though limited by their nature in scope, did, at least, provide a glance into the internal workings of the Wehrmacht and what the war was like for the common German soldier. By the early '60s, many of these works had been translated and had become widely available to the military analyst, historian, and the general public. At this time, the primary focus of study was on what the German army and the German soldier had done. A decade later, all that changed.

In the wake of the debacle of the United States in Southeast Asia, a critical eye was turned upon the U.S. military for clearly not all was perfect with the army that had swept the "Nazis" from the field. This led to a sober reassessment of the U.S. Army's performance in World War II and a more accurate and realistic assessment of its German opponent that revealed that the achievements of the German Army were even greater than previously (and grudgingly) acknowledged. There arose a newfound professional respect for the German soldier that in some quarters bordered dangerously close to admiration. The focus of study then shifted from what the German soldier had done to how he could have done it, given the overwhelming odds that he faced.

Well-written analyses of the Wehrmacht's organization, doctrine, tactics, weapons, and even cultural factors all contributed to the body of knowledge and did propose some interesting hypotheses but no definitive answers, leaving the military analyst still shaking his head in astonishment as he attempted to comprehend the hardships suffered and the accomplishment achieved by the German soldier of that generation.

Whereas these previous studies generally dealt with the Wehrmacht as a whole or its campaigns and battles, a more recent trend is that of individual unit histories concentrating primarily on the divisions of the Waffen-SS or the panzer force. Unfortunately, the infantry divisions that made up nearly 80 percent of the Wehrmacht land forces have been largely ignored.

What follows is the history of the Rhineland-Westphalian 6th Infantry Division. Among the first divisions created by the Wehrmacht in 1934, it went on to establish one of the longest and bloodiest records of continuous combat of any division during the war—Allied or Axis. Engaging in its first combat within weeks of the outbreak of World War II, the division fought literally to the last hour of the war. Although it won its first laurels in the French campaign of 1940, the division received its reputation as one of the best three divisions of the Wehrmacht while on the Eastern Front as it engaged its Soviet opponent in combat, the extent and savagery of which has yet to be fully appreciated by Western analysts.

This present work recounts not only the story of the 6th Infantry Division but, perhaps more important, that of the men who served in its ranks. Their story is told not from the author's objective point of view but from theirs—from the general down to the common Landser, neither of whom had the luxury of detached objectivity. In a similar vein, the story is presented in the spirit of the times in which it occurred, leaving intact and without comment or condemnation the attitudes, beliefs, impressions, and emotions as well as the prejudices and misperceptions prevalent during that period. Only by being aware of the world in which the German soldier lived and how he viewed that world and himself can one hope to achieve any understanding of his actions and motivations and perhaps answer not only the questions of what the German soldier did and how he did it, but the more critical question of "why?"

## Silesian Prelude

Neustadt, Upper Silesia. 8 May, 11:50 p.m.

The general sat alone in his headquarters in a small house in a small town yet untouched by the war. In the dim light of a table lamp, he stared into the dying flames of the fireplace as the last of the documents burned away. Outside, the night was quiet. For the first time in six years, a silence reigned. In the flickering flames, he saw the years of his life burn away, and at times he saw again the faces of the young men he had sent into battle—all the young men he had sent to their deaths. Had he done right? As a soldier, he had fulfilled his oath. As a soldier, he had done his duty to Volk and Vaterland—but had he done right? That question would only be answered when he stood before God, and he was certain that that moment was near. He watched as the burning papers became crumpled grey ash—a bleak reflection of the war, the nation; his life.

Outside he heard a commotion in the street—vehicles, commands, boots pounding on cobblestones. They were coming for him. In a moment, the door would be flung open, and then? Perhaps a drunken Ivan, who would immediately riddle his body with a burst of submachine gun fire, or perhaps a sergeant or junior officer who would appreciate what a prize catch a general would be. No matter, but in a way, he preferred the former.

He rose from his chair, placed his gold-braided officer's hat on his head and adjusted the Knight's Cross, which hung from his collar. Then he turned to face the door, and calmly awaited his fate.

# 1

# From the Ashes

November 11, 1918: the day the guns fell silent and, indeed, a silence did descend along the entire Western Front from the English Channel to the Swiss border. Yet in the great cities of Paris, London, New York, and Rome, there was no great silence as church bells rang and crowds filled the streets to celebrate the end of a four-year nightmare of slaughter that had engulfed the nations of Europe. Any celebrations in Germany, however, were short-lived, particularly when it became apparent that the terms of the armistice were tantamount to admitting defeat.

The Kaiser was gone, the war lost, and the German Reich, which had come into existence only five decades before, was threatening to collapse, but the army yet remained, and to the military elites the army had to be preserved whatever the cost. In their view, the army was Germany. The army had created the German nation, the army had unified the German nation, and without the army, the German nation was lost.

If the terms of the armistice had been harsh, the terms of the Treaty of Versailles the following year were harsher still. In addition to being stripped of its colonies and one-sixth of its territory, Germany was forced to accept the blame for the war and was saddled with a reparation bill of 130 billion marks.

It was left to the politicians—not the generals—to sign this humiliating treaty for the army was to remain blameless. Its soldiers marched back to the Reich in the same manner they had left it—rank on rank, arms shouldered, and heads held high. For four years, they had suffered and died at the front. They had done their duty only to be "stabbed in the back" by Marxists, social democrats, and other traitors at home.

However, it would seem that not even the army would escape the vengeance of Versailles. Over a six-month period, the once mighty Kaiserheer was required to reduce its ranks to a mere 100,000 men—perhaps sufficient to maintain stability at home, but never again would the Prussian Army be allowed to threaten the peace of Europe. The military had no choice but to begin disbanding its regiments and send the soldiers home. Not all went home. As the military elites had feared, in the wake of defeat and the demise of the army, the nation was being torn apart by revolution and the threat of secession by some of its member states. Many of the demobilized troops—old "Frontkämpfer" who had grown so accustomed to war that they could not imagine a world without it, young leutnants whose youthful patriotism had been tempered into hardened steel and who refused to accept defeat, and older officers of the military caste who despised Marxism even more than they did liberal democracy—formed the various Freikorps and set about crushing the revolutionaries at home and battling Bolsheviks in eastern lands.

In the meantime, the army now renamed the Reichswehr got on with living under the restrictions of the Treaty of Versailles. Not only was the army limited to 4,000 officers, 20,000 non-commissioned officers, and 76,000 enlisted men, but the terms of services were extended to twenty-five years for the officers and twelve years for all other ranks, which would make it essentially impossible to build up a force of trained reserves available at short notice to expand the ranks of the Reichswehr.

The head of the new German Army at this time was Chief of Staff General Hans von Seeckt, a Schleswiger by birth, who had begun his military career in 1885 in the 1st Regiment of Grenadier Guards "Kaiser Alexander." During World War I, he had served as chief of staff to various corps and armies and had been the last Chief of the General Staff of the Kaiserheer in 1918. For him, his task was not to live within the restrictions of the Treaty of Versailles but to operate outside them and not be caught by the Allied Military Commission.

Limited as von Seeckt was to only 100,000 men, he made certain that those enlisted were the absolute best that Germany had to offer, and considering the state of the nation's economy with its high level of unemployment, there was no shortage of volunteers, which allowed the army to be exceptionally particular as to who was chosen to wear the "graue Rock" or grey tunic. Only the highest qualified applicants were accepted; indeed, they were typically overqualified for the duties to which they were assigned to the extent that rather than being a standing army of 100,000 men, it was actually a training cadre for 100,000 officers and senior NCOs.

Organized into seven infantry and three cavalry divisions and based in the old garrison towns throughout Germany, the new army trained constantly, at times clandestinely with weapons forbidden them, at times in foreign lands such as the Soviet Union far from the prying eyes of the Allied Military Commission—and always in the pursuit of perfection. New weapons were tested and new concepts of warfare were discussed among the officers, but in this pursuit of excellence and modernity, the "Old Army" was not forgotten—how could it be? It was ever present. Each company of the new divisions had the duty of "Tradition bearer" of one of the imperial regiments of the past of which it honored the memory in solemn ceremonies and bore its flag on parade. The men were surrounded by the legends and heroes of the past—the storming of the Spicheren Heights, the Grenadier Guards at St. Privat, "von Bredow's Uhlans of Death," and the martyrs of the Great War. The ghosts were everywhere.

One advantage of a small army, unforeseen by the Allies but definitely appreciated by the German military elites, was the greater ability to control and indoctrinate the troops. In former years with the mass conscription of the male population, the military was forced to deal with human material from the entire range of the cultural, social, and political spectrum. Although the military prided itself on its ability to transform civilians into soldiers, it recognized that at the core, the recruits were still civilians and that the instilling of the correct military mindset into the rank and file or even the junior officers was at best both superficial and temporary. Now with the opportunity to carefully select, train, and educate its recruits, the military could be assured that its members would all possess not only the highest level of professionalism but also the correct attitude towards their duty and role in German society and would form a solid core of a future German Army when the time came for the shackles of the Treaty of Versailles to be broken.

The time came in 1933. A new government had come to power, led by an Austro-Bavarian who had risen to prominence on the promises that he would tear up the Treaty of Versailles, restore Germany's greatness, and, most important, rearm the nation. He had made other promises as well, but unfortunately neither the military nor the German public paid these promises much heed.

The new chancellor, Adolf Hitler, was true to his word. Within a year of becoming chancellor, he had withdrawn from the League of Nations, repudiated the Treaty of Versailles, reintroduced conscription, and directed the Reichswehr to expand first to twenty-one divisions with 300,000 men and then to thirty-six divisions with 500,000 men.

Even though the National Socialist regime in its efforts to unify the nation into a single "Volksgemeinschaft" sought to minimize cultural differences, the military traditionalists persisted in the practice of referring to the divisions of the new army according to their regional origins. They also continued the custom of "Tradition bearer." As for the Rhineland-Westphalian 6th Infantry Division, its 18th Regiment bore the traditions and flags of the Westphalian 55th "Graf Bülow von Dennewitz" and the Lotharingian 158th Infantry Regiments. The 37th Regiment bore the traditions of the Ost-Friesen 78th "Herzog Friedrich von Braunschweig" and the Unter-Elsass 138th Infantry Regiments, and the 58th Regiment was entrusted with the banners of the Westphalia 15th "Prinz Friedrich der Niederlande" and the Westphalian 17th "Graf Barfuss" Regiments as well as those of the Westphalian 7th Jäger Battalion.

In addition to bearing the legacy of illustrious regiments of the past, the 6th Infantry Division could boast a pedigree of its own. Its 18th Regiment (established January 1, 1921) had been one of the original nineteen regiments of the Reichswehr. Formed from the Freikorps Gabke, Pfeffer, Hacketau, and Lichtschlag, it had been sent off in the spring of 1921 to battle communist uprisings in Saxony and Thuringia, where it quickly restored order. Three future feldmarschalls (von Reichenau, Model, and Busch) had served in its ranks as company commanders during the '20s. On November 4, 1938, the 18th Regiment received the distinct honor of being "given" to none other than the scion of the Prussian military, Generaloberst Gerd von Rundstedt, upon his retirement from the army (the first of several). As titular Kommandeur of the 18th Regiment, he would continue to wear the field-dress uniform and insignia of a regimental commander throughout the war even after he had been promoted to generalfeldmarschall.

If anything, the Rhineland-Westphalian 6th Infantry Division was representative of the "Old Army" with its traditions and attitudes deeply rooted in the aristocratic Prussian past. A full 10 percent of the division's officer corps was of the nobility either by birth or patent.

Although the rapid expansion of the armed forces demanded by the new chancellor would quite naturally bring to its ranks, ideas, and viewpoints not necessarily in conformity with those of the military establishment, the army made it quite clear in a proclamation of Reichspräsident von Hindenburg on May 24, 1934 how it saw its role in German society and what it expected of the German soldier.

> The Wehrmacht is the arms bearer of the German People. It is the protector of the Reich and Fatherland.... Service in the Wehrmacht is honorable service to the German People. A soldier's honor lies in his willingness to risk his life for the German People. The highest soldierly virtue is that of an aggressive spirit that demands hardness and decisiveness. Cowardice is shameful, hesitation unsoldierly. The basis of the Wehrmacht is obedience and the basis of obedience is trust.... Achievement in war or peace comes only from the unshakable bond between officer and man.
>
> Confident yet modest, loyal and upstanding, God-fearing and honest, discreet and incorruptible, the German soldier shall be a model of manliness to The German People.

Loyalty to the German nation and the German people. Obviously, very little had changed in the attitude of the military since the creation of the German Army in 1871. However, the Führer, as the new chancellor was now called, was not entirely satisfied with this proclamation and soon after the death of Reichspräsident von Hindenburg (August 2, 1934) required of the army an oath of loyalty to him personally:

> I swear by God this sacred oath of unconditional obedience to Adolf Hitler, the leader of the German Reich and German People and the Supreme Commander of the Wehrmacht and as a brave soldier shall be ready at all times to risk my life for this oath.

At the time, this oath caused no great concern among the ranks of the Wehrmacht, but in later years, there were those of the officer corps who found themselves having to choose between loyalty to the German people and loyalty to Adolf Hitler.

Faced with the task of expanding the armed forces, the new Wehrmacht had to consider the question of what type of armed force it would be. During the Reichswehr period, there had been no lack of discussions analyzing the cataclysm of the previous war, a war that had resulted in stalemate as the massive amounts of firepower made available by the industrialization of warfare prevented armies from advancing without suffering prohibitive losses. The problem was how to get the armies moving again. The solution seems to have been the armored tracked vehicle. First introduced by the British at the Somme in 1916 and later employed by the Western Allies, the tank had succeeded in allowing the armies to advance, but only slowly and still at a horrendous cost in lives. In and of itself, the tank could not be said to have been a war winner. In the final analysis, Germany succumbed to attrition in the field and starvation at home.

As is often the case, the vanquished—having no laurels upon which to rest—learn the most from the war. The western allies had come away with the notion that tanks supported the infantry advance, whereas the Germans, who had been on the receiving end of tank attacks and consequently in a better position to appreciate the threat that tanks posed, viewed the tank as a decisive weapon in its own right. Rather than distributing tanks among the infantry and advancing on a broad front, the war theorists of the Reichswehr gave thought to the idea of concentrating tanks to break through on a narrow front then thrusting deep to wreak havoc far behind enemy lines, cutting communications and rendering the enemy incapable of exercising command and control of his forces—in other words, "Blitzkrieg."

Among some in the Reichswehr, particularly those who had experienced the horrors of the trenches first hand, the enthusiasm for this new concept of warfare was so great that in view of the restrictions of the Treaty of Versailles, consideration was given to the idea of creating a highly mobile elite strike-force of only 100,000 men supported by what would essentially be a national militia. To these "reformers," the huge armies of mass conscripts that by their very size had become unmanageable and incapable of maneuver were relics of the past. The emphasis of the new style of warfare was to be on mobility and the rapid maneuver of specialized (armored) forces.

However, to the older generals—traditionalists to the core—the idea of dethroning the "Queen of Battle" and relegating the infantry to a subsidiary role was out of the question. In any future struggle, the German infantry would do as it had in the past—march steadfast upon the enemy and crush him. To ensure that the infantry would have a relevant role in modern war, its divisional structure was redesigned and organized on the basis of balance, flexibility, and firepower.

The standard German infantry division at the beginning of World War II had a regulation strength of 17,000 officers and men, and in brief consisted of three infantry regiments, an artillery regiment, a reconnaissance battalion, an anti-tank (Panzerjäger) battalion, a battalion of engineers, a replacement and training battalion, plus the various service units (communications, ordnance, medical, veterinary, transport, and supply).

The three infantry regiments, each with a strength of 3,000 officers and men, were divided into three 800-man battalions that were made up of three rifle companies and a heavy machine-gun company with six heavy machine guns and six 8.1-cm mortars. The twelve companies, with the 4th, 8th, and 12th Companies being the heavy machine-gun companies, were numbered consecutively throughout the regiment as follows: I Battalion (1–4); II Battalion (5–8); III Battalion (9–12). In addition, each infantry regiment had a howitzer company (13th) with six 7.5- and two 15-cm infantry howitzers and a Panzerjäger company (14th) with twelve 3.7-cm anti-tank guns.

As with most armies, the basic infantry unit was the company. A German rifle (Schützen) company had a combat strength of 180 men divided into three fifty-man platoons plus a weapons section with three anti-tank rifles and two heavy machine guns. The platoons in turn were divided into four ten-man squads plus a 5-cm mortar team. The firepower of a typical German infantry company was considerable consisting as it did of twelve light machine guns, two heavy machine guns, thirty machine pistols, three mortars, three anti-tank rifles, and some 100 rifles, giving it a decided advantage in sheer volume of fire over its counterparts in both the East and West.

Throughout the history of warfare, armies had always sought the concentration of forces and weapons to achieve victory on the battlefield. As concerns weapons, the German Army of World War II turned this long accepted and commonsensical maxim on its head. The distinguishing characteristic of German divisional organization was the deliberate dispersal of heavy or support weapons down to the smallest unit practical. Whereas in most armies a rifle squad consisted of ten men armed with rifles with perhaps one armed with a magazine-fed automatic weapon, in a German division, the lowly squad was provided with fire support in the form of a belt-fed light machine gun, ensuring that in a squad-on-squad collision the German squad would hold the advantage in firepower. At the next level, a German platoon even had its own "artillery support" in the form of a 5-cm mortar. Companies were provided with heavy machine guns and tank defense and battalions with medium mortars.

A German regiment was essentially a small division with its own infantry howitzers, anti-tank guns, and assault engineers. This decentralization or dispersal of heavy support weapons was in accordance with the German military doctrine of chaos, opportunity, and initiative ensuring that in the chaos of battle an enterprising unit commander from regimental Kommandeur down to the simple squad leader would have the necessary support weapons close at hand to take advantage of a local opportunity.

As regards the other divisional units, the artillery regiment was made up of four Abteilungen (battalions): three with twelve 10.5-cm howitzers and one with twelve 15.5-cm howitzers or 17-cm cannons for a total of forty-eight guns and a personnel of 2,700 officers and men. The reconnaissance battalion of some 600 men consisted of a motorized company, an infantry company mounted on bicycles, and a Reiter Schwadron (cavalry company). The Panzerjäger battalion was armed with thirty-six 3.7-cm anti-tank guns and had a unit strength of 600 men. The engineer battalion of 800 men was divided into three companies of which one was motorized. The training and replacement battalion (Feld Ersatz Battalion) of 500 men, though not normally counted in a division's troop strength, often functioned in the capacity of divisional reserve. The services and supply units of a division amounted to some 3,000 men, and although infantry divisions were provided with some motor transport, they still required the services of some 4,000 to 7,000 horses that, though seeming outmoded, later proved of great value during the campaign in Russia.

This basic structure of the standard German infantry division was maintained until 1942 when casualties and the increasing demands of the war necessitated alterations in organizations, personnel, and weapons.

From the ashes of defeat, the German Army had risen anew. As challenging as the demands of the Führer had been for the rapid expansion of the military, in only seventeen months—that is, by October 1936—the Wehrmacht had increased its numbers to over 500,000 men organized into twenty-one infantry and three panzer divisions. Over the next two years, these numbers would triple.

The generals had done all that had been demanded of them. They had delivered into the hands of their Führer the most advanced army in the world. They could only pray that he would use it wisely.

2

# Mobilization and War: First Blood

On August 25, 1939, the Rhineland-Westphalian 6th Infantry Division received its mobilization orders. Throughout Wehrkreis VI, the quiet garrison towns of Bielefeld, Osnabrück, Detmold, and Lingen awakened to a sudden surge of martial activity as the division prepared for war. Although hurried, the activity could in no wise be described as "frantic," for as in all matters concerning the Wehrmacht, mobilization had been painstakingly planned—if not to the last minute, then certainly to the last hour. The troop trains would run on time; the war would run on time.

The details of casting an entire nation into war had been worked out over a generation before, and the mobilization of 1939 followed closely that of 1914. The troop strengths of the regiments were halved as companies were detailed off to form the core of newly raised divisions. The regiments were then brought back to full strength by calling in the reservists. The war had come at an advantageous time, for even the newest levy of recruits (called up October 1938) had already received a year of military training.

Even though the procedure of mobilization echoed that of the previous war, the mood of the nation did not. The earlier generation had marched off to the slaughter like lemmings, accompanied by stirring marches and young, joyful faces beneath flower-bedecked Pickelhauben—but not this time. The world now knew what modern industrial war meant, and a sense of dread descended upon the German nation. During the last days of August 1939, the Rhineland-Westphalian 6th Infantry Division marched off to war under the cover of night with the steady crunch of hobnail boots on cobblestones and pale young faces in the shadow of their Stahlhelme.

In 1914, Europe had understood that mobilization meant war, but this was 1939, and despite the overhanging gloom of an approaching war, there still flickered among the civilian population an unspoken hope that somehow war might yet be averted. The year before, during the Sudeten Crisis, the army had been mobilized, but at the last moment, a deal had been struck and Europe had breathed a sigh of relief. The shadow of carnage had been lifted, and the troops had marched back to their garrison towns to either enjoy the soldier's life or suffer the boredom of the barracks. Could it not happen this time as well? Except for a few minor skirmishes between border guards, there had been no great violence with Poland. Had not the Führer always achieved his goals without war? The Rhineland, Austria, the Sudetenland. Why not this time?

In the first two days of mobilization, the men of the 6th Infantry Division had had little time for such considerations, but now, as they sat in the crowded troop trains awaiting departure, alone with their thoughts, they had much to ponder. As soldiers, they accepted the inevitability of war rather than entertained hollow hopes of its avoidance. Their thoughts were of a more realistic nature. As with their fathers before them in August '14, they could not help but ask, "East or West?" If East, then perhaps the war would be restricted to Poland, but if West—that was their greatest concern—that would mean war with France and Britain and another Great War.

Just before noon on August 27, the troop trains pulled out of the station and headed west, more precisely southwest, 150 km to the Saarpfalz region, where, as part of the First Army, XXIV Army Corps, they took up positions near the French border between Saarbrücken and Zweibrücken with divisional headquarters at Homburg. The troops were immediately set to work improving the existing defenses (which, as part of the "West wall" had been erected more for propaganda purposes than for actual defense). The divisional engineer battalion, under Oberstleutnant Wiese, cleared fields of fire, built auxiliary bridges in the rear areas and laid out minefields (for the time being, the mines were left unarmed). Civilians were quickly evacuated from the "Red Zone," so quickly, in fact, that often doors were left unlocked, livestock unfed, and cows unmilked. Some men of the 6th Infantry Division were actually detailed to tend the animals and milk the cows.

Civilian refugees, deserted villages, abandoned farms all had the appearance of war, and yet there was no war. But on September 1, reality confirmed the appearance as the German nation heard the fateful words from Berlin: "Seit 4:45 wird zurückgeschossen." Germany was doing far more than "shooting back." Two Army Groups with six panzer, eight motorized, and twenty-seven infantry divisions began the pulverization of the Polish nation.

In the West, war arrived two days later on September 3, when Britain and France declared war on Germany. Although war had arrived, the German troops along the West wall were given definite instructions that the responsibility for initiating hostilities was to be left to the British and French: "Under no circumstances should the first rounds fired come from the German side." To avoid any laxity on the part of the troops that might ensue from such a directive, the men were also instructed to maintain the highest vigilance and combat-readiness for the French or British could attack at any time.

"Anytime" came September 8. In the early morning hours, twenty French soldiers were observed crossing the German border in the vicinity of Habkirchen and Reinheim. The "Schiessverbot" was immediately lifted, the landmines armed and the bridges at Reinheim blown. At 6 a.m. the next morning, French troops advanced trough a heavy fog to attack the positions of the 6th Infantry Division at Reinheim.

So began what is often referred to as the "Phoney War in the West," but in this "Phoney" War, young men on both sides would die. The Reconnaissance Battalion and the engineers with artillery support successfully defended their positions and brought in the division's first prisoners of the war. The French continued their attack the next day with Moroccan units and the division suffered its first casualties. The commander of the 3rd Company, 18th Regiment, Oberleutnant Dr. von Kopczynski and several of his men were killed, as was Schütze Geters of the 6th Company, 58th Regiment. Leutnant Mintrop with the 7th Company, 18th Regiment, succeeded in halting the enemy attack and threw them back with an immediate counterattack.

Certain that the French would launch increasingly heavier attacks with artillery support, Generalleutnant Freiherr von Biegeleben pulled his exposed forward units back to the Main Battle Line under the cover of night, but not without first having his men mine their former positions.

In the morning, as the young men of the 6th Infantry Division peered out from their trenches, foxholes, and bunkers, they saw a landscape reminiscent of their fathers' war—a no-man's-land inhabited only by the enemy dead—and they had pause to reflect on the past two days, the first days of combat. They were no longer "virgin" soldiers. They had received their Feuertaufe—baptism of fire—and they could be pleased with their performance. Although they had withdrawn from the forward positions (but only under orders), they had held the Main Battle Line and had flung the enemy back, and even if the Frenchman still stood on sacred German soil, the men were confident that when the time came, they would send the enemy packing.

For the next month, the Saarpfalz sector remained quiet, interrupted only by an occasional Stoßtruppunternehmen (trench raid), conducted mostly by the Germans or patrols colliding in the night. Quiet though the sector may have been, young men still died: Schütze Kemper at Erfweiler, Gefreiter Gläsker at the stone quarry near Kaltenberg, and at Rubenheim, Leutnant Jobst von Limburg.

On October 16, aerial reconnaissance reported what appeared to be rearward movements by French units. In accordance with the German military doctrine of aggression at all times, the 37th and 58th Regiments, without waiting for instructions, launched attacks against an enemy seemingly preparing to withdraw. The 37th Regiment retook Seyweiler, while Regiment 58, after overcoming stiff resistance, seized the Will-Wiesen, but not without losses. Schützens Kollmeier, Herold, Kaefer, and Müller, Gefreiter Rolfmeyer, and Unteroffizier Keute, all from Regiment 58, were killed.

Encouraged by the rapid success of his young soldiers (it was, after all, their first offensive action), Generalleutnant von Biegeleben ordered a general assault for October 18 to sweep the last enemy soldiers from German soil. They would not be alone. Joining them in this effort to secure the Saarpfalz region would be the Hessian 53rd and Pomeranian 75th Infantry Divisions of the XII Army Corps, as well as their sister division from the XXIV Army Corps, the Rhineland 36th Infantry Division.

At 8 a.m. on October 18, the German Sturm-Kompanien (assault companies) left their jump-off positions and in a pouring rain advanced toward the enemy. The attack was a complete success. The French units were quickly thrown out of their positions and rolled back across the German border. Left behind, in addition to the dead, were eleven officers and 366 men as prisoners of the Wehrmacht. (The 6th Infantry's share was three officers and eighty-four men.)

A.O.K 1 (Armee Oberkommando) A.H.Q. 18.10.39
Army Order No.26
In a two-day battle in the Saarbrücken-Zweibrücken Sector, the 52nd and 75th Infantry Division of the XII Army Corps and the 6th and 36th Infantry Divisions of the XXIV Army Corps, exhibiting exemplary audacity drove an equally strong enemy force back over the border. The French were forced to leave behind eleven officers and 366 men as prisoners in our hands. The considerable amount of captured material has yet to be ascertained.

In their first attack on the Western Front our German soldiers have clearly proven the superiority of our leaders and troops over those of the enemy.

To all the participating staffs and troops I express my recognition.

You have demonstrated that you are the equals of those of the Great War and our troops fighting in the East.

This order to be read out to all troops of the First Army during assembly.
To be distributed at company level.

Generaloberst von Witzleben

Perhaps a bit overdone for what was a relatively minor affair. After all, in the East, the German forces had completely crushed the Polish army in less than a month. Even so, the "battle" of Saarbrücken was definitely a morale booster for the young soldiers in the West and a propaganda victory for Hitler, who with some justification could claim that Germany had no quarrel with the West, and that France, not Germany, had been the first to attack, leaving the German soldier with no choice but to righteously defend his homeland.

After two months at the front, the 6th Infantry Division was relieved by the recently raised Silesian 252nd Infantry Division on 27 October. The time had come for another collection of "virgin" soldiers to receive their share of frontline experience. As the men of the 6th Infantry Division marched to the rear, they could hold their heads high and perhaps, with a certain degree of smug superiority, look down on the relief troops passing by. In their initial test, they had performed well, adding the first of many victories to their regimental flag. There had been no major foul-ups or failure of leadership. All had gone as clockwork, like a "Scharf-Schießen" (live-fire maneuver), and had been critical to the confidence building in young soldiers entering their first battles. The Wehrmacht's training, tactics, and doctrine had proven sufficient for the conditions of modern war.

But if the now battle-tested young men of the 6th Infantry Division thought that they would be returning home to flower-strewn streets and a hero's welcome, they were soon disabused of such a notion. The division was withdrawn only a few kilometers north to the Hunsrück region, where they spent the bitter winter of '39–'40 engaged in rigorous training. The division's artillery regiment remained emplaced near the front to provide support should the French attempt another incursion. The engineer battalion was sent off for special training—not in the construction of fortifications or the laying of land mines, but in the assaulting of concrete bunkers and the various uses of the flamethrower, which gave the engineers the suspicion that their next mission would have little to do with defending the sacred soil of Germany but, instead, with taking the war into the lands of the enemy.

# 3

# “Kameraden, Wir Marschieren im Westen”

“Soldaten der Westfront! The hour of the decisive battle for the future of the German nation has arrived.”

With these words, Adolf Hitler unleashed his war in the West. There followed a litany of past transgressions on the part of France and England against the German nation and the German people:

> France alone has declared war on Germany thirty-one times in the past 200 years.
>
> For 300 years it has been the goal of the power holders in England and France to prevent any consolidation of Europe and above all to keep Germany weak and ineffective.
>
> For decades it has been the goal of the English rulers to prevent the unification of Germany under any circumstances and to deny Germany the basic necessities required by a nation of eighty million.
>
> It has always been their goal to shatter Germany and to divide it into small states. That is why they declared war on us 3 September of last year and have rejected all my offers of peace.
>
> We have no hatred of the English and French people.
>
> It is a matter of whether we will live or perish.

Such was the Führer’s address to his soldiers in the early morning hours of May 10, 1940 as they waited in their bunkers, trenches, and jump-off positions along the Franco–German border. “Der Tag” had come. This is why they were here; this is what they had trained for: to hurl themselves at the arch-enemies of the German Volk. As aircraft droned overhead in the pre-dawn sky and the engines of 2,500 tanks roared to life, the infantry buckled on their gear, shouldered their rifles, and slipped grenades under their belts. Not one of them had any doubts concerning the justness of their cause.

"Soldiers of the Westfront! The hour has come. The struggle beginning today will decide the fate of the German nation for the next thousand years. Now, do your duty!"

Hitler had actually wanted to begin his campaign in the west much earlier. The Polish campaign had barely concluded when on October 10, he directed his staff to devise a plan at the earliest possible date for the destruction of the Western Powers. Pressed for time and not overly confident that Germany could prevail in a war against France and Britain, Hitler's staff presented a plan calling for a sweep with the main body of troops through Holland and Belgium and into northern France—little more than an unimaginative rehash of the failed Schlieffen plan of the previous war. Although unimpressed, Hitler agreed to the plan and only the vagaries of the weather, which caused one postponement after another, and a stroke of fate saved the German Army from exercising what was certain to be a failed undertaking.

On January 10, a German courier carrying the plans for "Fall Gelb" ("Case Yellow") was being flown from Münster to a planning session in Cologne when his pilot became disoriented in the fog along the Rhine and mistakenly landed in Belgium. Unsuccessful in destroying the top-secret documents, the courier along with the pilot and the plans for the upcoming invasion of France were taken into custody by the Belgian authorities. Although Belgium was officially neutral, a summary of the German war plan was delivered to the French. Hitler and his staff, uncertain as to whether the courier had been able to destroy the war plan, had to assume that it was now in the hands of the enemy. A new plan would have to be drawn up.

Someone on Hitler's staff remembered that during the initial planning of Fall Gelb a certain Generalleutnant von Manstein had proposed an entirely different plan which, instead of a sweep through the Low Countries, called for a thrust through the center of the French line in the wooded region of the Ardennes and then a sweep north to the English Channel, trapping the northern Allied armies and cutting them off from the rest of the French forces. The plan was bold and imaginative, and, more important, Hitler liked it. He immediately ordered the details for such a plan to be worked out.

Throughout the period of the Phoney War, the Western Allies had set about devising a plan to counter a German offensive if matters ever did come to a real war. Having experienced the effectiveness of strong fortifications during the Great War, the French had previously constructed a massive belt of forts that stretched along the French frontier from Switzerland to just north of Luxembourg. This essentially ruled out the possibility of any serious German offensive action along the southern half of the French line, thus enabling the French to concentrate the bulk of their forces in the north.

Even before they had come into possession of the German plan, the Western Allies had assumed that the Germans would opt for a Schlieffen-like sweep from the north across Belgium. The plan they adopted to counter this attack was "Plan D." At the commencement of the German offensive, four French and British armies would advance north into Belgium to the Dyle River and establish a defensive line from the coast to Dinant and then back west to the French border. A more disastrous plan could not have been provided the Allied armies if the Germans themselves had devised it.

At first glance, the balance of the opposing forces did not appear to favor the Germans. A total 141 German divisions faced 144 Allied divisions. The Germans possessed 2,335 tanks while the Allies could field 3,383. Not only did Allied tanks outnumber German ones, but the German tanks were of the lighter types (PzKWI and PzKWII), being little more than armored scout vehicles with cross-country capability. However, the Germans did have 4,000 aircraft to the Allies' 3,000, and the German forces were under a single command whereas the Allies were a coalition of four nations, four governments, and four command structures. Most important was the reality that Germany was willing to wage war, and the Allies were not.

Since 1934, the responses of the Western Powers to Hitler's expansionist policies had been passive and weak, revealing that their primary goal was to avoid another general European war. Britain and France had declared war on Germany when Hitler invaded Poland, but other than a quick sortie into the Saar, followed by a hasty withdrawal, they had only engaged in war about the edges. (The disastrous invasion of Norway in April had been an effort to deprive Germany of vital resources rather than a head-on collision of military might.) The collapse of Poland at the end of September 1939 removed the reason for which Britain and France had gone to war with Germany in the first place. What possible reason now could the western democracies give their people for a major war with Germany? Why die for a country that no longer existed? Understandably, there was simply no stomach for war and, hence, no real plan for defeating Germany. "Plan D" was essentially defensive in design. The Allies would advance to the Dyle, but there they would defend, not attack.

Why die for Danzig? Germany had already taken Poland. Why not let her keep it? Anything but another bloodbath between major industrial nations. Had not the German Führer himself said back in October that he saw no reason for war between Germany and France and England?

On May 10, 1940, two opponents faced one another: the one not wanting war, the other seeking to crush its enemies once and for all. Was there any doubt as to which would prevail?

The German forces poised to strike France were divided into three army groups. In the north was Army Group "B" under Generaloberst Fedor von Bock with twenty-nine divisions (three panzer divisions). In the center, the main striking force, was Army Group "A," commanded by Generaloberst Gerd von Rundstedt, with forty-four divisions (seven panzer and three motorized divisions). Facing the Maginot Line in the south was Generaloberst Ritter von Leeb's Army Group "C" with nineteen divisions.

In boxing terms, the plan devised by the Germans was that of a right feint followed by a left hook. On the right, von Bock's Army Group "B" would sweep through Holland and Belgium, and as the French and British armies in the north advanced to confront him, Army Group "A" would deliver the left hook, smashing through the Ardennes and then rushing to the Channel coast behind the Allied Armies in Belgium, thus cutting them off from the rest of the Allied forces. Meanwhile, Army Group "C" would maintain its watch on the Maginot Line.

When Hitler unleashed his armies that May morning, the Allies found themselves confronting a war they did not understand. The Germans were doing more than launching an offensive. They were letting loose all hell—speed, initiative, and, above all, total aggression. Throughout the French campaign, one gets the impression that the Western Allies and the Germans were fighting two different wars with two very different doctrines: one seeking to manage the chaos of battle, the other seeking to create chaos—and to exploit it.

In the north, the divisions of von Bock's Army Group "B" swept across Holland, quickly seizing the critical canals and bridges with either paratroopers or fast-moving reconnaissance units. The Dutch army of eight regular and two reserve divisions, which were neither equipped nor trained for modern war, could offer little resistance.

Alerted by the Dutch and Belgians that the German offensive had begun, the Allied command ordered that "Plan D" be put in effect. One British and four French armies marched northeast into Belgium to confront what was believed to be the main German force. They marched straight into the German trap, for to the south, the panzers of von Rundstedt's Army Group "A" were crashing through the "impassable" Ardennes. In two days, the panzers reached their first objective, the Meuse River. On May 12, the river was crossed and the German armored forces began their drive north to the English Channel, slicing behind the French and British armies in Belgium.

There were stops and starts during this headlong dash north, as both men and machines required rest and repair or generals argued over the pace of the advance. Even though they had invented "Blitzkrieg," the German generals were becoming concerned about the rapid progress of their attack as their exposed flanks became longer, and the infantry struggled to keep pace with the panzers. Nevertheless, by May 20, forward units of the German armored force had reached the English Channel, and the Allied armies, which had advanced into Belgium, now found themselves trapped between the forces of Army Group "B" cascading down from the north and von Rundstedt's panzers. Resistance in the north soon collapsed. Holland had already exited the war on May 15, Belgium capitulated May 28, and the British decided to withdraw to the coast and evacuate what they could of their army. Between May 27 and June 4, 224,320 British and 141,842 French troops were evacuated from the beaches of Dunkirk to England. France now stood alone.

All too often, studies of the French Campaign of 1940 tend to end with the British evacuation at Dunkirk. The remainder of the campaign, in which many thousands more would die, is sadly confined to brief epilogues or footnotes. As of June 1, 90 percent of France remained as yet untouched by the invader. France still had forty-nine divisions in the field and a further thirteen fortress divisions manning the Maginot Line. The Battle of the Frontiers had ended. The Battle of France began and with it the entrance of the Rhineland-Westphalian 6th Infantry Division.

When the men of the 6th Infantry Division heard the Führer's words early on the morning of May 10, they, like the other soldiers along the 400-km front, hurriedly buckled on their equipment, slammed their helmets on their heads, checked their weapons one more time, and steeled their nerves for the coming battle. Der Tag had finally arrived. However, if they thought they would be hurling themselves upon the enemies of their beloved fatherland, they were soon disappointed. The 6th Infantry Division was placed in Wehrmacht Reserve. They were to be one of the "follow-on" divisions that would be fed into the battle at a later stage, if needed.

As they assembled on the roads and marched off, they watched the sun rising off to their right and it became immediately obvious to them that despite the rousing refrain "Wir marschieren im Westen," they were definitely not marching west, but rather, north through the sleepy villages of the Hunsrück. As the few awakened villagers watched their young Rhinelanders and Westphalians march off, they could only wonder: were they returning to their northern barracks? Had peace been declared? Certainly they were not retreating and leaving them to the mercy of the French.

The first two days made no great demands of them: 20 km the first day, 25 km the next. For German infantry, that was nothing—a "march in the park." Beautiful spring weather, still on German soil, more akin to summer maneuvers than war. On Pentecost Sunday (May 12), the troops were even allowed to rest in order to enjoy the traditional Pfingstkuchen provided by the company cooks.

All that quickly changed. At the conclusion of church services, the division marched off at 11 a.m. A glance at the march records of the 58th Regiment reflects the heavy demands placed upon the men:

May 12: 52 km
May 13: 42 km
May 14: 30 km
May 15: 65 km
May 16: 45 km

May 17: 55 km
May 18: 45 km
May 19: 37 km
May 20: 30 km
May 21: 38 km

On May 22, a rest day was ordered for the men. In ten days, their heavy jackboots had eaten up 385 km of road, uphill, downhill, and under an increasingly hot sun. At times, the men (and officers) had found it necessary to hitch themselves to the wagons and help the horse teams pull their burdens up the steep roads. Some days, the troops had marched a full twenty-four hours straight. On other days, they had slogged along having had only two to four hours of sleep. Horses had dropped dead on the road. Men had dropped out of the ranks due to "Marschkrankheit" (another name for heatstroke and total exhaustion).

Prior to World War I, the German Army had considered marches of 20 km per day sufficient for the then-expected pace of war. Troops could, of course, be pushed harder, but not if they were expected to be capable of fighting at the end of the march. Yet in the first weeks of World War I, marches of 40 to 50 km per day had been demanded of the German soldiers, many of whom were reservists who were quite out of practice. The result had been that troops went into battle marched to the bone and utterly exhausted.

Envisioning and planning for "fast war," the Wehrmacht realized that for infantry to play any role, the men would have to become inured to marches of 50 km or more per day. Consequently "March Training" received almost as much emphasis as weapons and tactics instruction during the training of a new recruit. The result was a jackbooted marching machine unmatched by any other army.

For nearly a month now, the 6th Infantry Division had done nothing but march—30 to 50 km per day. Footsore, under a merciless sun, they marched, their minds dulled by the monotonous metallic clanking of their gear. Through villages where German was spoken, then a turn to the west where they heard the Flemish tongue, and on May 18, they entered a land where the country folk spoke French. The men continued the march to the sound of the feldwebels' command of "Watzen, watzen" or to the refrain of Soldatenlieder. There were hundreds of marching songs in the Wehrmacht's repertoire of martial music, and by now, the men of the 6th Infantry Division were certain that they had sung each one a half-dozen times.

But still no battle occurred. Throughout their march, they could hear the dull booming sound of war, but always far off in the distance. The men began to wonder if they would ever catch up to the war, or if the war might end without their having caught sight of the enemy once.

On June 6, the division crossed the Somme west of Amiens, and again the enemy was nowhere to be seen. The greatest difficulty had been to coax the mistrustful horses across the hastily erected auxiliary bridge. The division continued its march through the peaceful countryside, but as the lead units emerged from the village of Bussy-lès-Poix, up went the shout, "Alarm, panzer!" Twelve French tanks, three of which were the heavy Char B model came surging toward them from the right. Oberst von Daniels' 18th Regiment was vanguard, and its 14th (panzerjäger) Company immediately swung into action. They were joined by a battery of light howitzers from the artillery regiment and in a bitter, half-hour fight, all twelve tanks were destroyed.

The advance continued, but with nerves a bit rattled. Senses long dulled by exhausting marches were now quite sharp. Helmets usually hung casually from the belt were now firmly planted on the head. So this was modern war—battle without warning at any time or place, no matter how peaceful the countryside nor how quiet the village. "Jetzt wird's ernst," coursed through every mind. Now things were definitely serious.

At the town of Poix, the division encountered stiff French resistance. The division's Reconnaissance Battalion and the 1st Battalion of the 18th Regiment forced the enemy to withdraw, but the commander of the Reconnaissance Battalion's bicycle company, Oberleutnant van Laer, was killed. Despite the combat that day, the division was still able to advance 43 km.

## Crossing the Seine

The next day, June 7, the division set out in pursuit of the withdrawing enemy. Unlike the previous day, their only opposition was in the form of occasional French artillery rounds lobbed from great distance at the marching columns. Unnerving perhaps, but the only casualty was a communication vehicle destroyed by a random shot.

June 8 promised to be another day of strenuous marching and random destruction. At 9 a.m. after only five hours' sleep, the men took to the road and were soon introduced to a new terror to marching columns: bombing and strafing attacks by French aircraft. Early in the campaign, as "follow-on" troops, they had been spared such attacks, but now as the advance guard of the German drive to the Seine, they had become the primary target of desperate French attempts to slow the advance. Unlike the random artillery fire, these air attacks could not be ignored with fatalistic indifference. At the cry of "Jabos!" the troops had to scatter and seek cover. The headquarters staff of the 58th Regiment's 3rd Battalion was nearly wiped out in one of these attacks, suffering two dead and thirteen wounded out of its twenty-man force.

That afternoon, as the 18th Regiment settled down in the village of Morgny for a two-hour rest, the commander of the 1st Battalion, Hauptmann Riecke sent Leutnant Hunold Dietrich, Feldwebel Jacob Elfes, and three men to scout out the area off to the right. Not knowing where the enemy might be, they carefully made their way along a roadside ditch towards the village of Quenois. As they entered the village, it appeared deserted, but as Feldwebel Elfes rounded a corner, he came face to face with a French first lieutenant, who promptly raised his hands in surrender. The French officer informed Elfes that there were a number of men from a Zouave regiment who wanted to surrender. Elfes assured the officer that if he fetched in the Zouaves without their weapons, they would be well treated. In a few moments, the five-man German patrol found themselves surrounded by thirty-one Zouaves, happy to be out of the war. Their surrender posed a problem: what to do with them?

Lock them in the church, of course. They certainly could not drag them along on a scouting mission. Joined in the church by the priest and village mayor, Leutnant Dietrich informed the two that the prisoners were their people and that it was their responsibility to look after their needs. The French officer gave Dietrich his "*Parole d'Honneur*" that he would turn himself and the Zouaves over to the next German unit that arrived.

Feldwebel Elfes thought it time to continue their mission, but then Leutnant Dietrich caught sight of the church organ. Such an opportunity could not be passed up. With Elfes sweating away at the bellows, Dietrich began to play the organ, hesitantly at first, his fingers a bit stiff, but soon the church was filled with the music of Bach, Hayden, and Brahms. All too soon, the time came to depart. Dietrich and Elfes took their leave of the priest, whose cheeks streamed with tears, and the mayor, who stammered repeatedly, "You are not Huns!"

Outside, the villagers, drawn by the music, had emerged from hiding. "Is the war over?" they asked Dietrich and his party.

No, the war was not over. This had been but a brief interlude of beauty and humanity amid the ugliness of war. Leutnant Hunold Dietrich would be killed in action the next day.

Despite the air attacks and random artillery fire, the regiments of the 6th Infantry Division covered another 30 km. Late in the evening of June 8, the exhausted infantry stumbled off the roads to bivouac in the nearby fields. Rumor had it that they had outstripped the neighboring divisions, which meant they would have to wait until the other divisions caught up, and waiting meant resting—perhaps for an entire day.

However, at 3:05 a.m. on June 9, urgent orders arrived at headquarters: the division was to make itself "Marschbereit" at the earliest possible moment; advance 60 km to the Seine; seize the bridges at Andé, Les Andelys; and establish a bridgehead on the west bank—all of this by evening.

Freiherr von Biegeleben and his staff looked at one another in stunned silence. Had the order been sent to the wrong headquarters? A 60-km sprint to seize bridges from a surprised enemy was a mission one would normally assign to a fast-moving panzer or motorized unit, not to a division of foot sloggers, but

"Befehl ist Befehl"—an order is an order. The stunned silence did not last long. Von Biegeleben and his chief of staff, Hauptmann Reissinger, studied their maps. They knew their men were exhausted, but there was no choice in the matter. The bridges must be taken and somehow the worn-out legs in the worn-out boots would have to manage it.

The plan von Biegeleben and Reissinger devised and the subsequent assault might best be described as "making war on the fly." An infantry division plodding along at 4½ kph simply would not suffice. One way or another, the "Stoppelhopsers" would have to be transformed into a mobile strike force.

First, the assignment of objectives: the northern bridge at Andé was assigned to von Hartmann's 37th Regiment, the central bridge of Le Andelys to von Daniels' 18th Regiment, and the southern crossing at Courcelle to von Tresckow's 58th Regiment. Achieving these objectives was a question of speed and strength. The mobile component of the division (i.e. the Reconnaissance Battalion) was fast enough but not strong enough, whereas the infantry regiments were of sufficient strength but in no ways fast enough. The solution was to create three "Vorgeschobene Abteilungen" (forward-thrusting battalions) from any and all mobile units at hand and assign one to each of the three regiments.

Von Biegeleben borrowed the reconnaissance battalions from the neighbor divisions (27th and 41st Infantry) and from his own division's resources. Added to each was a panzerjäger company, a motorized engineer company as well as a company of bicycle-mounted infantry raised by each regiment. (In rural France, there was certainly no lack of bicycles available for requisitioning.) These "Vorgeschobene Abteilungen" were to race forward with all speed, reach the Seine before the French could react, seize the bridges intact, establish a bridgehead on the opposite bank, and hold it until the infantry regiments arrived.

At 6 a.m. on June 9, Generalleutnant Freiherr von Biegeleben wished these units "Godspeed" as they set off on a risky and uncertain mission. The *ad hoc* units presented a curious sight as they marched west: expert horsemen of the Reiter Schwadron beautifully mounted, the trucks of the engineer company loaded with inflatable rubber boats, the panzerjägers with their guns in tow, infantry on bicycles clumsily trying to manage their equipment and their balance, and not-so-expert or beautifully mounted infantrymen on requisitioned draft horses. Westward they marched, a mixture of old, new, and downright odd.

By 9 a.m. the heat of that June day had already become nearly unbearable. At the crossroads west of Gourney, von Biegeleben watched the young men of the infantry regiments march by. He saw the exhaustion in their sweat-streaming faces. He noticed the shuffling gait of the horses, their heads hung low. With 60 km to go and a battle to fight, something had to be done. The general stood up in his staff car and pointed stiffly to the west.

"Darunter müssen wir heute, Jungens, heute noch schlagen wir Frankreich!" Neither Blücher nor Steinmetz could have expressed themselves more succinctly—or more Prussian.

Near midday, elements of the Vorgeschobene Abteilung in the center reached the town of Les Andelys, which was still burning from an earlier attack of German dive bombers. Oberstleutnant Wiese, the commander of the division's engineer battalion came upon the scene and perhaps seeking the honor of being the first to capture a bridge over the Seine, immediately collected several men and an anti-tank gun and led an assault against the manned barricade blocking the bridge. With hand grenades raining down on them from over the barricade, the French defenders hastily vacated their position and fled across the bridge to the safety of the west bank. They did not make it. Panicked hands on the opposite bank pressed the plunger and sent the bridge and the fleeing *poilous* flying into the air. As the explosion echoed away and the last bits of debris fell from the sky and splashed into the waters of the Seine, Oberstleutnant Wiese and his companions stared in stunned silence from atop the barricade. Had it all been for naught?

Wiese was then joined by a couple of machine gun teams and a platoon (four 3.7-cm guns) from the division's Panzerjäger Abteilung, who had dragged their guns through the burning streets of Les Andelys. As the machine-gun teams engaged in a duel with their French counterparts across the river, the panzerjägers pinpointed the enemy's positions and began taking them out, one by one.

When von Biegeleben received reports that some of his units were battling along the Seine, he could no longer content himself with standing at the crossroads encouraging his men and directing traffic. Accompanied by his driver and Hauptmann Reissinger, he sped off in his staff car to Les Andelys.

As they made their way through the burning town, they suddenly came upon a French armored scout car. "Reverse!" Biegeleben ordered his startled driver, "and take cover!" Fortunately, the French armored car had not seen them and drove off. The general and Reissinger proceeded alone on foot through the town. At some point, they became separated. The division's doctor, Oberfeldartzt Paul Walter, later discovered the general sitting on a low stone wall. He had suffered a heart attack. As the burning timbers of the buildings were falling about him, he greeted the doctor with a smile and calmly remarked, "Es geht wieder." ("It's going again.") Whether the general was referring to his heart or the assault on the Seine, the doctor could not tell.

Meanwhile, back at the destroyed bridge, more German units came scrambling to the scene—panzerjägers, engineers, some infantrymen who had hitched a ride on the towed anti-tank guns, and, most important, light infantry howitzers from the Reconnaissance Battalion. The French opposition was soon silenced. At 3:20 p.m., Hauptmann Reissinger, who had made his way forward, summarized the situation and ordered a water-borne assault of the opposite shore. All available boats lying about were promptly "requisitioned" and panzerjägers, engineers, and infantry piled into the clumsy wooden fishing boats. Using their rifles as paddles, they paddled for all they were worth toward the far bank. Normally a risky if not suicidal mission, but this time the machine gunners and heavy weapons had done their job well. The troops landed unopposed and immediately established a defensive perimeter as more troops were ferried across.

With a bridgehead now established at Les Andelys, the main body of the division's Reconnaissance Battalion swept to the southwest in hopes of seizing the bridge at Courcelles undamaged, but again, after a brief firefight, the men of the Reconnaissance Battalion watched as the bridge flew into the air. Undeterred, Oberleutnant Freiherr von Böselager led his cavalry squadron a couple of kilometers downstream to Mousseaux where, at 2:30 p.m., the Reiters swam across the river on their horses. Not to be outdone, the bicycle company of the Reconnaissance Battalion crossed over with the aid of inflatable rafts.

In the north, the bridge at Andé still stood. Oberstleutnant Wiese sent a panzerjäger platoon under Leutnant Stahlschmidt to the bridge. Perhaps a bridge over the Seine could be captured intact, but as the panzerjägers approached, the bridge was detonated and dropped into the river. On the way north, Leutnant Stalschmidt had noticed a ferry station at Muids. It was worth a try. With his men, he sped back south where he found the ferry mid-stream, filled with refugees seeking to reach the west bank. Stahlschmidt persuaded the ferryman to return to shore where the civilians were ushered off and replaced by panzerjägers and their equipment. One panzerjäger humorously wondered aloud if their commander, who earned a leutnant's salary, could afford the fare. Despite artillery fire dropping into the water about them, the crossing succeeded. When the Reconnaissance Battalion, borrowed from the 27th Infantry Division, arrived, they found that Stahlschmidt had already established a bridgehead on the western shore.

Although none of the three bridges had been captured, the main objective of crossing the Seine had been achieved. As the various units of the division arrived—infantry, panzerjägers, cavalry, and cyclists—engineers quickly ferried them across in inflatable boats to reinforce and expand the bridgeheads. One such unit was the 2nd Company of Regiment 18, commanded by Leutnant Dietrich, who the day before had entertained the populace of Quenois with an organ recital.

Early on the morning of June 9, the call had gone out from the 18th Regiment for volunteers to form a bicycle company. Even though the nature of their mission was not revealed, there was no lack of willing volunteers. Any mission would be preferable to another day of foot-burning, forced marches. Eventually informed of their task, Leutnant Dietrich and his cyclists peddled off through the French countryside and arrived at Les Andelys at 7 p.m., where Dietrich, sixteen men, two light machine guns, and an anti-tank rifle were quickly ferried across the Seine.

Once ashore, they were sent off to the west, where a French artillery unit was still lobbing rounds into the river. Dietrich's group fanned out into a skirmish line and, guided by the sound of the French artillery, advanced through the tall grass. After a few kilometers, they located the French position, and Leutnant Dietrich ordered an immediate assault. As the two light machine guns provided covering fire, Dietrich and his men stormed the enemy position with rifles, spades, and grenades. The surprised French were quickly overwhelmed, and Dietrich's men found themselves in possession of thirty prisoners, one light machine gun, and a 20-cm artillery piece—a quick success that Leutnant Hunold Dietrich did not live to enjoy. He had been cut down by a burst of fire as he rushed forward alongside Gefreiter Friedrich Schultwessel. Sending the prisoners back under guard, Gefreiter Schultwessel and the men formed a defensive circle around the body of their young leutnant and dug in for the night.

Meanwhile in Les Andelys, Generalleutnant von Biegeleben had recovered from his heart attack and was assessing the day's action with his staff. None of the three Seine bridges had been captured intact, but despite this failure, the river had been successfully crossed at Les Andelys, Muids, and Mousseaux. Bridgeheads had been established on the western bank and were being reinforced by the hour as troops were ferried across as soon as they arrived. At Les Andelys, the divisional engineer battalion was already in the process of erecting a pontoon bridge capable of bearing heavy traffic.

The problem facing von Biegeleben was that all three crossing points and bridgeheads were located in the central sector (18th Regiment). If he directed the other two regiments to converge on the center in order to cross the river at Les Andelys, a logistical nightmare would be created that even a general directing traffic at a crossroads could not overcome. The 37th and 58th Regiments would have to find their own way over the Seine in their respective sectors.

In the north, the 37th Regiment had already selected a point near Herqueville for a forced night crossing. At 1:50 a.m., the 6th Company under Leutnant Deppe began paddling across the Seine in rubber boots provided by the engineers. They splashed ashore and, after a sharp fight, overcame the French defenders, who, though few in number, had offered stout resistance. A bridgehead was quickly established, and by dawn, two of the regiments, three infantry battalions, and a panzerjäger company had been brought across to the west bank.

As for the 58th Regiment to the south, it was spared the drama and denied the honor of storming across the Seine. Due to a communication failure, the regiment had gotten off to a three-hour late start the morning of June 9, after which followed what was described as "insane chaos" as infantry, artillery, trucks, and horse-drawn transport became entangled on the narrow country roads. Not until noon the following day was the regiment able to reach the Seine.

The difficulties encountered by von Tresckow's 58th Regiment actually solved much of von Biegeleben's problem. By the time the 58th Regiment had arrived, the bulk of the 18th Regiment had already crossed over to the west, thus allowing the 58th Regiment to utilize the crossing points in the central sector.

By the evening of June 10, the near-impossible objectives thrust upon the 6th Infantry Division the morning of June 9 had all been achieved. The Seine had been crossed. Paris was now doomed, and the last hope of the French to halt the German invader had been crushed.

The 6th Infantry Division's crossing of the Seine provides an excellent example of the Wehrmacht's doctrine of war: mission, initiative, and total aggression. Von Biegeleben was given a mission: "Cross the Seine." He was not instructed how it should be done. That was entirely up to him. In a like manner, after the general had organized the Vorgeschobene Abteilungen and assigned the objectives to his regiments, he had simply pointed west and shouted, "Today we strike France!" As for the assaults themselves, whoever arrived first on the scene did not wait for instructions from higher command, but on their own initiative immediately formulated a plan of attack to carry out the mission: an engineer oberstleutnant leading a grenade assault on an enemy barricade; Freiherr von Böselager's cavalrymen swimming across the river on their horses; Leutnant Stahlschmidt hijacking a civilian ferry boat; and, everywhere, units and individuals in time-honored Prussian tradition marching to the sound of the guns and adding their weight to the attack.

To the French defenders, the German assault of June 9 must have appeared wild, chaotic, and completely disorganized—and so it was, by design. With various German units arriving piecemeal and haphazardly from all directions, the attack was a modern version of the Prussian "swarm-tactics" used in the Wars of Unification during the previous century.

To effectively counter an enemy attack, the defender must ascertain the enemy's intentions and the probable objectives of the attack, but if the assault appears disorganized and without any discernible plan, the recognition of the enemy's intentions is made all the more difficult and often results in "Paralysis of the Defense." Along the Seine, the French defenders made no efforts to counter the German attacks other than holding in place until overwhelmed.

The storming of the Seine not only exemplifies the German doctrine of war, but also how infantry could best be utilized in the age of Blitzkrieg. With Hitler's overall military strategy being essentially offensive in nature and with infantry divisions making up more than 90 percent of the Wehrmacht's land forces, there was no other alternative but that these "foot-sloggers" be capable of offensive operations rather than be relegated to the defensive role of occupying and holding ground so typical of other armies.

Von Biegeleben and the men of the 6th Infantry Division proved at the Seine that the German infantry was equal to the task, and they would carry out this task for as long as the German Army remained on the offensive.

As brilliant as their achievement had been in crossing the Seine, the men of the 6th Infantry Division were not allowed to rest on their laurels. No sooner had their boots dried out than they were ordered to advance to the Eure River, fight their way across, and establish bridgeheads on the far bank. Unlike the hell-for-leather plunge across the Seine, the Eure assault followed a more traditional pattern of infantry attack with the division's three regiments advancing in line abreast, each putting two battalions forward and holding one back in reserve.

On June 11 at 7 a.m., the regiments advanced west out of their respective bridgeheads along the Seine. On the right flank, von Hartmann's 37th Regiment, which had the least distance to cover (5 km), had an easy go of things. By 10 a.m., they had reached the high ground overlooking the Eure. A few sporadic attacks by French tanks were driven off by the panzerjägers, and the regiment was able to quickly seize the bridge at Louviers, cross the river, and spend the rest of the day widening and strengthening their bridgehead on the west bank.

In the center, von Daniels' 18th Regiment stepped off the start line on schedule at 7 a.m. Initially they met with no resistance, but when they entered the forested region east of the Eure, they encountered their first opposition—not from the enemy but from the dense undergrowth. Cursing and crashing through the brush (there was no quiet way to proceed), the companies lost contact with one another. Only with a compass were the platoon and company commanders able to maintain direction. Now and then a bullet zinged through the branches above them, and leaves came floating down. Immediately the cry went up "Baumschütze"—"Snipers!" (For some reason when fired upon, troops in forested or jungle terrain illogically assume that enemy snipers have suicidally perched themselves high up in a tree.) The zinging bullets were most probably either parting shots from French stragglers or the overflying rounds from a distant battlefield.

When they emerged from the woods, Oberfeldwebel Weihrauch and Feldwebel Nolte were sent out with a patrol to reconnoiter the planned crossing point at Les Planches. Here they found the bridge still standing and promptly crossed over and entered the village, where they were surprised to meet up with Leutnant Kiesgen, who had crossed over the bridge earlier with his platoon. They found the village empty of French troops, but, as they moved out of the village to the west, they were suddenly attacked by an entire battalion of French infantry, supported by tanks, determined to throw the Germans back across the Eure.

Kiesgen and his small band would have been wiped out if other German units in the area had not "marched to the sound of the guns." Squad after squad, platoon after platoon clamored across the bridge and came to the aid of their comrades. The French attackers were driven off and the crisis averted.

South of Les Planches, the 18th Regiment's 2nd Battalion, commanded by Major Freiherr von Sass, forded the Eure near La Chappel then swung north and attacked the French defenders of Heudreville from the rear and drove them out. The main bridge there was now in German hands. Oberleutnant Schwerter and the battalion adjutant Leutnant Rhein with three NCOs and three enlisted men went out scouting to the west. In a small village, they came upon two French armored cars and twenty infantrymen. Schwerter and his group immediately attacked. Surprised, the French fled under a hail of machinegun fire, leaving behind nine prisoners. Leutnant Rhein hurled a grenade at one of the armored cars, bringing it to a halt. The French crew panicked and baled out, leaving Rhein with an undamaged armored car as a war trophy.

On the left flank of the division, von Tresckow's 58th Regiment did not begin their advance until 7:30 a.m. Despite the half-hour delay they made good progress. Their only opposition was the occasional French artillery round exploding off to their right, and soon they had outstripped the 18th Regiment, who were battling their way through the underbrush. By 11 a.m., the 1st Battalion had reached the heights above Cailly, from where they observed the French departing the village post-haste. Even if the bridge had been prepared for demolition, von Tresckow was certain that the enemy would not detonate it until all French troops were safely across the river. Perhaps with a sudden attack, the 58th Regiment could achieve what had not been possible at the Seine—capture a bridge intact and cross a river without getting their feet wet. The 1st and 2nd Companies were sent to ford the river north and south of the village to flank the defenders. The 3rd Company was brought up from reserve and directed to attack Cailly head-on.

The moment had come: "Augen zu und hinein!" The 3rd Company swept into Cailly and soon found themselves engaged in what all infantry dread—house-to-house fighting, where doctrine and training provided no great advantage to either side. Relying heavily on grenades, the 3rd Company slowly blasted their way through the village, but not until noon were they able to reach the bridge, which remarkably had not yet been destroyed. However, getting across it would be no easy task. In a house at the far end of the bridge and along the street that ran perpendicular to the bridge, the French had emplaced several machine guns that mercilessly raked the bridge and the street leading to it. A crossing *en masse* was not possible. Several "Teufelsjungen" (daredevils) courting death made the attempt in groups of two or three. Few succeeded.

A platoon of panzerjägers arrived and wheeled their four 3.7-cm guns into action. Firing HE rounds, they either eliminated or drove off the French machine gunners, all except for one stubborn *poilu* in the house at the end of the bridge, who continued to rake the bridge with his *mitrailleuse*. Word arrived that the 1st and 2nd Companies had failed to find a useable ford across the Eure and now the 3rd Company had no alternative but to storm across the bridge alone, machine-gun fire or not.

The sound of the NCOs' whistles pierced the air, and the 3rd Company raced across the bridge, their hearts thumping, boots pounding the surface of the bridge—all rather anticlimactic. The stubborn *poilu* at the end of the bridge had fallen silent. Either he had run out of ammunition or had decided that he had done enough to satisfy French honor and had withdrawn.

With the bridge now secured, the 1st and 2nd Companies returned to Cailly and crossed over behind the 3rd Company, and the three companies pushed on to Irreville, where at 3 p.m. they were instructed to dig in.

South of Cailly, the 58th Regiment's 2nd Battalion advanced towards its objective: the bridge at Autheuil. Its commander, Major zum Eschenhoff, had opted for a narrow front with only one company (6th) in the lead and the remaining four companies following behind in line. As the battalion approached the village of La Haute Boulaye, the point-leader of the 6th Company, Feldwebel Renzel spied French troops entrenched along the edge of the village. Imbued with the spirit of "Vorwärtsdrang" and seeing no reason why swift daring action should be the sole purview of young leutnants, he commandeered a Kübelwagen from the panzerjägers, loaded up a machine-gun team, and sped off toward the village. The French, totally unaware that the German advance had reached so far west, took little notice of the vehicle speeding down the road towards them, assuming it was just another group of French officers heading to the rear. Suddenly they found themselves staring into the muzzle of an MG-34 and quickly scattered in all directions. As Renzel and his men combed through the village, they rounded up fourteen prisoners.

The advance continued without opposition. By 10 a.m., the 2nd Battalion had crossed the Eure at Autheuil and by 11.15 had reached within 500 meters of Mesnil. However, off to the north, patrols had discovered that French forces still occupied the village of Reuilly. Instead of the advance being paralyzed by a threatened right flank, zum Eschenhoff saw an opportunity to surround and destroy a sizeable French force. Two platoons of the 6th Company were sent off to the northwest. Leutnant Henze with one of the platoons supported by three anti-tank guns was to attack the village from the west while the other platoon under Oberfeldwebel Merzhauser came in from the northwest.

When the attack went in, the French (a cavalry unit of the 4th Hussars) attempted to escape south where they were caught in the murderous fire of German machine guns, which had been set up as a blocking force. What occurred on the main road south out of Reuilly was reminiscent of a scene from the previous century. Riders were knocked out of the saddle; panicked, riderless horses careened about; the road was littered with dead and wounded—both man and horse. The battle was over in minutes. An entire squadron of cavalry had been annihilated, 100 French had been killed, and seven officers and ninety-eight men, most of them wounded, had been taken prisoner. German losses had been remarkably light. Only Leutnant Henze and seven other men had been wounded.

With all three regiments having crossed the Eure, Generalleutnant von Biegeleben ordered his men to halt, dig in, and rest. In three days, they had fought their way forward 75 km, crossed two rivers, taken 2,100 prisoners, and had captured or destroyed fifteen tanks and twenty-one aircraft. More importantly, they had broken through the "Seine barrier," and with their advance beyond the Eure had extinguished any hopes the French might have had to restore the Seine Front. The gateway to the rest of France now lay open to the German invader. The men of the 6th Infantry Division deserved a day of rest.

## Into the Loire Valley

They did not rest long. On the evening of June 13, von Biegeleben received his orders for the final phase of the French campaign: a 180-km thrust southwest to the Loire. For the march-hardened "Stoppelhopser" of the 6th Infantry division, who had already pounded over 500 km of French roads, that was at most a five- or six-day march. On the day that they set off south, German troops entered Paris. Did this not mean that "*La guerre est finie*?" No, Paris was lost; the war was lost, but no one told the French troops in the Loire Valley. For them, the war was definitely not "*fini*." Why they continued to fight at this stage of the campaign is difficult to understand. Perhaps to preserve some shred of French honor. Perhaps to prevent the hated Hun from trudging on one more meter of sacred French soil. Whatever the reason, the advance south was no "march in the park" for the men of the 6th Infantry Division.

With speed a necessity and with many rivers to cross, von Biegeleben reconstituted the Vorgeschobene Abteilung system, which had proven so effective at the Seine crossing. The Reconnaissance Battalion, reinforced with a company each of panzerjägers and engineers, was sent out to range far ahead of the marching columns while within the regiments themselves, as many infantry as possible were either loaded into any available transport or mounted on bicycles.

The first day's advance got off to a good start. The Vorgeschobene Abteilung sped south and in a surprise attack seized the bridge over the Avre River at Acon and established a bridgehead. Nearby, the bridge at Ilou was captured intact by Platoon Müller of the engineer company, but only after a hard fight.

As the march south continued, there was a noticeable stiffening of French resistance. On the morning of June 16, even the impetuous advance of the Vorgeschobene Abteilung was brought to a halt by a French artillery battery whose crews were determined to go down fighting. In the spirit of Ziethen and von Bredow, Freiherr von Böselager led his cavalry squadron in an audacious attack, which eliminated the French guns and proved once again that when properly used, aristocratic cavalrymen still had a role to play in modern warfare.

The determined resistance of the French artillerymen was not the only surprise that the day held in store for the division. The 58th Regiment had set off that day at 4:20 a.m. for what appeared to be another long march in the heat of a mid-June sun. A rest was ordered 36 km later in the forest just south of La Ferte Vidame. The men stumbled off the forest path and stretched out in the cooling shade alongside the ruins of an ancient castle. After an hour of rest, they resumed their march, but no sooner had the lead company emerged from the woods than it was struck by artillery fire. Five men of the lead squad immediately became casualties. Then, from a distant bocage, three heavy Char B tanks came rolling across the fields towards them. The cry went up, "Panzerjäger vorn!" and two platoons (eight guns) swung into action. Round after round they hurled at the charging tanks only to discover that their 3.7-cm guns had no effect on the 32-ton behemoths. The tanks returned fire, putting half the anti-tank guns out of action with direct hits. Two 10.5-cm howitzers were brought forward to join the unequal struggle, but howitzers were never designed to sharp shoot moving targets. One howitzer was quickly destroyed by a direct hit, and the battery commander, Oberleutnant Heinz, was severely wounded. Two more howitzers were wheeled forward, and the Abteilung commander, Major Kruger, personally directed their fire. After a prolonged exchange of fire, the French tanks retired back to the bocage, leaving the Germans to lick their wounds. For the 58th Regiment, June 16 had been the costliest day of the entire campaign. In addition to six anti-tank guns and three howitzers destroyed, the regiment lost four officers, five NCOs, and seventeen men killed.

The following day was far less bloody. As the division continued its advance south, it met only weak opposition—a few shots of defiance from scattered groups of French troops, who fired and then quickly melted away. Another noticeable difference was that when the marching columns entered the villages, they no longer discovered that a terrified populace had fled the dreaded Huns. Instead, the men were greeted by villagers offering bottles of wine and inviting them to join in a toast, "*La guerre est finie*." The rumor soon circulated throughout the ranks that the new French government had asked for the terms of an armistice—a rumor that was not confirmed until 5 p.m. when the Deutschlandsender normal program of martial music was interrupted by the Führer's voice announcing that the newly-formed French government expressed its intention to cease hostilities and had requested Germany's conditions for peace.

However, the "intention" to cease hostilities does not necessarily cease hostilities, and the 6th Infantry Division was ordered to continue its drive to the Loire. Early the morning of June 19, the Vorgeschobene Abteilung reached the bridge over the Loire at Ingrandes and immediately began racing across the 300-meter structure. The lead elements had just reached the third span when behind them came an explosion dropping the first two spans of the bridge into the waters of the Loire.

Undeterred, Oberstleutnant Becker ordered a Seine-style assault. As panzerjägers and machine gunners blanketed the opposite bank with their fire, engineers paddled infantry assault troops across the river in rubber rafts. Once ashore, the assault troops drove off the French defenders and established a bridgehead. The bridge was ingeniously restored. Soldiers replaced the fallen spans with a pontoon bridge and then connected it to the still-standing third span with a ramp, making the bridge at least serviceable for infantry. Over the next two days, von Biegeleben hastened his infantry across the Loire. Despite the looming armistice, the 6th Infantry Division was directed to continue the push south.

On June 25 at 11:35 p.m., as Generalleutnant von Biegeleben and his staff were setting up their headquarters in Beaupreau, the radio suddenly resounded with the trumpet notes of "Das Ganze halt," followed by the Führer's announcement of the "Waffenstillstand." France had agreed to the terms of the armistice. For the weary men of the Rhineland-Westphalian 6th Infantry Division, the French War had come to an end.

The news of the armistice spread quickly throughout the division, and the celebrations began, aided, of course, by liberal quantities of excellent French wine. The younger officers congratulated one another. In six weeks, they had achieved what their fathers had not done in the four years of the Great War: the iron ring forged by the enemies of the German nation, which for seven decades had threatened to crush the Fatherland, had now been forever shattered. The German people had been freed; the German Army redeemed.

As for the troops in their bivouacs amid the fields, the armistice was first greeted with the elation due a battle won, eventually replaced by feelings of relief and thoughts of a more reflective nature. In its simple grandeur, the traditional hymn of victory and thanksgiving, "Nun danket alle Gott," rose into the night sky across the Valley of the Loire. For the first time, the young Rhinelanders and Westphalians knelt beside their officers, bare-headed, hands folded on knee, and gave thanks to God for victory. They would never do so again.

Unfortunately, the very brevity of the French campaign creates the impression that it was somehow near bloodless. It was not. Nearly 100,000 French soldiers were killed in "Case Yellow" and another 200,000 wounded. German losses were 27,074 killed, 18,384 missing, and 111,034 wounded. When one adds in the British, Dutch, and Belgian casualties, the butcher's bill amounts to nearly half a million men killed, wounded, or missing in action—and all of this in forty-seven days.

With the end of hostilities, the formal celebrations began. Back home in Germany, the Führer had his victory parade through flower-strewn streets of Berlin while the crowds cheered, and in Paris, the army marched past the Arc de Triomphe while the Prussian generals saluted. Despite the recognized achievements during the campaign, the 6th Infantry Division participated in neither. Von Biegeleben had been assigned the duty of overseeing the demarcation line between what later became Vichy France and the Occupation

Zone. Not bad duty in one of the most beautiful regions of France, but here the troops faced the final "terror" of the campaign—the young women of France. Make-up, lipstick, and red-painted nails were a considerable shock to the young Westphalians, most of whom hailed from small rural villages of the North German Plain. What confronted them now appeared a validation of the German mother's warning to her soldier son to beware the women of France. However, as Feldwebel Elfes observed, upon closer fraternization, these "terrors" were actually decent young girls with names like Aline, Marcelle, and Odette.

In early September, the division was pulled from the beautiful Loire country and sent 350 km north to the Cotentin Peninsula where along the windswept rocky coast, they first organized the defense against the unlikely invasion of France by the British, and then trained for the even more unlikely German invasion of Britain.

Although the guns had grown silent and French civilian and German occupier had settled into a form of "normal" co-existence, the war still had one more victim to claim from the ranks of the 6th Infantry Division. On October 11, Generalleutnant Arnold Christian Rudiger, Freiherr von Biegeleben, suffered a second heart attack and this time, it did not "geht wieder." He was fifty-seven years old and had served the Fatherland for thirty-nine years. Recently the Führer had awarded him the Ritterkreuz for his division's achievements during the Seine crossing. He was laid to rest on foreign soil in the cemetery at Jullouville.[1] As he was lowered into his grave, the young men he had led in battle sang the traditional lament "Ich hatt'einen Kameraden"—a lament which would become all too familiar to the Rhinelanders and Westphalians of the 6th Infantry Division.

# 4

# Barbarossa I: Into the Unknown

In March 1941, the men of the 6th Infantry Division, who were just beginning to enjoy the arrival of spring in sunny France, were loaded on to troop trains and transported across Europe to East Prussia, which still lay in the icy grasp of winter. Snow blanketed the ground, and the numerous lakes were frozen to the depth of 65 cm. Winter is a long time passing in the East. The troops were billeted among the many small villages, the names of which sounded strange to their Rhineland and Westphalian ears, the rural dialects even more so. The accommodations awaiting them were no more welcoming than the weather. However, the lack of amenities was more than made up for by the correctness and hospitality of the rural East Prussian populace.

Besides the weather and scenery, there were other changes. Fifty-three-year-old Generalleutnant Helge Auleb now commanded the Division. The 37th Regiment's Kommandeur, Oberst von Hartmann, had been promoted to generalmajor and given command of the Lower Saxon 71st Infantry Division. His replacement was Oberstleutnant Hennicke, who had commanded the regiment's 1st Battalion. Oberst Edler von Daniels relinquished command of the 18th Regiment when he took over command of the 239th Regiment of the Rhineland 106th Infantry Division.[1] The 18th Regiment was now led by Oberstleutnant Carl "Corle" Becker from the 37th Regiment.

At the time, neither man nor officer had any idea of why they had been transported 2,500 km to this rural backwoods. Whatever had happened to the invasion of Britain? If all they were going to do was to train, why could they have not been dropped off in their garrison towns and train at home?

There were rumors—"latrine parole"—concerning a possible invasion of Russia, but that made no sense. Did not Russia and Germany have a "friendship" treaty of sorts? Did not thousands of tons of Russian grain and oil cross the German border daily? Why should there be war with Russia?

Something was definitely in the air. The arrival of new equipment such as the motorized 2-cm anti-aircraft guns and 5-cm anti-tank guns told them as much. Their training exercises and the exchange of rubber-tired transport for wooden-wheel "Panje wagons" all indicated that the target was Russia. The appearance of Russian translators confirmed their suspicions, but not until June 15 did the 6th Infantry Division receive its directives for Operation Barbarossa—the German invasion of the Soviet Union.

The German invasion of the Soviet Union in June 1941 was the greatest military operation the world had yet seen; 3 million men, 3,580 armored vehicles, 750,000 horses, and 7,184 pieces of artillery lay concealed in the forests and hollows along a 1,300-km front from the Baltic to the Black Sea. Opposing this force were 4½ million Russian soldiers. Perhaps to impart a certain crusading element to the invasion, Hitler had christened the undertaking "Operation Barbarossa," after the legendary German King and Holy Roman Emperor Friedrich Barbarossa, and had boasted that when the attack commenced, "The world will hold its breath." He was not far wrong.

The German invasion force was divided into three army groups, commanded by the generals who had so quickly dispatched France. In the north was Army Group North under Generalfeldmarschall Ritter von Leeb with three panzer divisions, three motorized divisions, and twenty infantry divisions. Von Leeb's task was to sweep northeast through the Baltic states and take Leningrad.

Next came Army Group Center, commanded by Generalfeldmarschall Fedor von Bock. Its nine panzer, five motorized, and thirty-five infantry divisions were to destroy the Soviet armies of the central front and advance on Moscow.

The southern invasion force was Army Group South, commanded by Generalfeldmarschall Gerd von Rundstedt, with five panzer, four motorized, and twenty-eight infantry divisions (plus three security, fifteen Romanian, two Hungarian, and two Italian divisions). Army Group South was to drive to the Black Sea and seize the natural resources-rich regions of the Ukraine and the Don basin.

In brief, those were the objectives given to the German Army groups, but Leningrad, Moscow, the Ukraine are merely geographic points on the map. The primary objective of German arms—obvious to the commanders in the field—was the quick destruction of the Red Army. This objective had to be achieved in weeks, a few months at the most, and not only because of the dreaded Russian winter but also because Hitler's generals understood that Germany with its limited resources could never prevail in a protracted struggle.

Although the generals understood the military objectives of Operation Barbarossa, they were far less certain of the Führer's overall war aims and political objectives. Other than a determination to destroy Bolshevism, Hitler had never clearly outlined his goals. This lack of clarity would cause serious problems later in the campaign as political objectives clashed with purely military objectives.

As part of Army Group Center, the 6th Infantry Division was assigned to Generaloberst Hoth's 3rd Panzer Group, who in conjunction with Generaloberst Guderian's 2nd Panzer Group, was to encircle and annihilate the Soviet armies north of the Pripet Marshes. On June 18, Generalleutnant Auleb was informed that "nulltag" had been set for June 22, and over the next two days under the cover of night, the division's units moved into their jump-off positions.

Their task for the opening phase of Barbarossa was to break through the Russian border defenses at Mariampole and by June 23 reach and cross the Njeman River at Prienai, 70 km away. This directive is indicative of what the German Army expected of its infantry divisions when used in an offensive role. The staff of the 6th Infantry Division received the directive with no great concern. Only a year ago they had raced pell-mell 60 km to the Seine and crossed it—all in one day.

The attack sector of the 6th Infantry Division was a 10-km stretch of ground from the eastward-flowing Šešupė stream in the south to the wooded area near Sudawskie in the north. The terrain on the Russian side of the border was gently rolling and interspersed with woods. Observation and aerial reconnaissance revealed concrete bunkers scattered throughout the sector. Unfortunately, enemy numbers and unit types could not be determined. They might be simple border guards or fanatical members of the Komsomol.[2]

For the attack, all three regiments were deployed in line abreast with the 37th Regiment on the right (southern) flank, the 18th Regiment in the center, and the 58th Regiment on the left (northern) flank. In this manner, whichever regiment first succeeded in breaking through the Soviet defensive zone, the other two regiments could more easily be shunted in behind it to form a single Schwerpunkt of advance. Because speed was of the essence in reaching the Njeman, the troops were instructed not to waste precious time overcoming strong points but, following the Stoßtrupp tactics of World War I, they were to bypass them and move quickly through the defensive belt. Special units of the engineers would deal with the strong points.

The night of June 20–21 was a typical summer evening, warm, almost sultry, and quiet. As the men of the 6th Infantry Division lay concealed in the dense East Prussian forests, there was little more they could do but listen to the croaking of frogs and the rustling of leaves. Above them the moon slid in and out of the passing clouds. In silence, they watched the luminous dials of their wristwatches tick away the night hours. It would not be long now. The summer nights in Russia are short.

At 3:05 a.m. came a distant droning sound from high in the sky. The sound came closer then passed overhead—German bombers flying east. Suddenly, the eastern horizon was lit up by pillars of flame as bombs rained down on the Russian positions. Behind them, the air was rent by the roar of their own artillery. The troops watched the glowing cylinders scream overhead joining the "Höllentanz" that had erupted before them.

Dawn revealed a heavy mist shrouding the combat zone. At the command of "Grenzsprung!" the men of the 6th Infantry Division rose from the ground and advanced towards the east. Squad by squad, platoon by platoon, they disappeared into the mist.

It was perhaps fitting that the land was shrouded in mist the morning of June 22 when the Germans advanced into Russia—into the unknown, into that primitive mysterious land of primeval forests and swamps; the home of Cossacks, Tatars, and other wild tribes. For centuries, the very thought of the East had aroused a sense of dread in the German psyche. Now they were entering that strange land, and, although confident of their abilities, the German soldiers could only hope that the Führer knew what he was doing. Beyond this hope, there remained only "Gott mit uns" and "Gott hilf uns."

With their eyes glued to their scissor-telescopes, the regimental commanders and their staffs watched as their troops were swallowed up by the mist. Would the Grenzsprung be successful, or had they sent their young men into a hornet's nest of interlocking fields of machine-gun fire? Out of the mist erupted the sound of gunfire and the muffled blast of hand grenades. Contact! With increasing anxiety, they awaited the first reports. They did not have to wait for long. On the right flank, Regiment 37 had taken Hill 192 and the village of Jurgezeriai. To the left, Regiment 58 had seized Hill 245 and were presently marching through the burning village of Liubavas. By 7 a.m., the regiment had reached Budvietis—they were through the Soviet defense zone.

In the center, the attack was not proceeding as smoothly. Even though the 18th Regiment had quickly taken Hills 208 and 220, as it advanced on Galbanowka, the 1st Battalion encountered stiff opposition in the woods just east of Hill 220. Within an hour, the 2nd Company had lost twenty-four men. The 2nd Battalion's advance was brought to an abrupt halt when it ran up against the concrete bunkers of the Soviet defenses before Akmenynai. Oberleutnant Grote, commander of the 6th Company, destroyed two Soviet armored cars with hand grenades while Leutnant Mintrop, a platoon leader in the 7th Company, led several assaults against a concrete bunker without success. Leutnant Stock was killed while attempting to thrust a stick-grenade into the firing port of a bunker, and Leutnant von Schrader was seriously wounded. As he lay bleeding, the occupants of the bunker rushed out and brutally murdered him. Not only had the 18th Regiment's advance been stopped, but the Russians had also mounted a counterattack. The attack was repelled and sixty prisoners taken.

Seeing that the 58th Regiment had already broken through the enemy defensive zone, Generalleutnant Auleb concentrated his Schwerpunkt on the northern line of advance. The 37th Regiment was directed to swing around behind the stalled 18th Regiment and fall in behind Regiment 58. The 18th

Regiment was ordered to leave a battalion behind to deal with the bunkers and have the rest of the regiment follow the 37th Regiment.

The sun had risen high into the sky. The mist had burned away, and now that they were through the border defense zone, the regiments fell into march column on the road and advanced towards the Njeman. In the open country the Russian defenders melted away or contented themselves with long-range potshots from distant woods and groves. Around noon, fifty Soviet aircraft were observed, approaching the marching columns, a situation that could have spelled disaster had not five German fighters (Bf 109s) swooped down on the Russian formation. In five minutes, they shot down five Russian aircraft and scattered the remainder. Unfortunately, one of the downed aircraft had slammed into the ground next to the road and had burst into flames, killing a doctor and several other men from an artillery unit.

The march continued. Aerial attacks were not the only threats with which the men of the 6th Infantry Division had to contend. Even if serious resistance appeared to melt away, the enemy often left behind "suicide squads," concealed among the wheat fields and commanded by fanatical commissars. These units, under the threat of the commissar's pistol, fought to the last and had to be dealt with up close with hand grenade, spade, and rifle butt. Doctor Heinrich Haape of the 18th Regiment came across one such group of four men and a commissar lying dead among the trampled grain. Their heads had all been bashed in.

At 10:30 p.m. on the evening of June 22, the regiments reached the day's assigned objective of Liudvinavas and bivouacked in the open fields. For the men of the 6th Infantry Division, the first day of Operation Barbarossa had been both long and successful. In eighteen hours, they had broken through the Soviet frontier defenses and advanced 42 km into that wild and mysterious land—but at a cost. Von Daniels' 18th Regiment had lost two officers and twenty-nine men killed, one officer and fifty-seven men wounded, and three men missing. Von Tresckow's 58th Regiment suffered losses of one officer, one doctor, and eighteen men killed. Although these losses would be dwarfed by those suffered later in the war, they were sufficient to convince the troops that the Führer's crusade in the East would be no walkover.

From the moment of first contact, the German soldier realized that he was confronting an enemy unlike any other he had faced before. The Russian soldier fought. He did not merely offer token resistance, firing off a few rounds to satisfy honor then quickly surrender. Willingly or under the threat of a commissar's Nagant pistol, the Russian soldier resisted until killed or wounded. The Germans reacted with anger and frustration at the stubbornness of their new opponent and complained of his use of "gangster" tactics. Isolated individual Russian soldiers, instead of surrendering to approaching Germans, would lie concealed, allow the Germans to pass, and shoot them in the back. And then there were the reported atrocities. A German doctor, treating six wounded men in a shallow where they had been brought to safety, came under fire, and when the doctor stood up to wave his Red Cross banner, he was cut down. The Russians then hurled grenades into the shallow, blasting the wounded to bits. Accurate or not, this and other accounts spread rapidly through the ranks and from early on served to increase the overall brutality of the war in the East.

At 6 a.m., the 6th Infantry Division resumed its advance to the Njeman. With speed being critical in seizing a bridge over the river, Generalleutnant Auleb recreated the Vorgeschobene Abteilung system, which had proved so effective at the crossing of the Seine. Redesignated as "Vorausabteilung," it consisted of the divisional Reconnaissance Battalion, a motorized company of engineers, a motorized company of panzerjägers, plus whatever infantry units could be made mobile with either bicycles or motor transport.

With the Vorausabteilung ranging far ahead and the infantry regiments strung out in march columns behind, June 23 proved to be a day of torturous marching along roads, ankle-deep in powdery sand. Above the columns hovered a heavy cloud of dust, visible for miles. After a 30-km march, the division reached the forest just west of Prienai on the Njeman, and the men were ordered to take a two-hour rest while commander and staff considered plans for an assault.

The forest lay on high ground and was assumed to be occupied by the enemy. Auleb decided to send the Vorausabteilung straight through the forest but directed the Reiter Schwadron of Freiherr von Böselager to take up position in a valley village to the south. Should the Vorausabteilung be unable to quickly fight its way through the forest, then von Böselager's Reiters were to swing around the forest and, using the valley as cover, sweep into Prienai and seize the bridge over the Njeman. However, at the last moment, Auleb was ordered by VI Corps headquarters to keep the Reiter Schwadron with the Vorausabteilung. Higher command interfering with the tactical deployments made by the commander on the scene was a noted departure from German military doctrine, and although Auleb's reaction to this departure was not recorded, one can well imagine its nature.

Fortunately, the Vorausabeilung was able to quickly fight its way through the forest and reach Prienai at 3:30 p.m., but as its lead vehicles approached the bridge, a massive explosion sent it flying into the air. After the experiences of the French campaign, a blown bridge was hardly a novel situation for the 6th Infantry Division to face, and they dealt with it as they always had—swiftly. Experienced machine gunners flung themselves down along the riverbank and quickly suppressed any defensive fire from the opposite shore, while engineers slid their rubber rafts into the Njeman and rowed the infantry across. In short order, a bridgehead was established on the eastern bank, allowing the engineers to apply themselves to the task of building an auxiliary bridge for the approaching marching infantry columns.

In two days, the 6th Infantry Division had broken through the border defenses, advanced 70 km, and crossed a river, proving yet again that a division of foot-sloggers had a role to play in the age of Blitzkrieg.

The engineers needed a day and a half to complete a bridge sufficient to carry the division's heavy equipment across the river, which meant a day and a half of rest for the men, and for the officers, the opportunity to discuss the disturbing order that had recently come down from higher command—the infamous "Kommissar Befehl"—which directed that any political commissar taken prisoner was to be "shot on the spot." The justifications given were:

1. Commissars were political officers, not military officers, and, therefore, not members of the Red Army. That they were armed and participated in military actions put them in violation of the Rules of Warfare.
2. Reports revealed that the commissars were responsible for either ordering atrocities against German soldiers or had committed such acts themselves.
3. Commissars often forced the Russian soldier to fight against his will and did not allow surrender.

In the discussions, some of the officers rejected the Commissar Order outright. Others indicated that they would simply ignore it, but not necessarily on humanitarian grounds. To them, the execution of a captive without any determination of guilt was an affront to their personal honor as a German officer. There were common sense, practical military reasons, as well, for ignoring the order. Were word to get out that every commissar had a death sentence hanging over him, they would only become more fanatical and less inclined to surrender or allow troops around them to do so. One also had to reckon on immediate retaliation against German prisoners. Another consideration was that if any German soldier had the right to murder a captive, the situation could get out of hand and seriously affect troop discipline.

The extent to which the 6th Infantry Division carried out or ignored the Kommissar Befehl cannot be determined by existing records or accounts. Commissars found dead on the battlefield were assumed to have been killed in action, have committed suicide to avoid capture, or have been killed by their own men. Captured commissars were generally sent along with the other prisoners to the collection centers. What became of them later, one can only guess.

At sunrise on June 25, the 6th Infantry Division crossed the Njeman, the same river that Napoleon had crossed to begin his fateful invasion of Russia 129 years before. Officers and men were well aware of this historical fact, and the march continued under a somber and reflective mood.

When the river crossing was completed, Generalleutnant Auleb received his new order. The division was to advance 350 km, break through the heavily fortified "Stalin Line," and cross the Duna at Polotsk.[3] This time, the division set no new daily march records as they had in France; 30 km and often less was all the men could manage on the Lithuanian roads, which were little more than sandy trails above which hung the ever-present cloud of dust kicked up by the marching columns. The sand tortured the muscles of the legs and the dust tortured the eyes and throats while the relentless summer sun tortured the rest of the body. They soon discovered that their wagons were totally unsuited to these road conditions. They were too heavy and often sank up to their axel hubs. Horses dropped dead from heat and exhaustion. As in France, the men had to harness themselves to the wagons to aid their four-legged Kameraden, but still the horses died.

Throughout the advance, the division encountered only sporadic opposition, which was easily brushed aside. For the most part, the men simply rounded up Russian stragglers at a rate of 100 per day. Their one relief from the exhausting marches was the welcome they received from the local inhabitants. Lithuanians, Poles, and even Russians lined the roads and showered them with flowers, hailing them as their liberators from the hated Bolsheviks. In the streets of Nowosiółki, the local dance troop performed for their new guests, and the 3rd Battalion of the 18th Regiment arranged a dance fest with the local villagers.

With good reason, the inhabitants welcomed the Germans as liberators. They had suffered enough in the Bolshevik "Workers' Paradise," which had all too quickly become a proletarian hell. From the people, the Germans learned for the first time how the communist system operated. On the collective farms, each family was allowed to keep one cow and one hen; the rest belonged to the commune. Likewise, farmers could keep only one-third of their harvest; the rest was taken by the state. They had to sell one-half of what they were allowed to keep in order to purchase what they needed.

The forced collectivization had only been the first step. Soon people began disappearing, never to be heard from or seen again. On July 9, Generalleutnant Auleb visited a prison in Wilejka, which had housed 1,600 individuals who had disappeared. Just before the German troops had arrived, the communists had fled with their prisoners, but not before executing 200 of them who had been judged incapable of marching. They had been forced to lie down, side by side, their heads overhanging a stone gutter, and had been dispatched with a single pistol shot to the back of the head. The bodies had been tossed into three potato pits and covered with a thin layer of dirt. Family members in the region had come there to find their loved ones, but identifying the dead in the tangled mass of limbs and bodies had been no easy task. The Bolsheviks had executed another 200 prisoners who had been unable to keep up the pace, 10 km east.

In the Jewish village of Oszmiana, the inhabitants reported to the 3rd Battalion of the 18th Regiment that before the Bolsheviks left, they had executed a number of villagers. These and other such reports of atrocities gave early warning to the young Rhinelanders and Westphalians of the nature of their enemy and the bitter ideological struggle into which they would soon be drawn.

While the 6th Infantry Division was struggling along the primitive roads on their way to the Old Soviet Frontier, events along the rest of the 900-km front were beginning to give shape to Operation Barbarossa.[4] There had been some surprises—the stubborn and at times skilled defense conducted by the Russian soldier; road conditions that were even worse than expected; and the appearance of Soviet medium and heavy tanks, which were superior to any tank possessed by the Germans. Despite these surprises, the operation was proceeding according to plan, albeit at a price. By June 30, German losses included 8,886 men killed.

In the north, von Leeb's army group had quickly broken through the Soviet border defenses and had begun its race through the Baltic countries. As early as June 26, von Manstein's LVI Panzer Corps had plunged ahead 150 km to cross the Duna at Dugavpils, but here the panzers were ordered to halt until the remainder of the Soviet forces along the Baltic coast had been eliminated. The coastal city of Liepāja was captured after a four-day battle. Riga fell to the Germans on July 1. Between June 24 and 27, the Soviet 3rd Tank Corps, representing the bulk of Soviet armored forces in the Baltic was destroyed with a loss of 200 tanks. On July 2, Army Group North began the advance on Leningrad.

South of the Pripet Marshes, von Rundstedt's Army Group South was advancing, but at a much slower pace. The Soviet High Command (Stavka) had always assumed that if Germany attacked the Soviet Union, the main thrust would be in the south with the primary objective of seizing the fertile grain fields of the Ukraine and the natural resources of the Don Basin. As a result, the area south of the Pripet Marshes was the most heavily defended sector of the entire front with four armies, 2,400 tanks (*versus* von Rundstedt's 600) and a series of defensive belts of well-constructed concrete bunkers. Unlike the Grenzsprung in the northern and central sectors, where German assault troops had smashed through the border defenses in a day, von Rundstedts forces were having to gnaw their way through the deep Soviet defensive belts while warding off heavy Russian armored counterattacks. In ten days of fierce fighting, the units of Army Group South had only advanced 100 km.

The slow advance in the south raised concerns at the Führer's Headquarters, but, since Operation Barbarossa sought a rapid decision north of the Pripet Marshes, the lack of progress on the port of Army Group South did not at the time present a crisis.

In the central sector of the front, there were no such concerns at the Führer's Headquarters. Von Bock's Army Group Center was rapidly achieving its primary objective: the destruction of the Soviet armies north of the Pripet Marshes. The Blitzkrieg doctrine of armored warfare tested in France was now being applied with near perfection by Army Group Center's two powerful panzer groups. On the northern flank, Generaloberst Hoth's Panzer Group 3 had quickly broken through the border defenses and pushed 300 km east while on the southern flank Generaloberst Guderian's Panzer Group 2 was rapidly advancing northeast. Between June 28 and July 1, the two panzer groups linked up at Minsk and Borislav, trapping four Soviet armies in the Białystok–Minsk pocket. The Soviet losses were enormous: 287,704 prisoners; 2,585 tanks destroyed; 1,449 artillery pieces; and 242 aircraft captured or destroyed, plus tens of thousands of Russian soldiers killed. This was the campaign's first great battle of encirclement and annihilation. There would be many more to come.

On July 11, after more than two weeks of marching, the 6th Infantry Division was within striking distance of the "Fortress of Polotsk." This "fortress" was actually a heavily fortified defensive belt 35 km long and 12 km deep, situated 20 km southwest of the city. Within this defensive belt lay 150 one- and two-story concrete bunkers connected by fieldworks and surrounded with deep belts of barbed wire. Complicating any assault were the numerous lakes and impassable swamps, not to mention nature's own version of wire entanglements—deep, thorny thickets.

As intimidating as the defenses were, they were also flawed. Following an outmoded doctrine of defensive fortification, which sought to maximize fields of fire, the bunkers had been more or less built out in the open rather than utilizing the natural features of the terrain (ravines, ridges, low hills, etc.) to conceal them. They had also been constructed with firing ports only to the front (the direction from which no self-respecting assault engineer would ever choose for an attack) and without any plan of interlocking fire or mutual protection.

For two days, July 13–14, the division reconnoitered the enemy defense zone. The Reconnaissance Battalion engaged elements of the Soviet 12th Rifle Division 18 km upstream from Polotsk. Reminiscent of a bygone age, Freiherr von Böselager sent the fortress commandant in Polotsk a formal request to surrender. The request was refused.

Unlike earlier actions, the 6th Infantry Division would not be able to achieve its objective through a surprise attack by swift-moving *ad hoc* units. The "Fortress of Polotsk" would have to be taken through a direct frontal infantry assault, which could easily become a blood bath for the division. However, infantry assaults against fortifications can be successful with careful planning and execution, and the men of the 6th Infantry Division would hardly have been considered amateurs.

The operating principle of the assault on the Fortress of Polotsk was that of maximum flexibility of attack. The deployment of the division reflects the axioms of opportunism and reinforcement of success (again, the Stoßtrupp tactics of the Great War). All three regiments were deployed in line abreast along a 20-km front with Regiment 18 on the right flank, Regiment 37 on the left flank, and Regiment 58 in the center. There were two roads leading through the Soviet defensive belt to Polotsk; one in the attack sector of the 18th Regiment at Gomely, the other in Regiment 37's sector at Lessiny. Von Tresckow's 58th Regiment would actually be withheld from the assault either to intercept any attempted counterattack or to be available to quickly follow on whichever of the other two regiments was first successful in penetrating the defensive zone. The object of the attack plan was to pierce the defenses on a narrow front, reach Polotsk as quickly as possible and seize the bridge over the Duna. For the actual assault, the regiments were instructed to employ the least number of units (in this case, one assault company per regiment), but the maximum number of heavy weapons.

At the Führer's Headquarters, 1,000 km away, Hitler insisted the attack be launched on July 14. Generalleutnant Auleb refused. The necessary artillery so vital to the success of the assault was not yet in place. He had already been interfered with once before by "higher command." This time, he held firm. The attack would commence the morning of July 15. Hitler never forgave Auleb's intransigence and saw to it that the general never received the Ritterkreuz.

The night of July 14, the "Sturmkompanien" (assault companies) quietly moved into their forward positions and bedded down for the night amid the cornfields and thickets. The officers noted a distinct enthusiasm among the troops. They seemed eager for battle—anything was a welcome relief from the torturous marches of the past weeks.

At 5 a.m., the air was rent by the crash of the division's thirty-six light howitzers and twelve heavy howitzers and cannon. They were not laying down a massive area barrage, but a closely coordinated, well-directed Zerstörungsfeuer (destructive fire) that shifted from point to point as deemed necessary by the attacking regiments. The primary targets were the trenches and field fortifications that stretched between the bunkers. To deal with the bunkers, the division employed a new tool—the 8.8-cm anti-aircraft gun from the division's Flak Company, which was now to be used as a "bunker buster." Each of the attacking regiments had been provided with two of these versatile guns, which had been brought forward to as close as possible to their targets and carefully concealed. Their task was to take out the bunkers with direct fire or, at least, render them "Sturmreif"—that is, softened up so as to be "ripe" for assault.

As the shells roared overhead, the assault companies readied themselves, shedding any superfluous gear—harness, gasmasks, mess kits, and even cartridge pouches. The troops would go forward in traditional "Sturm" style: rifles slung, pockets crammed with ammunition, and two sand bags filled with stick-grenades slung about their necks.

At 6 a.m., the feldwebels blew their whistles and the assault troops bounded toward the enemy positions. In the attack sector of Regiment 18, its Kommandeur, Oberstleutnant Becker, personally led his Stoßtruppen and engineers armed with flamethrowers against six bunkers that lay on either side of the road to Polotsk. They made quick work of the bunkers. Grenades and explosive charges thrust through the firing ports took out some of the bunkers, while in other bunkers, the occupants who had been battered near senseless by the direct fire of the flak guns, quickly surrendered at the approach of the jetting flames of the engineers' flame throwers. In the course of the day, the assault teams of Regiment 18 captured or destroyed fifteen bunkers.

Contrary to instructions, Oberstleutnant Hennicke, 15 km to the north near Lessiny, sent forward two companies of infantry and one of engineers. Here in the attack sector of Regiment 37, the direct fire of the flak guns and the divisional artillery was also proving its worth. Wherever the assault teams encountered resistance, concentrated artillery fire was quickly brought to bear. An attempted counterattack by the Russians was smashed by artillery fire as the enemy were assembling in a patch of woods. By 11 a.m., the assault groups had broken through the defense zone and were rolling up the remaining enemy positions from the rear.

Once through the Soviet defense belt, Hennicke set his regiment on the march to Polotsk. He assembled a small Vorausabteilung from whatever mobile units at hand, and sent them racing to Polotsk. With luck, they might succeed in capturing the bridges there. But luck was not to be had. As so often in the past, when the Vorausabteilung got to within 200 meters of the bridge, it exploded and dropped into the Duna. Following what by now had become standard procedure, the machine gun teams and panzerjägers blanketed the opposite shore with fire as the engineers paddled the infantry across the river to establish a bridgehead. The bridgehead was quickly established and the engineers set about constructing a bridge.

Despite failing to seize an intact bridge over the Duna, the 6th Infantry Division's assault on its "Fortress of Polotsk" was a considerable success. The much-vaunted Stalin Line had been broken in the course of a morning. A total 104 bunkers had been destroyed and 800 prisoners taken, and all of this with incredibly light casualties: eleven dead and thirty-six wounded.

Early on the morning of July 18, the engineers completed their 154-meter bridge over the Duna, and the regiments crossed over and marched into Mother Russia. The troops were appalled at the level of poverty of the local population. The villages consisted of one-room, wooden huts, often inhabited by as many as twelve people and, of course, the family cow. Any Landser unfortunate enough to have to enter one of the shacks soon discovered himself infested with fleas and other vermin. At first, the villagers reacted with fear to the grey columns marching by, but when they realized that the Germans had not come to slit their throats, they became a bit more approachable—but only to a point. Twenty years of communist repression had reduced them to a dull indifference as to who ruled them.

After crossing the Duna, the 6th Infantry Division was ordered to close the ever-widening gap between the far-ranging panzers of Hoth's Panzer Group 3 and the infantry divisions of the Ninth Army that were struggling to keep up with the pace of Blitzkrieg in the East. No easy task. Not only did the racing panzer divisions grab all the headlines, they also grabbed all the best roads, leaving the infantry to toil along on the primitive "dust tracks," which at times were little more than rural cow paths.

On they marched, ever eastward, past Obol, Gorodok, Witebsk, and countless villages with unpronounceable names. Witebsk had been nearly burned down by the Komsomol cadets before they withdrew from the city. Only the city center, built mostly of stone, had survived. The older inhabitants asked the newly appointed German commandant for permission to reopen the cathedral for services, which he promptly granted. The great bronze bell of the cathedral rang out over the still smoldering ruins of the city and the service was well attended, although the younger generation attended more from curiosity than devotion.

On July 29, after two weeks of marching beneath the heat of a midsummer sun, the 6th Infantry Division closed the gap with Panzer Group 3, not because they had managed to catch up with the panzers but because the panzers had stopped. Army Group Center's two panzer groups had already plunged 600 km into Russia. At Minsk they had destroyed three Soviet armies, and then in the Smolensk sector they had encircled three more armies of some fifteen divisions and were set to annihilate them. However, this would have to be left to the infantry divisions because for the time being, the panzer and motorized divisions were a spent force; the men were exhausted, their equipment broken down. Hoth reported that his Panzer Group 3 had already lost 60–70 percent of its fighting vehicles to either enemy action or mechanical failure. His divisions needed to be refitted and resupplied and their casualties replaced. Panzer Group 2 was in a similar condition and would not be operational until August 15. The rapid advance of Army Group Center had come to a temporary halt.

The 6th Infantry Division was diverted 40 km northeast to Kanats, where they were to relieve the Saxon 14th Motorized Division, which was essentially "abgekämpft" ("fought out"), and take up defensive positions along the Mesha River. Defensive? Did the troops even remember what the word meant? They had not manned defensive positions since the first few weeks of the war back in '39. Since then, the men had marched across France, stormed across the Soviet border zone, broken through the Stalin Line, and advanced 600 km into the Russian homeland. Now they were expected to go over to the defensive? To most of the troops, an entrenching tool was what one used for in-close fighting instead of a bayonet.

The senior officers of the division, who understood that a division is only a small cog in the great machine of a campaign that can be shifted about the battlefields without explanation, accepted the new directive with little concern. As for the men, going on the defensive meant relief from the endless marching, but among the junior officers, young men with active minds, there arose a feeling of uneasiness. Up to this point, they had known nothing but marching from victory to victory or, at least, hearing of great triumphs from other sectors of the front. One can forgive their questioning as to whether all was not going well in the Russian War. In a sense, their concerns were justified.

Since July 15, discussions had been taking place at the Führer's Headquarters, concerning what to do next in Operation Barbarossa. In addition to the great disparity in the size of the military forces and available resources of the warring parties, the original plan for the eastern campaign with its three primary objectives (Leningrad, Moscow, and the Ukraine) had created problems of its own.

In war, one normally seeks the convergence of one's forces at a decisive point in order to overwhelm the enemy. Operation Barbarossa, with its far-flung objectives, assured the divergence of German forces. This problem had been appreciated by the planners of Barbarossa, who realized that at some point in the campaign the powerful panzer groups of Army Group Center might have to be diverted from their advance on Moscow and be "loaned out" to Army Groups North and South to enable them to achieve their objectives.

Not only were the primary objectives geographically divergent, but they were also divergent in their very nature. In the planning of Barbarossa, Hitler had always maintained that Leningrad, the "birthplace of Bolshevism," was a political objective; the Ukraine with its natural resources, an economic objective; and Moscow with the bulk of the Soviet forces defending it, a military objective. The question arising at the Führer's Headquarters concerned which of the three objectives was to be achieved first? In the last half of July and the first half of August, new directives and amendments to these directives began emanating from the Führer's Headquarters. At times in these directives Leningrad appeared to be the primary objective, at other times the Ukraine, while emphasis remained that the destruction of the Soviet armies of the central front was still paramount. These confusing and at times contradictory directives created concerns among the army and army group commanders—not because of the decisions made by Hitler but by his seeming inability to make a decision. Did the Führer not know what he actually wanted to achieve?

Hitler had once remarked during the planning of Operation Barbarossa that "One only needs to kick in the door and the whole rotten structure will collapse." His armies had certainly "kicked in the door," but when one kicks in a door, one does not know what one will find within. The German Army hoped to find a collapse of the Red Army; Hitler hoped to find a collapse of the entire Soviet political system. Both hopes were to prove illusory.

On July 29–30, the 6th Infantry Division relieved the "fought-out" 14th Motorized Division and took over a 40-km front along the Mesha from Kanats in the west to Wassiljowa in the east—40 km of front for a single division, twice what the training manual allowed and, even worse, the division's new home was a swampy woodland. Accustomed as the men were to the well-tended forests of their homeland, they now found themselves in the midst of a primeval forest and confronted with a style of warfare for which they had no training. (Even the German Army could not persuade the powerful German Forestry Service to allow military maneuvers in their precious idyllic forests.) Due to the extent of the front, the division could only cover it by using widely spaced strong points between which patrols moved constantly back and forth. A fine opportunity for any young German wishing to live out his Karl May fantasies, but instead of confronting imaginary Indians, here the men were dealing with NKVD units, Cossacks, and the ever-present partisans.[5] If any of the young Rhinelanders and Westphalians had ever thought that by going over to the defensive they would get a respite from the war, they were soon to be disabused of that notion.

The day after they had taken over the sector, they had to fight off strong and aggressive Russian patrols (NKVD), who being familiar with the area, could easily infiltrate the thinly held German line and appear as if from nowhere. On August 1, two squadrons of Cossacks attacked the outposts of the 2nd Company of Regiment 18, forcing the men to evacuate their position. Leutnant Wasmuth was killed and four men were missing. The next day, the regiment's 3rd Company was attacked by strong Cossack units that had infiltrated around behind them. Hauptfeldwebel Bernhausen and eighteen men of the 1st Platoon were cut down and another seventeen went missing. Later a patrol discovered eleven of them in shallow graves. All had been severely beaten and then shot in the head. According to local civilians, the Cossacks had led off the other six missing men with their hands tied behind their backs.

In the afternoon, Russian units bypassed the 18th Regiment's 2nd Company and pushed deep into the German defense zone. Hauptmann Höke, commanding the 2nd Battalion held in reserve, sent the 7th Company forward in a counterattack. They were able to drive the enemy back and restore the original front line. In the sector of the 1st Battalion near Schischowa, a strong enemy force unable to break through the German defenses, sidestepped them, and pushed deep into the defense zone all the way to the supporting artillery positions. Having fired off all their ammunition, the artillerymen were engaged in a close combat infantry battle using carbines, machine-pistols, and spades.

A critical situation had arisen and once again, the cavalry rode to the rescue. Freiherr von Böselager's Reiter Schwadron caught the Russians by surprise with a flank attack. The infantry and artillerymen were able to follow the progress of the attack from the muzzle flashes and signal flares rising in the night sky. By 10 p.m., the gunfire had ceased and von Böselager's cavalrymen bivouacked on the ground they had won. His victory though was soon overshadowed by the death of his elder brother. Two days later, Freiherr Antonius von Böselager, who served as a reserve officer under his younger brother, was severely wounded and died at the battalion aid station. The head of the von Böselager family had fallen. He would not be the last from this aristocratic family to die in Hitler's war in the East.[6]

Over on the left flank the welcome received by von Tresckow's 58th Regiment in the Mesha sector was little different from that of the 18th Regiment. At mid-morning on August 2, the Russians attacked in strength the regiment's strong points at Ordyna and Poshogi. The attacks were repelled, but Generalleutnant Auleb deemed it prudent to reinforce the 58th Regiment with the 2nd Battalion of the 18th Regiment and the 3rd Battalion of the 37th Regiment.

The next day, the enemy concentrated his attacks on the 3rd Battalion of Regiment 58. The attacks were beaten back, but the 9th Company lost two men killed and thirteen wounded plus an anti-tank gun destroyed by a direct hit. The regiment's 2nd Battalion was ordered to drive the enemy back. They succeeded but paid a high price: eleven dead, four officers and twenty-nine men wounded, and one officer and twenty-six men missing for a total of seventy-one casualties (breaking through the "Stalin Line" had cost the entire division only forty-seven casualties.) A total 200 Russian bodies were counted amid the dense undergrowth. An estimated 100 enemy wounded had been carried off by their comrades.

The pattern was now set for this battle in the swamps and forests along the Mesha. The Russians launched battalion strength attacks against the German strong points or bypassed them and drove deep into the defense zone. Then the Germans counterattacked and pushed the Russians back. Although in time, the Germans would become masters of defense, at this stage of the war, the German soldier was doctrinally and psychologically incapable of anything other than attack. Each Soviet attack was met by an immediate counterattack, and the dead began to pile up on the forest floor. The action reports of the 58th Regiment reflect the growing intensity of the fighting:

| | |
|---|---|
| 9 August. | Enemy attack supported by four tanks. 10th Company loses four dead. Two Russian tanks destroyed. |
| 10–12 August. | Enemy patrols. Regiment loses four dead. |
| 13 August. | Regiment losses: three dead, one wounded, one missing. |
| 18 August. | Enemy attack beaten back with hand grenades. Two dead, eight wounded, one missing. (Enemy losses: thirty-eight dead and thirty-six prisoners.) |
| 19 August. | Two battalions attack Katkowo. Immediate counterattack drives enemy back. Regiment loses sixteen dead. |
| 21 August. | Reinforced Russian company attacks Katkowo. Forty-five Russians killed, 100 wounded, five taken prisoner. Own losses, one dead. |
| 22 August. | Soviet attack in regimental strength on Kanat-Katowo position with armor and artillery support. Situation critical. Division commander arrives on scene. Attack finally repelled. Own losses: four dead, fifteen wounded. Enemy losses 200 dead, |

180 wounded, five prisoners. [In this single action, the 58th Regiment expended 32,035 rounds of rifle ammunition; 1,310 machine-pistol rounds; 329 5-cm mortar rounds; 299 8-cm mortar rounds; seventy-five stick grenades; and forty-five egg grenades. And still the attacks continued.]

23 August. Four enemy attacks supported by tanks. Fifteen NCOs and men killed. Two officers and forty-four men wounded. Enemy losses, 120 dead, 200 wounded, and eleven prisoners.

27 August. Russian 243rd Infantry Division breaks through 37th Regiment. Its commander, Knight's Cross holder Oberstleutnant Hennicke killed in action. Parts of Regiment 58 drives enemy back and seals the gap. Regiment 58 loses twenty-one dead, twenty-five wounded, and two missing. Regiment 37 loses ten officers and 162 men killed, thirteen officers, and 113 men wounded and thirty-six missing.

With losses totaling 382 officers and men, August 27 was the costliest day the 6th Infantry Division had experienced since the beginning of the war. On August 30, one month after taking over the Mesha sector, the division's two chaplains, Bongards (Evangelical) and Freiherr Geyr von Schweppenburg (Catholic), held the division's first mass burial. As the men sang "Ich hatt' einen Kameraden," 200 men of the 37th Regiment were laid to rest in the recently established German cemetery at Punewo. The 200 birch crosses in the forest clearing were a grim reminder of the determined and at times brutal enemy the men of the 6th Infantry Division were now facing.

While the 6th Infantry Division was occupied with the incessant attacks and counterattacks in the green hell of the Mesha, other infantry divisions of Army Group Center were crushing the Soviet forces in the Smolensk pocket. Marshal Timoshenko's efforts to break through the German iron ring from the outside and rescue the three trapped Soviet armies had all failed and von Bock's Army Group Center claimed another great victory: 320,000 Russian soldiers marched off in captivity, leaving behind 3,205 armored vehicles, 3,120 artillery pieces, and 1,098 aircraft either captured or destroyed. The path to Moscow lay open, and hope existed that the war could be finished before winter arrived.

This hope was dashed when Hitler decided that the economic goal of the Ukraine was to take precedence over any advance on the central front toward Moscow. Despite the pleadings of Guderian that now was the moment to strike at Moscow, on August 21, Hitler directed that Guderian send his Panzer Group 2 south and, in conjunction with Army Group South's Panzer Group 1, destroy the Soviet forces defending the Ukraine.

For the 6th Infantry Division, this meant spending another month in the swampy forests of the Mesha sector. At least this time the men would be in a different swamp. Between September 4 and 9, the division relieved their neighbor on the right, the Hessian 129th Infantry Division, and took up positions in the Ossotnja sector. As before, strong points connected by constant patrols were utilized to cover a 40-km front, and also as before, the division received a similar reception in their new position. On September 11, a force of 250 Russians attacked the 3rd Battalion of the 18th Regiment. The attack was smashed by a rapid concentration of fire from Artillery Group Sommer and then finished off by a counterattack led by Leutnant Kiso, and 120 dazed Russians were taken prisoners. On September 15, a Russian assault company preparing an attack was attacked first by elements of the 37th Regiment and the Reconnaissance Battalion. Ninety prisoners, including five officers, were taken. The rest of the Russian assault company had been killed. In addition, seventy of the excellent Russian machine pistols (PPSh-41) were hauled off as war booty and quickly distributed among the troops. The next day, a strong enemy attack succeeded in breaking through a section of the 37th Regiment's line, but the breach was quickly sealed off, and the greater part of the enemy force was killed. Only a few managed to make it back to their own lines.

Having had their noses bloodied in these first engagements, the Russians decided to leave the 6th Infantry Division alone. Apparently these "fascist bandits" had learned how to fight in a Russian forest.

After these initial clashes, the division mostly had to deal with the ever-present threat of partisans. If there was one thing that the German soldier had learned so far in the eastern campaign, it was that forest plus swamp equaled partisans. From their natural habitat of woodland and marsh, partisan bands unleashed deadly ambushes deep behind German lines particularly aimed at the supply troops as they moved along the forest paths bringing supplies to the front lines. These partisan bands were not the result of a spontaneous reaction of the Russian population to an invasion of their homeland by a hated enemy but formed a part of Soviet military strategy to counter any invade. Well-organized and led by committed communists, the partisans and the "Banditenkrieg" they waged became far more than a nuisance as the Germans were forced to commit increasing amounts of their limited resources to counter the partisan threat.

Although normally left to the responsibility of the Security Divisions or Police Battalions, at times front-line units found it necessary to conduct "partisan hunts" or "partisan sweeps" behind their own lines. In mid-September, the 37th Regiment was alerted by local villagers that a sizeable force of some 500 partisans and Russian soldiers were hiding in a nearby woods. Specially selected men were sent out on patrol to locate the enemy, and then elements of the Reconnaissance Battalion accompanied by engineers moved in rapidly to surround and crush this danger lurking in their rear. Some escaped; many were killed; and 100, most of whom were wounded, were taken prisoner. Generalleutnant Auleb visited the aid station to see the prisoners as they were being treated by German medical personnel. Observing them lying on the ground smoking cigarettes given them by their captors, he could not help but be impressed by their stoic demeanor. A number of them were clad in civilian clothes—obviously partisans—but in view that they had been fighting alongside regular Russian troops, Auleb ordered that they be treated as prisoners of war and not executed.

Except for the occasional harassment fire of the Soviet artillery, the Ossotnyja sector remained quiet and the officers noticed that the men were making substantial improvements to their living quarters. The aggressive "always forward—always attack" mentality drilled into the German soldier made him fundamentally adverse to superfluous improvements to temporary defensive quarters, but now the men were lining the walls of their dugouts with birch staves and covering the floors with straw. What could all this mean?

By this point, even the dullest Landser understood why their advance had been halted six weeks ago. The panzers had been sent off south to conquer the Ukraine. The men also understood that it was mid-September and the nights were growing cooler. By the time the panzer units returned, there would not be sufficient time to resume the advance and capture Moscow before winter set in—and winter comes early in Russia.

Rumors had been circulating that the division was to spend the winter where it was and resume the advance in the spring. Nothing could have been further from the truth. On September 16, news arrived of a great victory in the south. At Kiev, Army Group South had destroyed six Soviet armies, taken 665,000 prisoners, and had captured or destroyed 3,718 artillery pieces and 884 tanks.

Then, the Führer's personal address was read out to the troops by the company commanders.

> Soldaten an der Ostfront!
>
> Since 22 June when I called on you to remove the threat from our homeland, you have engaged the greatest military power in the world. We know now that it was the intention of the Soviet Union not only to overrun Germany but all of Europe.
>
> Meine Kameraden!
>
> Thanks to your bravery, in three months you have taken 2,400,000 prisoners, destroyed or captured 175,000 tanks of all sizes and 21,600 artillery pieces. In addition, during this time 14,300 aircraft have been shot down or destroyed on the ground.
>
> Meine Kameraden!
>
> Before us now stands the last great decisive battle of this year—the Battle for Moscow.

The words of the Führer came as a shock to the officers and men of the 6th Infantry Division. They would not be going into winter quarters. The advance would continue, even if it was rather late in the season to begin the "final campaign."

However, in due course, they accepted the Führer's directive with the professional calmness expected of the German soldier. As they thought more of it, they convinced themselves that the Führer would not have ordered the advance on Moscow if he had not thought it possible—and the Führer had not been wrong yet.

5

# Barbarossa II: The Volga and Beyond

Code-named Operation Typhoon, this "last great decisive battle of the year" was to be conducted in two phases. The first phase called for the destruction of the remaining Soviet forces on the central front. The second phase was the actual assault on Moscow. As in previous operations, the panzer and infantry divisions of Army Group Center were to conduct battles of encirclement and annihilation. Panzer Group 3 and Panzer Group 4 (on loan from Army Group North) were to destroy the Soviet forces north of the Smolensk–Moscow highway while Panzer Group 2 eliminated those forces located to the south. Once these objectives were achieved, Moscow would be left defenseless, which opened the possibility that Stalin might be willing to seek terms, or "the whole rotten structure" might collapse, leading to a new regime seeking peace. Either way, a winter assault on Moscow itself might not be needed.

The 6th Infantry Division's role in Operation Typhoon was to cover Panzer Group 3's northern flank as it thrust eastwards, but first the division would have to "kick open the door" in the Ossotnja sector to allow the panzers through.

During the last week of September, the men watched as the preparations for the assault took place around them. Understanding that the road conditions would be horrible (the autumn rains had already arrived), the division's motor transport was replaced by horse-drawn. With the expectation of large numbers of Russian prisoners, who would need at least one meal before they marched off to the collection centers, Generalleutnant Auleb ordered the field kitchens moved up closer to the front line. The ambulances were replaced by one-horse "Panje wagons" lined with straw and provided with a thatched roof. Although they could transport only one wounded man at a time, they had the practical advantage of being able to be positioned within 100 meters of the front, thus allowing for the rapid evacuation of casualties. In addition to stockpiles of ammunition and hand grenades, 800 fresh replacements from the division's

Field Training and Replacement Battalion arrived to fill out the rifle companies. Unfortunately, the last group of 400 replacements arrived the day before the attack and could not be adequately "worked in" to their new units. By the end of September, all was in readiness for the 6th Infantry Division to "kick open the door" for Hoth's Panzer Group 3. Everything had arrived. Everything, that is, except for winter clothing. In the coming weeks and months, the men would be facing the harsh Russian winter with little more on their backs than what they had worn during the heat of summer.

The Ossotnja sector through which the 6th Infantry Division was to attack was a 10-km stretch of swamp 90 km north of Smolensk. The division was to get across the swamp, seize the vital causeways, and then break through the main Russian line of resistance located along the eastern edge of the swamp, thus opening up the way for the Thuringian 1st Panzer Division. For the assault, Auleb deployed his division in the standard two-up, one-back arrangement with Becker's 18th Regiment attacking on the right flank, von Tresckow's 58th Regiment on the left, and the 37th Regiment held in reserve to either exploit success or to add impetus to a stalled attack. Each of the attacking regiments was supported by an artillery Abteilung, and the 58th Regiment had been provided with an additional infantry battalion from the 18th Motorized Division.

Facing them was the 242nd Soviet Rifle Division. German reconnaissance, however, had not been able to determine if any Soviet armor was present nor the extent and location of enemy artillery support. Besides the swampy terrain, the other difficulty confronting Auleb's regiments was the presence of two critical heights: Hill 220 in the center of the 18th Regiment's attack route and the high ground near Dewjataja on the left flank of the 58th Regiment. From these two vantage points, Soviet artillery observers would be able to view the entire attack zone and direct heavy fire down upon the Germans as they sloshed their way through the swamp. Both heights would have to be captured quickly if the division wished to avoid heavy casualties. The time and date of the attack was set for 6 a.m., October 2.

On the night of October 1, as the men were making their final preparations, the company commanders read out to them a message from the Führer:

> The last great decisive battle of this year will destroy the enemy and finally remove the threat from Germany and all of Europe which has hung over the continent since the time of the Huns and the Mongol horde. In the coming weeks the German people will be with you more than ever before.

The message was received in silence. Tomorrow was not simply a leap across another Russian swamp but the commencement of the "last great decisive battle of this year." For many a young Rhinelander and Westphalian, it would be their last battle.

By 2 a.m., the assault companies of the two attacking regiments had moved into their forward positions. Each platoon was then divided into two Stossgruppen, one led by a leutnant, the other by a senior NCO. Each Stossgruppe consisted of twenty men and two light machine guns. A few hours before the scheduled attack, these Stossgruppen were to crawl towards the Russian lines where they would lie in concealment 100 meters or less from those points of the enemy defenses which had been selected for the break-in. As soon as the artillery barrage lifted, the machine-gun teams would blanket the enemy positions with heavy fire while the rest of the Stossgruppe rushed forward with grenade and spade. This was a tried and true tactic dating back to the Stoßtruppen of the Great War but also one fraught with risk and which could only be conducted by highly trained, experienced troops—something the Landsers of the 6th Infantry Division certainly were.

The night passed slowly. The nights were longer now in Russia than they had been back in June when the division had first entered this vast country. The black night sky gradually changed to a gun-metal grey, and a thin ribbon of red appeared across the eastern horizon. The ribbon grew wider and wider. Then, "crash!" the artillery ripped apart the stillness of the dawn and rained fire down upon the Russian lines. Halfway through the planned fifteen-minute barrage, the guns concentrated their fire on those positions lying directly before the Stossgruppen. At 6:15 a.m., the shelling abruptly ceased. A moment of silence descended, and then "Los, sprung!" The machine guns clattered away at the rate of 900 rounds per minute, and the Stossgruppen stormed the enemy lines.

In the attack sector of the 58th Regiment, the Russian defenses along the western edge of the swamp were quickly overrun. In the center of the sector (2nd Battalion), there appeared to be a path leading through the swamp, and it was immediately chosen to be the Schwerpunkt of the attack. The 2nd Company of engineers was rushed in to reinforce the 2nd Battalion, and the artillery concentrated its fire at the base of the path. After a few minutes of devastating fire, the companies of the 2nd Battalion plunged into the swamp. The going was not easy, but by 8:40 a.m., they had fought their way through to the eastern edge of the swamp.

The regiment's 1st Battalion on the left and the 3rd Battalion on the right were not as successful. Their advance was halted by heavy Russian resistance. Many of the wounded drowned in the swamp. Their comrades, pinned down by heavy enemy fire, were unable to help them. Their bodies were not recovered until the following day.

From his command post, Generalleutnant Auleb could observe the 2nd Battalion emerging from the eastern edge of the swamp and, choosing to reinforce success, ordered the artillery to concentrate its fire on the village of Spiritschino, 1 km east of the battalion. At 9:15 a.m., the 2nd battalion moved into what remained of the village. Then, on his own initiative, the battalion commander, Hauptmann Witte, swung his units 2 km to the south and attacked the village of Jessennaja. After overcoming stout opposition, Hauptmann Witte could report at 1:15 p.m. that the village was firmly in German hands.

Meanwhile, the other two battalions of the 58th Regiment had succeeded in fighting their way through the swamp but had been unable to bring any of their heavy weapons (infantry howitzers and anti-tank guns) with them because the enemy had blown two large gaps in the causeway. Following again the doctrine of reinforcing success, Auleb directed the 1st and 3rd Battalions of the 37th Regiment to join in the advance of the 58th Regiment. During the course of the day, the 58th Regiment fought its way forward another 3 km and at dusk dug in along the western edge of the forest 3 km west of Baturino. In twelve hours of heavy combat, von Tresckow's regiment had broken through two Soviet defense belts, crossed an "impassable" swamp, and pushed 8 km eastwards—but at a heavy cost. Five officers and 104 men lay dead in the swamp and the fields beyond. Twelve officers and 360 men had been wounded, and another twelve men were missing. October 2 had been the bloodiest day for the regiment thus far in the Russian campaign.

Over on the right (southern) flank, Becker's 18th Regiment had also had a rough and bloody day. In as much as the regiment had been tasked with opening the way and protecting the flank of the 1st Panzer Division, it had been put under the command of the panzer division. The attack sector of the 18th Regiment had been considered the more difficult due to the fact that the swamp at this point was further away from the German front line than in the northern sector, giving the regiment a much wider stretch of open ground to cover under enemy fire. In addition, there were three commanding heights from which Russian artillery observers could call down fire upon the assault companies as they advanced: Hill 500 (2nd Battalion sector), Hill 220 (1st Battalion sector), and Hill 215 (3rd Battalion sector). If the assault were to succeed, these heights would have to be taken quickly.

The three battalions of the regiment were deployed abreast: 2nd Battalion on the left flank, 3rd Battalion on the right flank, and 1st Battalion in the center. At 6:15 a.m., when the artillery barrage stopped, the Stossgruppen leaped to their feet and stormed forward. They quickly overcame the Russian defenders west of the swamp. At 6:20 a.m., five minutes after the attack had begun, Hill 220 was in German hands. The 1st Battalion in the center and the 3rd Battalion on the right made good progress, fighting their way through the swamp, crossing the Ossotnja stream, and occupying the high ground near Storoshok.

However, on the left flank, the 2nd Battalion had run into difficulty early on. Initially, the assault had rapidly gained ground but then had been stopped cold by the increasing defensive fire. Oberleutnant Grote's 6th Company and the 8th (heavy machine-gun) Company eventually discovered a gap in the enemy defenses and were able to reach the western edge of the swamp at 10:30 a.m.

The battalion commander, Hauptmann Höke made his way forward and took personal command of the two companies. He led them through the swamp, seizing the causeway and reached the day's objective, the high ground northwest of Storoshok.

The other two companies of Höke's 2nd Battalion did not have the good fortune of finding a gap in the Russian defenses. Leutnant Focken's 3rd platoon of the 5th Company had encountered no opposition and had been able to reach the Shidiki road where they overran an enemy position, taking a lieutenant and six men prisoner, but then, advancing without orders, Leutnant Focken's platoon disappeared around 6:45 a.m.

The 1st Platoon, divided into two Stossgruppen commanded by Leutnant Späthe and Feldwebel Wallmeier, were able to cross a minefield without loss but then were confronted by a 2-meter-wide belt of barbed wire. Ignoring the enemy rifle and machine-gun fire raining down on them from nearby Hill 500, Oberschütze Moritz cut a path through the wire. Leutnant Späthe immediately ordered his twenty-man Stossgruppe to assault Hill 500. Under the covering fire of the group's two light machine guns, they raced 150 meters across a potato field and assaulted the hill. In hand-to-hand combat, they overcame the defenders. Meanwhile, Feldwebel Wallmeier swung off to the left with his Stossgruppe and cleared the woods adjoining Hill 500 to a depth of 150 meters, taking four prisoners.

Encouraged by his success, Späthe continued his advance eastwards, but no sooner had they left Hill 500 than they came under fire from every direction—artillery, mortars, machine guns, and snipers. Leutnant Späthe and two men were killed, an unteroffizier and three men were wounded. Unable to go either forward or back in the hellish crossfire, the remaining men of the Stossgruppe dug in where they were.

At this same time, Feldwebel Wallmeier's Stossgruppe in the woods found itself under attack by a superior Russian force and fell back to Hill 500. Time and again, the Russians attempted to retake the hill, but Wallmeier and his small group were able to beat back the attacks. By now, the Stossgruppe was down to two light machine guns and ten rifles. Their situation had become critical.

The commander of the 5th Company, Oberleutnant Rhein had already lost one of his platoons (Leutnant Focken's platoon was still missing) and saw that he was in danger of losing another. Despite the heavy fire, he had no choice but to send his last platoon across the same potato field that Leutnant Späthe had crossed. Covered by the fire of two heavy machine guns from Feldwebel Zesniak's heavy machine-gun troop, the men of the 2nd Platoon were able to reach Hill 500 with only two men wounded. Feldwebel Zesniak then brought his troop forward to join them.

Not wanting to risk another costly attack on the new reinforced German position, the Russians attempted to simply blast the German defenders off Hill

500 with artillery, mortars, and machine-gun fire. Worse still were the Russian snipers, who fired at the slightest movement. Unteroffizier Burger was killed by one of these well-concealed marksman.

At dusk, the Russian fire slackened and the German defenders prepared for another attack, but nothing happened. Minutes passed and the men looked at one another in puzzlement. Oberleutnant Rhein quickly made up his mind. If the Russians were not going to attack him, then he would attack them. Anything was better than lying here waiting to be blown into oblivion. At 7 p.m., Rhein ordered an assault on the woods. Covered by two light and two heavy machine guns, the men rushed down the hill into the woods, only to find the enemy gone.

With nothing to impede their advance, Rhein's 5th Company pushed forward to reach the other companies of the 2nd Battalion at Storoshok around 8 p.m., where they took up position in the cemetery north of the village—an appropriate billet for the end of a long and costly day. The 18th Regiment had lost three officers and forty men killed and eight officers and 117 men wounded.

The battle of the Ossotnja Swamp cost the 6th Infantry Division a total of 673 men killed, wounded, or missing. As usual, most of the casualties fell upon the rifle companies. There were several reasons for the heavy casualties: the effectiveness of the Soviet artillery fire directed by observers on the high ground near Dewjataja, which being some 7 km behind the front line, could not be neutralized in the early stages of the attack; the tenacious defense of the Soviets 242nd Rifle Division most of whose members went down fighting in the fields, woods, and swamps of the Ossotnja sector. Another reason for the heavy losses may have been the insufficient time available to adequately "work in" the 800 replacements who had arrived only days before the assault.

Despite the losses, the 6th Infantry Division had again successfully completed its assignment. In the opening phase of Operation Typhoon, the door had been kicked open through which the panzer divisions could now pour and complete their assignment—the annihilation of the Soviet armies before Moscow.

The next morning at 5:30 a.m., the regiments were ordered to fall in and continue the advance east. Wearily the men gathered up their gear, shuffled into line, and set off toward the rising sun. They had gotten little sleep. After an exhausting day of combat they had spent much of the night eliminating isolated pockets of resistance and rounding up Russian stragglers. They had been given no time to grieve or reflect. Their fallen comrades had been left behind to be buried by troops of the rear services. It may have been comforting to know that the divisional chaplains, Bongards and von Schweppenburg, would read the eulogy, but "Ich hatt' einen Kameraden" would be sung by strangers to the fallen, men who had never known them, eaten with them, or fought alongside them.

As the 6th Infantry Division advanced to the east, it encountered only weak and scattered resistance. The Soviet forces who had fought so tenaciously against them in the Ossotnja sector had been utterly destroyed, and what few units that remained were retreating rapidly northeast to avoid encirclement.

The primary resistance to the advance came from the Russian weather and the Russian land—or lack thereof. With the arrival of the autumn rains, the Russian landscape seemed to have disappeared beneath a sea of mud, the "Rasputiza," which made the movement of vehicles on the primitive roads nearly impossible. Even the one-horse "panje wagons" had a difficult time. Marches of 30–50 km per day were a thing of the past, but the scant dozen kilometers the division managed per day was no less demanding on the men. The division had marched off without much of its heavy equipment, which was still stuck in the Ossotnja Swamp and would remain there until November—not only because of road conditions but also lack of fuel. This lack of fuel was soon accompanied by another shortage—food, something the men quickly noticed under the physical demands placed upon them by the road conditions and worsening weather. Foraging and requisitioning were made difficult by the abject poverty of the local populations. (One certainly could not take a family's only cow or hen.) These shortages were the first indication that Germany's resources had become stretched quite thin by the demands of Barbarossa.

On the morning of October 6, as the division set off to the northeast, the men were greeted by the first snow, but it was only a tease. The dreaded Russian winter had not yet arrived, and by noon the snow had melted away, leaving the roads in even worse condition than before. After a 15-km march, the division was suddenly ordered to swing southeast and seize the bridge over the Djneber at Slepzowo, 30 km away. The next day, October 7, the temperature dropped, and the snow fell in earnest—this time, no tease. The Russian winter had arrived, but the winter clothing had not. In addition to being totally inadequate, the men's summer uniforms had become somewhat thread bare and had long since faded from Feldgrau to a piss-yellow green.

Despite the weather and the miserable roads, Becker's 18th Regiment reached Slepzowo on October 8 and seized the bridge undamaged. The Russian demolition team arrived too late and was easily driven off. The bridge at Slepzowo was hardly what would come to mind when one heard the word "bridge." The structure was a crude and flimsy walkway 150 meters long, 2 meters above the river's surface, supported on piles driven into the river bed. It resembled some makeshift crossing of a country stream built by local farmers of a previous age to get their produce to market.

As Generalleutnant Auleb watched his troops cautiously making their way across the primitive structure in the cold and the pelting snow, he was reminded of the French Emperor and his *Grande Armée*. He turned to his staff and spoke with a sense of both *déjà vu* and premonition:

> I have learned in school that it is cold here in winter, much colder than in Germany. And I have also learned what happened to Napoleon when in 1812 he attempted to wage war in Russia. If this idiot in Berlin orders us to make a second advance on Moscow without considering the arrival of winter, then that is nothing more than stupidity—and a crime.

Auleb then added, "Gentlemen, none of us will ever see our homes again. You will all remember my words."[1]

For all too many of the men of the 6th Infantry Division, the general spoke true.

After two of his regiments (18th and 58th) had crossed over the Dnieper, Auleb received orders that were rather puzzling. He was to halt his eastern advance and strike north with all speed. What was this all about? Simply put, success. Army Group Center was already thinking in terms of phase two of Operation Typhoon—the assault on Moscow itself. By October 7, Hoth's Panzer Group 3 and Hoepner's Panzer Group 4 had already completed the encirclement of five Soviet armies at Wjasma. Reinhardt's XLI Panzer Corps was no longer needed and was directed to swing north to take Kalinin (160 km northwest of Moscow), thereby severing the Leningrad–Moscow highway. The VI Corps (6th and 26th Divisions) was again to act as flank cover for the XLI Panzer Corps.

At 4 a.m. on October 10, the division began its advance north with the 58th Regiment astride the road to Ssytschewka, the 18th Regiment deeply echeloned to its left. The weather was bitter cold, but at least the roads were frozen, making the going easier than in the previous days. Still suffering from a shortage of fuel, the mobile communication units had to be left behind. In the upcoming battle, reports and orders would be transmitted in the old manner—horse-mounted couriers. The anti-tank guns, likewise, had to rely upon horses for transport.

By 9:30 a.m., the 58th Regiment had covered 15 km to reach the high ground just south of Ssytschweka and prepared for an immediate assault. The attack on Ssytschweka bore an eerie resemblance to that earlier campaign in Russia nearly a century and a half before. The falling snow, officers and couriers rushing about on horseback, the guns being pulled to the front by horses, their crews cursing while manhandling the guns into position—only this time, the obscenities were shouted in German rather than French. Similarly, instead of holed up in a command post kilometers behind the front awaiting reports, Generalleutnant Auleb could view the entire battlefield from the heights south of Ssytschweka and as in earlier times personally direct the battle. All that seemed missing were the bugle calls and colorful uniforms.

Respecting the strength of the enemy defenses before him, Auleb had no intention of ordering the 58th Regiment into a costly frontal assault—the lives of his men were too dear to him. He left the 1st Battalion to fix the enemy in place and shifted the other two battalions around to the left to occupy the high ground northwest of the town. When the Russians realized that they were being outflanked, they began a hasty withdrawal. At 1 p.m., the 2nd Battalion swept down from the heights into the town, where they quickly overcame the enemy's rearguard units. Twenty-seven artillery pieces and 600 prisoners were taken as well as a huge story of supplies, including rations only half-burned by the retreating Russians, which provided the men of the 58th Regiment the first "cooked" meal they had tasted in days. At 4 p.m., with the last Russian defenders rounded up, the 58th Regiment dug in along the heights north of the town. The day had cost the regiment nineteen dead and thirty-four wounded. Tomorrow, the men were certain, they would resume the advance north. Next stop: the Volga.

But as the 6th Infantry Division marched off north the morning of October 11, it had only gone a few kilometers when Auleb received orders from VI Corps Headquarters to halt march and form front facing west. Sizeable Soviet forces, which had been bypassed and cut off during the German drive east, were now attempting to escape to the northeast. Their very presence posed a serious threat to the flank and rear of the XLI Panzer Corps as it pushed north. Auleb was charged with intercepting and halting the escaping enemy forces. To do so required the 6th Infantry Division to cover a 50-km front that stretched from near Rzhev in the north to Ssytschewka in the south. As so often before, the division could only accomplish this by establishing strong points along the most likely avenues of escape.

For the next two days, the division repelled one Russian attack after another. The weather was horrible, the Russians desperate, the fighting fierce. Reports circulated that often Russian soldiers, in order to avoid capture, committed suicide by lying on a grenade and pulling its pin. On the afternoon of October 13, the 18th Regiment had to fight off three near-suicidal attacks over a four-hour period. Ten battalions of Russian infantry with artillery support stormed against the German positions time and again, always with the roaring shout of "Urrah!" a shout that would haunt the nightmares of many a veteran long after the war.

The ammunition situation became critical. By mid-afternoon, the German machine gunners had fired off all their standard ammunition and were forced to use their specialized armor-piercing rounds against the waves of human bodies rolling towards them. The light infantry howitzers of the 13th company were wheeled up to the front lines and fired directly into the dense enemy ranks with horrendous effect, but soon they were down to the last two rounds. For the first time in the eastern campaign, the shout went up, "Seitengewehr aufplflanzen!" Finally, at 10 p.m., a resupply of ammunition arrived, and after a brief barrage, the companies of the 18th Regiment stormed forward in a counterattack and drove the enemy back into the woods from which he had launched his attacks. The Russian losses were described as "horrific."

On October 14, the 6th Infantry Division was relieved of its defensive duties by the 26th Infantry Division. The past two weeks, though hard fought, had been successful. Since the plunge across the Ossotnja Swamp, Auleb's division had captured 4,500 prisoners, forty-five artillery pieces, thirty-two mortars, ten anti-tank guns, one tank, and two armored cars.

The next morning, the division resumed its advance north to the Volga. The road conditions, as usual, were horrible. One day the roads were ice covered, the next day swallowed by mud. Even worse, the division was following in the path of the XLI Panzer Corps, whose tracked vehicles had churned the road into an unrecognizable muddy porridge. The fuel shortage continued and the division's transport still remained 150 km to the rear. The food shortage continued as well. More and more the men found themselves dependent on the land. The Russian bread (chleba) was too coarse—even for German stomachs—and provided more illness than nutrition. The horses had acquired their winter coats, but the men had not, and their faded threadbare uniforms had begun to fall apart.

Despite these conditions, the morale of the men remained high. Their advances and victories sustained them. On October 17 came news of the great battle of Wjasma-Bryansk. Seven Soviet armies of eighty-one divisions had been annihilated, and 332,000 Russian soldiers had been killed and 668,000 taken prisoner. The road to Moscow now lay open.

On that same day a few kilometers south of Rzhev, the 6th Infantry Division was diverted northeast, denying the men the opportunity to view the historic city. However, in a few months they would see quite a bit of Rzhev—a city with whose name the Rhineland-Westphalian 6th Infantry Division would be forever bound in the annals of war.

Three days later, on October 20, the division reached the Volga, and without awaiting orders the men of the 58th Regiment gathered up whatever boats they could find in the area and paddled across the 164 meters to the opposite shore. They had done it. They had crossed the Volga, the great "Mother River of Russia"—even if only in rotting fishing boats. The following day, the engineers threw a bridge across the river at Ultino, allowing the other two regiments to cross over to the northern shore.

General Reinhardt arrived that day and on behalf of his XLI Panzer Corps expressed both thanks and recognition of the 6th Infantry Division's outstanding achievements. He brought with him fifty Iron Crosses 1st Class and 400 Iron Crosses 2nd Class to be awarded to the men. He also brought the division a new assignment. To adequately protect his flank, Reinhardt needed Auleb to push his division another 20 km north and establish a 30-km front along the Tma River. The more distance and rivers that could be put between the Soviet 29th Army to the north and the extended flank of the XLI Panzer Corps, the better.

Before the assault on the Tma could take place, the Volga bridgehead first had to be expanded and deepened. This was not accomplished until October 24.

The attack then was scheduled for dawn the next day. The Russian weather, as capricious as ever, had changed again. The snow had melted away and the rain had returned—a cold, bone-chilling rain.

At 7:30 a.m., the regiments began their advance. In contrast to previous assaults, the attack did not proceed smoothly. On the left, the 37th Regiment encountered stiff opposition and could only make slow progress. On the right, the 58th Regiment faced the greatest difficulty. The Oldenburg 110th Infantry Division, which was to have advanced on the regiment's right, was still in the process of crossing the Volga and not yet ready for the attack. This left the 58th Regiment's right flank open and necessitated having to echelon units to the right rear to cover its own flank. Worse, the further the regiment advanced, the more units were needed as flank guard, thereby weakening the spearhead of the attack. As a result the 58th Regiment could only make limited progress.

Only in the center with Becker's 18th Regiment did the division enjoy a measure of its accustomed success. By nightfall, the regiment had fought its way forward 12 km and had reached the Tma opposite Durulino but found that the bridge there had already been destroyed. No matter, they would cross in the morning.

The night of October 25 was cold and rainy, which proved to be good preparation for the next day's assault. The engineers arrived with their indispensable rubber rafts, and the men of the 13th Company emplaced their four infantry howitzers directly across the river from Durulino.

A heavy mist hung over the Tma River when at dawn the howitzers opened fire on the Russian positions. Pinpoint accuracy was not necessary for a barrage that was only a diversion. Both upstream and downstream from Durulino, the engineers quietly slid their rafts into the water and, concealed by the mist, transported the 1st and 2nd Battalions across the river. Once across, they hit the Russian defenders from the rear. Having expected a frontal attack, they panicked and fled north to the Eremkino on the north bank of the Ratshaja River.

One river crossed, why not another? Taking advantage of the enemy's panicky flight, Oberleutnant Rhein led his 5th Company forward. Without hesitation the men plunged into the meter-deep icy water of the Ratshaja and waded the 25 meters to the opposite bank. They quickly overcame the Russian defenders, who could not have imagined that the Germans had followed so closely on their heels. That men who had already spent a day and a night out in the open, pelted by a freezing rain, would plunge into waist-deep, icy water and storm an enemy position is indicative of how deep the spirit of aggression had been ingrained in the German soldier.

The following day, the 18th Regiment advanced another 10 km north and cut the Toroshok–Stariza highway. Despite the success of Becker's Regiment, the overall situation of the 6th Infantry Division was not good. The open right flank of the 58th Regiment precluded any further advance. Just how precarious the situation was, was confirmed October 28 when eight Soviet tanks and an infantry company from the Soviet 8th Tank Brigade suddenly appeared at the village of Tredubje, 10 km behind the front. They had easily passed through the thinly held right flank and slid around behind the 58th Regiment.

The Soviet tanks, four of which were T-34s, went roaring down the main street of Tredubje with all guns blazing. Two 3.7-cm anti-tank guns that by chance were in this rear area, unwisely chose to combat these 34-ton monsters. The panzerjägers wheeled their puny "Türklopfer" (door knockers) into the street and fired for all they were worth only to see round after round ricochet off the metal beasts; 50 meters, 30 meters, 20 meters, then "Raus!" and the gun crews leaped aside and watched their guns flattened into compact piles of twisted metal beneath the 34 tons of steel.

The lead tank stopped and its commander rose out of the hatch for a look around. One of the division's veterinarians, suddenly trapped in a street duel with tanks, took aim with his carbine and fired. The tank commander slumped back down inside, and the tank rolled off onto a side street. The other tanks about-faced and drove off out of the village—not that they were fleeing from a horse doctor and his carbine. Most probably they were looking for other targets worthy to crush.

Alerted to the threat, General Auleb requested an air strike that arrived twenty minutes later. As the Stukas swept down upon their prey, the Russian tanks and infantry scattered in all directions. For the moment, the threat had been averted, but the incident made clear that the division's situation was untenable. At any time, a powerful enemy force (and the Russians seemingly were capable of conjuring up forces at will) could come smashing through the weak right flank and cut off not only the 6th Infantry Division but the entire VI Corps.

Auleb decided to halt the 58th Regiment's northward advance and, in conjunction with the 110th Division (which had finally gotten across the Volga), push east and clear the Tma-Volga sector of enemy forces, thus securing the right flank. Meanwhile, the 18th Regiment would have to be withdrawn back across the Tma. Reluctantly, the men of the 18th Regiment prepared to pull back. They had relinquished hard-won ground in the past but only to German units sent to relieve them. Never had they abandoned a position to the enemy. A somber mood hung over the men in the rubber rafts as the engineers paddled them back across the Tma. For the first time, the Landsers had doubts concerning a successful outcome for the Führer's war in the East.

And well they might. What had just occurred on that small sector of the Eastern Front foreshadowed what would take place a month later along the entire front during the last phase of Operation Barbarossa.

Towards the end of October, the German forces in the Tma-Volga sector (6th, 26th, and 110th Infantry Divisions) were directed to go over to the defensive, but they were instructed not to regard this as going into winter quarters. At any time, they could be called upon to conduct operations as the situation demanded. But before going on the defensive, the sector first had to be secured by pushing further east and clearing out any Soviet forces still operating between the two rivers. This action was carried out by the 58th Regiment, and it was not done cheaply. During the last days of October as the regiment eliminated the remaining pockets of Soviet resistance, it lost eighty men killed, including Oberleutnant Josef Saliter (11th Company) and Oberleutnant Richard Hoppe (13th Company).

Although the troops had been advised that they were not going into winter quarters, winter had arrived. The days of alternating frost and thaw were past. Temperatures fell below freezing and remained there. The ground froze to a depth of 1 meter and the snow continued to pile up. Most western armies had always regarded winter as a nuisance, something that made the lives of the troops more difficult and hindered operations against an enemy. In Russia, winter was the enemy and one more deadly than one's armed opponent. Throughout the Eastern War, the German soldier struggled not only to survive against his Russian foe but also against the very land itself.

For a month now, the 6th Infantry Division had been living off the land, gleaning whatever the men could find in the frozen fields—oft times expending more calories in the hunt than what their meager harvest would provide. In time, they acquired the appellation of the "Steckrube Division" or "Turnip Division" for their agrarian efforts.

On November 9, the long absent supply train finally caught up to the division, bringing the much-needed supplies—unfortunately, nowhere near what was needed. The standard daily requirement for an infantry division was 30 tons; the supply train could only manage 15 tons, and since ammunition received top priority, the men's stomachs continued to suffer. The division did what it could to remedy the situation. In the area, there were numerous wild horses grazing in the fields. With the deepening snow, these creatures would eventually perish. The Germans sought to prevail upon the local farmers to take them in, but they refused for they had no extra fodder—nor did the Germans, who could barely feed their own horses. Reluctantly, the company butchers were sent out to harvest this available source of protein. For over a month, the men of the 6th Infantry Division sustained themselves on horseflesh.

Perhaps more serious than the shortage of food, fuel, and ammunition was the lack of winter clothing. The men did have their greatcoats, but the German greatcoat for all its stylishness is remarkably thin—adequate for standing guard on chilly nights in the Potsdamerplatz, but woefully unsuited for winter warfare in Russia. Missing were the gloves, vests, pullovers, and long underwear. Many reasons (i.e. excuses) were later given for this lack of winter protection: the lack of transport that necessitated the prioritization of supply—ammunition, fuel, food, and clothing, in that order. Also, supposedly the Führer had denied the request to distribute winter clothing (normally done in October) for fear of giving the troops the impression that the Russian war would not be concluded before winter set in. Whatever the reason or excuse, the men were the ones who suffered.

Quite naturally, the men were also the ones who remedied their situation—by stripping the enemy dead. The barbaric conditions of the Eastern Front gave rise to barbaric measures not seen since the Dark Ages, and over the next few years, the Russo–German War would follow the course of ever-increasing barbarity. Whenever possible, the men acquired the enviable Russian winter clothing, although at times the frozen bodies first required some thawing out. Fur coats, fur hats, felt boots quickly replaced the thread-worn, inadequate German clothing often to the extent that one could not distinguish friend from foe. Those unable to acquire or those lacking the necessary callousness to strip the dead wrapped themselves in blankets, tablecloths, or whatever rags they could filch from Russian huts. Worn over it all were the white bed linens to provide some degree of camouflage. The mighty Wehrmacht that had overrun Europe now had been reduced to a field-gleaning, potato-stealing army of ragged vagabonds.

As the 6th Infantry Division settled into its defensive positions in the Tma-Volga sector, serious discussions were taking place 300 km to the south at the headquarters of Army Group Center in Orsha. Feldmarshall von Bock, his army commanders, representatives of Army Groups North and South, and Generaloberst Halder, Chief-of-Staff of the German Army, who had flown in from the Führer's headquarters, were debating what to do next in the Eastern Campaign.

Since June 22, the German armies had achieved incredible success. They had advanced over 1,000 km across the Russian landscape, sweeping the Soviet armies from the field; 200 enemy divisions had been destroyed and over 3 million casualties inflicted on the Red Army. In the north, Leningrad was under siege while in the south von Rundstedt had overrun the Ukraine and his armies now stood on the shores of the Sea of Azov. On the central front, von Bock's divisions had eliminated the Soviet forces before Moscow and had pushed to within 50 km of the city. But still the "whole rotten structure" had not yet collapsed.

What was collapsing were German resources. By November 1, Operation Barbarossa had cost the German Army 686,000 men killed, wounded, or missing. A total 65 percent of the tanks and other vehicles had either been destroyed by enemy action or had fallen out through mechanical failure. Divisions on average had lost 20–30 percent of their regulation strength. Food, fuel, clothing, and spare parts were all in short supply. The machines were breaking down; the men were breaking down.

The question facing the participants at the Orsha conference was: should one last effort be made to take Moscow this late in the season or should Army Group Center dig in for the winter and finish the enemy off in the spring? Could malnourished, poorly clothed, exhausted troops be asked to somehow summon up the strength to push through blinding snowstorms and temperatures 30 to 40 degrees below freezing in a final effort to capture Moscow?

On November 13, the decision was made. The Moscow offensive would resume. "Nulltag" was set for November 19.

As Army Group Center resumed its advance on Moscow, the 6th Infantry Division again served as flank guard. At least, on this occasion they were given a more manageable sector to hold, only a 16-km front along the Tma River between Tuchini and Matjukowo. Even though the division had gone over to the defensive, this should not give the impression that the front was quiet. Throughout November as the weather deteriorated, the men were under constant harassing fire from artillery and mortars and the object of frequent enemy attacks in company and battalion strength supported by tanks. The majority of these attacks fell upon the division's eastern flank held by the 58th Regiment as the regiment's war-diary records:

> 2–3 November. Night attacks repelled.
> 3–4 November. Night attack by 170 Russians; most are killed.
> 5 November. Night attack at Tutani beaten back.
> 9 November. Numerous attacks repelled.
> 17 November. Four attacks in battalion strength warded off. Temperature drops to minus 30 degrees.
> 27 November. Several attacks in platoon strength from Soviet 508th Regiment.
> 28 November. Four attacks in battalion strength leaves 300 Russians dead. Own losses, eleven men killed.

These attacks, which appeared random and with no obvious objective, were more than mere harassment. In addition to depleting the strength of German companies, these attacks were intended to keep the Germans in the Tma–Volga sector on edge and on the defensive.

November 19: "Nulltag" for the final assault on Moscow. With the stirring exhortations of the "Tagesbefehl," which spoke of "Decisive battle … final victory … every ounce of determination … glorious conclusion," still ringing in the men's ears, the divisions of Army Group Center rolled off to the attack—or, rather, shuffled off into the blowing snow and ice fog of that fateful November morning. They were no longer the divisions of June 22. To call them shadows of their former selves borders on overstatement. They were far more like mirages or pale reflections. Most could only muster one-third of their original strength. The Bohemian 10th Panzer Division, for example, possessed a mere twenty-eight tanks and ten howitzers. Its two infantry regiments counted fewer than 500 men in their ranks. Cold, hungry, still no winter clothing worthy of the name and these were the men who were expected to achieve the final victory?

The attack went forward but only slowly. The swift advances of summer were now a distant memory. The enemy would not yield. With his back against Moscow, the Russian soldier defended in place and he died in place. The weather grew even worse. On November 27, the temperature fell to -40 degrees. Divisions were losing 40 percent of their manpower from frostbite alone. Casualties, once considered light, were sufficient now to render a division unfit for further action.

Despite this, the men at Army Group Center fought their way forward, through the cold, the snow, and through the last belt of the Russian defenses. They fought their way to within a few kilometers of Moscow. But as the temperature continued to fall, vehicles froze, weapons froze, hands and feet froze until on December 5, the attack on Moscow froze to a halt. After two weeks and 150,000 casualties, the "decisive, final battle" was over. There was no epic clash to signal its end. Only a deathly silence that descended upon the battlefield as the drifting snow slowly covered the dead.

Operation Barbarossa had failed. The Soviet Union had not been defeated in a single swift campaign. The "whole rotten structure" had not collapsed, and an exhausted and greatly weakened German Army now found itself stretched out across a 1,500-km front, marooned in a hostile land, unable to advance and unwilling to retreat. The enormity of the failure weighed heavily upon the Führer and his staff, who could only ask themselves, "What now?"

Stalin would soon answer their question.

# 6

# A Winter in Hell

Even before the Germans had commenced their final advance on Moscow, Stalin and his High Command had been planning their next move. Stalin had been informed by his extensive intelligence network that Japan had no intentions of joining its German ally in the war against the Soviet Union, but instead was planning to attack British and American interests in the Far East and the Pacific.

Back in June, Stalin had ignored his spies' warning of the impending German invasion. He did not make that mistake again. Assured that he need not fear a Japanese attack, Stalin felt confident to transfer thirty divisions of his Far Eastern Army to the Moscow Front. These divisions, the so-named "Siberian Divisions," were excellently trained and superbly equipped for winter warfare and would form the spearhead of the great counteroffensive that Stalin was planning.

Nor were these the only divisions available to him. Despite having lost over 200 divisions and millions of soldiers, the Soviets had been able to raise another 350 divisions. Granted, many of these divisions were little more than cannon fodder. Over the next few months, these untrained and often unarmed conscripts would be hurled against the Germans in suicidal charges as though their bodies were to be used as sponges to absorb as much of the limited German supply of ammunition as possible. As for the shortage of rifles, that posed no problem. As the casualty figures rose, there would be more than enough rifles to go around.

As the last exhausted German units sputtered to a halt in the ice and snow before Moscow, Stalin unleashed the Great Soviet Counteroffensive against von Bock's Army Group Center. On Friday, December 5, at 5 a.m., the first Russian shells rained down on the Rhineland-Hessian 36th Motorized Division's positions along the northern flank of Army Group Center. Over the next weeks and months, the Soviet counteroffensive would spread like a fire across almost all the 1,200-km Eastern Front.

During this first winter of the war, the most brutal fighting took place under the most brutal of conditions as Russians and Germans battered one another amid blinding snowstorms with temperatures of -40 and -50 degrees. Little quarter was given, and the wounded quickly froze to death under the inhuman conditions. German divisions, with weakened and exhausted men, attempted to hold their lines, but against a human tidal wave, they were forced to give way. The German front was broken through in numerous places. German units would find themselves surrounded, then desperately fight their way free only to find themselves surrounded again. Their dead they left behind unburied, something unthinkable a scant week before. Good comrades of a dozen battlefields soon disappeared beneath the drifting snow.

German weapons were no better protected against the cold than were the men. Tank engines refused to start, the hydraulic recoil systems of artillery froze solid, rendering the guns useless. The machine gun might fire, or it might not. One did not know until it was too late. Even the firing pins of the ever-reliable Mauser carbines froze tight. The grenade, the spade, the bayonet, and the brutal instinct for self-preservation were the only reliable weapons.

Fearing the disaster of a Napoleonic retreat, Hitler demanded that the front hold fast, but the overwhelmed German divisions began withdrawing if only to avoid encirclement and annihilation. Concerns arose at the Führer's headquarters that the entire front was in danger of collapse. The concern was unnecessary. The German Army might die, but it does not collapse. Bowing to reality, Hitler finally authorized a withdrawal on the central front to the "Königsberg Stellung," which was nothing more than a line drawn on a map at the Führer's headquarters, which ran from Rzhev south to the Moscow highway.

This withdrawal ushered in the next step down in the barbarity of the Russo–German War. The German High Command ordered that all useable shelter (i.e. every house, hut, and even barn) be destroyed before the troops withdrew. This "Scorched Earth" policy of the Wehrmacht has often been greatly criticized, if not criminalized, but only by those with no appreciation of winter warfare in Russia. That a retreating army leaves nothing of military value behind for the enemy to seize is a well-known and universally accepted axiom of war. Armor, artillery, infantry weapons are either destroyed or rendered inoperable; supplies and rations are burned; and railroads, bridges, and communications are likewise demolished. Nothing is left to the enemy. In Russia in winter, shelter is a military necessity. Deprived of it, the enemy will perish, but so, too, the civilian population.

Many German commanders in the field objected to this policy on both military and humanitarian grounds. (Again, as in the "Commissar Order," the moral objections may have had more to do with personal honor than with any genuine concern for the Russian peasant.) Unit commanders from the squad-level up understood that setting structures alight just prior to withdrawal did nothing more than alert the enemy that a withdrawal was taking place and thereby inviting an immediate attack when the retreating unit was at its most vulnerable. In addition, the Russian soldier was well clothed against the elements, and with the abundance of forests and his native abilities, he could easily construct a serviceable wooden shelter in the space of an hour. All the hardship inflicted upon the civilian population and the resulting animosity would have been to no purpose.

The 6th Infantry Division was not spared the ferocity of the Soviet onslaughts. Their situation was particularly difficult, having, as they did, both an exposed northern and eastern flank that were the targets of constant attacks. Any Russian penetration of either flank endangered not only the 6th Infantry Division but the entire 9th Army.

On December 28, the VI Corps (6th, 26th, and 110th Divisions) received orders to withdraw from their exposed Tma–Volga sector to Stariza, 50 km to the southwest, and establish a permanent defensive line from which no further retreat would be allowed. These orders raised more than a few eyebrows among the members of Auleb's staff. They were familiar with the area, having passed through it during the advance to the Volga, and knew that it was less than an ideal choice for a defensive line due to its locations and terrain.

The division requested that the withdrawal be conducted in a single 40-km leap, reasoning that the Russian artillery would be unable to keep pace with their pursuing infantry, who, deprived of artillery support, would be less inclined to mount major attacks against the division's retreating units. The request was denied. The withdrawal was to be carried out in short 5-km marches that unfortunately resulted in Auleb's division being subjected to constant savage attacks throughout the entire withdrawal.

Just after dark on the evening of December 20, the 6th Infantry Division began the withdrawal. The temperature stood at -30 degrees. Hungry, exhausted men, bundled up in whatever rags they could find, shuffled off into the falling snow. Some pulled sleds piled high with equipment, others clung to the snow-decked manes of the horses in an effort to share the animal's warmth. Outwardly Napoleonic, a haunting reflection of that disastrous retreat a century and a quarter before. But if the Russians thought that they would have an easy time following upon the heels of a defeated army, picking off stragglers at their leisure, they soon learned that the German soldier was no less dangerous in retreat than he was in attack.

As Auleb and his staff had feared, the Russians were able to maintain contact with the division as it executed as directed the "short hop" withdrawal. On the first day of the retreat, Oberleutnant Graff von Kagenek's 3rd Battalion of the 18th Regiment had to ward off numerous attacks on the right flank along the Volga. On December 23, the village of Tredubje on the left flank was attacked from the north, south, and east. Despite the efforts of the 37th Regiment, the village had to be given up. At 4 p.m., the Russians launched an attack on the 18th Regiment just as it was preparing to withdraw. After several hours of combat, the attack was repelled, but it had caused a serious disruption of the division's timetable of retreat.

December 24 (Christmas Eve), Heiligabend, the village of Iwanischi. Hauptmann Höke's 2nd Battalion of the 18th Regiment had reached the village at dawn that day, and throughout the day had awaited the inevitable Russian attack. The temperature stood at -25 degrees. At 3:45 p.m., as darkness was falling, Hauptmann Höke visited his men huddled together in their trenches and foxholes. He distributed Iron Crosses and reminded the men of the meaning of Christmas Eve. At 6 p.m., the forward outpost reported no unusual enemy activity. At 7 p.m., they reported the same. Perhaps on this, the holiest of nights, the Russians would leave them in peace.

But in Russia in December 1941, there was little chance of that. At 8 p.m. came the rattling fire of a Russian machine pistol, the crash of mortars and the deadly "Ratsch-bum."[1]

"Sie kommen!"

In dense masses, the Siberians of the 912th Rifle Regiment stormed the outskirts of the village. The cold night resounded with their shouts of "Urra!" They quickly overran the forward positions of the 7th and 8th Companies and occupied the houses and barns along the outer edge of the village. Hauptmann Höke ordered a counterattack. Leutnant Keller was to seal off the breach immediately with his two squads of engineers, and when Oberleutnant Grote arrived with the battalion reserve (1st Platoon of the 6th Company), they were to drive the enemy out of the village.

Meanwhile, the commander of the 8th Company, Oberleutnant Thummes, took matters into his own hands. Rushing to the breach in the German line with six men and a heavy machine-gun team, he quickly brought the Russian attack to a halt. Then acting as loader to a mortar team, Thummes slid round after round down the barrel. The effect was devastating. A Russian officer was seen standing, attempting to drive his men forward until a mortar round blasted him off his feet. The Siberians scattered and took shelter in the surrounding barns.

At that time, Leutnant Keller arrived with his engineers. He did not wait for Oberleutnant Grote to arrive with the battalion reserve, but headstrong as always, he charged one of the barns. For fear of hitting Keller and his men, Thummes ceased his mortar fire and joined the attack with his men. In hand-to-hand combat, they took the barn, the Siberians all dead or fled. Leutnant Keller was shot through the knee and carried back to the battalion aid station. Oberleutnant Grote continued the attack and drove the Russians out of his sector of the village.

However, along the eastern rim of Iwanitshi, the Russians had gained a firm foothold and had no intentions of allowing themselves to be driven out. To avoid casualties he could ill afford, Hauptmann Höke ordered his two heavy infantry howitzers to soften up the enemy prior to the counterattack. The howitzer commander objected; only a few meters separated the enemy from their own troops. Höke had no choice. The risk had to be taken, and he ordered the howitzers to fire away. The 15.5-cm shells screamed over the heads of the Landsers and crashed into the houses and barns. A chorus of screams rent the night air.

Time to attack. The howitzers lifted their fire 200 meters east. In one of the barns, the Siberians held fast. Oberfeldwebel Weischede of the infantry howitzer platoon wheeled his 7.5-cm gun into the middle of the street. He was an old hand at close infantry support. As the men of the 2nd Battalion had always said, "Wenn Weischede schiesst, dann bleibt kein Auge trocken." ("When Wieschede shoots, the tears roll.") As bullets whizzed past his ears, he calmly gave orders to the gun crew. Several rounds from the gun's stubby barrel smashed into the barn. Wood splinters, shingles, and body parts rained down on the street. Some of the Siberians attempted to flee and were cut down to a man by machine-gun fire.

Oberleutnant Grote pointed out another barn filled with Russians, and again Weischede went into action, A few rounds and the barn burst into flames. This time no enemy attempted to escape but burned alive amid the flames. Oberfeldwebel Weischede was badly wounded and transported to the rear. His skill and daring would be sorely missed in the coming days.

Oberleutnant Grote barely had time to report the village "Feindfrei" (free of the enemy) when the Russians launched an attack on the southern edge of Iwanischi. The attack was stopped in its tracks by the murderous machine-gun fire of Grote's and Feldwebel von Sassen's platoons. Limping from a painful ricochet wound, Oberleutnant Grote stood up and with a sniper rifle fired away at the fleeing Russians, dropping several of them in the snow.

At midnight, after four hours of intense combat, the night fell silent, but no one much felt like singing "Stille Nacht." The grey light of that Christmas morning revealed the night's carnage—smoking timbers of the burned-out houses and barns, blackened shell craters dotting the snow, the frozen bodies of dead Siberians. The defense of Iwanischi had cost Höke's 2nd Battalion nine dead and eighteen men wounded, and 142 Siberians lay dead in the village streets; no one bothered to count the enemy dead in the surrounding fields.

At least the 18th Regiment would be left in peace on Christmas Day, but not so the division's other two regiments. On Christmas Eve, von Tresckow's 58th Regiment had to fight off four strong Soviet attacks on the village of Stanischino at a cost of seventeen dead and sixty-seven missing. The 3rd Battalion's commander, Major von Issendorf; the 1st Battalion's commander, Oberstleutnant Mattusek; and Assistant Surgeon Dr. Aengenheyster had all been wounded. A fifth attack forced the regiment to give up the village and retire eastwards.

Christmas morning found the 58th Regiment occupying the villages of Ramoikowo and Wassilewkoe. At 7 a.m., the Russians attacked with two rifle regiments. The 3rd Battalion in Wassilewkoe was able to drive off the attackers, inflicting heavy losses, but at Ramoikowo, the Russians took advantage of a heavy ground fog and attacked from a woods near the edge of the village. They quickly broke through the defenses and drove the 1st Battalion out of Ramoikowo. Despite repeated attempts to retake the village, it remained firmly in Russian hands. With the enemy in Ramoikowo, the 3rd Battalion was in danger of being cut off and was ordered to abandon Wassilewkoe and take up positions a few kilometers to the west. Christmas Day had cost von Tresckow's regiment thirty-one dead and forty missing. These were losses that the weakened battalions could no longer afford.

On the northern flank, Christmas was no kinder to Oberstleutnant Hirsch's 37th Regiment. Its three battalions had spent Christmas Eve escaping one potential encirclement after another. By midnight, the 2nd and 3rd Battalions had managed to link up, but the 1st Battalion found itself isolated to the northwest in the village of Vukontowo. At 12:45 a.m., a Russian regiment attacked the village from the south and southwest. Heavy Soviet mortar fire rained down on the village causing heavy losses among the horses of the artillery and transport units. The Russians fought their way into Bukontowo and reached the area near the church. Here Oberstleutnant Hirsch mounted a last-ditch defense. Carbine in hand, he personally directed the fighting. Despite two grazing head wounds, he remained with his men.

As the pressure mounted and the situation became desperate, Hirsch led a counterattack to the northeast in an attempt to outflank the Russian attackers. Using hand grenades, often the only reliable weapon they possessed, they bombed their way forward to the northeast corner of the village, but the small force left behind under command of Leutnant Dunker to defend the church was driven entirely out of the village. They established a new line among the two batteries of Hauptmann Stiewe's 10.5-cm howitzers, who were emplaced just west of Bukonbowo. Ignoring the bullets whistling overhead, Stiewe stood among his gunners and directed point blank fire into the western edge of the village, dissuading the enemy from attempting any further advance.

At 3:30 a.m., Oberstleutnant Hirsch and the rest of the 1st Battalion suddenly appeared. They had succeeded in battling their way out of the northeast corner of the village and had circled around west to join up with Leutnant Dunker and Hauptmann Stiewe. Hircsh was determined to retake Bukontowo, but despite the support of Stiewe's howitzers, his two attempts failed.

Shortly afterwards, the other two battalions of the regiment arrived upon the scene. They had been wandering about in the snow most of the night and had, for the lack of a better phrase, "stumbled to the sound of guns." With his battalions reunited, Hirsch considered another go at the village but eventually decided against it, choosing instead to continue the withdrawal west before daylight arrived. Because most of the regiment's horses had fallen victim to the Russian mortar fire, the howitzers had to be left behind. Ever since the appearance of artillery on the battlefield, the loss of one's guns to the enemy had been a serious matter. Reluctantly Hauptmann Stiewe ordered the destruction of the guns that had served the regiment so well, and then he and his gunners joined in with the infantry columns as they trudged off to the west.

There was yet one more drama to be played out that Christmas Day. A stranger had arrived at the headquarters of the 6th Infantry Division. He was assumed to be an officer, but bundled up as he was and covered with snow, it was not possible to recognize his rank. His demeanour, however, was unmistakable—irritable and ill-humored.

"Oberst Grossmann to see General Auleb."

The stranger was ushered in to the general's quarters. From outside, the staff could overhear a long excited exchange. After the stranger left, the staff learned the reason for his visit: Generalleutnant Auleb had been relieved of his command. Oberst Grossmann was to immediately assume command of the Rhineland-Westphalian 6th Infantry Division.

General Auleb was not the only commander to go that winter. The Führer was cleaning house, or rather, scapegoating for what was beginning to look like a military disaster. These officers, these arrogant Prussian aristocrats, had let him down, had betrayed his genius. Feldmarschals von Leeb, von Bock, and von Rundstedt and Generals Guderian, Hoeppner, and Strauss all were relieved of their commands. One by one, the men who had led the Führer's armies to victory after victory were either unceremoniously dismissed or retired "for reasons of health." Whatever the official reason was, they all had one thing in common: they had either too often quarreled with or had been critical of Hitler.

Oberst Grossmann's ill humor can well be understood. Relieving a fellow officer of his duties—especially a highly respected senior officer—is hardly a pleasant task. A further inducement of his ill humor was the fact that he was a stranger, taking over a division whose officers and men he did not know, in the middle of a complicated withdrawal with no knowledge of the immediate situation and no real idea where his regiments might actually be in this vast Volga landscape.

New commander or not, the retreat of the 6th Infantry Division continued. After five days, they had only covered little more than half the distance to Stariza. Nor did the Russians show any sign of letting up the pressure. They seemed determined to wipe the division out to the last man, and if things continued as they were, they might very well do so. The battalions of the division were down to an average combat strength of 100 men (from a regulation 800). Death and wounds had taken many; frost and exhaustion had taken the rest.

Stalin had instructed his troops to attack at night because the Germans did not like fighting at close quarters in the dark. For purposes of boosting confidence such stereotypical nonsense about one's enemy is often told to inexperienced troops before going into battle for the first time. That Stalin knew very little about the German soldier would soon be made very clear to the young men of Soviet Rifle Regiments 1241, 1243, and 1245 at the little town of Schitinkowo.

The brief peace granted the 18th Regiment on Christmas day did not last long. December 26 was spent fighting off Soviet attacks on the positions of the 1st and 2nd Battalions at Kosnakowa. The weakened companies were only able to man a thin line of outposts and only through the effective fire of artillery support were the enemy's attacks halted.

The morning of December 27 the Russians unwisely attempted a daylight assault on the 3rd Battalion at Schitinkowo. The battalion commander, Oberleutnant Graf von Kageneck, calmly allowed the enemy to close to within 80 meters before giving the order to fire. A few rapid bursts of machine-gun fire, and in minutes the fight was over. One officer and sixty men lay dead in the snow at the edge of the village. At 9 p.m., under cover of darkness, 400 Russians attacked the northeast corner of Schitinkowo. The two German companies there possessed only ten light machine guns, two mortars, and twenty-eight rifles. There was desperate fighting, much of it hand to hand, but the German defenses held. A quickly organized counterattack drove the enemy back. The attack had cost the Russians two officers and eighty men killed.

The next day was relatively quiet. Graf von Kageneck used this period of calm to issue the distasteful order to drag the Russian dead into the village and strip them of their quilted jackets and felt boots. A gruesome task since the 173 bodies brought in were frozen stiff and required thawing out by the ovens before the desperately needed clothing could be removed. By noon, Graf von Kageneck's troops were as well protected against the cold as any Siberian unit.

Shortly after the moon went down that night, the Russians attacked the eastern and northeastern edge of the village with two battalions. Although the Germans had tried to keep the machine guns warm near the ovens in the huts, the ice-cold night still caused many of them to jam. With a ten-to-one superiority, the Russians were able to fight their way into the village. Attempts to drive them out were unsuccessful. Oberleutnant Böhmer, commander of the 2nd Company, went down wounded and was carried back to the aid station.

Then unexpectedly two Russian companies attacked the northwest corner of the village as another company struck the southern edge. Schitinkowo was all but surrounded. So began the night in hell as Germans and Russians battled one another in the darkness among the houses and narrow streets of Schitinkowo. The fighting was at close quarters, often hand to hand. A flare would briefly illuminate the night, followed by a murderous cacophony of machine-gun, rifle, and machine-pistol fire as the combatants were able to make out the shadowy figures of their opponents. Then the flare would burn out, the night grow dark again, and the firing abruptly cease only to be followed by the "crump" of hand grenades that did not need a precise target.

Despite the efforts of von Kageneck's men, the Russians with their overwhelming superiority in numbers pushed relentlessly towards the center of the village where the battalion aid station was located. Battalion Surgeon Dr. Haape could hear the fighting approaching from three directions, but there was nothing he could do. He was far too busy with the business at hand. The aid station was already overfilled with forty wounded. A Landser bleeding heavily from a hip wound staggered in. "Die Russen sind da!" he gasped. "The Russians are here!"

A near panic arose among the wounded. They knew what their fate would be if the Russians reached them. So did Dr. Haape. He had heard the accounts of what had befallen the German wounded when the Russians had overrun Kalinin. The German doctors had been executed and the wounded flung naked out the windows into the snow. Those who had survived the fall had been immediately dispatched with a shot to the head. He was determined that his wounded would not suffer a similar fate. Every capable wounded man was armed and tasked with defending the aid station. Meanwhile, he took his machine pistol and a couple of hand grenades and went out to assess the situation.

In the darkness, he confronted a Russian soldier. The doctor was quicker and the Russian, stitched with bullets, dropped in the snow—so much for the Hippocratic Oath. The greatest threat appeared to be coming from the east, but as he proceeded in that direction, a flare suddenly illuminated the darkness, and he heard a voice calmly order "Feuer." A German voice, a familiar voice—Leutnant Lammerding. All hell broke loose as Lammerding's men fired into the approaching Russians with everything they had: machine guns, carbines, machine pistols followed, of course, by a bevy of hurled grenades. Dr. Haape made his way back to the aid station. With Lammerding here, he need not worry that the Russians would break through from the east.

Back at the aid station, Dr. Haape ran into von Kageneck and explained the situation. The east and south were still holding for the moment, but the enemy was still pushing in close from the north. Just how close Haape and von Kageneck would soon find out.

Von Kageneck, who had a dozen men with him and a light machine-gun team, took up a position just outside the aid station along a low, stone wall. He fired a flare into the air, illuminating fifteen Russians standing directly in front of them. They were immediately mowed down. Von Kageneck located an artillery observer and ordered him to direct artillery fire into the village. (The howitzers were emplaced a few kilometers to the west.) But what of their own troops? They could not be helped; if the observer was unable to make out his targets, he was to direct fire on wherever he thought the enemy might be. Von Kageneck not only wanted to halt the enemy advance, but he also wanted to drive them completely out of the village with a counterattack.

As Dr. Haape returned to tending the wounded, he heard the artillery rounds screaming overhead and German voices outside shouting "Bravo!" with each detonation. Then came the ripping sound of machine guns and the cry of "Hurra!"—the counterattack. A few moments later, a heavily clad figure crashed through the door. A Russian? No, all the men were now wearing Russian clothing. The man exclaimed that his oberleutnant was lying outside in the snow. Head wound, but still breathing.

Dr. Haape hurried outside to where the crumpled figure lay. Graf von Kageneck, stunned, bloodied but still breathing. The doctor knelt down beside von Kageneck and assured him that the wound was not mortal. As he helped him back to the aid station, von Kageneck complained of feeling as though he had been kicked by a horse. In the aid station as Dr. Haape was bandaging his patient's wound, he told him that the time had come to evacuate the wounded who could walk. Von Kageneck agreed. The doctor also suggested that his patient should come with them. Von Kageneck did not agree. Out there in the streets his men were fighting and that is where he belonged. Von Kageneck placed his field cap upon his bandaged head, took leave of the doctor, and returned to the fight. From the doorway, Dr. Haape watched his friend make his way down the street, his progress made easily visible by the white head bandage. He watched him until he disappeared into the night.

A short time later, Dr. Haape marched at the head of twenty "walking" wounded, of whom some could only keep pace through the help of their comrades. All of them bore weapons should they have to fight their way through to the regimental aid station at Terpilowo. The twenty wounded too badly injured to be moved had been left behind in the care of the battalion dentist, Dr. Baumeister. As the column of wounded trudged through the deep snow, they gave a backward glance at the village of Schitinkowo—a nightmarish apparition. Burning houses, the flash of explosions, the clatter of machine guns, and flares constantly arching across the night sky. At least for now, they were well out of it.

The fierce, confused fighting raged throughout the night, but eventually the Germans gained the upper hand. With hand grenades and infantry howitzers they either killed or drove the enemy out of the village one house at a time. When dawn arrived, Schitinkowo—or rather, what was left of it—was once again in German hands. The grey morning light revealed a scene similar to that of Iwanischi four days ago—burned-out houses, a scorched, pock-marked landscape, and bodies scattered among the streets and smoking ruins. A total 349 Russians lay dead in the snow. One wounded officer and twenty-seven men were prisoners, who appeared stunned that they had somehow survived the carnage. No less stunned were the survivors of the 3rd Battalion that was now down to only 141 officers and men—less than a normal-sized company. Forty men had been wounded and fifty-two of their comrades had been killed. Among the dead was the battalion commander, Oberleutnant Franz Joseph, Graf von

Kageneck. He had not survived a second head wound. His white head bandage had made him an all-too-conspicuous target. Four days earlier, he had learned that his wife, Elisabeth Maria, Prinzessin von Bayern, had given birth to twin boys—boys who would never know their father.[2] Both Russians and Germans had paid a heavy price to possess the village of Schitinkowo. A village in the middle of nowhere that, after all, was nothing more than a way station on the long path of the German retreat.

The 6th Infantry Division still had another 15 km to go before it reached Stariza. A further 15 km of meter-deep snow, freezing temperatures, constant Russian attacks, and savage fighting in the ruins of countless Russian villages. Auleb's once powerful division had been reduced to a pathetic band of survivors, struggling through the blinding snow storms, dragging their akjas behind them, some piled high with their equipment, others bearing the frozen bodies of their comrades. German military tradition buries its dead on the field of battle, but here the ground was too deeply frozen and the time too short. Perhaps at Stariza the dead could be honorably interred.

Why these exhausted survivors did not simply give in, lie down in the snow, and mercifully allow themselves to peacefully pass into the next world is difficult to understand. Discipline, unit cohesion, and the will to survive all eventually have their physical limits. Perhaps to explain, one must reluctantly resort to stereotype and recognize the unique and at times unbelievable hardness of the German soldier of that generation—a hardness of mind and body which remains incomprehensible to a later more docile generation.

Although their hardness might sustain them, it could not sustain their numbers which became fewer each day. Regiments had become battalions, battalions were little more than companies, and companies had been reduced to less than platoon strength. With temperatures remaining 30 and 40 degrees below zero, sickness and the cold claimed as many victims as did Russian bullets. In ten days, the division had lost 677 men to frostbite alone.

Troop strength among the various units had dropped to absurd levels. Freiherr von Böselager's Reconnaissance Battalion had been reduced to a mere twenty-three men. The 2nd and 3rd Companies of engineers each numbered only one officer, four NCOs, and twenty-five men. In fifteen days the 58th Regiment had reported a loss of 796 officers and men. The combat strength of its three battalions was alarming:

1st Battalion 155 Officers and men
2nd Battalion 157 Officers and men
3rd Battalion 152 Officers and men

The Howitzer Company had three light infantry howitzers and forty-one men. The Heavy Machine Gun Company still had a respectable 116 men but no heavy machine guns. The division was forced to comb through the support units to find replacements. Drivers, cooks, blacksmiths, and even medical personnel were armed, outfitted, and sent off to the rifle companies. Units had become so weak that they could not sustain even single-digit losses. A burst of enemy machine-gun fire or a single mortar round dropping among a group of soldiers could seriously compromise the combat capability of an entire platoon.

The retreat continued. The next few days were no different from the previous days—the cold, the exhaustion, and the warding off of Soviet attacks. By now, the division had crossed over to the south bank of the Volga, but it still had to defend against attacks from the north and east by Soviet forces attempting to cut them off and annihilate them.

When the ragged, weary battalions of the 6th Infantry Division staggered into Stariza on December 31, they discovered what they had feared from the beginning. The "Stariza Stellung" was totally indefensible. Located at the bend of the Volga where the river turns sharply south, the position was already compromised by Soviet forces that had pushed across the river to the south.

New Year's Day brought more bitter cold (-50 degrees) and more bitter fighting. A Russian attack south of Stariza at Kolodino almost resulted in the capture of the division's headquarters. At Koronino, a battalion of Russian cavalry swept down on the aid station of the 1st Medical Company. Dr. Schulz and his medical staff succeeded in driving off the attackers but not before they had massacred a number of the helpless wounded. Meanwhile, the 2nd Battalion of the 18th Regiment was engaged in heavy fighting to the north and east of Stariza as they tried to keep open the roads into the city for straggling German soldiers and supply trains from other units. New Year's Day cost the regiment another nine dead and twenty-four wounded from its already depleted ranks.

At 4 a.m. on January 2, the division received the news for which it had been waiting: the "Stariza Stellung" was to be abandoned, and the division was to withdraw to the "Königsberg Stellung" at Rzhev. But if the men thought that this would be the end of their nightmare, they could not have been more wrong. What they had suffered so far was only a foretaste of what awaited them at Rzhev.

# 7

# The First Winter Battle of Rzhev

Rzhev, a city with a pre-war population of 54,000 lay on both sides of the upper Volga, approximately 300 km west of Moscow. Occupying a region rich in timber and other natural resources, the city had been fought over for centuries by the various Russian principalities. The bitter struggle for Rzhev that would take place over the next fifteen months had nothing to do with timber. Located where it was, as long as the Germans held the city, Moscow could always be threatened by a renewed German offensive. Understandably, Stalin demanded that Rzhev be taken regardless of the cost in blood.

The Königsburg Stellung was essentially a line drawn on a map at the Führer's Headquarters, to which Army Group Center had been permitted to withdraw but from which there was to be "kein Schritt zurück!"—not a step back. Its front extended from Rzhev in the north 280 km to Kaluga in the south. As impressive as its name may have sounded, echoing as it did that East Prussian Teutonic barrier against the Slavic east, in reality it was rather less so.

If the exhausted survivors of the 6th Infantry Division had imagined that they would be greeted by well-constructed defenses provided with heated bunkers, then they were sorely disappointed to discover that the Königsberg Stellung was indeed but a line drawn on a map. Only in a few of the villages along the Main Battle Line had anything resembling defenses been erected. Artillery emplacements, deep trenches, or heated bunkers were all lacking. For the most part, the men would again be forced to lie out in the open field, unprotected and at the mercy of winter and the enemy.

The sector assigned to the 6th Infantry Division was a 17-km front 15 to 25 km northeast of Rzhev, between the villages of Nemzowo and Krupzowo. The 37th Regiment held the left flank at Nemzowo, the 18th Regiment was on the right flank at Krupzowo, and the 58th Regiment occupied the center of the front. A front of 17 km was well within the defensive capabilities of a division—if it were a division, but by now, the combat strength of the 6th Infantry Division had dwindled to a mere 1,500 officers and men, which left fewer than 100 men per km of front.

Adding to the difficulties was the increased workload thrust upon the already over-taxed troops. With no existing fortifications the men were required to construct them themselves. With the ground solidly frozen, the men set about digging "snow trenches" in the meter-deep snow or erecting walls made of frozen blocks of snow, neither of which would protect them from enemy fire but they would shield them from observation.

The lack of manpower naturally increased the duties of those still remaining with their units. Sentry and listening posts needed to be manned and constant patrolling maintained. Due to the brutal cold, the regulation duty time had to be reduced from four hours to two, which doubled the number of shifts for a twenty-four-hour period. This cut in half an individual's off-duty or "recovery" time before he had to go back out into the cold. As a result, the men staggered about in a perpetual zombie-like state of exhaustion. Also, because of the extreme cold, the Horchposten or listening posts had to be manned in pairs. Otherwise, a Landser lying alone in the sub-zero weather could all too easily allow himself to drift off to sleep and never wake up. To alleviate the manpower shortage, the rear areas were again combed out for any available warm bodies. Supply troops, construction engineers, even members of the medical staff were armed and sent to the front line where they would either quickly learn to be combat riflemen or quickly die.

No sooner had the 6th Infantry Division occupied its positions in the Königsberg Stellung than the nightmare of the past two weeks resumed: arctic temperatures, blizzards, and the incessant enemy attacks. The Russian wolves that had constantly snapped at the division's heels during the retreat had caught up and immediately began launching wave after wave of attacks on the German-occupied villages.

January 2: the 18th Regiment's 5th Company (combat strength thirty-three men) and 6th Company had just settled in to their positions on either side of the Rzhev–Stariza highway at Krupzowo when, at 5:30 p.m., they were struck by a heavy barrage from Soviet 7.6-cm guns and heavy mortars. Thirty minutes later, two companies of Russian infantry attacked across the snow. Flares illuminated the night, machine guns clattered, rifles cracked, and Russian troops went down. By 7 p.m., the firing had ceased. The next morning, fifty Russians bodies were counted lying before the German positions. The Germans had lost five men badly wounded, including the commander of the 6th Company, Oberleutnant Grote (this was his fourth wound of the war). Worse was the loss of twenty-five men to frost bite.

The next morning, 6 km to the west, at the village of Gridino, the 18th Regiment's 3rd Battalion, discovered that at some time during the night, the enemy had infiltrated the thinly manned front line and occupied several houses along the northern edge of the village. The battalion commander Oberleutnant Böhmer ordered an immediate attack. There was fierce close quarters combat, but the enemy refused to budge. The Russians brought in reinforcements; the Germans brought in light infantry howitzers and blasted the Russians out of the shelter. Sixty-five Russians lay dead in the streets and shattered buildings.

A few hours later, the Russians attacked again. Unfortunately, too much time had elapsed since the earlier fighting, and the machine guns had refrozen in the frigid air. Quickly the weapons were doused with benzine and set alight. Would they thaw in time? They did, and once again Russian blood stained the snow. Under the hammering fire of machine guns, the enemy withdrew, leaving behind thirty of their number dead.

At 4 p.m., 400 Russians attacked in the growing darkness. There seemed to be no limit to the number of lives they were willing to sacrifice to possess a few ramshackle houses and barns of a tiny Russian village. But then, if they did not seize them, they would spend another night in the cold, and in Russia in winter, shelter no matter how meager meant survival. The first wave of attackers were mowed down, and the Russians shifted their assault to the northern side of Gridino. Leutnant Kiso, commander of the 10th Company, and a few of his men were trapped by the attack in one of the houses along the northern edge of the village. Despite assault after assault by what seemed to be suicide squads, Leutnant Kiso's small band held firm and prevented the enemy from penetrating into Gridino. Leutnant Kiso and four of his men were wounded.

Then came an attack from the northwest by two companies of infantry. This time the Russians succeeded in breaking into Gridino and occupying several houses. The order went out, "Gegenstoss!" The 11th Company launched a counterattack. Its leader, Leutnant Ohlig, charged forward only to be cut down at close range by a burst of machine-pistol fire. Leutnant Lammerding was badly wounded a few moments later. The counterattack stalled until reinforcements from the 37th Regiment arrived and added their weight to the assault. Several hours of vicious combat were needed to drive the enemy out of the village. Sixty dead Russians remained behind. Twelve Germans had been killed, twenty-four wounded, and eight other men needed to be treated for hypothermia.

The next day dawned like so many others had in the past few weeks: smoking ruins of a village, bodies lying in the streets and the adjoining fields, weary survivors staring blankly into nothing, others performing the ghoulish task of thawing out the Russian dead and stripping them of their winter clothing.

After what the men had been through the past twenty-four hours, indeed, the past two weeks, the 3rd Battalion at long last was to be relieved and taken off the front line—that is, what was left of it. When Oberleutnant Böhmer ordered the assembled men to count off, their voices fell silent after the count of ninety-nine. Ninety-nine men, barely the normal strength of two platoons.

"Ohne Tritt, marsch."

Without a word, the survivors of the 3rd Battalion shuffled off through the deep snow. They had a good 5 km to go before they reached the regimental headquarters at Malachowo. Shoulders bent under the weight of their weapons, beards hung with icicles, many clad in blood-stained Russian snow capes, they were burned-out, hollow shells of men, some on the verge of collapse. As they stumbled into Malachowo, the regimental commander, Oberst Carl "Corle" Becker, was standing outside the door of his headquarters with his adjutant, Oberleutnant von Kalckreuth, and saw the ragged band of survivors approach—and they saw him. Hushed voices ran up and down the ranks. "Der Oberst ist da." They could not allow him to see them like this. They had been relieved, not defeated. Finding the strength, they straightened their bent bodies and fell into step. Oberfeldwebel Albrecht Schnitger sang out the old Soldatenlied, "Von den Bergen, fliesst ein Wasser," and the men joined in, "Das ist lauter kühler Wein."

Oberst Becker was a hard man, who rarely gave way to emotion. This was his second war. In the Great War, he had been wounded five times and had witnessed all the horrors of the Western Front, but now as he watched his young men march by, their heads somehow held high, singing as though returning from a peace-time maneuver, tears trickled down his weather-beaten cheeks.

The experiences of von Tresckow's 58th Regiment were not less brutal than those of its sister regiment. Holding a 4-km sector between Fridino and Ranimza, the 58th Regiment's positions, like those of the 18th Regiment were thinly manned and for the most part based in the small villages of the area. During the withdrawal to the Königsberg Stellung, the combat strength of the entire regiment had been reduced by casualties and frostbite to only 621 officers and men—less than that of a normal-size battalion. To reinforce his depleted numbers, von Tresckow had received a company of sorts comprised of men from the communications battalion of VI corps headquarters who had traded their radios and teleprinters for rifles and machine pistols. The war diary of the 58th Regiment reflects the desperate fighting that took place during its first days in the Königsburg Stellung:

> 3 January: Receive company made up of communication troops from VI Corps. Leutnant Korte and seven men of 3rd Company killed.
> 4 January: Several enemy attacks repelled. Own losses, thirteen dead. Temperature minus 40 degrees. Still no winter clothing.
> 5 January: Only minus 5 degrees but heavy snowstorms. Defensive combat and counterattacks in woods near Sobakino.
> 6 January: 6:30 a.m., counterattack against Sobakino unsuccessful. Two Russian attacks, each of two battalions fought off. Three hundred enemy dead. Own losses, three dead, one missing.
> 7 January: More enemy attacks, including tanks. Own losses, three dead.

> 8 January: Heavy artillery bombardment. Russian ski patrol sighted.
> 9 January: Battalion-strength attack on Gridino, Klipukowo, and Sobakino. Heavy artillery and mortar fire. Four hundred dead.
> 10 January: More attacks on Ranimza and Sobakino. Leutnant Corts 3rd Company killed.

Bombardments, attacks, counterattacks—this was daily life in the Königsberg Stellung. By mid-January, the 58th Regiment had been reduced to a combat strength of only 135 officers and men. How much longer could this go on before the Rhineland-Westphalian 6th Infantry Division no longer existed?

Although the objectives of Soviet strategy and planning are both discernible and rational, the unit tactics employed by the Russians in the first year of the war are puzzling, to say the least. Even though during the winter offensive they possessed overwhelming superiority in men at most points along the front, they often did not effectively make use of this advantage. This is most apparent in the after-battle reports of German units. The Russian assaults appear as piecemeal and lacking any coordination. First, a single company is sent in to the attack; it is mowed down and then is followed by another company and then another, all suffering the same bloody fate as the first. It was as if the Russian commanders were deliberately feeding their men piecemeal to the German machine gunners. This gave rise to the widespread belief among German troops that the enemy was employing the sinister tactic of using Russian bodies to exhaust the limited supply of German ammunition.

However, there may have been a less sinister basis for the near suicidal "Urrah charges" of the enemy—the lack of competent leadership. In a pre-war purge, Stalin had devastated the Red Army's command structure. In addition to eliminating 90 percent of his generals, Stalin had also liquidated over half of his divisional and brigade commanders as well as 80 percent of his regimental colonels. Tens of thousands of officers had been executed for "high treason" so that when war with Germany came, the Red Army was still grievously suffering from a shortage of trained, competent leadership at all levels. The Russian soldier was brave, or, at least, forced to be so by pistol-waving commissars, but he was inexperienced and at times untrained. The lack of adequately trained and experienced company, battalion, regimental, and divisional commanders resulted in the clumsy and disjointed nature of Soviet infantry assaults. Sending men to attack across open fields time and again is not a tactic—it is murder.

The Great Soviet Counteroffensive of December 1941 had originally sought to drive the German forces on the central front from the gates of Moscow. By the end of December, this objective had been achieved and the Soviet High Command now saw the opportunity to perhaps obtain far greater goals, one of which was the destruction of German Army Group Center or, at least, a large part of it.

On the central front the Soviet attacks had pushed the German armies back various distances, resulting in an uneven front that presented the Russians enticing points of attack. One such point was the northern sector of the Königsberg Stellung. Here, the German 9th, 3rd Panzer, and 4th Panzer Armies were facing the enemy on both a northern and eastern front. The northern front (9th Army) ran from Rzhev back 75 km west to where it tied into the southern flank of Army Group North. The eastern front (3rd and 4th Panzer Armies) extended from Rzhev 150 km to the south.

At what would later become the Rzhev Salient, the Soviet Command focused its efforts to destroy the northern wing of Army Group Center. In the north, Col. General I. S. Konev's Kalinin Front with five armies (22nd, 29th, 30th, 31st, and 39th) was to break through the German northern flank and push south. On the German eastern front, Marshal Zhukov's Western Front with nine armies (1st Shock, 5th, 10th, 16th, 20th, 33rd, 43rd, 49th, and 50th) would attack in the sectors of the 3rd and 4th Panzer Armies and drive westwards. If these two Soviet forces were able to link up southwest of Rzhev, the German 9th, 3rd Panzer, and 4th Panzer Armies would be trapped and threatened with annihilation. To achieve this, the Soviets had amassed an impressive force of 688,000 men, 10,900 artillery pieces, and 475 tanks.

In the north the blow fell on the morning of January 4, 20 km west of Rzhez where in the frigid cold (-40 degrees), the assault divisions of Lt. General Maslennikov's 39th Army stormed across the frozen Volga and ripped open a 15-km wide hole in the German line in the sector of the Saxon 256th Infantry Division. Division after division, including those of Maj. General Shetsov's 29th Army, poured through the breach until two Soviet armies and a cavalry corps were deep behind the German front and were driving hard to the south. Some Soviet units peeled off east to attack the main German supply line of Wjasma–Rzhev while others wheeled back northeast to assault Rzhev from the rear. The capture of Rzhev was only prevented by the quick action of the 6th Infantry Division's supply officer, Major Disselkamp. The old cavalryman threw together a hodge-podge collection of rear-echelon service troops supported by a few anti-tank guns, and in a series of actions in which the division's Veterinary Company particularly distinguished itself, he drove off the Soviet attacks.

Despite the heroics of Major Disselkamp, the German front was coming apart under the massive Soviet blows. Powerful enemy thrusts had burst through the thinly held lines and had plunged deep into the hinterland. German divisions, corps, and even armies were in danger of being cut off and annihilated much the same as they had done to the Russians during the summer and autumn battles. However, in any battle there are two fronts: the defending front and the attacking front. When one observes the resulting position of the opposing forces with its confusing mosaic of interspersed Soviet and German units, one could just as easily remark that the Soviet front was coming apart. The Soviet divisions and armies, now deep behind the original front line threatening to encircle German units, were themselves in danger of being cut off and encircled. The situation maps present a picture of considerable chaos. Whoever could best exploit the chaos would emerge the victor.

The man who could do this was General der Panzertruppe, Walter Model, who took over command of the 9th Army on January 17 after its commander, Generaloberst Strauss, had been relieved of command for health reasons. Despite the chaos on the map in front of him, the task of the new 9th Army commander was clear: hold Rzhev, seal off the breach in the German line, and destroy the Russian forces that had penetrated deep behind the front.

The task may have been clear, but the method and the means to achieve it were far less obvious. With divisions the size of regiments and a shortage of food and munitions—not to mention the brutal weather and the snow-packed, near impassable roads—Model would have to become a one-man HL team, exhibiting the tactical brilliance of a Ludendorf and the unshakable steel nerves of a Hindenburg, and he would have to demand one last effort for the half-starved, exhausted men under his command.

For two weeks, the Soviet 39th and 29th Armies had been shoving division after division through the breach in the German line west of Rzhev and pushing them south. By January 21, elements of the 39th Army had penetrated as far as 80 km, and its units that had wheeled back to the north were only 8 km from Rzhev. Day after day, the German units on either side of the breach watched the steady stream of men, tanks, and vehicles pour past them. The German artillerymen stood by in frustration, their guns silent. The meager supply of ammunition still available had to be conserved to defend their own positions if the Soviets decided to widen the breach. What carnage their howitzers and cannons could have wreaked upon those dense enemy columns.

Because of the "Siberian cold" (-40 degrees), the blinding snowstorms, and lack of transport, the German effort to seal off the breach had been postponed time after time, but on January 22, in the midst of a howling blizzard, the attack finally got rolling. Elements of four infantry divisions (251st, 256th, 26th, and 216th) attacked from the east while advancing from the west to meet them were the Brandenburger 206th Infantry Division and the SS Cavalry Brigade Fegelein. At first glance, an impressive force until one considers that at this time most German divisions had been ground down to less than a quarter of their regulation strength. (The 206th Infantry Division had a total strength of only 2,283 men.) Despite the weakness in numbers, the attack caught the Russians by surprise. They had been so preoccupied with pushing south as far and as fast as possible, they had failed to appreciate the potential threat lurking in their rear.

At 12:45 p.m. on January 23, the spearheads of the two attacking German forces met at Ssolomina. The breach in the German line had been sealed off, and the Soviet 29th and 39th Armies were now trapped deep behind the front.

As for their destruction, there was no great hurry. The longer the Soviet armies were deprived of crucial supplies, the weaker they would become. Model would annihilate them in his own good time.

Although the critical fighting in this "First Winter Battle of Rzhev" had shifted to the west and south of the 6th Infantry Division, the Russians still maintained a constant pressure on the German front northeast of Rzhev. For the Rhinelanders and Westphalians the next two months would be no different than the previous month—sudden artillery barrages raining down on them and companies of Russian infantry storming across the open snow fields howling "Urra!"

These attacks were "holding attacks," designed to keep the German forces in the northern sector firmly pinned in place, preventing them from being employed at more critical points of the battlefield. The attacks would come at the Germans a single company at a time with no prospect of achieving any worthwhile success. Machine guns would mow them down, and as quickly as it had begun, the attack would be over, and a silence would descend, broken only by the pitiful cries of the Russian wounded. These also would grow quiet; the wounded did not last long in the cold. During battles in the western theatres of the war, truces of mercy were often arranged between the combatants to allow the wounded to be carried off the field, but not in Russia. Russia was its own type of war, a war of annihilation with prisoners seldom taken and the wounded often shot, which gave rise to an ever-increasing hardness among the troops of either side, occasioned not only by one's own suffering but also the suffering of one's enemy. The normal human capacity for empathy was extinguished by a self-protecting indifference. The battlefields around Krupzowo, Gridino, Guschtschina, and a dozen other villages presented an eerie tableau during the daylight hours with blackened, frozen limbs protruding up through the snow. But by next morning, they would be gone, buried by the windswept drifts of snow as though nature herself was sweeping the fields clean in preparation for the next round of slaughter.

The 6th Infantry Division held fast as it always had, refusing to give a meter of ground. A village was only given up when it no longer existed, when it had been reduced by battle and barrages to nothing more than a blackened scorch mark on the snow. The men's suffering was increased by the shortages, which had become commonplace. On January 28, the bread ration was reduced to 75 grams per day—and that for over-taxed bodies trying to generate sufficient heat to survive in sub-zero weather. Horseflesh had become a rare luxury. The few surviving horses were too necessary for transportation to be slaughtered for the sake of the men's stomachs. Only those horses that had collapsed from exhaustion found their way into the men's mess tins. In the shattered villages there was nothing left to either requisition or steal. Soon battle casualties and frostbite took second-place to illness as malnourished bodies fell prey to a host of maladies, the worst being typhus. There were only sufficient vaccinations to inoculate those men over fifty—that is, the senior officers and the older reservists of the support units. The young frontline officers and men had to do without such protection. To replace the sick, the rear area was combed through yet again, but the yield this time was only nine officers and eighty-four men.

On February 1, the men of the 58th Regiment witnessed a grisly scene. Wolves were sighted busying themselves among the Russian dead in the fields. A few shots rang out from those disgusted by the sight, but the starving creatures refused to be deterred. Further attempts to frighten them off were given up as a waste of precious ammunition.

Now and again there were a few occasions that lightened the men's mood. In early February, the first Christmas packages arrived as well as the winter clothing collected by Propaganda Minister Goebbels' appeal to the German public to support the troops. The empty stomachs greatly appreciated the "Weihnachtspäckchen" with their stollen, kuchen, and chocolates, but clad as they were in blood-clotted Russian clothing, the men could only look with a certain bemusement upon the odd assortment of civilian garb sent by Dr. Goebbels. Stylish perhaps and sufficient for an autumn stroll in the woods or awaiting a tram on a windy street corner but of hardly any use in the Russian Winter. At least, the home front had not forgotten them even if the people at home could have no concept of their suffering.

Far more appreciated than these bits of clothing was a battalion of replacements from Germany. For once, actual trained soldiers and not the truck drivers, blacksmiths, cooks, and medics dragged out of the support services. With these replacements came news from home—from the towns and villages across Westphalia and along the Rhine. But not all the news was uplifting. The 58th Regiment learned that all of their former comrades who had been sent off at the beginning of the war to help build the Rhineland 126th Infantry Division were now dead. Such news gave the Landsers pause to ponder—how long before the same would be said of them?

By the end of January, General Model judged that the time had come to deal with the two Soviet Armies deep behind the German front line. The plug he had fashioned in the front west of Rzhev was still successfully resisting Soviet attempts to reopen the breach and free their stranded armies. The 6th Infantry Division was yet holding firm northeast of Rzhev and along both sides of the Soviet corridor of advance, Model had been able to emplace several of his divisions. The Soviet 29th and 39th Armies were essentially surrounded on three sides.

Model's first victim was Shvetzov's 29th Army in the northern reaches of the corridor. The initial German attack drove a wedge between the two Soviet armies resulting in Shvetzov's army being trapped in a pocket of its own. Model then began reducing the pocket with concentric attacks. Due to the weakness of the individual German units involved, the attacks were conducted slowly and methodically—no lightning-like Blitzkrieg assaults this time. The Germans referred to the present method as the "Hackmaschine," and true to its name it hacked out the Russian positions one village at a time. The Rhineland 6th Panzer Division proudly announced that in the space of a month it had seized eighty villages from the enemy. Success was measured by the number of villages taken, again highlighting the unique feature of the Russian Winter War in which nothing had a higher military value than the villages and the physical shelter they provided. Dots on a map that during the spring and summer campaigns were little more than places to acquire forage or to march through indifferently were now the center of some of the fiercest combat.

The Soviet commander of the Kalinin Front, Col General Konev, spared no efforts to rescue his two trapped armies. The German XXIII and VI Corps along the northern Rzhev sector were the targets of countless attacks by the Soviet 22nd, 30th, and 31st Armies desperately attempting to break through to their trapped comrades. All in vain. The German front held and Model's "Hackmaschine" continued to hack up the Soviet 29th and 39th Armies.

With the passing of February and the arrival of March, the first hint of spring could be sensed in the air—not robins nor melting snows but an occasional day when the temperature rose as high as 0 degrees. The Siberian cold, however, was reluctant to relinquish its icy grip from the land. The "mild" days were often followed by days during which the temperature dropped to -34 degrees, and the storms howled. Enemy activity was as capricious as the weather. During periods of storms and frigid cold, the men of the 6th Infantry Division were left in peace, but on the "mild" days, the enemy returned with a vengeance.

On March 2, a strong enemy patrol—always a harbinger of a forthcoming attack—collided with a German patrol, resulting in seventeen Russians killed. The next day, the 1st Battalion of the 18th Regiment had to fight off three enemy attacks, one of which was only done so in hand-to-hand combat. On March 4, the 58th Regiment was attacked at Sobakina by a single Russian Company. The next day, the Russians repeated the attack with two companies. The attack was repelled and twenty dead Russians dotted the snow. On March 9, during an attack on the forward outposts of the 18th Regiment's 2nd Battalion, the battalion commander, Major Höke was wounded. Oberleutnant Rhein took over command. An early morning trench raid on March 18 by members of the Soviet 915th Rifle Regiment was driven off without loss. Fourteen Russians were killed and one taken prisoner.

Besides sensing a hint of spring, the Landsers also sensed a lessening of enemy pressure. Attacks were rarely in more than company strength and once repelled, they were seldom repeated. Nor were the enemy assaults pushed to the near suicidal extreme as before. They were more akin to the weakened thrashing about of a dying beast.

As the enemy activity declined, the troops attended to other pressing matters. Little remained of the villages in which they had been fighting the past two months. Deprived of shelter for much of the period, they had been forced to lie out in the open relying on snow trenches and snow walls to shield them from enemy sight. However, even in Russia, spring does eventually arrive, and with it, the melting away of these makeshift fortifications leaving the men exposed, "as though they were on the parade ground," one Landser described it. A new Main Battle Line was constructed 700 meters to the rear and this time at one of the division's own choosing and not haphazardly determined by the locations of this or that village, and it was a true defensive line with optimal fields of fire, genuine trenches, and underground bunkers.

Equally important as preparing the new defenses, was the preparation of the recently arrived replacements from Germany. As with all German recruits at this stage of the war, they had been excellently trained in weapons and tactics. Although what they had learned on the training grounds of Sennelager might have been sufficient for the virgin soldiers in the earlier western campaigns, the war in Russia was an altogether different war, and the new replacements would have to learn the brutal difference if they hoped to survive for more than a day.

Leutnant Mergelsberg of the 18th Regiment oversaw the advanced training of the new replacements at Shitinki, 12 km behind the front. The fresh-faced newcomers listened intently (and with some intimidation) to the ragged, bearded survivors of a hundred battles, most of whom were still wearing the bloodstained and bullet-ripped winter uniforms of the enemy. They heard tales of commissars and Siberians, of partisans and "G'nickschüsse," how the enemy fought and how he was to be fought, what to eat and what not to drink—all the things that one needed to know in the daily struggle to survive in the east.

In addition to the replacements, there was another arrival in March. The 2nd Company of the Engineer Battalion that had been "lent" to the Hessian 251st Infantry Division had returned to the division. They had marched off a company strong on February 2. Only three men returned, not a single officer or NCO among them.

There were departures as well. Oberstleutnant Hirsch, who had temporarily commanded the 18th Regiment before taking command of the Reconnaissance Battalion, was transferred to the Afrika Korps. From the snows of the steppes to the sands of the Sahara. He did not survive the war. Oberst von Tresckow, who had been with the 58th Regiment since 1938 and had been its Kommandeur since December 1939, now left to command his own division, the newly raised 328th Infantry Division. His replacement was Oberst Furbach, a stranger to the regiment, a stranger to the division.

By March 24, spring was no longer a hint in the air. Temperatures rose to above freezing and remained there. The heavy blanket of snow began to melt. First, a barely audible trickling of water, then a visible stream, and finally a veritable torrent. A landscape once frozen in white was transformed into a muddy-brown lake. The newly constructed bunkers and trenches flooded and required constant bailing out. To make matters worse, as the frozen ground began to thaw, the trenches collapsed, adding to the men's work load as they had to shovel out and shore up their shelters.

Despite nature's discomfort, one could sense a rise in the men's spirits. A feeling, a hope—almost imperceptible and that one feared to express openly—but a feeling that the nightmare had passed, that they had endured a hell never before experienced by a German soldier and they had survived.

So too had the Russian civilian population of the towns and villages behind the front. Over the winter months, a symbiotic relationship had developed between the civilians and their uninvited "guests"—a cooperation born of necessity and based on common sense. As far as the Russian peasant was concerned, the Bolsheviks and their commissars were gone—may they go to the devil. The Germans and their Ortskommandanten were masters in the land now. Why antagonize them? Far better to cooperate. The Russian civilians often helped in the hospitals and kitchens or built and cleared roads. The German paid well with Komissbrot (army bread), which, though it often choked a new German recruit, to the local peasant was a near delicacy compared to his own coarse, black bread. For those convinced that the commissars would never return, there was the German Reichsmark that was now the currency of the land. (When the communists did return, these poor, simple people would suffer a terrible retribution for simply trying to survive.) In a like manner, the German Landser had grown accustomed to his Russian "hosts," and having to deal with the Red Army, partisans, and the climate, he saw no reason to increase his present difficulties by unnecessarily antagonizing the local population.

In addition to the passing of winter and the melting of the snow, there arrived another sign of survival and renewed hope in the form of a delegation from the local populace requesting the division commander's permission to allow the people to once again celebrate Easter now that the Bolsheviks were gone. Generalmajor Grossmann was somewhat surprised at the request and not a little bemused by the near panic that arose among the women folk when he readily gave his permission. With only a week until the Holy Day, the good women could not see how they could ever procure all that was needed for the great Easter Feast and manage to prepare it in time.

But manage they did. On April 5, 1942, the people saw their Easter arise from the grave into which it had been cast by the Bolsheviks two decades ago. And for the first time in their lives, young Catholics from the Rhineland and young Protestants from Westphalia witnessed the solemn beauty of the Orthodox Easter.

At 11:30 p.m., the church bells rang out over the land calling the people to worship. In the newly reopened churches, the village folk assembled. Clad in their finest attire, they stood neighbor to neighbor, their uplifted faces illuminated by a hundred candles. At midnight, the priest appeared, clad in white and silver robes, and announced, "Christos Woskresse!" to which the congregation replied, "Woisstinu Woskresse!"

They embraced and kissed one another and exchanged brightly colored eggs. Led by the priest and choir, the people emerged from the church bearing small candles. Seven times the candlelight procession circled the church and then the people departed to their homes. Once there, the candles were placed before the precious icons, and the Easter Feast began. And what a feast it was: ham and sausage, white cheese and onions, herrings and cucumbers, and, of course, Kulitsch, the special Easter bread. With joy and piety and no small amount of vodka, the villagers celebrated that Easter of 1942, a brief reflection of the time before the Bolsheviks.

"Woisstinnu Woskresse!"

But the reflection faded all too soon. There would be no Easter the following year nor for many decades to come.

Although the sector of the 6th Infantry Division on the northeast Rzhev front had remained relatively quiet since the arrival of the spring thaw and rains, heavy fighting had continued to rage to the west and southeast as both Konev and Zhukov launched attack after attack in the attempt to free the trapped Soviet armies. But in the end, due to the massive casualties and depleted stocks of munitions, the Soviet High Command called off the Rzhev offensive. The armies of the Kalinin and Western Fronts were directed to go over to the defensive. The trapped remnants of the Soviet 29th, 39th, and 33rd Armies would either break out on their own or perish.

The First Winter Battle of Rzhev had come to an end. The cost had been enormous. The "official" losses of the Red Army were put at 776,889 men killed, wounded, or missing (more recent studies indicate a casualty list of 918,000).[1] The losses of German Army Group Center were 330,000 killed, wounded, or missing which when added to the Soviet losses, presents a total butcher's bill of 1.1–1.2 million in human losses—and this was only the First Battle of Rzhev; there were three more to come.

# 8

# The Summer Battle of Rzhev

Not only had the Rzhev Offensive wound down, but the Great Soviet Counteroffensive begun in December had likewise ground to a halt along the entire Eastern Front. It had drowned in a sea of its own blood. To the near million casualties the Russians had suffered at Rzhev, 2 million more from the other sectors of the front could easily be added. The extent to which the Soviet High Command was willing to sacrifice Russian lives often defies modern comprehension. Even in the broad expanse of the Russian homeland there was a finite number of living souls. Exchanging three or four lives for every German life was not a winning strategy but rather a guarantee of mutual annihilation. However, this callous squandering of human lives had at least achieved its primary objective. The German advance had been halted, Moscow saved, and the enemy thrown back some 100–200 km along the front.

The irregular successes of the Soviet counteroffensive had resulted in a front with numerous pockets and corresponding salients that over the coming months and years the opposing forces sought to take advantage of or eliminate altogether. The "Rzhev Stellung" was just such a salient. Located 280 km northwest of Moscow, the Rzhev Salient jutted 160 km in a northeast direction and was 200 km wide at its base. Its convoluted front of 700 km was defended by some forty to fifty divisions of the German 9th, 3rd Panzer, and 4th Panzer Armies of Army Group Center. For the Germans, the salient could serve as a springboard for any renewed assault on Moscow and had to be held at all costs. For that very reason, to the Russians the salient presented a constant threat that had to be eliminated. Given its importance, is there any wonder that Rzhev would become the "Great Slaughterhouse of the Eastern Front?"

Over the next two months, a relative calm descended along the northeast sector of the Rzhev Salient. As the earth absorbed the melting snow and the fields dried out beneath an increasingly warm sun, the men of the 6th Infantry

Division set about repairing their trenches, training the recent replacements, and of all things, tending to the spring planting. Here again was another instance of the peculiar relationship between conquered and conqueror which at times arose during the Russian war—a relationship of mutual interest forced upon both by necessity. The Germans had horses; the Russian farmers had hay and fodder. Nothing could have been more logical than for the Germans to loan out their four-legged comrades for fieldwork and in return for the farmer to feed them the precious fodder which all too often was in short supply due to the overextended German supply system. Now that the Germans had put an end to the hated commune system, the farmers were eager to get into the fields. The land was theirs now not the state's, and if the Bolsheviks did not return, then a bountiful harvest would be theirs as well—except, of course, that which might be required and requisitioned by their "guests."

Despite it being a "quiet" sector for the time being, death took no leave of absence. German and Russian patrols continued to ambush one another, trench raids were carried out under cover of night, and there was always the harassing fire with artillery and mortar rounds dropping randomly from the sky and killing just as randomly. Random or not, between April 13 and May 22, the 58th Regiment lost thirteen men and one officer (Leutnant Hotan, 3rd Company) killed by this harassing fire.

For over a month, the Russians had occupied a strong point on a hill (K-Höhe) a couple hundred meters away from the 18th Regiment's front line. They posed no immediate threat, but from either boredom or bravado Feldwebel von Sasson decided that the Russians must go. On the night of May 3, von Sasson and a small group of volunteers crept silently up to the crest of the K-Höhe. At the prescribed moment came a flash-barrage from the regiment's heavy infantry howitzers, and then von Sasson and his men leapt into the enemy position. With Ballenladungen, they quickly destroyed the four Russian bunkers and then scurried back to the safety of their own lines dragging along six prisoners—all without suffering a single casualty.[1] The number of Russians killed was not known. After a trench raid, one does not linger to count the enemy dead.

Prisoners were always a prized trophy of such raids. They were a good source of information, especially during "quiet" periods when the enemy's intentions were less obvious. Another source of information was the occasional "Überlaufer" or defector. The 6th Infantry Division had set up loudspeakers along their sector of the front, and with the aid of two translators and a defector, the Russian positions were bombarded with propaganda broadcasts in hopes of inducing more of the enemy to defect. These broadcasts did not spew out hate or threats but instead promised good treatment and good food, and, most important, announced the abolishment of the commune system. When Germany won the war, the communist overlords would be gone, and every peasant would own his own land. The effort bore fruit, especially after the "Schlammperiod" (mud period) had ended when an "Überlaufer" could more easily traverse the ground which separated the opposing lines.

These "Überlaufers" were great talkers, in part to both ingratiate themselves with their new comrades and to justify this treason to their own conscience. Some of the information was useful, but much of it had to be taken with a heavy dose of salt. Detailed information was rare. The average Russian soldier knew almost nothing beyond his own immediate circumstances. The more recent recruits had little idea of where they were or even to what unit they belonged. More illuminating were the overall impressions and attitudes expressed by these defectors:

> The recent recruits have no training; second lieutenants only one month.
>
> Only 400 g of bread a day and watery soup.
>
> People fed up with Bolshevism because of food shortages. Red Army takes everything, at least the Germans feed themselves.
>
> The men all know about the end of the commune system, people only want their own land.
>
> Only the officers want to fight, not the men.
>
> Many more commissars at the front.

Although these remarks concerning the present status of conditions and morale may have been comforting to the ears of some intelligence officers, to the "Alten Hasen"—the old front-line veterans—the mere presence of these defectors told them that something was in the air. The faint-hearted usually defect just prior to a major operation in hopes of taking themselves out of harm's way before the shooting starts rather than afterwards when surrendering to the enemy is far riskier. The uneasiness of the "Old Hares" would prove to be well founded.

The Soviet High Command may have called off the Rzhev Offensive and the men of the 6th Infantry Division may have been busying themselves with hauling in deserters, but for Generaloberst Model, there was yet a final chapter to close in the Winter Battle of Rzhev. The Soviet 39th Army and 11th Cavalry Corps were still wandering about in the forests and swamps deep behind the German front. Although cut off and insufficiently supplied, these 60,000 troops still posed a serious threat—especially if the Soviets were to launch another attack against the Rzhev Salient.

Now that the pressure of the Soviet attacks had eased along the Rzhev Front and the German lines had stabilized, Model was able to assemble a force of seven infantry and four panzer divisions to eliminate this threat. Code-named Seydlitz after Friedrich the Great's audacious cavalry commander, the German attack like its namesake would indeed bring down "Morderei" upon the Soviet 39th Army and 11th Cavalry Corps. Again, the German attack plan called for concentric attacks and carving up the Soviet forces into smaller slices thus depriving the trapped Russian units of mutual support or the ability to organize a coordinated defense.

Model, however, would not be there to carry out his meticulously planned operation. Always a "hands-on" general, he was never content to isolate himself in his headquarters. During battles, he was all over the front actively directing operations and speaking with his officers and even ordinary Landsers so as to have a first-hand feel of the battle. On May 23, while flying in a Fiesler Storch over the scene of the upcoming battle, he and his pilot were wounded by Soviet ground fire, the general seriously so. Model's life was only saved by an emergency blood transfusion carried out at the field hospital of the 1st Panzer Division at Belyj. He would be away from the action for three months. Meanwhile, command of Operation Seydlitz was taken over by General der Panzertruppe von Vietinghof.

The German attack began July 2, and despite torrential rains, swarms of mosquitoes, and a stubborn opponent desperately fighting for survival, the attack rolled on relentlessly. By July 5, the northwest corner of the pocket had been hacked off, and two days later, the remaining area had been sliced in half. The trapped Russian units mounted desperate attempts to break out to the east, west, and south, all to no avail. Eleven days after it began, Operation Seydlitz had achieved its goal. The Soviet 39th Army and 11th Cavalry Corps had been crushed. Even though as many as 18,000 Russians had been able to slip through the German encirclement to safety, 50,000 remained behind as prisoners. In addition, the Germans destroyed or captured 226 tanks, 763 artillery pieces, and 1,955 mortars and machine guns. How many young Russians lay dead in the swamps and forests perhaps may never be known. Now, over fifty years later, their remains are still being found.

With both sides having fought themselves to exhaustion during the winter battles, the question now was which side would first regain its breath and what would it do when it had done so? For Germany, the question was critical. Operation Barbarossa had failed. The Germans had kicked in the door, but nothing had collapsed. Instead, the Russians had kicked the door right back in their faces. Germany's only real chance of victory—the swift destruction of the Red Army—was gone and now Germany found itself in the precarious position of waging a protracted war not only against the Soviet Union and the British Empire but against the United States as well. The situation necessitated a complete reassessment of Germany's war aims and strategy. Blitzkrieg, with its primary objective being military, was no longer feasible or relevant. Henceforward, the objectives of the Wehrmacht would have to be strategic in nature in order for Germany to acquire the resources with which it could continue the struggle and perhaps attain a political settlement.

Little wonder then the pessimism among some of the German generals in view of Germany's present situation. But generals are tasked by their masters to wage war and so somehow they would have to devise a plan for future operations. Remaining on the defensive in the East was not an option. The Soviet Union had withstood the shock of Barbarossa and was now mobilizing its vast resources of manpower and industry that dwarfed those of Germany. Ceding the initiative to the enemy was tantamount to placing one's head on the chopping block and waiting for the blow to fall.

The plan drawn up by the German High Command for the summer of 1942 reflects not only a shift in strategy but also the degree to which German military resources had been dangerously overextended. With much of Europe having to be occupied and a campaign ongoing in North Africa, a Barbarossa-type offensive in the East involving the entire front was beyond Germany's present capabilities. Operation Blue, as the plan was named, involved only one sector of the front—that of Army Group South—and had but one objective: oil. The armies of Army Group South were to strike east to the Volga and once the Volga Front was secured at Stalingrad, they were to plunge south into the Caucasus and seize the rich oil fields of the Baku region. Although Operation Blue would not win the war for Germany, it most assuredly would allow Germany to continue it.

During the first few weeks of June, the 6th Infantry Division's sector had its relative "quiet" disturbed by several enemy attacks that seemingly were as random and as pointless as the harassing artillery and mortar fire of the past two months. The night of June 3, the 1st Engineer Company fought off an enemy attack at close quarters. The rising sun revealed fifty-nine dead Russians sprawled on the ground before the engineers' foxholes and trenches. As war booty, the engineers collected twenty-four machine guns, twenty rifles, and a mortar. On June 17, after suffering a heavy bombing raid during the night, the positions of the 37th Regiment were attacked by infantry supported by fighter bombers and a dozen tanks. The fighting lasted throughout the day. In all, ten enemy assaults were repulsed. Obergefeiter Waldeyer and Gefreiter Schneider went tank hunting with magnetic mines and Ballenladugen. Nine burning Soviet tanks illuminated the night. These attacks and the continued appearance of deserters raised concerns as regards the enemy's intentions.

But these concerns were soon forgotten by Grossmann's Landsers as word came down on July 18 that the 6th Infantry Division was to be taken off the front line and actually sent to the rear for rest and replenishment. For the first time since the morning of June 22, 1941—378 days ago—the men would not be waking up and facing the enemy. As the war diary of the 58th Regiment expressed it, "No howling of artillery shells, no rattling of machine guns nor the high pitch whining of ricocheting bullets." However, there was a catch. They would have to march the 50-km trek back to the rest area just west of Ssytschewka—50 km, what was that to them? They had marched 2,000 km to the Volga and beyond, so 50 km would be nothing more than a leisurely stroll in the country.

In high spirits and anticipating several weeks of rest and relaxation, the men packed their gear on the morning of July 19 and marched off to an "oasis of peace" and a well-deserved rest. Had they been able to see but two weeks into the future, their spirits would not have been quite so high.

The earlier concerns of the old "Frontschweine"—that uneasy feeling that something was in the making—was well founded. Undeterred by the previous failure in the "Winter Battle of Rzhev" with its near 1 million casualties, the Soviet High Command was already planning a second Rzhev Offensive. What was human life as compared to the survival of the Bolshevik State? The plan produced could hardly be considered imaginative. The Soviet Kalinin Front was again to attack the northern face of the Rzhev Salient and take Rzhev while the Western Front was to break through the salient's eastern flank and drive on Wjasma. The guiding principle of Soviet military doctrine seems to have been "If at first you don't succeed, keep throwing in more lives until you run out of lives, then gather more bodies and repeat." For the second Rzhev Offensive, the Soviets had amassed a force of forty-three rifle divisions, seventy-two rifle brigades, twenty-one tank brigades, sixty-seven artillery units, and thirty-seven battalions of 'Katyushas' (rocket launchers). In all, 486,000 men and 1,715 tanks.

When the 6th Infantry Division reached the rest area near Ssytschweka on July 23, the men were rather disappointed (though they would have expressed it quite differently). Two days of torrential rain had transformed the "oasis of peace" into a swamp. The men were forced to pitch their tents in this morass and sleep on the sodden ground or take shelter in the few filthy dilapidated huts in the area. Nor was there much in the way of rest. The German soldier is not allowed to rest and grow stale. The men were plagued with constant drill and training exercises. A young replacement, Schütze Reiner Niemann of the 58th Regiment describes the conditions of this "oasis of peace" in a letter to his parents:

> On 21 July we were relieved by another unit and pulled out of the front. Then in two days we marched 90 km to the south and moved into rest quarters in a deserted village that was more lice-ridden and vermin-ridden than ever before. Because of the rain and swampy terrain, we couldn't even pitch our tents. The higher command would not leave us in peace. They hounded us and drilled us in water that was almost over the top of our boots—all under the name of "Tactical Maneuvers." This finally reached the high point and end point on 30 July when we were sent out in the pouring rain to engage in live-fire maneuvers from 5 a.m. until 11 a.m. We didn't have a dry stitch of clothing either on our backs or in our hut. And so we sat until 2 p.m., soaking wet in our filthy huts and watched the stream rise and cut us off from the rest of the company. Then came the order for us to be ready in forty-five minutes. How we all cursed about that.[2]

If Schütze Niemann and his comrades had known why they had to be ready in forty-five minutes, they would have cursed a great deal more.

At 6:30 a.m. on July 30, thousands of Soviet guns, mortars, and rocket launchers rained down hell along the northern Rzhev Front. The Summer Battle of Rzhev had begun. After a ninety-minute barrage, the assault divisions of the Soviet 29th and 30th Armies smashed into the sector of the Saxon 87th and 256th Divisions; 5 km due north of Rzhev at Polunino, the Russians broke through the front line and drove a wedge between the two German divisions. A crisis had arisen—alarm!

The 9th Army Headquarters immediately thought of the 6th Infantry Division "resting" near Systschweva and directed that it be transported north with all haste to stabilize the front. At 12:30 p.m., the division received the order to assemble its units and proceed to the rail station at Ssytschewa where they were to be loaded onto trains and transported north to Rzhev. Neither rested nor replenished, the men of the 6th Infantry Division hurriedly made themselves "Marschbereit" and set off for Systschweva. Easier said than done. For two days, the rain had been coming down—and still was. The streams and creeks had become rushing rivers that in many places had washed away the bridges. To make matters worse, the divisional transport, both horse-drawn and motor-driven, was still in Rzhev though they would have been of little use for the torrential rains had turned the roads into impassable quagmires. However, the situation was so critical that the division was ordered to leave its heavy weapons and equipment behind and depart immediately. The men marched off with only their personal weapons, the individual allotment of ammunition (120 rounds per man), and one hand grenade apiece.

The 1st Battalion, Regiment 58, was the first to depart. At 8 p.m., it set off in the rain and increasing darkness. Schütze Niemann continues in his letter to describe the ordeal:

> While we were packing our kits, the Russians had to go out in the rain and build a causeway over the stream. But it wasn't done quickly. We couldn't march off until evening and only for two kilometers because we could see that neither the baggage train nor the foot soldiers would be able to cross the river. So we marched off without our baggage in another direction. Still in the pouring rain we marched two kilometers through swamps with water up to our belt buckles. Then fifteen kilometers on a road to the next supply depot. This turned out to be only eleven kilometers from our original starting point in the village.[3]

Soaking wet and hungry, the 1st Battalion did not reach Ssytschewka until 6 a.m. on July 31. So desperate was the situation at the front that the decision was made to immediately transport to Rzhev whatever units happened to arrive at the rail station without waiting for them to organize themselves. The 1st Battalion was quickly loaded onto trains and it arrived at Rzhev at 11:30 a.m. At 7:45 p.m., they were ordered to attack the enemy positions east of the village of Golachowo and re-establish the original front line. Oberst Furbach marched north with his "regiment," which consisted of the 1st and 2nd Companies of the 1st Battalion, two platoons of the 4th (heavy machine-gun) Company, one light infantry howitzer, two companies of engineers from the 742nd Division, a labor battalion from the RAD and two Sturmgeschütze.[4, 5]

Not until midnight was he able to get his hodgepodge collection of troops organized and go into the attack (the two Sturmgeschütze never did arrive). The night was pitch dark and rainy. The Russians, probably exhausted after a day of heavy fighting and not expecting an attack in the pouring rain, were taken by surprise. Oberst Furbach's *ad hoc* regiment rolled up three lines of entrenchment, killing 200 Russians and taking another fifty-one as prisoners. In an effort to preserve their hand grenades, Furbach's men had mostly employed their knives, spades, and small arms to clear out the enemy, which now left them dangerously low on ammunition.

Throughout the course of the day (August 1), as other units of the 58th Regiment arrived, the regiment extended its front eastwards to link up with the 256th Division, and the men dug shallow trenches in the rain-soaked ground. The night's action had cost them eleven dead, including the regimental adjutant, Oberleutnant Hüttmann, and the regimental clerk, Oberfeldwebel Eggersmann. Leutnant Ikels of the 3rd Company was wounded as was Oberst Furbach (though only lightly in the hand).

Meanwhile, Hauptmann Petersen's 2nd Battalion of the 18th Regiment had arrived in Rzhev after an arduous journey through torrential, swampy terrain, and near impassable roads. Late on August 1, without any rest, Petersen's battalion was sent 6 km northwest to the village of Chanino, where it was to restore the original front line. This redeployment became a mad dash through hell since the entire area between the front line and the Volga was under continuous fire from Russian artillery and rocket launchers. The men could only make their way forward by leaping from shell crater to shell crater. That they were able to reach Chanino as a cohesive unit was a feat in itself.

Later that night, the 2nd Battalion relieved the battered units of the 87th Division and occupied their trenches and bunkers—and just in time. At 5 a.m., heavy artillery fire rained down along the entire front of Petersen's battalion. For an hour, the ground shook and the air was filled with dust and smoke. Then the detonations moved rearwards, a clear signal that the time for the attack had arrived.

"Aus dem Bunker, los!" The men scrambled out of their bunkers and manned the trenches. Hastily, both heavy and light machine guns were set in position, canisters of ammunition flung open, the metal belts clamped into the gun breaches. But there was nothing to be seen of the enemy. A heavy fog hung over the battlefield. In the distance, the sound of tank engines and the clanking of their tracks could be heard. The tension mounted as the sounds came closer. Then the fog suddenly lifted, and there, on the ridge directly opposite the right flank of the battalion was an entire battalion of Russian infantry supported by four tanks preparing to attack.

Petersen's battalion was not alone. Far to the rear, the artillery regiment of the 87th Division stood ready to support them. Forty-eight barrels of medium and heavy guns roared and sent their projectiles into the Russian ranks. Briefly a panic ensued as the Russian soldiers scattered. Order was quickly restored and the advance continued. Then suddenly thirty German Ju 88 bombers swept down out of the sky and released their deadly cargo across the front of the enemy advance. Forced on by pistol-waving commissars, the greatly thinned Russian ranks rolled forward while the tanks provided them fire support. Only about 100 of the enemy reached the German lines and attempted a final assault. "Urra!" The assault quickly collapsed under the withering fire of German machine guns and carbines.

In a fit of reckless bravado, two T-34s with mounted infantry came roaring toward the village, tank and infantry firing away. A 7.5-cm anti-tank gun took the lead tank in its sights. "Crash!" The first round left its barrel. The Russian infantry immediately bailed off the tanks and scattered. A second 7.5-cm round scored a direct hit, and the tank burst into flames. The 2nd Battalion's "Panzerbrechers" (volunteers specially trained to combat tanks) went after the second tank with their magnetic mines and rendered it out of action. Later two crewmen emerged from the tank and fled off into a ditch, followed by two of their comrades, obviously wounded, who limped off after them. The Panzerbrechers let them go unharmed. Those poor devils had had enough for one day.

By noon, the Russians had regrouped and received reinforcements. They launched a two-pronged attack on Chanino, defended by Oberleutnant Otto Hellweg's 6th Company. Wave after wave of "Urra"-screaming attackers were mowed down but more kept coming. The Russians were able to constantly bring up reinforcements and shelter them in a depression located directly in front of the village. Oberfeldwebel Lauhöfer reported that the mortar crews had shot off the last of their ammunition. Deprived of high-angle mortar fire, there was nothing the German defenders could do about the Russian assault groups massing in the depression. Three times, the enemy attacked and three times he was stopped—but only just. The situation was becoming desperate. Now all the men of the 6th Company were low on ammunition. Oberleutnant Hellweg sent an urgent message to Battalion headquarters requesting ammunition and reinforcements. "Lage Ernst!" situation serious. Hauptmann Petersen knew his company commander well, and when Otto Hellweg said "Lage Ernst," then the situation was indeed serious. Two squads from the 7th Company and one squad from the 5th Company with a 3.7-cm anti-tank gun fired Sprenggranaten

(HE) rounds into the enemy's ranks, but it was not enough. The attacking wave shouting "Urra!" stormed into the village, and the men of the 6th Company shouted "Hurra!" and met them head on with carbines, machine pistols, and grenades. Some of the Russians sought shelter in houses and sheds, but hand grenades dealt with them quickly enough. Two enemy tanks that had entered the village were knocked out by the anti-tank gunners. As the day came to an end and the Russians withdrew, Oberleutnant Hellweg reported to battalion, "Position firmly in our hands." He had chosen to say "Position" rather than "Chanino" for good reason. The village now was nothing more than a heap of smoking rubble.

While the 2nd Battalion of the 18th Regiment was engaged in the bitter struggle for Chanino, the 1st Battalion, 58th Regiment, was busy improving its entrenchments in the rain-sodden ground of its sector. In the distance, they observed what appeared to be an enemy force massing for an attack 4 km north of Galachowa. The regiment's howitzer company took them under fire that seemed only to stir up a hornet's nest. Two heavy KV-1 tanks and three lighter T-70 tanks with infantry support came charging across the fields. German artillery and mortar fire soon broke up the attack but not before the 58th Regiment had lost twelve of its men killed. Leutnant Voss, 1st Company commander, was seriously wounded.

Later that evening, the 3rd Battalion arrived and extended the regiment's front to the east. (Due to the heavy losses during the winter fighting, the division's infantry regiments had been reduced to only two battalions of infantry each.) Unfortunately, the 3rd Battalion had already suffered the loss of four experienced NCOs. Feldwebels Texforis and Steinbach, Oberfeldwebel Wilmshorst, and Stabsfeldwebel Karger had been killed while conducting reconnaissance patrols.

At 5:30 a.m. the next day (August 3), the Russians launched a battalion strength attack on the village of Polunino. The attack was repelled. Two other attacks later that day were likewise beaten back with heavy Soviet losses. The 58th Regiment suffered only four men killed, but these losses were serious in that two of the killed were company commanders: Leutnant Berghaus of the 1st Company and Leutnant Heidekamp of the 10th Company. Another company (3rd) commander, Leutnant Dietrich, was wounded. In three days, the 58th Regiment had already lost to death or wounds half of its company commanders—and the Summer Battle of Rzhev had only begun.

August 4 would prove to be a bloody day. By now, all three regiments of the 6th Infantry Division were deployed in the front line and were occupying a 6-km sector from Bernikowo in the west to Polunino in the east. The 37th Regiment (minus one battalion being held in VI Corps reserve) held the left flank at Bernikowo. The 58th Regiment occupied the right flank at Polunino while the 18th Regiment held the center at Fedorkowa.

Throughout the morning, the 58th Regiment had been observing considerable enemy activity north of Polunino. The sound of tanks revving up their engines indicated that an attack was imminent. At 1:45 p.m., Russian attack-aircraft swept down on Polunino and released their bombs. Ten minutes later the enemy unleashed a heavy artillery barrage along the sector of the 3rd Battalion. At 2 p.m., the attack began. Two battalions of Russian infantry and thirty T-34 and KV-1 tanks assaulted the positions of the 9th, 10th, and 1st Companies. Three tanks penetrated the defenses of the 9th Company while the other tanks remained at a distance and fired away at the German positions, providing the Russian infantry with cover fire. The infantry assault was driven back, at many points in hand-to-hand combat. Nine Soviet tanks were destroyed and another three damaged before they also withdrew.

At 3 p.m., the enemy renewed his attack on Polunino with ten tanks and both mounted and dismounted infantry. The attack was quickly brought to a standstill. Only one platoon of Russian infantry got to within hand-grenade range before they were wiped out. At 4 p.m., the Russians attacked again, this time with three battalions of infantry supported by ten tanks. The infantry assault was first stalled and then driven back by artillery, mortar, and machine-gun fire. The tanks rolled through the German lines, but finding themselves without infantry, they abruptly about-turned and drove off. Without infantry support the tanks felt themselves highly vulnerable to those damned "Panzerbrechers," who seemed to be lurking in every shell crater. Another attack in battalion strength on the right flank of the 3rd Battalion was likewise repelled.

That had been the fourth attack of the day. The men of the 58th Regiment slumped down in their trenches and foxholes, exhausted, their faces and uniforms dust-covered, their red-rimmed eyes staring into nothing, the shouts of "Urra" still echoing in their heads—heads now devoid of any thought. How much longer could this go on? Certainly Ivan would have to run out of bodies sometime.

Ivan did not. More reinforcements arrived and were packed into the jump-off positions as the Russians prepared for a fifth assault. Alerted of the enemy's preparations by the forward observers, the Landsers rose from the bottom of their trenches, foxholes, and shell craters and took up firing positions. They checked their weapons, neatly laid out their stick grenades with the caps unscrewed and the pull cords exposed, thrust their sharpened spades into the dirt beside them, and waited for Ivan to come.

At 7:50 p.m., five heavy and five light tanks came rolling across the shell-cratered landscape toward them, but without infantry support. No shouts of "Urra!" this time, only the ominous clanking of metal tracks. Puzzled, the Landsers looked at one another. "What the hell was Ivan thinking?" In contrast to the earlier attacks, the Russian tanks did not pull to a halt and begin lobbing shells from a distance at the German positions; instead, they came crashing at full speed directly into the defense zone. As though in a fit of bestial rage seeking revenge for all their heavy losses that day, the tanks rolled up and down the

German line attempting to collapse the trenches and foxholes and crush the inhabitants to a pulp.

As night fell, seven of the monsters, having satisfied their rage, drove back to their own lines. Three, not yet finished with their game, remained behind. Now came the moment of the "Panzerbrechers" of the 2nd Engineer Company. Like primitive hunters of the Stone Age, they stalked these modern iron mastodons in the darkness. By 10 p.m., the hunt was over. Two of the beasts had been "slain." The third unfortunately escaped.

So ended August 4. The 58th Regiment had withstood five heavy attacks in the course of ten hours, destroyed seven T-34s and two KV-1 tanks, and inflicted heavy losses on the Russian infantry, but the cost had been high. As the war diary of the 58th Regiment cryptically noted: "Das Regiment velor heute 30 Tote." ("Today, the regiment lost thirty dead.") And tomorrow the killing would begin all over again.

August 5, 3 a.m.: in what could only be described as a probing attack or a "reconnaissance in force," a Russian infantry company without tank support (or any chance of success) attacked the 10th Company. For an hour, the sound of battle reverberated in the murky grey light of dawn. By 4 a.m., the attack had petered out without having achieved anything more than adding to the number of brown-clad bodies lying in the fields and ensuring that the German defenders were now wide awake and fully alert.

In the woods south of Romano, three battalions of infantry and seventeen tanks were observed assembling for an attack. At 10:50 a.m., Soviet fighter-bombers attacked the regiment's command post, and although no casualties were suffered, one of the two Sturmgeschütze assigned to the regiment was heavily damaged. This presented a problem. Sturmgeschütze were forbidden to operate alone, which meant the remaining "Stug" would not be available for what was obviously coming.

At 12:45 p.m., six more tanks were spotted assembling in the woods. Now was the time for the German artillery to act. Sixty light and heavy howitzers sent salvo after salvo into the woods in the attempt to smash the Soviet attack before it could begin. The attempt failed. At 2 p.m., Soviet artillery and rocket launchers answered with a brief but intense preparatory barrage. Ten minutes later, two companies of infantry supported by tanks charged the positions of the 3rd, 9th, and 10th Companies. In the sector of the 3rd Company, the attack was quickly brought to a halt by German artillery, whereas the Russians got to within 50 meters of the 10th Company and 100 meters of the 9th Company before being thrown back with heavy losses.

By 5 p.m., the Russians had reorganized and launched another attack on the 10th Company with twelve tanks and infantry. Four T-34s rolled through the German lines at Timofojewo and destroyed two 7.5-cm anti-tank guns. Then one of the tanks got stuck and fell prey to the roaming Panzerbrechers. Alerted to the presence of their nemesis, the other T-34s promptly withdrew. One, however, got stuck and was quickly rendered out of action.

Fifteen minutes later, eighteen tanks with mounted infantry attacked along the entire front of the 1st Battalion. One tank was immediately knocked out by the anti-tank guns and the rest driven off. Another attack by tanks against the 10th Company resulted in five Soviet tanks destroyed by the deadly 8.8-cm Flak guns. At 7 p.m., the Russians launched what would be their sixth and final assault of the day. Twelve tanks broke through the lines of the 9th Company while infantry attacked the company's left flank. Four of the tanks were set ablaze by the anti-tank guns, three rendered immobile, and another became stuck in a shell crater. The remaining four tanks withdrew but not before two of them were destroyed by the ever-present Panzerbrechers. By 7:35 p.m., the attack was over and quiet descended over the battlefield.

Another long and bloody day for the 58th Regiment. For over sixteen hours, its two battalions had fought off six armor and infantry attacks. Eighteen soviet tanks had been destroyed by the anti-tank guns and three more were credited to the Panzerbrechers (two were accounted for by Gefreiter Schulte-Strathaus). The regiment lost eleven dead, including another experienced NCO, Feldwebel Theo Schneider of the 12th Company, and dozens more wounded, but the line had held. Two dozen tanks and hundreds of Russian lives had been sacrificed and not a meter of ground gained.

August 6 was a near repeat of the previous day. Only hours after the fighting had died down on the night of August 5, the front exploded again. At 3:15 a.m., the exhausted men of the 58th Regiment were awakened by a thunderous barrage of artillery, mortar, and rocket fire bursting around them. Then silence followed by the bellowing roar of "Urra!" when a battalion of Russian infantry supported by four tanks came storming through the pre-dawn darkness against the 10th Company. Forty-five minutes later, another battalion supported by five tanks assaulted the 9th Company. For two hours, furious fighting raged along the front of the 9th and 10th Companies until, with their ranks decimated, the Russians withdrew under the covering fire of their tanks.

Throughout the day, the Russians launched attack after attack against the companies of Furbach's 58th Regiment. The crash of artillery, the clanking of tank tracks, the rattling of machine guns, shouts of "Urra!" and "Sie kommen!" rang out along the entire front until well after dusk when the fighting mercifully died down. None of the attacks had succeeded in penetrating the German defenses, and the Russian losses were described as "gewaltig" ("massive"). The 58th Regiment's losses that day were fourteen killed and dozens wounded.

August 7: on this day, the God of War rested and surveyed his domain. For the moment, the Russians had apparently run out of bodies to feed into his greedy hands, but he could be well pleased with his handiwork thus far. The smoldering hulls of thirty-one tanks littered the shell-cratered landscape. Hundreds and hundreds of brown-clad bodies lay amid the trampled grain fields, and thousands more lay screaming in the dressing stations—music to his ears. The scales, however, were unequal. Only eighty-six corpses wore the Feldgrau—but no matter, the battle had only begun. There would yet be time to balance the scales.

And how had the opening scene of the Summer Battle of Rzhev played out for the rest of the 6th Infantry Division? A glance at the war diary of the 18th Regiment tells the same bloody story as that of the 58th Regiment.

4 August: 3 p.m. Attack on 1st Battalion. Two tanks break through Main Battle Line. One of them rolls over battalion command post.
5 p.m. Three attacks on Hill 200 repelled.
6:30 p.m. Two attacks with ten tanks and infantry on left flank of 2nd Battalion smashed by heavy mortar fire from Mortar Battalion 848.

5 August: 5:30 p.m. Infantry attack with six tanks on Hill 200.
7:15 p.m. Infantry attack with eight tanks on Hill 200. Infantry driven back. Tanks remain on Hill 200 and fire on our positions with devastating effect. Unteroffizier Siekmann allows tanks to approach to closest possible range and quickly destroys three type T-60 tanks with his 3.7-cm anti-tank gun. Four tanks destroyed by Panzerjäger Company of Regiment 58.

6 August: 5 p.m. Enemy concentration on Hill 200 smashed by our artillery.

10 August: 4:30–5:30 a.m. Drumfire along entire regimental front. Attacks against 2nd Battalion at Fedorkowo and 1st Battalion on Hill 200 driven off in close combat.
12:10 p.m. Enemy rolls over right flank of 1st Battalion. Battalion Commander Hauptmann Petersen wounded.
4 p.m. Two enemy tanks pierce Main Battle Line at Hill 200. Leutnant Frowein killed.
6:40 p.m. Two enemy companies attack Hill 200. Oberleutnant Böhmer wounded. Heavy losses: twenty dead, forty-two wounded, two missing.

In short order, the Russians were able to amass new bodies to cast into the blood mill at Polunino. Many of these replacements were recently conscripted males (and some females) from areas overrun by the Soviet advances during the winter. They had been given a uniform, a cap, and a rifle, and if lucky, might have been shown how to load it. Other than that they had received almost no training. That was of little concern to the commissars, who suspected that the new recruits had all collaborated with the fascists and were now being given the opportunity to redeem themselves.

All through the night of August 9–10, Soviet aircraft droned overhead and unloaded bombs along the entire front as well as deep in the rear areas of the 6th Infantry Division. This bombing, combined with repeated clashes with Russian patrols, indicated that Ivan was back and planning another attack. At 4:40 a.m. on August 10, artillery, mortar and rocket fire crashed down on the German positions. At 5:15 a.m., after thirty-five minutes of drumfire, the first attack of the day began. Two infantry battalions supported by armor assaulted the 3rd Battalion of Regiment 58. By 5:37 a.m., a Russian tank had already broken into the defense sector of the 9th and 10th Companies and following the usual tactics, was rolling up and down the front line peppering the entrenchments with machine-gun and cannon fire or attempting to crush them with its heavy tracks. For over an hour it clanked back and forth until it was finally destroyed by the panzerjägers.

At 7 a.m., the Russians launched a three-company attack against the 1st Battalion. Four Russian tanks remained outside the defensive zone and gave cover-fire for the infantry. At 7:10 a.m., the regiment suffered a severe blow: Hauptmann Thummes, commander of the 3rd Battalion and one of the bravest and most competent officers of the regiment, was killed by artillery fire while on his way from his command post to the front line. Oberleutnant Lepin of the 13th Company took over command of the battalion. With the aid of supporting artillery fire, the 3rd Battalion succeeded in driving back the enemy attack by 7:40 a.m. Less than forty minutes later, the battalion was hit in the left flank (9th Company) by two battalions of Russian infantry supported by fifteen tanks. The infantry had been able to get up close to the German line by crawling through a cornfield. With a shout and a sudden rush they broke into the defense zone of the 9th Company. Even though by 9:15 a.m., nine Soviet tanks had been destroyed by anti-tank guns and Panzerbrechers, there still remained five tanks within the defense zone which made a counterattack impossible.

Meanwhile, the neighboring 10th Company had its hands full repelling two strong attacks and destroying five tanks. The situation of the 3rd Battalion was becoming serious. An airstrike was requested, and at 10:04 a.m., Ju 87 dive-bombers plunged out of the sky and unloaded their bombs, most of which unfortunately landed short. Hauptmann Friedrich Müller and the entire company troop were killed when a bomb landed directly on the 9th Company's command post. Only one Russian tank had been destroyed. The gap in the German line had widened to 200 meters, and 1,000 Russian infantry were seen massing to exploit the breach. A second airstrike was ordered, and again the bombs fell short of their target. At 4:40 p.m., a battalion of Russians attacked the 8th Company, and an hour later, two more battalions joined the attack. A German counterattack failed. Soviet heavy tanks rolled about the defense zone, inflicting heavy casualties. To stem the crisis, the Germans threw all that they had into the fight. Artillery and mortar fire pounded the Russians both within and outside the defensive zone. Another dive-bomber attack was ordered. Two platoons of engineers added their weight and tank-busting skills to the German counterattack. At 6:50 p.m., the 3rd Battalion was able to report to regiment that the enemy had been thrown back and the original frontline restored.

August 10 had been the most serious day yet of the battle for the 6th Infantry Division. Ten days of unrelenting combat and the ever-increasing enemy pressure was beginning to take its toll. For the first time, the division's lines had suffered a serious breach, and a crisis had been only narrowly averted. The day had cost thirty-three dead and thirty-seven missing. Four more experienced officers had been lost through death or wounds. The burning hulks of twenty-five Russian tanks and the regiment's courage and tenacity being lauded in the all-important Wehrmachtsbericht was small consolation to the brain-numbed men of Oberst Furbach's 58th Regiment.

For the next three weeks, the battle played out in the same unrelenting fashion—at dawn, a half hour of drumfire followed by air attacks, then repeated infantry attacks in company and battalion strength, often as many as six a day. At times the enemy would break into the defensive zone, a crisis would arise, and a desperate counterattack with whatever troops available would throw the enemy back. And the next day the scenario would be repeated.

The German units along the northern Rzhev Front were gradually being ground down, burned to cinder. Respected, experienced leaders and old comrades from the beginning of the war were disappearing at an alarming rate. Battalions became companies, companies became platoons, and platoons were little more than a couple of squads—and there were few reserves remaining, even at Corps and Army levels. For that there was a reason. On August 4, the Soviet Western Front had opened its offensive against the eastern face of the Rzhev Salient. The Soviet 20th and 31st Armies and the 6th and 9th Tank Corps with 949 tanks launched their assault against the German XXXVI Panzer Corps both north and south of Pogoreloe–Gorodishche. By August 6, the Russians had torn open a 30-km wide hole in the German defenses. By August 23, they had widened the breach to 80 km and had reached to within 12 km of Systschevka, threatening the main German supply route. Generaloberst Model, who had returned to duty on August 10 after recovering from his wound, once again found himself in the midst of a crisis on the Rzhev Front. All available forces were flung into the battle along the eastern Rzhev Front to avert the looming disaster. The northern Rzhev Front would have to manage on its own.

To remedy the absence of available reserves the divisions on the northern Rzhev Front were forced to adopt the less than satisfactory measure of replacing a depleted unit with one of their own less-depleted units and rotating the former to the rear where it could rest and replenish its losses. On the night of August 18, the 1st Battalion of the 58th Regiment, which had been reduced by some 300 casualties from 450 to only 140 men, was relieved by the 1st Battalion of the 37th

Regiment. Six officers, twenty-six NCOs, and 118 men wearily marched the 7 km back to the rest area at Shoporowo just west of Rzhev. They were not there for very long.

As a result of the heavy Soviet pressure on the northern Rzhev Front, the 6th Infantry Division's neighbors to the east, the 256th Infantry and the 14th Motorized Divisions, had been forced by August 20 to withdraw to the south bank of the Volga, leaving the division with an open right flank. The 1st Battalion of the 58th Regiment, after only forty-eight hours of rest, was thrown back into the battle. The battalion had received 250 replacements, who were described as "inexperienced, quickly trained, and hadn't ever thrown a live grenade." Nevertheless, Oberstleutnant Hollinde's 1st Battalion was now 400 strong. It relieved its sister battalion, the 3rd, which had lost 75 percent of its manpower and was down to only 103 officers and men.

When Hollinde's battalion returned to its old positions at Polunino and Galachowo, the men found that little had changed. Thirty minutes of pre-dawn drumfire followed by air attacks and the ceaseless infantry and armor attacks until nightfall. August 27 was another bloody day. Oberstleutnant Hollinde, who twenty-seven days before had led the 1st Battalion in to the Summer Battle of Rzhev, was grievously wounded while leading a counterattack (he died the next day). At 8 p.m., a truck containing seventy-five Teller mines parked near the regimental headquarters was struck by a shell splinter and exploded, flattening headquarters and lightly wounding Oberst Furbach. That day, the regiment—that is to say, the 1st Battalion—lost thirty-six dead and 121 wounded.

To the left of the 6th Infantry Division, a Soviet attack in the sector of the 87th Division had broken the German line and had driven a wedge between the two divisions. Hauptmann Ernst Rhein with part of his 1st Battalion of Regiment 18 and whatever other units he could collect mounted a counterattack to seal off the breach. Hauptmann Rhein was severely wounded, and his counterattack was only able to stop the Soviet advance just short of reaching the Volga.

By now it was obvious that the battered and depleted divisions of the VI Corps could no longer hold the Rzhev Front north of the Volga. On the right flank, the 256th and 14th Divisions had already withdrawn to the south bank of the river, and on the left flank, the 87th Division would soon be forced to do the same. Only in the center was the 6th Infantry Division holding strong, but with both flanks exposed, it would be forced to withdraw. On August 31, Grossmann's Landsers bid farewell to the hellholes for which they had been fighting and dying the past four weeks. Polunino, Galachowa, Federkowa, Chanino—names etched in their regimental histories, names seared into their souls. Their casualties reflected the ferocity of the fighting. When Oberst Furbach led his 58th Regiment into battle on August 1, it had a troop-strength of 988 officers and men. Thirty days later, when it was pulled off the front, the regiment counted only 458 in its ranks, despite having received 601 replacements during the course of the battle.

This reflected a loss of 1,131 officers and men, killed, wounded, or missing—71 percent! In recognition of its courage and sacrifice, the 58th Regiment received: two Knight's Crosses (Oberst Furbach and Unteroffizier Möller); seven German Crosses in Gold; eighty-eight Iron Crosses I Class; 570 Iron Crosses II Class; and forty Panzer Close Combat Badges.

Not surprisingly, many of the medals were awarded posthumously.

The casualty report of Becker's 18th Regiment was almost as grim. Of the 1,418 officers and men who fought under the flag of the 18th Regiment those first thirty days of August, 746 became casualties. Records for the 37th Regiment do not exist, but its casualty list was undoubtedly quite similar to those of its sister regiments. Divisional records show that for the period August 1–22, the 6th Infantry Division lost 565 officers and men killed; 1,745 wounded; and 192 missing, for a total of 2,502. Over 9,000 Russian dead lay across the 6-km front of the 6th Infantry Division, more than one for every meter. Little wonder that the Russians referred to this shell-cratered landscape as the "meat grinder of Rzhev," and this meat grinder still had another month and a half to grind.

The new German front line of the northern Rzhev Front ran along the southern bank of the Volga, except in the center of the line at Rzhev. Here in the "Neu-Kohlberg Stellung," the 6th Infantry Division defended a protective arc about that part of the city that lay north of the Volga. At places called the "Stadtgut," "Handtuch," "Seidenfabrik," and "Panzerstrasse," the division would add more of its blood to the Summer Battle of Rzhev.

When the division withdrew to Rzhev during the first days of September, the men saw that the city had changed considerably since they had hurriedly passed through it a month ago on their way to the front. Indeed, the city was barely recognizable. Like the Landsers in their forward trenches and foxholes, Rzhev had been the target of non-stop shelling and air attacks as the Russians sought to disrupt the German movement of troops and supplies to the front. The streets were near impassable, filled as they were with shell craters, the rubble of collapsed buildings, and the skeletons of burned-out vehicles. In Rzhev North, hardly a building remained intact; certainly none of their roofs. The city was little different from the half dozen or more shattered villages that the division had recently vacated.

Was this what they had been fighting for the past eight months? This "Jewel of the Volga," this smoldering heap of rubble? Was this what Ivan had been dying for in the tens of thousands? Briefly the Landsers questioned the value of the sacrifice—but only briefly. The Führer had commanded that Rzhev be held, and hold it they would no matter the cost.

In the Neu-Kohlberg Stellung Generalmajor Grossmann deployed his regiments along the defensive arc about the northern half of the city with Infantry Regiment 423 (subordinated to the 6th Infantry Division) on the eastern flank between the Volga and the Stadtwald, Regiment 58 between the

Stadtwald and the Chalinka Creek, and Regiment 18 from the Chalinka Creek back to the Volga. The 37th Regiment was dug in on the south bank of the Volga west of the city. Over the next six weeks of battle, the regiments would be flung about the battlefield as the situation or crisis demanded, and they would be rotated out of the fighting as their heavy losses required.

If the men of the 6th Infantry Division had hoped that they might enjoy a brief respite from battle once they had withdrawn to their new position, they were quickly disappointed. Their Russian adversaries had followed closely upon their heels, and no sooner had they arrived and taken up position than the Russians began launching attacks all along the Neu-Kohlberg Stellung. Nothing had changed. Heavy artillery barrages and air strikes followed by repeated infantry and armor attacks. On September 2, 7, 8, and 9, Soviet attacks were beaten back with heavy loss. On September 14, a powerful Russian assault broke into the center of the German line at the "Stadtgut." Only with the greatest difficulty and the aid of the engineers' flamethrowers were the Russians thrown back and the front line restored. Fifteen Soviet tanks were destroyed in the fighting.

September 21, 6 a.m.: drumfire along the entire Neu-Kohlberg Stellung followed by mass infantry attacks supported by armor. The enemy broke through the German defenses and penetrated into the northeast corner of the city. A counterattack by the 2nd Battalion of Regiment 18 drove the enemy back but was unable to re-establish the original front line. A further attempt mounted the next day by both battalions supported by Sturmgeschütze also failed to restore the front line. This time, the Russians simply would not budge.

During the second phase of the Summer Battle of Rzhev, an improvement in the Russian performance was noticeable as well as a decline of German combat dominance. The Russians were repeatedly able to breach the German defenses and gain a lodgment, and more often than not, the German counterattacks were less than a total success. The Russian commanders had learned to quickly reinforce any break-in, which reflects an increased ability to coordinate their attacks and move their units about the battlefield. No longer did their supporting tanks go wandering here and there attempting to pot-shoot the German defenders hunkered down in their holes. Instead, the tanks dug themselves in almost to their turret rings within the defense zone and awaited the inevitable counterattack. This made them difficult targets for the German anti-tank guns and Sturmgeschütze.

The decline in German combat effectiveness can be attributed to a month of non-stop combat and the resultant heavy casualties. The companies and battalions were not only weakened units of one-third normal strength but were now for the most part composed of recent replacement with inadequate training and no combat experience. Fewer and fewer of the old hands and the experienced NCOs and officers remained. They were either resting beneath Birkenkreuzen in the numerous cemeteries about Rzhev or in base hospitals throughout Germany.

Replacements from training companies back in Germany were slow in coming. The 6th Infantry Divisions own Field Training and Replacement Battalion had long since been emptied out, and the service units, which had been combed through time and again since December, had little left to give. These service troops, who at first had been looked down upon by the old hands, were now almost regarded as hardened veterans after surviving a single clash with the enemy—but even these "veterans" were becoming rare.

However, replacements were being found—and what replacements they were. A recent arrival of three officers, five NCOs, and 123 men destined for the 18th Regiment was described as consisting mostly of factory workers with only seven weeks' training. Of the officers, only one had any experience at the front. The other two were retrained Luftwaffe ground personnel. Most serious was their noted lack of eagerness for combat. Another batch of fifty replacements was led by a thirty-eight-year-old leutnant. The unit's two NCOs had no experience of the front, the one only having wielded a pen in his service to the Fatherland and the other's knowledge of war came from what he had heard on the radio. As for the men, they had no understanding of machine guns and knew of hand grenades only from rumor. The division's Chief of Operations, Major John, reported that of fifty-eight replacements for the 58th Regiment: "Only a couple possessed the necessary qualities to be trained for any leadership role and consequently the re-building of the regiment is not possible."

Although the replacements might not have been up to the 6th Infantry Division's standards, the old hands—the "Alten Hasen"—were as effective and as deadly as ever. One such "Alter Hase" was Oberfeldwebel Albrecht Schnitger of the 18th Regiment. Already ascribed near legendary status not only in his regiment but throughout the entire division, he was a typical example of the Wehrmacht's pre-war class of professional, non-commissioned officers. Reliable, resourceful, dedicated to the wellbeing of his men and in battle utterly fearless.

On September 24, a critical situation had arisen in the northeast sector of the Neu-Kohlberg Stellung. At 2 a.m., a Russian force of 100–150 men had broken into the German defenses near the Rzhev–Stariza rail line and had dug in along the railroad embankment. If this force was reinforced, it could easily drive into the city, for all that stood between the Russians and Rzhev was Oberfeldwebel Schnitger's "Kampfgruppe" of a mere fifteen men. The squad on the left had already been weakened when it had clashed with a strong enemy patrol. They had pulled back 50 meters and were down to three men, a jammed light machine gun, and no grenades. Schnitger quickly assessed the situation. If Ivan attacked, his small force would be crushed, and the enemy would be in the city. In accordance with the Wehrmacht's general maxim "If in doubt—attack," Schnitger placed a two-man, 5-cm mortar team on his right flank and brought up a heavy machine gun to replace the jammed machine gun of the squad on the left flank. With six men, he crept up close to the railroad embankment. Seven men against more than a hundred, but Schnitger was confident that they could bring it off in typical infantry fashion—up with a shout and then go in with hand grenades and machine pistols.

At 2:40 a.m., Schnitger gave the order to the mortar team, "Feuer frei!" Round after round dropped out of the night sky into the densely packed Russians while the heavy machine gun raked back and forth across the railroad embankment. Schnitger's six men lay there, their eyes riveted on their leader. He turned to them and nodded. The time had come. Hand grenade first, then "Los!" With a shout of "Hurra!" they leaped over the embankment, machine pistols blazing, yelling for all they were worth. Schnitger later confessed that he had never shouted so loudly and so much in his life. Stunned by the mortar rounds and hand grenades and confused by the howling devils in their midst, the Russians panicked and fled, leaving Schnitger and his devils in possession of the rail junction. The crisis had been averted by a handful of "Alten Hasen" with the daring and the expertise to still get the job done. And in a few days they would do it again.

September 27: throughout the day, the Russians had launched company- and battalion-size attacks supported by tanks against the north and northeast face of the Neu-Kohlberg Stellung. Most of the attacks had been repelled, but only with the greatest difficulty and with heavy losses. Near the "Seidenfabrik," the enemy had broken in and quickly entrenched. Several counterattacks failed. On the morning of September 28, an assault group from the 252nd Division attempted to drive the Russians out but was unsuccessful. Overnight, the Russians had reinforced their position and were preparing to push into Rzhev. Another crisis was looming and again Albrecht Schnitger and his "Kampfgruppe" was called upon to rescue the situation.

His Kampfgruppe consisted of three unteroffiziere and fourteen men, two of whom had been gleaned from the supply company. Armed with machine pistols, two light machine guns, and 200 hand grenades carried in washbags slung over their shoulders, they set out for the "Seidenfabrik." This time they were not alone. Two Sturmgeschütze had been assigned to support the counterattack.

At 4:30 p.m., German artillery laid down a short barrage of smoke shells to conceal the Kampfgruppe's advance. Schnitger's men crawled to within 50–70 meters of the Russian position, but the enemy spotted them through the smoke and raked them with machine pistol and rifle fire. The Sturmgeschütze rolled forward giving cover fire and Schnitger and his men leaped into the attack. A wild *mêlée* erupted in the smoke-shrouded entrenchments. Machine pistols barked, grenades exploded, Russians shouted commands, and Germans shouted "Hurra!" Two Russian flamethrowers shot tongues of flame at Schnitger's men, but they were quickly put out of action with well-aimed grenades and with horrifying result. In minutes, Schnitger's left-hand group had rolled up their section of the enemy position, but his right-hand group had been unable to advance. Then the covering smoke drifted away and the two Sturmgeschütze withdrew. Two heavy Soviet tanks were seen approaching in the distance, and the "Stugs," without a traversable turret and mounting only a short-barrel 7.5-cm gun, did not dare to take on the enemy tanks without the cover of smoke. Schnitger and his men would have to finish the job themselves.

The two men from the supply company came crawling over to Schnitger, dragging two washbags full of grenades. Schnitger and another man began hurling grenade after grenade into the Russian entrenchments. Three other men caught up in the fury of battle leaped into the trench with their machine pistols and, as Schnitger described it, "rolled it up like a carpet." The Kampfgruppe then quickly organized for defense. Ninety Russians had either been killed or wounded and another twenty taken prisoner.

Two weeks later, at a presentation ceremony, the division's commander, Generalmajor Grossmann, and the regimental Kommandeur, Oberst Becker, affixed the Ritterkreuz about Oberfeldwebel Albrecht Schnitger's collar. This outstanding soldier already held both Iron Crosses and the German Cross in Gold. When congratulated by his commanders on his most recent decoration, he replied with typical Landser Galgenhumour, "Das nächste Kreuz ist das Birkenkreuz." ("The next cross will be a wooden cross.")

Throughout the first two weeks of October, the battalions of the 6th Infantry Division were rotated in and out of combat as the situation and their casualties demanded. When their numbers had been worn down to a level at which they were no longer effective, the battalions were relieved and sent to a rear area to rest and replenish their numbers. Almost without fail, after but a few days, a crisis would arise, and they would be flung back into the fight without having rested or been able to instruct the new replacements in even the most basic techniques of ground combat and survival in the "meat grinder of Rzhev" attrition.

The majority of the crises occurred in the northeast sector of the Neu-Kohlberg Stellung, where the Russians had succeeding in pushing back the German line and strongly establish themselves in the "Stadtwald." From here, they had launched numerous assaults that had threatened to break into the city itself. Repeated German attempts to eliminate the "Stadtwald" position had all failed, and the Germans were forced to live with this thorn in their side and the constant threat it posed to the Neu-Kohlberg Stellung.

After the middle of October, the Summer Battle of Rzhev slowly began to wind down. Both sides had battered one another into senseless exhaustion, and the appearance was that the Russians had again temporarily run out of fresh bodies to feed into the blood mill of Rzhev. On both the northern and eastern face of the Rzhev Salient, Soviet attacks became less frequent and less intense until one day they ceased entirely. Like the previous Winter Battle of Rzhev, the Summer Battle of Rzhev, begun and waged with such ferocity, died away with barely a whimper.

As with all campaigns on the Eastern Front, the cost had been enormous. German losses are difficult to determine since no overall figures are available.

The fact that the sixteen divisions involved lost on average 60–80 percent of their personnel tells one nothing for certain because the German divisions, still not rebuilt since the previous battles had rarely attained more than 50 percent of their regulation strength. This and the constant inflow of replacements only complicate further determination of German losses. Estimates vary from 50,000 to over 100,000. Whatever the number, Germany could hardly continue to bear such casualties.

Russian losses were, of course, many times those of their opponent. Lives had again been squandered at an incredible rate; 300,000 dead, wounded, and missing is considered low by modern reckoning. General Grossmann provides a more detailed assessment of Soviet losses: 380,000 dead and wounded, 13,770 prisoners, 2,956 tanks destroyed or damaged, and 870 aircraft shot down.

The Soviet Summer Rzhev offensive did, however, achieve some gains. Except for the city of Rzhev itself, the Soviet assault had forced the Germans back across the Volga. On the eastern face of the salient, the German front had been pushed back 40 km, and Russian forces now stood only 12 km from the all-important Rzhev–Ssytschevka supply line. But despite the massive efforts and the equally massive losses, the Russians still had not achieved their primary objective: the elimination of the Rzhev Salient and the destruction of the German 9th, 3rd Panzer, and 4th Panzer Armies. The salient had been battered and crumpled in like a tin can, but the Germans still held Rzhev.

The Soviet Commanders of the Kalinin and Western Fronts may have bowed to the reality that their summer offensive had ground to a halt, and the German defenders may have been able to heave a sigh of relief at having averted another catastrophe, but the Summer Battle of Rzhev still had one final bloody scene to play out. In the northeast corner of the Neu-Kohlberg Stellung, where the Russians were stubbornly clinging to their foothold in the Stadtwald, the Germans decided that they could no longer live with this thorn in their side.

From all three regiments and the engineer battalion of the 6th Infantry Division, enough men were collected to form a Stossgruppe to eliminate the "Stadtwald" position once and for all. Commanded by young Leutnant Dieckmann of the 37th Regiment, the assault group launched its attack the night of October 15. Although Leutnant Dieckmann was killed in the first rush, the operation was a complete success. The Russian "Stadtwald" position was eliminated and the original German front line was restored. A total 120 Russian soldiers were killed and a further ninety-six taken prisoner. Reports were that the flamethrower teams of the engineer battalion had greatly distinguished themselves—one can well imagine what horrors that entailed.

# 9

# "Wir Halten Rshew!" The Second Winter Battle of Rzhev

Even before the Summer Battle of Rzhev had consumed its last victims, the Soviet High Command was making preparations for yet another Rzhev Offensive. Rzhev, however, was not the only concern of Stalin. There was still the matter of the German offensive in the south. One German army had already reached the Volga at Stalingrad. Two other armies were now deep in the Caucasus, and German mountain troops had planted the Nazi flag high upon Mt. Elbus. But to Stalin and his staff, this was not a time of despair but rather one of opportunity. The German southern offensive was dangerously over extended. Its flanks were being protected by Italian, Hungarian, and Romanian armies, and whatever their combat capabilities might have been, they were not Germans.

In the Southwestern, Don, and Stalingrad Fronts the Soviets had 1.1 million men and 1,463 armored vehicles, giving them a sufficient superiority over their opponent to be confident in the success of a powerful counteroffensive. With the code name of Operation Uranus, the Soviet plan called for smashing through the Romanian, Hungarian, and Italian armies on either side of Stalingrad, entrapping the German 6th Army within the city and then pushing on southwest to the Sea of Azov, cutting off the two German armies in the Caucasus.

Such was Stalin's thinking, but Zhukov, now the Deputy Supreme Commander, still maintained that the decisive victory of the war was to be achieved on the Central Front. He wanted another crack at Rzhev. With the elimination of that troublesome salient and the destruction of German Army Group Center, the northern and southern wings of the great fascist force that had invaded the motherland would wither away. On the Kalinin and Western Fronts (and the Moscow Defence Zone) stood a force of 1.9 million men; 24,642 artillery pieces and mortars; 3,375 armored vehicles, and 1,170 aircraft—far more than what was available for Operation Uranus in the south. On September 26, Stalin gave the go-ahead for the planning of two great winter offensives.

For the renewed attack on the Rzhev Salient, the Kalinin and Western Fronts had at their disposal nine armies with 702,924 men; 10,900 artillery pieces and mortars; and 1,718 armored vehicles. Appropriately named after the blood-greedy God of War, Operation Mars, like the previous Rzhev offensive, could hardly be described as imaginative. Again powerful attacks were to be made against the western and eastern faces of the salient and an attack on the northern Rzhev front. Having butted their foreheads bloody against the solid wall of the Neu-Kohlberg Stellung, the northern Soviet attack was redirected some 50 km further to the west of Rzhev.

Despite the lack of originality, Zhukov was confident of success. He definitely possessed the force superiority necessary for victory: four to one in men, ten to one in tanks, and two to one in artillery. In addition, he was certain that the German 9th Army against whom most of his forces would be directed had suffered heavily over the past ten months. The divisions now were but shells of their former selves and the men exhausted. Zhukov well appreciated the near superhuman hardness of the German soldiers, but even they had to have a breaking point.

The Soviet Deputy Supreme Commander was correct in his assessment of the German 9th Army. It had suffered horribly in the winter and summer battles. In the 9th Army sector, Model possessed sixteen infantry divisions, two panzer, and one motorized divisions. To oppose Zhukov's offensive, the 9th Army could only field a force of 140,000 men, 1,900 artillery pieces, and a mere 125 tanks. Zhukov was also correct in believing that the German divisions had been hollowed out. Replacements had not been able to keep pace with casualties. A "strong" division was one that could boast being at one-half regulation strength (*c.* 7,000–8,000 men). Most were far less than that. However, the Soviet Supreme Deputy commander was wrong in one assessment; the German divisions may have been hollow. The men were not. The German soldier was still rock hard—die he might, but break he would not.

In an effort to boost the morale of the depleted German infantry regiments, the Führer had decreed on October 15 that henceforth all infantry regiments were to be redesignated as grenadier regiments, echoing the glory of those stalwart elite units of the imperial past. All infantrymen were now to be known as grenadiers and the ranks of schütze and oberschütze were changed to grenadier and obergrenadier respectively—not that these new grenadier regiments would be receiving any additional grenadiers or obergrenadiers.

Perhaps a greater boost to morale than this echo of the past was the issuance of the new wonder weapon—the soon-to-be legendary MG-42. This machine gun with its incredible rate of fire of 1,200 rounds per minute provided a German squad with overwhelming fire power which could not be matched by any opponent during the war. Although the high rate of fire took some getting used to, in the hands of a skilled Maschinengewehrschütze it was a terrifying weapon and took a heavy toll of victims.

Another boost to morale was the arrival of winter clothing. With winter approaching, many a survivor of the previous winter shuddered at the thought of another Russian winter. The clothing that arrived was not the normal woolens and scarves nor the pathetic grab-bag of donated civilian garb, but instead was specialized protective gear designed for winter combat: quilted jackets and trousers in camouflage white, felt boots, fur hats, and shooting mittens. No longer would the men need to shuffle about like tramps wrapped in bed linens, table cloths, and other bits of rags pilfered from Russian huts or pull on blood-stained, bullet-riddled clothing stripped from the enemy dead. Now they could walk about actually resembling the German soldiers that they were. Naturally, there was not enough of the specialized clothing for all the troops. The men of the rear services would have to settle for the newly designed greatcoat, which was longer and blanket-lined. The quilted snowsuits were reserved for the men on the front line.

After twenty days on the northern Rzhev Front, the 18th Regiment was relieved on October 25 and rotated back to a rest area at Tolstikowo just south of Rzhev. Since the beginning of the Summer Battle of Rzhev, the regiment had lost forty officers and 1,372 men. The survivors deserved a rest. Three days later, the regiment received the newest batch of replacements and set about the task of teaching the newcomers the brutal realities of combat at Rzhev. Also arriving was a disturbing directive from divisional headquarters: the regiment was to make itself as mobile as possible through means of troop carriers, light vehicles, panje wagons, and even skis. The meaning of this directive was obvious. In any upcoming battle, the regiment would be employed as a mobile strike force to be rushed from crisis to crisis.

On the evening of October 31, the Kommandeur of Regiment 18, Oberst Becker, was visiting divisional headquarters when the phone rang. Generaloberst Model wished to speak with Oberst Becker. The room fell silent. Over the past few months a phone call from Model had usually meant "Alarm! Regiment Marschbereit!" As Becker picked up the phone, the only thoughts passing through his mind were the men are not rested, the equipment not repaired, the new replacements not yet trained, and now we are to be thrown back into the inferno?

For a moment, Model's words did not quite sink in. "Congratulations … the honor of the regiment … Ritterkreuz…." As the general rang off, Becker stood there stunned. In recognition of the achievements of Grenadier Regiment 18, the Führer had awarded him the Knight's Cross. Becker understood that the award was not for him alone. It was for the regiment—his regiment. As "father" of the regiment, he would wear that piece of tin about his neck for the fallen and the maimed, for the exhausted Landser, and for the young leutnant, who in the six weeks of hell at Rzhev had grown old before his time. Accordingly, the next morning, "Corle" Becker announced to his men, "Kameraden, das Regiment

18 hat das Ritterkreuz bekommen!" ("Comrades, Regiment 18 has gotten the Knight's Cross.") Perhaps more important to the men was that the regiment was not immediately being rushed back to the front.

While the 18th Regiment was enjoying its well-deserved rest, the division's other two regiments returned to the front. On November 1, they arrived at their old positions in the Neu-Kohlberg Stellung. The men knew the area well. The "Stadtwald," "Stadtgut," "Seidenfabrik," and "Ziegelei" were all still there, or what was left of them. Very little had changed: rubble and shell-cratered earth still littered with Russian corpses, blackened hulls of burned-out tanks, and memories and horrors that could not be expressed in words.

Soon after they had settled into their old positions, several of the men of Regiment 58 decided the time had come to pay Ivan a visit to let him know that the "58th" was back. On the night of November 5, Unteroffizier Nilazny of the 10th Company assembled a Stoßtrupp and slipped off into the darkness towards the enemy lines. In a masterfully conducted trench raid Nilazny and his men rolled up 200 meters of trench, destroying twelve enemy bunkers and three munition dumps. Then grabbing three prisoners, the raiders hurried back to their own lines leaving behind fifty dead Russians—all at no cost to themselves. For this action, Unteroffizier Nilazny was named to the Honor Roll of the German Army and received the Honor Roll Clasp.

The enemy retaliated the next morning with an ill-advised company-strength attack against the 11th Company. The attack was quickly swept away by the rapid-firing MG-42s. Those not cut down were sent scurrying back to their own positions. On that day, winter arrived with its sub-zero temperatures and snowstorms. Gradually the fighting in the Neu-Kohlbeg Stellung died down—except, of course, for the usual sniping and harassing artillery and mortar fire. Although relatively quiet, the month of November cost the 58th Regiment forty-five dead and two men missing.

There was good reason that a calm had descended upon the Neu-Kohlberg Stellung. Zhukov was preparing to unleash his Operation Mars in yet another attempt to crush the Rzhev Salient. Originally scheduled for mid-October, the offensive had been postponed for a month as a result of the autumn rains that had turned the landscape into a quagmire. With the onset of winter and the hardening of the ground, the attack could proceed.

At 7:15 a.m. on November 25, after two hours of drumfire, Operation Mars commenced on the eastern face of the Rzhev Salient. In the midst of a snowstorm eight Soviet rifle divisions and three tank brigades smashed into the German line 15 km northeast of Ssytschevka in the sector of the Württemberg 78th Grenadier Division and the Silesian 5th Panzer Division. For all its fury, the gains of the attack were minimal. Despite overwhelming superiority in men and materiel, the Russians had only succeeded in opening a 30-km-wide breach in the German line and advancing 3 km before being brought to a halt.

That same day, the armies of the Kalinin Front launched their attacks against the northern and western fronts of the Rzhev Salient. In the north, 50 km west of Rzhev, the Soviet 39th Army was able to break through the thinly held 42-km-wide sector of the weakened Potsdamer 206th Grenadier Division and threatened to cut the Olenin–Rzhev highway. The motorcycle battalion of the "Grossdeutschland" Division was rushed to the front and immediately counterattacked. Reinforced the next day by other elements of the "Grossdeutschland," the counterattack continued, and although unsuccessful in restoring the original front line, the Soviet advance was halted for the moment and the crisis averted.

Along the western face of the salient, 60 km to the southwest, the Soviet 22nd Army breached the defenses of the Rhineland 86th Grenadier Division and pushed into the Lutschessatal. The Germans responded quickly by sending in Kampfgruppe Köhler from the "Grossdeutschland" Division to stymie the Russian attack. Over the next few days, bitter fighting raged amid swirling snowstorms as the Germans threw into battle additional mobile units from 9th Army Reserve. The Soviets continued their advance, but only slowly.

Near Belyj, 50 km to the south, the 41st Soviet Army was able to push aside the Hessian 246th Grenadier Division and 2nd Luftwaffe Field Division and create an 8-km-wide gap in the German front. Two Soviet mechanized corps thrust through this gap and achieved the deepest penetration of all the Soviet assaults during the opening phase of Operation Mars. Once more the Germans brought up mobile reserves to contest the enemy advance.

In the first few days of the Soviet offensive, the pattern for the battle had emerged. The Russians would attack and enjoy initial success, and then the Germans would throw in mobile reserves and bring the advance to a halt. More Russian forces would pour in, and their advance would start rolling again though only at a snail's pace.

On the eastern Rzhev Front, the Soviet 20th Army was so determined to push through the German defenses and cut the vital Wjasma–Rzhev supply route that they brought up the second echelon consisting of the 8th Guards Rifle Corps, 2nd Guards Cavalry Corps, and the 6th Tank Corps and shoved them forward into the narrow gap in the German front. There the dense Russian columns became the target of devastating German artillery and mortar fire coming at them from three directions and creating a slaughter yard. Even in the blinding snowstorm, a German gunner could not miss. Russian bodies were stacked up by the thousands in the gullies and ditches where they had sought cover. Entire regiments were decimated, but still the attack continued. By November 27, elements of the Cavalry and Tank Corps had fought their way over the Wjasma–Rzhev rail line and were pushing west. However, by this time, the 6th Tank Corps had lost over half its tanks.

Early on the morning of November 28, Oberst Becker received a phone call at his headquarters, and this time the voice on the other end of the line made no mention of Knight's Crosses or congratulations. The words "Marsch und Einsatzbereit!" were still ringing in his ear when he replaced the receiver. His regiment was to be march- and combat-ready by noon. The 18th Regiment had recently completed the directive of making its units mobile and for the better part of a month had sat in reserve just south of Rzhev. This was the longest the men had been off the front line since the war in Russia had begun, and now a mere three days into the enemy's newest offensive they were to be thrown into a crisis.

The regiment was ordered to proceed 25 km due south to Ossuga "with all possible speed," seal off the enemy penetration, and restore the Wjasma–Rzhev supply route. On the afternoon of November 28, Kampfgruppe Becker, as the regiment was now called, set off on what the men would later refer to as their "Winterreise"—or winter tour. They soon discovered that they were not as mobile as they had hoped. The snowstorms over the past several days had rendered the roads (when they could be found) nearly impassable. The sleds so vital for transportation in the Russian winter had never arrived, which left man, beast, and vehicle to struggle the best they could through the meter-deep snow. The painstaking progress that they were making was insufficient for the present crisis. At 10 p.m., the decision was made to load Kampfgruppe Becker onto trains at Papino and rush it south to Ossuga.

Becker's units arrived in Ossuga the morning of November 29 and spent the day organizing themselves for the mission, all except for the 14th (panzerjäger) Company that had not arrived. With its lighter vehicles, it remained hopelessly stuck in the snow far to the north. For support, Becker was promised a company of tanks.

At 7:15 a.m. on November 30, Oberst Becker sent his grenadiers into the attack. The 2nd Battalion advanced south along the east side of the rail line while the 1st Battalion advanced along the west side. With the platoons deployed in standard wedge formation, the battalions went forward—and with no small amount of apprehension. They were, after all, dealing with a Soviet Tank corps, and they did not have any anti-tank weapons, not even a single, miserable 3.7-cm gun. The promised tank support never showed up. Of small consolation was the lone Sturmgeschütz, which, having wandered about for hours in the snow, joined the advance south.

Although puzzling at first, a more important addition to Kampfgruppe Becker's attack was the arrival of a "freight train" that actually turned out to be a Panzerzug or armored train. A veteran of World War I (as was its commander), it had been disguised as a freight train after the war in order to be hidden from the Allied War Commission and to avoid the restrictions of the Treaty of Versailles. Hauled back into service, this "freight train" brought with it incredible firepower: thirty-two machine guns, two 2-cm flack guns, four mortars, and two anti-tank guns.

With the newly arrived source of support, the attack proceeded. The 2nd Battalion swept away the enemy forces east of the rail line and advanced 5 km to the train station at Loshki, where it crossed over to the western side, turned, and advanced north to meet the southward-driving 1st Battalion. Caught between the two German forces and hammered by the guns of the "freight train," the surviving Russian defenders fled off into the woods to the west. By nightfall, Kampfgruppe Becker had successfully completed its mission. The Wjasma–Rzhev supply route had been restored and the Soviet forces that had broken through were now trapped in the forest west of Ossuga.

The action had cost Kampfgruppe Becker twelve dead and thirty-two wounded. Unfortunately, many of the casualties were "old hands." All too often when units go into action with a high proportion of inexperienced recent replacements, as was the case with Kampfgruppe Becker, the older experienced men find themselves out of necessity taking on greater responsibilities and risks and consequently suffering high losses.

With the Wjasma–Rzhev rail line again in German hands, the Soviet 6th Tank Corps and 2nd Guards Cavalry Corps were now cut off and surrounded. There were no options remaining to them but to launch desperate attempts to break out to the east and reach Russian lines. A few were successful; most were not.

The Second Winter Battle of Rzhev raged on for another three weeks as the Russians sought in vain to exploit the initial breakthroughs they had achieved back on November 25. The Soviet commanders continued shoving fresh units and fresh bodies into the battle, determined to eventually force a decisive breakthrough—whatever the cost. The cost was horrendous, an estimated 8,295 casualties per day.[1]

On the eastern Rzhev Front, the Soviet 20th Army had only advanced 10 to 12 km. Briefly they had succeeded in cutting the Wjasma–Rzhev supply route as previously mentioned, and they had paid a heavy price for that meager achievement. In the north, after the initial breakthrough, the Soviet forces had only been able to advance 12 km. Along the western face of the Rzhev Salient, the Soviets had achieved the greatest penetrations: 20 km for the 22nd Army in the Lutschessatal and 50 km for the 41st Army south of Belyj. All at a terrible price. In four weeks, the 41st Army's 50-km advance had cost 50,636 casualties. In other words, 12,500 casualties per week per 12 km advance.

There was something rather Somme-like about the Soviet Rzhev offensives—the application of ever greater amounts of mass and materiel with ever-diminishing returns. The operations and tactics mirrored those of the Great War and so did the results.

As with the previous offensives, the Second Winter Battle of Rzhev slowly ground to a bloody halt. The God of War had fully satiated himself and like the River Scamander could accept no more victims. Operation Mars, which had begun in the pounding fury of "Trommelfeuer," gradually echoed away in the swirling snow and ice mist of the Russian landscape. The Russian attacks grew more sporadic and weaker—much like the thrashing of a beast wounded to death, until in the end they died away completely. By mid-December, even Zhukov was forced to concede that the offensive had failed and he ordered his forces to withdraw or, if entrapped, to break out.

On December 20, the Second Winter Battle of Rzhev officially ended. The cost had been great and remains a matter of debate among historians. The Soviets put their losses at 215,700, of whom 70,000 were listed as killed or missing. The Germans estimated their opponent's losses at 200,000 killed and wounded plus 1,847 tanks destroyed. More recent estimates speak of over 300,000 men killed, wounded, or missing—and all that in less than thirty days.[2]

What did this great expense of human lives achieve? Although Operation Mars utterly failed in its objective of capturing Rzhev and destroying the German armies in the Rzhev Salient, Zhukov maintained that by putting such heavy pressure on the salient, Operation Mars had prevented German Army Group Center from shifting any of its forces south to combat the Soviet Stalingrad counter-offensive. Perhaps one might grant him that point, but conversely the 750,000 men committed to the Rzhev Offensive and the 300,000 lost were prevented from assisting the Stalingrad counteroffensive. The First Winter Battle of Rzhev had forced the Germans to withdraw to the Königsberg Stellung and at times had threatened the German armies in the salient with catastrophe. In the Summer Battle of Rzhev, the Russians had, at least, pushed forward to the banks of the Volga on either side of Rzhev. Operation Mars, for all its fury and losses, could claim no such successes. In the end, the front had changed but little, and the German Landser could yet boast, "Wir halten Rshew!"

Even though the Neu-Kohlberg Stellung, where the 37th and 58th Regiments were stationed, had been spared much of the violence of Operation Mars, no staff officer could have ever reported to headquarters, "Im Norden nichts Neues." Oberst Furbach's Regiment 58 had seen to that. While to the southeast, west, and southwest, the battle raged, the grenadiers took it upon themselves to wage their own battle in the form of the Stoßtruppunternehmen or trench raid. This deadly style of warfare had been brought to the level of art by the German infantryman and was conducted almost as a competitive sport among the companies. Encouraged by senior officers to prevent troops from becoming dull and complaisant during extended periods of defensive warfare, these raiding parties seldom lacked for volunteers. The newer men felt the need to prove themselves to the old hands, and the "Alten Hasen," who already knew themselves to be living on borrowed time, still took part in these raids in order to lend their expertise and to maintain their aura of invincibility.

In addition to preserving the aggressive nature of the troops, the trench raids often brought back useful information in the form of enemy prisoners. Besides the identification of units and their locations, the mere physical appearance and demeanor of these prisoners could reveal a great deal concerning the enemy in one's sector. Overage and underage prisoners with indifferent attitudes indicated that one was facing second-class units and need not fear that a major attack was imminent whereas prisoners young, fit, and excellently outfitted could well mean trouble in the near future.

The participants in the Stoßtruppunternehmen also brought back bits of enemy equipment, often purloined with inexplicable risk. After a hit-and-run raid, one would assume that quickly reaching the safety of one's own lines would be paramount. Pausing to snatch and lug back an enemy machine gun, radio set, or even a mortar appears foolhardy at best. But the German soldier had to have his war-booty as proof of his exploits if not for bragging rights. Much like their Teutonic forbearers, these raiders victoriously returned "home" dragging captives and proudly displaying their trophies of war. In some respects, war at the basic level had changed very little since ancient times. All that seemed missing was the deep roar of the aurochs' horn announcing the heroes' return.

On the night of December 2, Feldwebel Anders and a group of men from the 1st and 2nd Companies raided the Russian lines, destroying two bunkers, eight machine gun emplacements, and a disabled T-34 tank that the enemy had been using as an observation post. At least fourteen Russians had been killed. As booty, Feldwebel Anders' Stoßtrupp brought back two prisoners, one light machine gun, and eight rifles. Anders' group lost not a single man.

Not to be outdone, on December 9, the commander of the 3rd Company, Leutnant Thünemann, led a Stoßtrupp on a trench raid west of the Dobraja road. Without casualties, the raiders destroyed three bunkers, accounted for fifteen enemy dead, and made off with one light and one heavy machine gun. However, one does not indefinitely enjoy good fortune. A raid on the night of December 12 near the "Stadtgut" sector did not fare well. Although the raiding party blew up nine bunkers, seven machine-gun emplacements, and nabbed two prisoners, they lost twelve of their men killed and two missing. Leutnant Alois Thünemann was killed by an enemy sniper when he went out to receive his returning raiders.

The Stoßtruppen of the 3rd Company took a grim revenge. On the night of December 22, a raiding party led by the new company commander, Leutnant Richter, broke into the Russian positions on either side of the Dobraja road. Explosions rocked the night as the raiders rolled up 250 meters of trenches. They destroyed seven bunkers, four emplacements and grabbed two prisoners and a light machine gun. Without loss, they returned home leaving behind fifty enemy dead.

Heiligabend, Christmas Eve 1942: peace had descended along the entire Rzhev front. The Soviet Offensive had come to an end, and even the aggressive Stoßtruppen of the 58th Regiment had ceased their nocturnal forays. This was the 6th Grenadier Division's second Christmas in Russia; it was the first Christmas that they would actually be allowed to celebrate. They had warm clothing, warm bunkers, and, most important, peace and quiet—so very different from the previous year during the withdrawal to the Königsberg Stellung when any contemplation of the Savior's birth had been swept away by the wind, cold, and the war.

This year, they would genuinely observe the Holy Days, as genuinely as they could 1,500 km from their homes and families. Even Ivan was strangely silent, though unlikely out of any respect for the German Weihnachten. Why wake the beast? If Fritz was celebrating, then, at least, his dreaded Stoßtruppen were not quenching their thirst for violence.

The men of the 6th Grenadier Division were well provided for this Christmas. The company cooks and bakers (those not already serving in the front lines) had outdone themselves. There was no shortage of sausages, kuchen, or stolen, and certainly no shortage of alcohol. For once the Weihnachtspost had arrived on time, and the hardened Landsers generously shared out the precious delicacies sent from home. Those without family naturally received their "Führerpakete." In each of the bunkers stood a tiny spruce creatively decorated with candles and strips of foil. During the evening, the company commanders made their rounds of the bunkers, followed by the regimental commander passing out Christmas cheer and Iron Crosses. A chorus of traditional Weihnachtslieder rose into the night sky, taking away some of the chill in the air. Ivan remained quiet, respectfully listening if not understanding.

As the candles burned low and the alcohol took its toll, the men grew quiet and reflective as their thoughts turned to home, family, and fallen comrades. One thought that drifted through each Landser's head was the hope that this would be their last Christmas in Russia. For far too many of them, it would be.

# 10

# Operation Büffel

The 6th Grenadier Division rang in the New Year in a lively fashion, one that would become tradition for the remainder of the war. At daybreak on January 1, every carbine, machine gun, mortar, and even 2-cm Flak gun fired away at the Russian positions in front of them. Ivan did not return the New Year's greeting, hunkering down instead in bunkers and trenches fully expecting a major attack. Then the guns fell silent and the smoke drifted away. After all, it had all been in good fun.

The Führer and the German General Staff were in a far less celebratory mood that New Year's Day. The Rzhev Front may have withstood the Soviet winter onslaught, but far to the south on the Stalingrad and Caucasus Fronts, a disaster was staring them in the face. In mid-November, Zhukov's other offensive, Operation Uranus, had smashed through the Romanian armies, entrapped von Paulus' 6th Army in Stalingrad, and was pushing southwest to the Sea of Azov, threatening to cut off the other two German armies in the Caucasus. Von Paulus had requested permission to attempt to break out of the encirclement, but the Führer had denied the request. The 6th Army would fight where it stood. Hitler had given assurances that he would somehow rescue the 6th Army. He did not. Two months later, von Paulus and the remnants of the 6th Army surrendered. A total 91,000 freezing and starving skeletons shuffled off to Siberia; a scant 5,000 of them would ever see Germany again.

Although short of catastrophic, the German defeat at Stalingrad was a severe blow to the Wehrmacht. Depending on the sources, dates, and extent of the campaign considered, Axis losses in killed, wounded, or taken prisoner range from a quarter to over a half million men. Whatever the number, after three and a half years of war these were losses that Germany would be hard put to replace.

History likes its drama and the Battle of Stalingrad has often been called the "turning point" of the war. Accurate or not, the defeat was certainly indicative that Germany had reached, if not overreached, the limit of its power. Hitler might still have been determined to win the war, but more sober minds at the Führer's Headquarters and in the field were now thinking more in terms of how not to lose the war. The defeat and heavy losses at Stalingrad were soon to directly affect the defenders of Rzhev.

Early in January, the "prodigal sons" of Regiment 18 returned from their "Winterreise." For the past month as part of 9th Army's mobile reserve, they had been flung about the battlefield to wherever a crisis had arisen. At Ossuga and in the Lutschessatal, they had suffered heavy casualties. Thirteen officers and 407 men had been killed, wounded, or were missing (40 percent). As Becker's grenadiers trudged northwards through the snow, they caught sight of a road marker, "Rshew 27 km," and despite the memories of the horrific summer battles, many a Landser strangely experienced the feeling of returning home. Due to the regiment's losses, it was not immediately reunited with its sister regiments at the front. The regiment was directed to its old rest area at Abramkowo south of Rzhev, where it readied replacements and set about the task of rebuilding its depleted ranks.

Here, the men received unwelcome news—they were soon to become orphans. They were losing the "Father" of the regiment. Oberst Carl "Corle" Becker had been promoted to generalmajor and was leaving them to take command of the Rhineland 253rd Genadier Division. Becker had commanded the regiment since December 1940. He had led the men across the Russian border that fateful June morning of 1941 and had been with them every step of the way—across the Njeman, the Duna, to beyond the Volga. With them he had endured the harshness of the winter and the brutal battles of Rzhev. For most of the men of the regiment, he was the only "Vater" they had known.

The sadness of Corle's upcoming departure was soon replaced by a feeling of near panic among his staff. If the Kommandeur was leaving them, then he would have to be given a proper send-off; that is, a formal military farewell with regimental band, parade, and the final review of the troops. But who today among the ranks could remember the spit and polish of the parade ground? The troops of the companies now had only been schooled for combat. What could they possibly know of the beauty and artistry of the Prussian military culture with its cuffed and braided Waffenröcke, the gleaming helmets, the mirror-polished jack boots, and the white gloves? Here at the front the men had only their ragged and torn winter combat jackets, white-washed and dented helmets, and insulated felt boots. And what of the music? Musikmeister Ruhland's regimental band had long since been converted to infantrymen and scattered among the companies. Had even enough of them survived to form a quartet? There was nothing for it. Somehow the regiment would have to pull it off. And, somehow they did—perfectly.

In a forest clearing, the regiment formed up on three sides of a square. At the open end stood the regimental flag flanked by two infantry howitzers. To the accompaniment of the "Präsentiermarsch," Oberst Carl Becker reviewed the grenadiers of the 18th Regiment for the last time. The men stood ramrod stiff in the snow, palms pressed against the trouser seam, eyes right. As the Oberst drew level with each grenadier, the helmeted head snapped eyes front. Becker looked directly into each man's eyes, and in that moment—as in the old days—man, regiment, and Kommandeur were bound together as one.

With the formal review of the ranks concluded, there remained one final act to play out. The stern voice of a hauptfeldwebel rang out across the forest clearing, "Vorbeimarsch!" The moment the staff had dreaded had arrived.

They need not have worried. As the troops marched past their Kommandeur, rank on rank, they performed the Paradesteckschritt flawlessly despite their clumsy felt boots. The ranks straight, not a man out of step, as though they were on the parade ground of Bielefeld. A Hohenzollern guardsman would have been proud. As the last notes of "Preussens Gloria" drifted away into the surrounding woods, Oberst Carl Becker took his final farewell of Grenadier Regiment 18 and departed, well-pleased and touched by the ceremony, this brief echo of a nearly forgotten past. Twelve years would pass before he ever saw any of his grenadiers again.

Shortly after ringing in the New Year, the men of the 58th Regiment resumed their customary nocturnal activity of paying Ivan a "visit." At 5:30 a.m. on January 5, Leutnant Josef Kleinemeier and a Stoßtrupp from the 2nd Company "visited" the Russian position north of the "Kolonie." Often engaging in hand-to-hand combat, the raiders rapidly rolled up the entire trench. Unfortunately, Leutnant Kleinemeier was seriously wounded in the *mêlée* and died three days later.

The 2nd Company was unable to avenge Leutnant Kleinemeier for on January 14, the 58th and 37th Regiments turned over their positions to the Hessian 129th Grenadier Division and moved a few kilometers west to take over the "Wolga Stellung." Their new sector ran west for 8 km along the south bank of the Volga from Rzhev to the Lepeticha Bend. Regiment 37 dug in along the eastern half of the sector while Regiment 58 held the western half. The "Wolga Stellung" was considerably calmer than the "Neu-Kohlberg Stellung." The enemy was no longer breathing down their necks but was entrenched on the other side of the Volga some 800 meters away. With the enemy at a distance the men's greatest struggle was against the heavy snowstorms that filled their trenches and required constant shoveling out. This exhausted the men particularly since the temperatures had dropped to -30 degrees. As with the 18th Regiment, Regiment 58 was also losing its Kommandeur. Oberst Furbach, who had led them through the summer battles at Rzhev and had been awarded the Ritterkreuz for his regiment's exploits, had been called away to 9th Army Headquarters for special assignment.[1] His replacement was Major Zorn, the commander of the division's Panzerjäger Abteilung.

Although the Volga lay between them and the enemy, the river was frozen over and provided no defensive barrier. The 37th and 58th Regiments had not been in their new positions for two weeks before the Russians, well aware of their newly arrived opponents' pugnacious nature, attempted to deliver the first blow. On the night of January 30, a Russian raiding party complete with flamethrowers attacked the 37th Regiment but was stopped dead in its tracks by a hail of artillery and mortar fire. Oberleutnant Althage organized an immediate counterattack and wiped out the survivors. Triumphant, his group brought back five prisoners, one flamethrower, four light machine guns, eight machine pistols, and sixteen rifles.

Angered that the enemy had beaten them to the punch, the Landsers retaliated soon enough. On February 6, Leutnant Karl Rindfleisch of the 11the Company of Regiment 58 led a Stoßtrupp across the frozen Volga and without casualties rolled up 200 meters of entrenchments, destroying two bunkers, inflicting heavy losses on the enemy, and bringing back one prisoner. For the next two weeks, Ivan did not attempt any new trench raids.

After an absence of two and a half months, the 18th Regiment returned to the division February 12. The ranks had been replenished, and the men appeared eager to return to the front. Anything was better than serving as a mobile reserve and enduring another "Winterreise." The regiment took over the eastern half of the "Volga Stellung," relieving Regiment 37, which was placed in Corps Reserve. The new commander of the 18th Regiment was Major Heinrich "Steppan" Höke, who had previously commanded the regiment's 3rd Battalion. Höke was an old "Achtzehner." He had been with the regiment since 1924 when he had been accepted into the Reichsheer as a nineteen-year-old volunteer. He had risen in the ranks from lowly Landser to Kommandeur of Grenadier Regiment 18, and the men he now led looked upon him as "one of their own."

In mid-February, the 6th Grenadier Division as well as all the divisions in the Rzhev Salient received the puzzling directive to carefully pack all unnecessary equipment and send it to the rear. The men were even instructed to rid themselves of any superfluous personal gear. In addition, a ban on home leave and out-going mail had been imposed. Something was definitely in the air. There was, of course, the usual "Scheisshausparole" or latrine rumors circulating among the ranks, but they were seldom any more reliable than small-town gossip. The troops could only continue to wonder what it all meant.

What it all meant was that after fifteen months the Germans were finally leaving Rzhev. The aftershocks of the Stalingrad disaster were being felt along the entire Eastern Front. More important is that they were being felt at the Führer's Headquarters. For over a year, Hitler had insisted that the Rzhev Salient be held at all costs and not only because of his aversion to anything that smacked of retreat. He had stubbornly clung to his illusion that one day the Rzhev Salient would serve as a springboard for a renewed advance on Moscow. Even though the salient had been battered and dented by Zhukov's offensives, it still possessed a frontage of over 500 km requiring twenty-nine divisions to man its defenses. After the heavy losses at Stalingrad, this "springboard" and the illusion of a future assault on the Soviet capital had to be given up. Hitler's Chief of Staff, Generaloberst Zeitzler, sought to convince his Führer that by withdrawing from the Rzhev Salient, the front could be reduced from 500 to only 150 km thereby freeing up many divisions that could either be employed elsewhere or used to build up a reserve. Hitler eventually bowed to reality and reason and on February 6 authorized the 9th Army and 4th Panzer Army to withdraw from the Rzhev Salient.

Code-named Operation Büffel (buffalo), the withdrawal was not to be a "devil-take-the-hindmost" bug-out, but rather a meticulously planned and executed operation. Evacuating long-held defensive positions in the face of a numerically superior enemy is perhaps the riskiest maneuver that a military force can undertake. If at any point during the withdrawal the enemy catches wind of the operation and opportunistically seeks to take advantage of the situation by launching a serious attack upon troops now in the open, a carefully planned withdrawal can quickly be turned into a catastrophic rout.

When the magnitude of Operation Büffel is considered—the abandoning of 500 km of front, withdrawing twenty-nine divisions, some of which had to travel 150 km and establish a new defensive line—one can appreciate the extraordinary efforts required for its success. The heaviest burden of the planning and preparation fell upon the army corps and divisional staffs and the always-overworked engineers. Timetables, routes, and distances had to be worked out in minute detail. Any confusion or jam-up of withdrawing columns could prove disastrous. As for the engineers, the labors of Hercules lay before them: 200 km of motor-vehicle roads and 600 km of roads for horse-drawn transport had to be constructed and kept clear of the ever-drifting snow (a task usually performed by Russian volunteers); 450 km of new communication cable needed to be laid and 1,300 km of existing cable pulled up; 1,000 km of railroad dismantled, and, most important, for each step of the withdrawal, a new line of fortifications had to be built. The engineers' most devious task, the installing of mines and booby traps, would, of course, wait until the last minute.

Not only were the Germans leaving Rzhev, but a sizeable portion of the previous year's harvest was leaving with them. Thousands of tons of wheat, potatoes, oats, and hay, as well as, several thousand head of livestock had to be transported out. Nothing could be left to the enemy. Once again the war had reverted to the Dark Ages.

To avoid the enemy becoming suspicious, the troops in the front line were instructed to continue their normal activities (i.e. trench raids and patrols). The artillery and mortars were to maintain their usual pattern of harassing fire. The men, however, were to be kept in the dark concerning the withdrawal in case any of them should be taken prisoner during their forays.

Despite all the precautions and efforts to mask the operation, reports from partisans and spies soon alerted the Russians that the Germans were most likely planning a withdrawal, but the extent and the date remained unknown. The increased activity of Russian patrols and the repositioning of units, particularly the armored forces, told the German intelligence officers that Ivan had gotten wind of the operation. Their suspicions were confirmed when on February 18, Russian loud speakers blared out across to the German front lines, "The 9th Army is packing its bags and getting ready to leave!" Nonetheless, Operation Büffel would take place on schedule as planned.

Or so the staff officers thought. After weeks of feverish activity working out march routes, timetables, and a thousand other details, the overworked staffs of the 9th and 4th Armies found themselves confronted with a serious problem that threatened the entire operation. At the last moment, some 60,000 Russian civilians were demanding that they be evacuated with the troops. Having worked for or, at least, having cooperated with the Germans, they had no desire to be liberated by their countrymen. Even those who had merely tolerated the enemy were aware that they could be denounced by a neighbor seeking to save his own neck from the commissar's rope or "G'nickschüss." The staff officers had no choice but to rework their plans. If the civilians were not accommodated, they would leave on their own initiative, clogging the roads with their overloaded panje wagons and upsetting the carefully worked-out timetables. Such an exodus would endanger the entire operation.

While the staff officers redrew their plans, the 6th Grenadier Division maintained its normal activity in the "Wolga Stellung." On February 23, Stabsfeldwebel Anders with a Stoßtrupp from the 11th Company of Regiment 58 slipped across the frozen Volga and paid Ivan a visit. With grenades and bunker-bombs they rolled up 450 meters of trenches, destroying three bunkers and twelve dug-outs, and inflicting an estimated fifty casualties without suffering a single casualty. As booty, they hauled back one light machine gun, one machine pistol, eight rifles, and one prisoner.

The 18th Regiment, which had returned to the front February 12, now felt itself sufficiently settled in to launch a trench raid of its own. At 9 p.m. on February 26, a demolition team of one officer, two NCOs, and five men with a support team of two NCOs and eight men with two light machine guns carefully made their way over to the Russian side of the river. Well-concealed in their Schneehemden, they crawled in single file through the snow, the demolition team in front, support team close behind. When they were 15 meters from the enemy trench, a Russian sentry, having grown suspicious, came towards them to investigate. He was quickly rendered unconscious by a stick grenade wielded as a club.

The support team rapidly deployed one machine gun to the left, one to the right, and both slightly forward. The demolition team leaped forward and slid over the parapet and down into the trench. Oberfähnrich Max Hunzinger hurled a 3-kg explosive charge into a bunker and all hell broke loose. Shouts, screams, and detonations broke the stillness of the night as the Stoßtrupp rolled up 100 meters of trench, destroying a heavy machine gun bunker and a dug-out. They blasted their way along another 50 meters before they were brought to an abrupt halt by a sudden barrage of enemy mortar fire. Five of the raiders were wounded, two of them seriously. Ivan had come up with a rather brutal remedy for these thuggish fascist trench raids—heavy mortar fire on one's own position, friendly casualties be damned.

The raiders had hoped to take out a command bunker, but now it was time to get out and to get out fast. Dragging their wounded (one of whom died *en route*) and the unconscious Russian sentry, they slid down the steep Volga banks and made their way back to their own lines. Though not a total success, they could, at least, console themselves with having killed fifteen of the enemy and brought back one heavy machine gun, a German MG-34, and several machine pistols and semi-automatic rifles, as well as one prisoner and a radio set. They would not have the opportunity to do better another time. The next day, February 27, word came that Operation Büffel would be set in motion at 7 p.m. on March 1.

March 1, 7 p.m.: for the past several days, the officers, particularly the staff officers, had been nervously eyeing the weather and the road. Recently temperatures had been gradually rising. The snow had softened from its normal hard crust, and water was collecting on the roads. Was the Russian winter set to betray them again? First, in 1941 by arriving too early, and now in 1943 by departing too soon. Half of the transportation was based on sleds. If the snow melted away, they would be useless, and if the roads thawed, the wheeled transport would be equally useless. But as darkness fell, the officers breathed a sigh of relief. The temperature was rapidly dropping, the roads were refreezing, and, better yet, the snow had begun to fall. Never had the harsh Russian winter been more welcomed.

In the Wolga Stellung, the men of the 6th Grenadier Division were making the final preparations for their departure. Positioned at the apex of the Rzhev Salient, they had the longest trek of any of the divisions in Operation Büffel—150 km. The first leg of their journey was a quick "hop" of over 30 km to the previously prepared position near Stupino. During the days of victory in the French campaign and Barbarossa, a march of 30 km would have been regarded as a casual stroll, but now after a year of defensive warfare and with legs no longer accustomed to such demands, 30 km through the snow would be no easy task.

As the grenadiers packed up their personal gear, the engineers busied themselves with arming the thousands of mines they had laid in the past week and installing the last of their diabolical booby traps. When Ivan returned to Rzhev, he would meet with a fiery homecoming.

On schedule at 7 p.m., the heavily laden grenadiers assembled on the icy roads and at the command marched off into the night. The thermometer continued to fall, and it had begun to snow again. With conflicting emotions the men tromped through the snow. Relieved, of course, to be out of the hellhole of Rzhev, they were, nonetheless, retreating—something the German soldier did not willingly do, orders or not. For fifteen months, they had held Rzhev against all the Red Army could throw at them. To the honored appellations of "Frontkämpfer" and "Ostkämpfer," they had added yet another to the military parlance of the day—"Rshewkämpfer." There would never be a badge, shield, or cuff band for the "Rzhev Fighters," but that mattered little, for as General Grossmann expressed it, "They wore the Rzhev shield on their brows." Behind them they were leaving a thousand bitter memories and thousands of fallen comrades, lying beneath their Birkenkreuzen in a dozen cemeteries scattered about Rzhev.

However, these were not the only comrades they were leaving behind. Back in the Lepeticha bend of the Volga, Oberleutnant Hötzel of the 58th Regiment deployed his Nachtruppen (rearguards) a mere three squads and two light infantry howitzers. Obviously such a small force was not a sacrificial last-ditch defense heroically buying time for escaping comrades. Their mission was to turn back enemy patrols and to convince the Russians that the Germans still held Rzhev. Hötzel and his Nachtruppen would have to hold their widely dispersed positions for twenty-four hours.

In the early morning hours of March 2, just as the men of the 6th Grenadier Division were reaching the prepared positions at Stupino, a Russian raiding party attempted to break into Hötzel's position. They were immediately thrown back. In the course of the morning, Hötzel's small force ran off several enemy patrols. Ivan was getting suspicious. At 12:30 p.m., heavy artillery and mortar fire crashed down on the Nachtruppen and 200 Russians leaped from a ravine and charged across the frozen Volga. The MG-42s ripped holes in their ranks, but still they came on. Some actually forced their way into the German positions and had to be dealt with by machine pistol, grenade, and the ever-handy spade. Among their foxholes and across the snow-covered ice of the Volga, Hötzel's men counted 138 enemy bodies. Four of their own comrades had been killed.

Hötzel's rearguard was not on a suicide mission. The division had left them adequate motor transport so that when the time came, they could make good their escape and catch up with their foot-slogging comrades—assuming, of course, that their luck had not run out. At 6 p.m., under the cover of darkness, Hötzel's Nachtruppen loaded up their vehicles and bid the Wolga Stellung a final farewell from the 6th Genadier Division.

The Russians were not long in discovering that the Germans were gone. All along the Rzhev Salient Russian patrols entered the deserted trenches and bunkers and soon became acquainted—to their great cost—with the hellish creativity of the German engineers. The fascist bandits had mined and booby-trapped everything: doors, beds, ovens, even stores of vodka.

Despite the mines and booby-traps, the Red Army did pursue its enemy. At 10 a.m. on March 3, a Russian forward unit of sixty men clashed with a six-man German patrol just north of Stupino. The patrol's machine-gunner took a heavy toll of the surprised enemy caught out in the open, cutting down forty of them before they could withdraw. Fearful of being outflanked, the patrol pulled back to Stupino. Seven hours later at 5 p.m., the Russians launched an attack with 300 men against the snowwall defenses of the 58th Regiment. The attack was beaten back with heavy loss; 100 Russian bodies dotted the snow. The 58th Regiment lost six men killed, among them Leutnant Martin Kruse, commander of the 3rd Company. He had been the backbone of the defense, encouraging his men and directing their fire, mindless of his own safety until a Russian bullet cut him down.

At 7 p.m., the 6th Grenadier Division began the second step of their withdrawal—another 30-km march in the snow in the direction of the rail center at Ssytschewka. The men lamented the fact that in the deeply frozen ground they were unable to give their fallen comrades a proper burial. They could only lay them in graves hacked out of snowdrifts. Perhaps in the spring a merciful enemy would find it in his heart to do them the honor. A rearguard was left behind under the command of Oberleutnant Helmut Lindemeyer of the 1st Company, Regiment 58.

The Russians attacked soon enough with a force of 200 men, supported by mortar. The attack was repelled, but not before Oberleutnant Lindemeyer and Feldwebels Rohde and Tiemann were killed. The enemy remained quiet the rest of the night, and just before dawn the rearguards loaded their wounded onto sleds and hurried off to catch up with their comrades.

The fourth day of Operation Büffel brought the grenadiers yet another exhausting 30-km trek. When they reached the snowwall fortification along the Bukatino–Chochlolowka line, they received orders to halt and hold the line. Although weary to the bone, the men immediately set about improving the defenses and mapping out fields of fire. They knew that Ivan was close on their heels and soon they would again be fighting off his near-suicidal attacks.

The next morning, their eyes were greeted by a strange apparition emerging from the frozen mist. Motor-sleds propelled by powerful aircraft engines were skimming across the snowfields toward them. Sheltering behind their snow walls, the grenadiers looked at one another in puzzlement. "What could Ivan be thinking?" Although the sleds were packed with infantry and armed with two machine guns, they had no armor protection and were out in the open fields—and the panzerjägers quickly shot all eight of them to pieces. A pity, had they been captured undamaged they would have been quite useful for the next leg of the withdrawal.

Undeterred by the destruction of their sleds, the Russian infantry continued the attack, suffering heavy losses before they drew back. No sooner had the fighting died down when the cry went up, "Alarm!" In the 58th Regiment's sector, a hostile force in company strength had been spotted marching in column upon the regimental command post to the rear. Somehow Ivan must have infiltrated the German line. Fortunately, the alarm turned out to be false. The hostile force was definitely Russian, but it was only a column of civilian refugees conducting their own Operation Büffel.

For the next three weeks, the withdrawal from the Rzhev Salient proceeded according to plan. But what did "according to plan" mean to the common Landser? Torturous night marches across a frozen landscape, dropping exhausted into the makeshift shelters of the new defensive line, and catching a few hours of sleep before the inevitable attacks by the pursuing enemy, and then once more, another night march.

As well-planned and executed as Operation Büffel might have been, this did not mean that there were not moments of crisis that threatened units with annihilation. On the twelfth day of the withdrawal, after an exhausting night march, the 18th Regiment found itself holding a sector far too wide for its numbers, which had been steadily diminished by casualties, sickness, and exhaustion. Worse yet, the supporting artillery and even the regiment's own infantry howitzers had no ammunition. The munition truck was far to the rear, stuck in the snow with a flat tire. The grenadiers could do nothing more than lie in the snow and watch as, in the distance, a sizable enemy force assembled for an attack.

At 2:14 p.m., just as the Russians were deploying for the assault, the munitions truck arrived, "Gott sei dank!" Feverishly, the crates of artillery ammunition were unloaded and distributed among the field-and-infantry howitzers—and not a moment too soon. Already, the waves of enemy were rushing forward, their shouts of "Urra" carried before them by the wind. In a cascade of howitzer fire, the Russian ranks were drastically thinned out and then driven back by a hail of machine-gun fire.

The Russians were not yet finished. At 10 p.m., a strong enemy force hit the 2nd Battalion and broke into the positions of the 6th Company. Leutnant Bewermeier scraped together some of his scattered troops and launched an immediate counterattack. He was cut down in the first few seconds of the assault—a hard loss for the regiment, another "old hand" gone. Enraged, his men drove the Russians back and restored the front line.

For the next two days, fighting raged up and down the Bukatino-Chocholowka line—attack, break in, counterattack. The bodies began to pile up on either side of the snow wall. On March 13, the 6th Grenadier Division suffered a heavy blow: Albrecht Schnitger had fallen. The news of this remarkable soldier's death spread quickly throughout the division. He had been struck down while leading a counterattack. Like all too many of the old hands, his luck had finally run out. Iron Cross, Knight's Cross—Birkenkreuz. Generalleutnant Grossmann called Major Höke and expressed his deepest sympathy for the regiment's loss. Corle Becker, now commanding the 253d Grenadier Division, immediately upon hearing the sad news, sent a telegram to his old regiment, stating that he stood by his old comrades in this dark moment. Five months ago, almost to the day, he and Grossmann had affixed the Ritterkreuz about the young man's collar.

Oberfeldwebel Albrecht Schnitger was not buried in a snowdrift. When the 18th Regiment pulled out that evening, they brought their comrade with them. As though from a scene in the Götterdämmerung, they lay his body on a bier and, borne by four stalwart grenadiers, Albreht Schnitger marched with his comrades for the last time while all around on the horizon, villages burned in the night and artillery rumbled in the distance. As one grenadier expressed: "It was as though we were Goth's bearing our slain king."[2] On March 15, after fifteen days of combat, the division was pulled out of action. Someone at 9th Army Headquarters took mercy on the men and provided them motor transport for the last leg of the withdrawal. There was no rejoicing or singing in the back of trucks as they jostled along the deeply rutted roads. The men simply sat and blankly stared at one another in numbed, exhausted silence. Although the withdrawal of German forces would continue for two more weeks, for the men of the 6th Grenadier Division Operation Büffel was at an end.

By the end of March, Operation Büffel had ended for all the German divisions of the Rzhev Salient. By any measure, it could be considered a success. The 530-km front of the salient had been reduced to 200 km. With minimal losses of men and material, twenty-nine divisions had successfully withdrawn, and more important, twelve infantry, three panzer, two motorized, and one SS cavalry division had been freed to be available for other operations. The generals and their staffs could certainly congratulate themselves on their remarkable accomplishment—a textbook example of tactical withdrawal. However, remarkable or not, a tactical withdrawal is still a retreat, something at which the Wehrmacht would become quite adept in the future.

Within days of the withdrawal, the propaganda machines of both sides kicked into high gear. Moscow acclaimed it a great victory achieved by force of arms. The invading fascists had been driven back 150 km, thousands of square kilometers of Russian soil and hundreds of towns and villages had been returned to the motherland. Rzhev, the "Jewel of the Volga," which had cost so much Russian blood, had at long last been liberated.

The German propagandists spoke of a "tactical redeployment" (which at this stage of the war could actually be stated without too much irony) and of the "desultory," if not "timid," pursuit by the enemy (something the men of the 6th Grenadier Division might dispute). Certainly the Soviet pursuit could not have been termed "Blücheresque," but the Red Army did pursue. Its casualties were proof of that. The Germans estimated that their enemy lost 42,000 men, the equivalent of six infantry divisions. Modern historians place the number more than three times higher at 138,000.[3] Whether Soviet victory or German achievement can be debated, but what is certain is that some 150,000 men, Russian and German, paid the final blood bill to the "blood mill" of Rzhev.

# 11

# Operation Freischütz

When the 6th Grenadier Division reached the new German front line, they were relieved that their labors were at an end and also to discover that the "Büffel Stellung," as it was now named, represented a genuine defensive line with adequate protective trenches and heated bunkers—so unlike the makeshift snow walls and igloo shelters they had been inhabiting the past two weeks. Like any new tenants, they naturally thought it necessary to add their own finishing touches: more barbed-wire entanglements, more trenches, more bunkers (which needed to be blasted out of the still-frozen ground), and, of course, mines. In a brief period, the division's engineers laid out 5,000 Schuh and Teller mines.

They were wise to have done so. Within days of the division's settling in to its new positions at Dorogobush, the pursuing Russians arrived and immediately began putting pressure on the forward outposts. Throughout the day of March 22, these outlying positions fought off twelve attacks. Suspecting a strong Soviet attack, Generalleutnant Grossmann ordered that the forward outposts be pulled back to the safety of the Main Battle Line. At 10 p.m., a force of over 200 infantry attacked out of the darkness. They were quickly repelled, suffering heavy losses in killed and wounded as well as seventeen prisoners. Those who had survived were observed frantically entrenching in an effort to escape the murderous German machine-gun and mortar fire. From long experience, the grenadiers knew that Ivan rarely launched a single attack, and so they remained vigilant the remainder of the night. They need not have bothered. It had only been a "reconnaissance in force" and one which had told Ivan all that he needed to know: this was the new German front line, not a temporary defensive position prior to another withdrawal, and it was a front line that the fascists intended to hold.

After this, the Dorogobush front quieted down. The Russians attempted no further attacks and the grenadiers did not even revive their customary trench raids, as though both sides had exhausted themselves and no longer had the stomach nor the taste for more blood-letting. Only the usual harassing artillery and mortar fire broke the calm.

On March 31, the "Schlammperiode" arrived. The snow began to melt and the Russian landscape was transformed into an impassable sea of mud, bringing to a halt any serious military operations.

In the first week of April, the grenadiers of Regiment 58 received welcomed news—they were no longer "orphans." For the past two months, they had been fighting under the temporary command of Majors Zorn and Lange. On April 5, the new "father" of the regiment arrived. To avoid disappointment among the troops, higher command had appointed Major von Issendorf as Kommandeur of Grenadier Regiment 58. He was an old "Achtundfünfziger"—"an old '58er'"—who had been with the regiment since 1937 and had fought through every campaign alongside the men until wounded at Stanischino on Christmas Eve 1941 during the nightmarish withdrawal from the Volga. Fully recovered from his wounds, he assumed command of the regiment much to the satisfaction of both officers and men.

For some three weeks, the 6th Grenadier Division had enjoyed a period of relative calm in its sector, but the calm eventually gave way to boredom. On the front of the 2nd Battalion of the 18th Regiment, the Russians had entrenched themselves on the crest of a previously unoccupied hill. It was an excellent observation post for them, but isolated as it was, it was also an inviting target for bored Stoßtruppen. On the night of April 13, Oberleutnant Otto Hellweg with a small party of men from the 2nd Battalion and a squad of engineers under Leutnant Hahn paid Ivan a visit. With grenade and bunker bombs, they quickly rolled up the enemy position, inflicting heavy losses, but such raids were never without risk. Leutnant Hahn was killed by an artillery round as the Stoßtruppen scurried back to their own lines.

On May 1, word came down from 9th Army headquarters that Grossmann's 6th Grenadier Division was to be relieved. This was the first time in nine months that the entire division was pulled out of action. Nine months—277 days. In that time, the division had withstood the onslaught of Zhukov's Rzhev Offensives and had fought its way back to the Büffel Stellung. It had seen its battalions reduced to nothing and rebuilt time and again. Old familiar faces had disappeared, new ones had arrived, and then they too disappeared like the others. Veterans of a score of battles had been welcomed back from the hospital only to be wounded again, or killed. The last time the entire division had been pulled off the front line, the men had enjoyed but a few days of rest before they had been flung back into the "blood mill" of Rzhev. Perhaps this time they would actually be allowed to rest and recover.

As word of the division's forthcoming relief leaked out, the "Scheisshausparole" network kicked into high gear. The men's battle-numbed brains recovered almost as quickly as their weary limbs, and their imaginations soared. Perhaps they would be going to France, perhaps to Denmark, or even Italy. When the panzer and Waffen-SS Divisions were pulled off the front to be rebuilt and refitted, weren't they commonly sent to sunny France or even sunnier Italy? Why not the poor bastard infantry?

Before Generalleutnant Grossmann could depart with his grenadiers to possible sunnier climes, he still had one last duty to perform at Dorogobush. Six Russian auxiliaries that had been with the division since September 1941 and had rendered valuable service as concerns battling spies, sabotage, and partisans, were presented with the "Tapferkeits und Verdienstmedaille in Bronze für Ostvölker" ("Bravery and Service Medal in Bronze for Eastern Nationals"). With the ceremony completed the division was loaded onto troop trains and bid a farewell to the front.

At first, the trains traveled west—that was a promising sign, but then the engines turned south and the hope of a sojourn in France promptly dissipated. A few kilometers north of Smolensk, the troops detrained and continued their journey on foot. German soldiers are well known for their recuperative abilities, and the men's spirits soon revived. The earth had dried out, spring had arrived, and the weather could have been no finer in France. Off to the right of the marching columns, the gilded domes of the cathedral of Smolensk glittered in the bright sunlight, and to the left the lush green fields were dotted with well-fed cattle. As the grenadiers marched, they broke into song. They were all old "Ostkämpfer" now; what did it matter whether Frankreich or Russland? If one was alive and had all his limbs, then life was good. "Mann an Mann marschieren wir, einerlei, wohin…"

When the men arrived at the rest area southeast of Smolensk, they were anticipating a few weeks of blissful rest. Divisional Headquarters had different plans. The German soldier was seldom allowed to rest and grow stale. The directive was sent out to regiment, battalion, and company that the men were to be brought to the peak of both physical and mental fitness. A rigorous program of retraining was instituted involving unit tactical maneuvers, marksmanship (especially for the machine-gun teams), and hand-to-hand combat. Not only did this retraining deprive the troops of their much-wished-for rest, but it also made clear that they would soon be cast back into the cauldron of combat.

For the sake of morale, the men were allowed some diversions. On regularly scheduled trips, groups of grenadiers were bussed into Smolensk for a bit of sightseeing or to take in a movie or variety show at the local Soldatenheim. For the most part, the local population was friendly and at times brought the men fresh eggs and milk—gifts, of course, for the Herrn Offizieri. As for the Landsers, they did not protest the inflated prices for such delicacies, the likes of which they could barely remember.

On May 11, the division's Chief of Operations, Oberstleutnant Gerstung, returned from a meeting at LV Corps Headquarters bringing with him the new directives for the 6th Grenadier Division. The mission laid out before Generalleutnant Grossmann and his staff was received with little enthusiasm. Code-named Operation Freishütz, it tasked the division in conjunction with other units to sweep free of partisans the area northwest of Brjansk. In other words, "Banditenkreig," a task for which the men were unsuited both by training and temperament. They were German infantry, irresistible in the attack, stalwart in the defense. They forded rivers under fire, rolled up hundreds of meters of enemy entrenchments in a single night's Stoßtruppunternehmen, or repelled repeated mass-wave attacks of Russian infantry. They hunted down tanks with magnetic mines and bundles of grenades. They were grenadiers, not gamekeepers chasing poachers through the brush. Such a task was best left to the security divisions or the Russian Volkswehr battalions.

However, an order is an order, and on May 11, after less than two weeks of "rest," Grossmann's grenadiers climbed aboard troop trains at Smolensk and traveled 50 km south to the staging area for Operation Freischütz at Shukowa. The zone of operations for this grand partisan sweep was an area 55 km long and 25 km wide northwest of Brjansk, infested with an estimated force of 3,000 partisans, who for the past year and a half had been attacking German supply units and terrorizing the local population. They were well supplied by airdrops with arms and ammunition. Food and other provisions they simply took from the villages. The extent to which the civilian population had been intimidated by these roving bands of partisans soon became apparent to the men of the 6th Grenadier Division. Unlike their previous experience, the people of the region were distant, suspicious, and uncooperative.

Operation Freischütz called for a converging advance of the 6th Grenadier Division from the north, the 5th Panzer Division from the south, and a unit designated as Oststab 455 from the east. In the west, the 707th Security Division and the Russian 1st and 2nd Volkswehr Battalions were to maintain an interception line to prevent any partisans from escaping west. In coordinated stages, the converging units would reduce the zone of operations down to a 5 × 5-km pocket in which the entrapped partisans could be annihilated.

Certainly a good plan on paper, but Operation Freischütz was not conducted on paper. It was carried out in the inhospitable terrain of a densely forested swamp. Planned and conducted in a manner similar to the future "sweeps" in Southeast Asia during the Vietnam War, the results were also similar.

On the morning of May 21, Operation Freischütz was set into motion and immediately the German units began to experience difficulties. As the men waded through the swamps and hacked their way through the dense undergrowth, all the while beset by the sauna-like heat and swarms of mosquitoes, they found it difficult to maintain direction or contact with neighboring units. Gaps in the line of advance were unavoidable, allowing the partisans to easily escape (especially at night). Stumbling upon a force of partisans or a cache of arms was mostly a matter of chance. While searching the few villages, the Germans often had to resort to force due to the uncooperative nature of the local inhabitants.

On May 30, after nine frustrating days of sloshing through the swamps and struggling through the thick woods, the advancing German units converged at Umysslitschi only to find no densely packed pocket of trapped partisans to destroy. Apparently the greater number of partisans had succeeded in slipping through the gaps in the German lines or had merely blended back into the civilian population. Although the Germans had destroyed over 250 "bunkers," no large number of partisans had been killed or captured. The list of arms and equipment seized was also disappointing: six machine guns, nine machine pistols, eighty-seven rifles, eight pistols, two telegraph sets, one radio, ten horses, and eight cows. With the exception of the horses and cows, this was little more than what the grenadiers could have bagged in a couple of well-executed trench raids.

The Germans would have been hard put to call Operation Freischütz even a "limited success." At best, Generalleutnant Grossmann could only describe it as having been "instructive," and in a way, his assessment was correct. Not since the crossing of the Volga and Tma Rivers back in October 1941 had the 6th Grenadier Division engaged in a division-size offensive operation. In the past year and a half, the division had only been involved in either withdrawals or defensive actions with a few (usually battalion-strength) counterattacks with local and limited objectives. In Operation Freischütz, the divisional and regimental commands had been tasked with coordinating the movements and actions of all the units of the division over the many kilometers of the advance in accordance to an overall plan—an excellent refresher course for staff officers grown too accustomed to defensive warfare. For company and platoon leaders, the operation had provided them the opportunity to work in cooperation with their fellow officers and, of equal importance, to get to know the men under their command—their strengths, weaknesses, or special talents. In addition, the companies, platoons, and even squads had for once the opportunity to adequately "work in" the recent replacements and acclimate them to the physical and mental strain of combat in the East—and with minimal losses. All too often in the past, these poor souls had of necessity been flung into the cauldron of battle too soon with few of them surviving long enough to replenish the ever-dwindling ranks of the experienced Ostkämpfers.

On May 31, Grossmann's grenadiers sloshed their way back out of the swampy forest and returned to Shukowa where they were loaded onto troop trains. They did not return to their rest area near Smolensk. Once again, the trains took them south to a place called Orel. The "refresher course" they had just received would prove to be most valuable in their next undertaking—Operation Zitadelle.

# 12

# Zitadelle

For Germany, the year 1943 had gotten off to a disastrous start. The summer offensive in the South had ended with defeat in the snow-swept, rubble-strewn streets of Stalingrad. An entire German army had been annihilated, and the armies of the Italian, Romanian, and Hungarian allies smashed. A half-million men had been removed from the Axis forces in the East. The two German armies that had plunged into the Caucasus had narrowly escaped their own destruction. The campaign designed to acquire the oil necessary for Germany's continuance of the war had failed to yield a single barrel. In addition, Hitler had been forced from necessity to relinquish the Rzhev Salient and with it his hopes of a renewed advance on Moscow.

In North Africa, the German military situation had seriously deteriorated. The Italo-German forces that had once stood on the Egyptian border threatening the Suez Canal had been pushed by the British back across the North African Desert and now found themselves essentially trapped in Tunisia with the Anglo-American forces before them and the Mediterranean Sea to their backs. Hitler refused to evacuate them, and by May, the campaign and a continent had been lost.

Although their sons were fighting far away to the East and the South, the war was now being brought home to the German people as the R.A.F. intensified its nighttime terror bombing of German cities. With the arrival of the American 8th Air Force and its heavy bombers targeting the German war industry during daylight raids, the German homeland was being pounded around the clock.

To replace the heavy losses suffered in the East, the Wehrmacht required 800,000 replacements, but even the most rigorous calling up could only yield 400,000 new recruits. Many of these had been combed out of the war industries and had to be replaced by foreign workers, both willing and unwilling. Despite the setbacks and heavy losses, the war could not yet be said to be irretrievably lost. Even with the less than adequate number of replacements, in the spring of 1943, the Wehrmacht stood at its highest level with 11.2 million men under arms. As a result of the reorganization of the war industry by the new Armaments Minister Albert Speer, the German factories were producing at a more realistic level required by the war. Whereas in 1942 only 350 tanks and fifty Stumgeschütze per month had rolled out of the factories, in 1943 the numbers had risen to a monthly production of 700 tanks and 200 Sturmgeschütze.[1] In addition, German scientists and engineers held out the promise of new and fantastic weapons, many of which would remain in the realm of fantasy, while others—such as the rockets (V-1 and V-2), jet aircraft, and the newer models of tanks—would become a deadly reality for the Allies.

As serious as the military situation on the Eastern Front had been in January and February, by April, the front had stabilized thanks to the exploits of Generalfeldmarschall von Manstein. After the Soviet armies of Operation Uranus had broken through the Don Front in November 1942 and encircled the German 6th Army at Stalingrad, Stalin and his High Command had become greedy and, as it turned out, overly ambitious. They had wished to push their forces all the way to the Sea of Azov, cut off the German armies in the Caucasus, and thereby create a "super Stalingrad." Von Manstein had not panicked. He allowed the Soviet spearheads to overextend themselves, and then with the forces he had assembled, attacked their flanks, cut them off, and ground them into pulp. By the time the "Schlamperiode" arrived and put an end to operations, von Manstein's forces had destroyed six Soviet tank corps, ten rifle divisions, and a half dozen independent brigades. Over 600 tanks, 400 artillery pieces, and 600 anti-tank guns had been captured or destroyed. A total 23,000 Russian dead were counted on the battlefield. Overall Soviet losses were estimated at 100,000. Von Manstein and the spring thaw had granted Germany a reprieve from what might have been an irreversible defeat.

In the course of the war in the East, a pattern had evolved in which during the summer the Germans launched their offensives and in winter the Soviets launched their counteroffensives, and 1943 would be no different. Even before the snows had melted, Hitler and the German General Staff were debating the question: what next in the East?

There were those (particularly Generaloberst Guderian, Inspector of the Armored Forces) who argued that Germany should forego any major offensive that summer and remain on the defensive for all of 1943, using the time to completely rebuild the armored forces. However, the words "Hitler" and "defense" rarely belonged in the same sentence. The German soldier does not defend, he attacks.

But where? A cursory glance at the map at the Führer's Headquarters answered the question quickly enough—Kursk. Although the Germans had successfully "straightened out" the northern half of the Eastern Front by withdrawing from the Demjansk and Rzhev Salients, the Soviet winter offensives and von Manstein's counterattack had resulted in the southern half of the front being full of dents and bulges, the largest of which was at Kursk. At 200 km wide at its base, the Kursk Salient thrust westwards 160 km into the German line between Army Groups Center and South. For the Russians, it represented an excellent springboard for either an attack north, slicing into the rear of Army Group Center, or a thrust southwards to the Black Sea, cutting off and trapping the German armies in the Eastern Ukraine, and like the Germans, who had desperately clung to their Rzhev springboard, the Russians had no intention of giving up the Kursk Salient.

The Germans certainly recognized the threat posed by the Kursk Salient, but Hitler and others also recognized the opportunities it presented. In the opening months of the Russian War, the panzer forces had to break through the enemy's front at various points in order to create huge pockets of Soviet forces to be encircled and destroyed. At Kursk, the Russians had created one for them. If the salient could be pinched off at its base by powerful armored thrusts, then perhaps another great battle of encirclement and annihilation could be achieved similar to those of the glory days of Barbarossa. The resulting heavy losses inflicted upon the enemy and the elimination of the salient, which would shorten the front by some 300 km and thereby free up dozens of divisions, could well restore the initiative to Germany.

The plan for the German 1943 Summer Offensive (code name Zitadelle) was simple enough. Model's 9th Army from Army Group Center was to attack the northern shoulder of the Kursk Salient and drive 60 km south to the city of Kursk, while Hoth's 4th Panzer Army of Army Group South struck the southern shoulder and pushed north to link up with Model's forces at Kursk. With the salient cut off, the entrapped Soviet forces would then be destroyed by concentric attacks. As simple as the plan was, time would be required to assemble the necessary forces. May 1 was viewed as the earliest possible date for the commencement of Operation Zitadelle.

If to the Germans the Kursk Salient was the obvious and logical target to attack, then to the Russians it was equally obvious that the salient was the target that would be attacked. Consequently, they began building up the defenses to the extent that the Kursk Salient would become one of the most heavily fortified defense zones ever constructed during the war.

As the earth dried out after the spring rains and the German preparations for the offensive continued apace, Hitler uncharacteristically became hesitant to launch the attack, always finding one excuse after another to postpone Operation Zitadelle. He protested that he needed more men, more guns, more tanks, and all the while the Russians were cramming more men, more guns, and more tanks into the salient until in the end, fully one-third of the Soviet field forces would be involved in its defense.

Perhaps in view of the failures of Operations Barbarossa and Blau, Hitler had come to doubt his claim of being the greatest warlord since Friedrich the Great, or perhaps he realized that Operation Zitadelle would be Germany's last chance to reverse the tide of the war, and if it failed, then what? Much like the Duke of Brunswick at Valmy Ridge in 1792, Hitler stared at the dispositions of the enemy forces before him and, paralyzed by indecision, could not bring himself to order the attack.

May arrived and passed, then came June, and still Hitler procrastinated. His field commanders—Kluge, von Manstein, Model, and Hoth—became concerned as daily they watched the enemy increase his defenses. Had the moment to strike already passed? Finally, on July 1, at a hurriedly arranged conference at the Wolfschanze, the Führer announced to his field commanders that Operation Zitadelle would commence in four days' time on July 5. In retrospect, perhaps Hitler should have reached the same conclusion as the Duke of Brunswick that "Hier schlagen wir nicht."

On June 1, the 6th Grenadier Division arrived in Orel, and throughout the month while the generals planned and the Führer procrastinated, the grenadiers resumed their training regimen, which had been interrupted by Operation Freischütz. For the men, who had spent most of the Eastern War in either filthy, lice-ridden villages or the shattered ruins of Rzhev, Orel was like being—to borrow a Landser's phrase—"auf einem anderen Planet." ("On another planet.") Here, there were broad paved streets, shops, street vendors, and well-dressed pedestrians—especially the young women in brightly colored summer dresses. Much of the previous war damage had been rebuilt although in a Western fashion. There were parks, fountains, a kindergarten, and even a home for the aged and infirm. For the soldiers, there were two cinemas and two Soldatenheime (soldiers' homes). To the average Landser, this was almost a return to civilization.

With the arrival of another batch of replacements, the companies attained what was described as a "respectable" troop strength (i.e. 100 men). This is not to mean that the division was anywhere near its original mobilization strength of 17,000. At best, it had but half that number. The regiments still could only field two battalions each. Even so, the division was stronger at this time than it had been in over a year. As for the training they were receiving at Orel, it was not the usual "loosening of the joints and scraping off the combat rust," but a regimen that was purpose oriented and noticeably more intense. In addition to the constant rifle practice and hand-to-hand combat instruction, there was an increase in company and battalion-size exercises, including joint maneuvers with tanks and Sturmgeschützen. Although the grenadiers knew nothing of Operation Zitadelle as yet, they sensed that whatever was coming was coming soon and the presence of tanks told them that it would be a grim and bloody affair.

On June 13, the 6th Grenadier Division departed the training grounds near Orel and in three night marches (absolute secrecy had been demanded for Operation Zitadelle) moved south 36 km closer to the Kursk Salient, where they resumed their training. The regimental Kommandeure and their staffs made fewer appearances on the training grounds for they were often called away to divisional headquarters to receive instructions and to work out details. Their absence was duly noted by the men and immediately understood: battle was not far off.

On July 2, the grenadiers packed up their gear and moved closer to the front. As they marched in the semi-darkness of the short summer night, they did not sing or speak among themselves—not even the usual crude gallows humor so common among the "Frontschweine." Only the metallic clanking of weapons and equipment accompanied the shadowy columns. The situation was too serious for any casual anxiety-releasing banter. Despite the ironclad secrecy imposed upon Operation Zitadelle, somehow the troops sensed that the upcoming battle would be as no other. Without a word being spoken, the gravity of the situation had been conveyed by the Führer to his generals and from his generals down through the ranks to the common Landser. Operation Zitadelle was the last chance for Germany to change the course of the war. If it failed, then "Gott hilf' uns."

Despite the misgivings concerning the success of the operation present among the German General Staff and the commanders in the field, Zitadelle would go forward as planned. To eliminate the Kursk Salient, the Germans had amassed a force of 900,000 men of whom 570,000 were allotted to the actual attacking forces; 10,000 artillery piece; 2,700 tanks and Sturmgeschütze; and 2,500 aircraft.[2] The southern attack force from Generalfeldmarschall von Manstein's Army Group South was comprised of Generaloberst Hoth's 4th Panzer Army (two panzer, four panzergrenadier, and four infantry divisions) and Armee Abteilung Kempf (three panzer and six infantry divisions). In the north, Generaloberst Model's 9th Army from Army Group Center had at its disposal four panzer and fourteen infantry divisions.

This assemblage of over 500,000 men and over 2,000 tanks on a combined frontage of the northern and southern attack sectors of 90 km was the heaviest concentration of military might that the Wehrmacht had ever achieved in the war. Could there be any doubts as to the success of Operation Zitadelle?

Yes, and serious ones at that. To oppose this powerful force the Soviets had amassed an even greater concentration of men and arms: 1,337,000 men; 3,306 tanks; 20,220 artillery pieces; and 2,650 aircraft. The attack–defense ratio was not in Germany's favor: three to two in men, three to two in tanks, and two to one in artillery. Hitler's two-month delay in launching the offensive had allowed the Russians to build up their defenses—and build they certainly had. Aided by 300,000 civilian workers, six deep defensive belts had been constructed, containing 5,000 km of trenches with the added horror of 2,700 anti-personnel and 2,400 anti-tank mines per kilometer and a half of front.[3]

Considering the forces opposing them, the Germans could hardly expect to achieve a swift breakthrough, and with such a heavy concentration of their own forces on relatively narrow attack fronts with pre-determined (and predictable) lanes of advance, the Germans were deprived of their greatest asset—flexibility of maneuver. Unlike the early days of Blitzkrieg with its swirling movements of forces, dramatic breakthroughs, and breath-taking dashes deep into the enemy's hinterland, the battle of the Kursk Salient would be a head-on collision of men and steel, a primitive slug fest with both sides fully aware of the stakes at hand—or as the men of the 6th Grenadier Division had foreseen, a grim and bloody affair.

Generalleutnant Grossmann's 6th Grenadier Division was but one of the twenty divisions of Model's 9th Army, but in accordance with their hard-won reputation as one of the best divisions of the entire Wehrmacht, they were given a leading role to play in the opening phase of Operation Zitadelle. Having a realistic appreciation of the Soviet forces arrayed against him and the extent of their defenses, Model, in order to spare his precious armor, opted for the tactic of employing infantry units to achieve the initial breakthrough, through which the panzers would then pour and push on to Kursk. Assigned to the XLVII Panzer Corps, the 6th Grenadier Division with the 20th Panzer Division would form the Schwerpunkt of Model's northern attack force. They were to break open the Soviet front line on a 6-km front between Werch-Tagino and Ssenkowo for the 2nd and 9th Panzer Divisions and then follow on as reserve. No easy task for Grossmann's grenadiers but certainly not beyond their capability even if they had not participated in a joint armored attack since crossing the Ossotnja Swamp in October 1941. To aid them in their critical task, they would have the artillery support of the three panzer divisions plus two Nebelwerfer (rocket launchers) Abteilungen. In the expectation of densely laid minefields, an additional battalion of engineers had been provided. For the initial assault, Grossman had at his disposal sixty-two Sturmgeschütze of the Sturmgeschütze Abteilungen 245 and 904 and, most important, twenty-six of the new heavy PzKwVI (Tiger) tanks of Major Sauvant's Heavy Tank Battalion 505. Generalleutnant Grossmann had never commanded such a powerful force before, and he and his staff can be forgiven their optimism as concerns Operation Zitadelle.

The night of July 4 was oppressively warm, the air made steamy by the most recent thunderstorm. The humid heat was especially oppressive for the men of the 6th Grenadier Division in their shallow trenches along the muddy banks of the slow-flowing Oka River. The night was also quiet, as nights are before a battle. The silence was almost as oppressive as the heat. Only the croaking of frogs and an occasional call of a night owl broke the stillness. Now and again a fish would splash the surface of the shallow waters of the Oka, its belly briefly flashing white in the moonlight. Then it would be gone.

The plan was set, the objectives defined, the final details worked out. Nothing remained for the men to do but to wait for the night hours to tick away. Some lay in the bottom of the trench, their eyes closed as though asleep, but it was only a self-imposed trance. Others stood along the trench wall and stared into the darkness, seeing nothing. Neither the "sleepers" nor the "watchers" were thinking of anything. The night before battle is not a time for thought—of home, family, or even the day's objectives. The brain must be devoid of thought; drained empty and allowed to return to its primitive state of an instinctual, reflexive muscle. Only then will the entire organism have any chance of survival in the coming battle.

The 6th Grenadier Division was at its strongest troop level it had been in over a year and was well rested. Among them were the "old hands"—the Alten Hassen—a few of them dating back to the French campaign and the early days of Barbarossa. Others had survived the "meat grinder" of Rzhev. These were men who had been wounded time and again, and time and again they had found their way back to their old regiment. The left side of their tunics was festooned with medals, their faces festooned with scars. Most were obergefreiters now, and that was as high a rank they would ever achieve—or aspire to. Men described by the military establishment as "possessing no discernible leadership qualities." Men whose true talents only rose to the fore when the air was filled with whizzing metal. They were the backbone of the combat formations. They were the men who would carry the attack forward.

Model's northern attack was scheduled to begin at dawn on July 5, and the Russian dawn comes early during the summer months, around 3:30 a.m. This night, however, would be cut short, and not by the rising sun. Aware that the German attack was imminent, the Soviet commanders in the Kursk Salient planned to disrupt it with a heavy pre-emptive bombardment of the German forward positions and the artillery emplacements farther to the rear. In the southern sector, General Vatutin, certain that the Germans would attack at dawn July 5, began his pre-emptive bombardment of the German positions at 11 p.m. on July 4.

In the north, the Soviet commander, General Rokossovsky, was not as certain of the timetable of the German attack—that is, until he received word that near Tangino a German engineer (Bruno Fermello) from the 6th Grenadier division had been captured while clearing mines, and, under interrogation, had yielded the information that the German attack was scheduled to begin at 3:30 a.m. Convinced, Rokossovky unleased his pre-emptive barrage at 1:10 a.m. As the shells crashed down on the forward positions, the Germans feared at first that the Russians were launching their own offensive, but when the guns fell silent an hour later and no attack occurred, the German commanders could breathe a sigh of relief. Although there had been casualties and some disruptions, Operation Zitadelle was to continue as scheduled.

Far more disconcerting to the 6th Grenadier Division than this surprise barrage, which had caused them little damage, was the order that the division's assault was to be delayed three hours behind that of the Mecklenburg-Pomeranian 292nd Grenadier Division on their immediate left. Apparently there were insufficient attack-aircraft to support both divisions' assaults simultaneously. Although the pre-emptive barrage had made obvious that the enemy was aware that the German attack was coming, what concerned Grossmann and his grenadiers was that the delay of their assault behind that of their neighbor meant that they would lose the immediate and local element of surprise, which was so critical for the success of any infantry assault. The first leap, the first rush across open ground, those precious first few moments, often determined the difference between success and failure and to the infantryman, the difference between life and death.

As the eastern horizon grew light on the morning of July 5, Operation Zitadelle, Germany's great gamble to regain the initiative in the Eastern War, was let loose. At 3:30 a.m., along the 50-km front of the northern attack sector, the medium and heavy artillery of Model's 9th Army belched their thunder and fire into the dawn sky. This hellish symphony was soon joined by the screaming sounds of the Nebelwerfers with its rocket trails arching high across the heavens. Even the infantry howitzers and mortars joined in the chorus as they took on targets of a more limited range. The German assault troops watched from their trenches as tons of metal rained down from the sky and explosions sent columns of smoke high into the air. They nodded to one another in grim appreciation. All too often in the past, they had been the recipients of such violence from the sky. Soon the Russian front line disappeared amidst a wall of fire and smoke, but if one thought that this devil's concert had reached its finale, it was shortly raised to an even higher level of violence. Up in the sky, German dive-bombers appeared. One by one, squadron by squadron, they gracefully heeled over and with their wing sirens screeching, they swooped down on their targets.

At 6:20 a.m., the devil's concert moved into the attack sector of the 6th Grenadier division. Two hundred guns of medium and heavy caliber, twenty-four Nebelwerfers, and the heavy infantry howitzers of the attacking regiments hurled their carnage at the Soviet 15th Rifle Division. Then the Stukas arrived and pounced upon their targets. After thirty minutes, this carnage was moved forward to the enemy's support trenches and artillery positions. The time had come. Amid the din of explosions trilled the Feldwebel's whistle. "Los! Auf!" The grenadiers leapt from their trenches and stormed forward.

The division advanced across its 6-km front in three Angriffskeile (attack wedges): on the left, the 58th Regiment; on the right, the 18th Regiment; and in the center, the Reconnaissance Battalion. Regiment 37 followed as divisional reserve. From his command post on the high ground west of Tangino, Generalleutnant Grossmann observed for the first time his entire division advancing into the attack. He watched as the assault troops rolled up the first enemy entrenchments, followed by the men of the weapons companies dragging forward their heavy machine guns, infantry howitzers, and anti-tank guns. "An uplifting sight for a soldier's heart," as Grossmann described it. For those down below amid the wheat and cornfields, the experience was not quite so "uplifting." Despite the fury of the artillery preparations and the Stuka attacks, the grenadiers had never been confronted by such hellacious defensive fire coming at them from all weapons and from all directions. Russian defenders, who had been passed by unnoticed in the corn and sunflower fields, suddenly rose up and fired into the backs of the advancing grenadiers. In these green hells of vegetation, a man did not see his enemy until he literally stumbled over him, and then one, or perhaps both, would die. In the open fields matters were no better. Here, the grenadiers were pounded by Russia artillery, rockets, and mortars or became targets of Soviet fighter-bombers sweeping low over the battlefield. But even in the face of the stubborn Russian defense, Grossmann's grenadiers somehow advanced.

Höke's 18th Regiment and the Reconnaissance Battalion pushed forward 1½ km to the village of Yasnaya Polyana and the Wiedehofwald while von Issendorf's grenadiers of the 58th Regiment quickly splashed across the shallow Oka and seized the village of Nowi-Chutor, but then as they advanced south, they began taking heavy flanking fire from the east. The regiment's neighbor to the left, the 292nd Division, had failed to advance much beyond its start line. The attack of the Mecklenburgers and Pomeranians, which had been launched three hours in advance of that of the 6th Grenadier Division, was firmly stuck before the Soviet defenses in the Oserki Forest. Grossmann directed the 58th Regiment to shift the weight of its attack more to the west and continue its advance south in conjunction with the Reconnaissance Battalion.

By 8 a.m., the 18th Regiment had pushed forward another 2½ km to reach the Kirchwald on the northern edge of the village of Podoljan. Although his left flank was still lagging somewhat behind, Grossmann decided that for the moment his grenadiers had done enough and the time had arrived to send in the tanks. The opportunity for an infantry general to have armored units at his disposal is rare enough, but the opportunity to have two companies of the new super-heavy Tiger tanks at one's beck and call would cause even an experienced panzer general to salivate. At 60 tons, the Tiger tank was neither fast nor particularly maneuverable, but with 80–100 mm of frontal armor and mounting a high velocity 8.8-cm gun, it did not need to be.

Grossman directed Major Sauvant and his forty-six Tigers to drive on Podoljan and the high ground south of the village; the grenadiers would follow in their wake. As Heavy Tank Battalion 505 rumbled through the ranks of Regiment 18, the grenadiers stared at these clanking behemoths in wide-eyed astonishment. They had heard rumors of these new super tanks but as yet had never seen them close up. Could anyone now be in doubt of victory? They shouldered their weapons once more and fell in behind the Tigers. A feeling of confidence surged through their ranks—that is, until swarms of Soviet T-34 tanks swept in like angry hornets and Höke's grenadiers found themselves trapped in the midst of a tank battle. There was nothing they could do but fling themselves to the ground and press their faces into the earth while the metal monsters battled it out all around them.

Major Sauvant's Tigers proved their worth, destroying a large number of T-34s, and driving off the remainder. The advance continued, albeit slowly. The same scenario played out the rest of the day: stubborn Russian defenders and constant Soviet armor attacks. In the open fields, the tanks fought their duels while the grenadiers plunged into the cornfields and fought their opponents man to man.

Slow though the advance was and bitter the fighting, by 8 p.m., the 18th Regiment and the Reconnaissance Battalion had advanced another 6 km and had reached the day's objective of Ssaborowka. In thirteen hours of relentless combat, the regiment had fought its way through 10 km of densely manned defensive belts and had inflicted heavy losses in men and material on the enemy. Their own losses, however, had not been light. In addition to the casualties among the men and NCOs, five company or platoon leaders had been killed or wounded. Company commander Oberleutnant Schüger, who had given up his cushy job as adjutant of the communications battalion to volunteer for infantry duty, had been killed while rolling up an enemy entrenchment. Leutnant Hellmond of the 14th (panzerjäger) Company had also fallen. Wounded were Leutnant Bremenkamp, commander of the 1st Company, Leutnant Lübbert, one of his platoon leaders, and Leutnant Fehlauer, a platoon leader in the 2nd Company.

Over on the division's left flank, the advance of the 58th Regiment had lagged behind though Grossmann could not blame his grenadiers. Their progress had been severely hampered by the failure of the 292nd Division to push its attack forward. The entire day the 58th Regiment's left flank had been "in der Luft" ("in the air"). Time and again von Issendorf had found it necessary to detail a platoon or company to deal with the incessant flanking fire. Worse still, the further the regiment advanced the more deeply it had to echelon units rearwards to protect its open flank, thus weakening its forward thrust. In spite of this difficulty, Regiment 58 had succeeded in seizing Hill 245.9 in a bloody assault and advance 4 km to the Herzwald by day's end. Twenty-one of its number, including the commander of the engineer platoon, Leutnant Dr. Hermann Grimrath, had been killed and several dozens more wounded.

As the sun set on the evening of July 5, Generalleutnant Grossmann and his staff assessed the day's progress. For the most part, he could be pleased with his grenadiers; they had succeeded in breaking open the Russian defenses on a broad front, and despite all that the enemy had thrown at them, they had fought their way through some of the heaviest defenses ever encountered by infantry. With acceptable losses, they had advanced, at the farthest, 10 km into the defense zone. However, in his heart, Grossmann believed that a great opportunity had been missed earlier in the day when after his grenadiers had broken through the first defensive belts, the 2nd and 9th Panzer Divisions had not been brought forward and unleashed. He was certain that the added weight of two panzer divisions would have caused the Soviet defense to disintegrate, and that by now the panzers would be well on their way to Kursk. But that had not been his call to make, and for the present, his concern was with tomorrow's attack. His lagging left flank was a problem that required correction, but not at the expense of holding back Höke's 18th Regiment until the 58th Regiment pulled even. The left flank would simply have to make better progress on the morrow. To facilitate this, Grossmann directed the 58th Regiment to reverse its advance and attack north into the Oserki Forest in hope of getting the 292nd Division's attack moving again. This required that the 37th Regiment be pulled out of reserve to take over the left flank advance. Unfortunately, this meant that tomorrow, the division would go into battle without any reserves to either contend with an emergency or take advantage of an unexpected opportunity.

July 6, day two of Operation Zitadelle. At 4 a.m., the regiments stepped off to the attack. Overhead, their own artillery and rockets went screaming and howling towards the enemy while they were greeted by the artillery and rockets of their opponents. The day was a repeat of the previous day. Kursk may not have been the largest operation of the Eastern War, but due to the heavy concentration of forces, it was certainly one of the most intense. In the cornfields and ravines, the infantry slugged it out man to man while all about them the tanks careened across the battlefield and shot one another into heaps of metal scrap. Above them, hundreds of Soviet and German aircraft battled for the skies.

That morning, both Generaloberst Model and Feldmarschall Kluge visited Generalleutnant Grossmann at his command post and congratulated him on the success of his division. "Stoppelhopsers" that they were, they were pulling this great armored attack forward.

As before, the 6th Grenadier Division's advance was a slow and brutal grind forward, but Grossman's arrangement was proving successful. The 37th Regiment, with its flank protected by the 58th Regiment's attack into the Oserki Forest, was gradually catching up with the 18th Regiment. Similar to the day before, the advance was hampered by Russians who, having been by-passed, raised up, and fired into the backs of the attacking units. The Russian soldier seemed not to know when to surrender. Eventually, this fire from the rear became so heavy that a battalion from the 58th Regiment had to be pulled out of the fight for the Oserki Forest and, in conjunction with six Sturmgeschützen, was directed to sweep across the rear of the advancing regiments and glean the fields of these troublesome Ivans.

At the village of Step near the center of the advance, forty Soviet tanks came charging towards the grenadiers. They were immediately engaged by Major Sauvant's Tigers and driven off with heavy losses. A Russian infantry attack into the left flank and rear of Regiment 37 was only stopped by the quick response of Leutnant Knopker and his reserve platoon. The division's attack pushed on past Step. Hill 231 was taken, and although the 18th Regiment had only managed a 1½-km advance by dusk, the 37th Regiment had done much to catch up the left flank. Having pushed forward 5 km to the outskirts of Ssnowa, the regiment stood only a kilometer behind the right flank.

The gains of July 6 had been less that spectacular, but the division had advanced. After two days of intense fighting, Grossmann's grenadiers had penetrated the Russian defense zone to a depth of 10 km, and still there seemed to be no end of enemy entrenchments, bunkers, and minefields. Could anyone blame the grenadiers for wondering if they would ever break out into the open?

That evening, Grossmann bid a reluctant farewell to Major Sauvant and his heavy tank battalion, who were being sent off to another sector at the battlefield. In the two days that his tigers had been attached to the division, they had racked up a score of forty-two Soviet tanks destroyed. In the coming days, Sauvant's Tigers would be sorely missed. On a positive note, the attack of the 58th Regiment into the Oserki Forest had been successful in allowing the 292nd Division to advance. The 58th Regiment could now return to divisional control and in the morning when the 6th Grenadier went forward, it would do so with all three regiments in line.

There was another farewell yet to be made that evening. Word was received that Hauptmann Jochem Kluge of the 18th Regiment had fallen at the head of his battalion. Formerly the regimental adjutant, he had taken over the 2nd Battalion when its leader, Major Höke, had been promoted to Regimental Kommandeur. A soldier poet in the mold of Walter Flex, Jochem Kluge had immortalized the "Rshewkämpfers" in his poem "Wir hielten doch Rshew!" His death was a heavy blow to the entire division from general to grenadier. He had been the Landsers' voice, expressing what they could not, and the soldiers' dirge "Ich hatt' einen Kameraden" never rang more true.

Late that night, a patrol sent out from Regiment 18 reported back that the Eiwald and Schmetterlingswald were weakly defended and argued for an immediate surprise attack. Although Grossmann had intended to hold up Regiment 18 until the left flank could pull even with it, the option of refraining from attack when an opportunity arose did not exist in German military doctrine. He granted permission for the attack.

Leutnant Spieker, who had already been wounded twice over the course of the past two days (his eighth and ninth wound thus far in the war) assembled a Stoßtrupp and led them into the Eiwald. As soon as they located the enemy position in the woods, Spieker ordered an assault. Flares illuminated the night and the Stoßtrupp's machine-gunner raked over the Russians. Spieker himself blazed away with his MP-40, emptying magazine after magazine into the enemy. Then, caught up in the frenzy of combat, he leapt into the entrenchment. Stunned, the fifteen surviving Ivans promptly surrendered to the wild-eyed German officer brandishing a machine pistol. A commissar handed Spieker his Order of the Red Banner and complimented him on his attack. No less stunned at the turn of events was Leutnant Spieker, who discovered that he did not have a single round left in his weapon.[4]

After Spieker's *coup de main* in the Eiwald, the 18th Regiment launched its attack into the Schmetterlingswald and found it rough going (the Russians had either strongly reinforced their position or the patrol's earlier report had been mistaken). Not until noon did the regiment succeed in fighting its way through to the southern edge of the woods.

For once, the greater progress was being made on the left flank where the 37th Regiment advanced 4 km that day overcoming enemy resistance in the villages of Ssnowa and Bitjug. Although at Kursk there was no such thing as an easy advance, one can fairly say that on July 7, the 37th Regiment had a far easier go of it than the 58th Regiment in the center, which had been charged with the taking of the heavily fortified Hill 257. On the first day of the Kursk Offensive, the regiment had captured Hill 245.9 and so the grenadiers knew what they could expect: well-concealed, well-protected bunkers dug deep into the hillside with mines scattered all about—and they also knew how to deal with it.

"Pioniere vor!" Engineers to the front. Heavily laden with their flamethrowers and explosive charges, the engineers organized their assault groups and moved up the hill under the covering fire of machine guns and infantry howitzers. As they were methodically burning and bombing out the enemy emplacements, ten Soviet tanks appeared as from nowhere and attacked their brother infantrymen down below. Where were Sauvant's Tigers? Fortunately, the Sturmgeschütze assigned to the division appeared, and although they preferred to operate from ambush, they took the Soviet tanks head-on, destroying several and driving off the rest.

Not until evening did the engineers clean out the last of the Russian defenders and claim Hill 257 as their own. The day's cost had been heavy for the 58th Regiment. Twenty-five of its ranks had been killed, including two experienced NCOs: Feldwebel Seiffer of the 9th Company and Feldwebel Hasse of the 13th (howitzer) Company. Two more company commanders, Oberleutnant Ranft (11th Company) and Leutnant Haverkamp (9th Company) were lost through wounds.

After three days of punishing combat against an enemy who chose to die in place rather than yield a meter of Russian soil, the 6th Grenadier Division had clawed its way through 11 km of Russian defense belts and presently occupied the line Kaschara-Karpunjewt. All three regiments and the Reconnaissance Battalion had pulled abreast, and their flanks were now covered by the 2nd and 9th Panzer Divisions, which, having been released into the attack, had finally caught up with Grossmann's Stoppelhopsers. The general felt that the battle had reached its critical point and he was optimistic concerning the coming clash. With his three regiments in line, and his flanks covered by the panzers, he was certain that on the morrow the Soviet defense would collapse and his grenadiers and the panzers would finally break through and break out into the open. Ironically, facing the 6th Grenadier Division in the morning would be the Soviet 6th Guards Division. The collision of German grenadiers and Soviet guards would indeed make for a grim and bloody affair.

July 8, the fourth day of Operation Zitadelle: Grossmann's regiments were not abreast. At the last moment, he had been directed to pull the 37th Regiment out of the line and hold it in reserve in a ravine to the northeast. Its former position on the left flank would be taken over by units of the 9th Panzer Division. This alteration did not dampen Grossmann's optimism for now he had both armor support close at hand and an entire regiment in reserve. The orders for the day were simple enough: advance and break the enemy's defenses.

Dawn arrived, and after a brief, though intense, preparatory barrage followed by a Stuka attack, the 6th Grenadier Division with the 2nd and 9th Panzer Divisions on its flanks went into the attack—an attack that went virtually nowhere. As with Grossmann, the Soviet commanders had sensed that the battle had reached its critical point. After three days of relentless battle, the nightmare that had haunted the Soviet High Command since the beginning of the offensive had not occurred. There had been no great German breakthrough, no revival of Blitzkrieg with hundreds of German panzers and thousands of German "devils" plunging deep into the hinterland. The defense belts had reduced the German advance to a crawl. The men had given little ground, and what ground they had yielded, they had drenched with their blood and that of the enemy. They may have died in droves, but they had not surrendered in droves. Stalingrad had proven that the German could be beaten. The time had arrived for Kursk to prove that he would be beaten.

In the center of the northern front, Rokossowsky had three tank corps and now instead of relying solely on the fanatical defense of his infantry to slow or halt the German advance, he intended to meet the enemy's assault head on with heavy armored attacks. The 2nd and 9th Panzer divisions spent the day engaged in ferocious tank battles as they struggled to fight off the swarms of T-34s that Rokossowky was throwing at them. They were hard-pressed to hold their own ground and were unable to make any appreciable advance. Grossmann's 37th Regiment, rather than being available as reserve, was instead involved in repeated Soviet attacks aimed at the division's left flank and rear. The other two regiments did manage to advance against incredibly heavy and stubborn defense, but their gains were meagre. By 6 p.m., Höke's 18th Regiment had only succeeded in pushing forward a kilometer and a half to occupy the village of Kutyrki. On the left, von Issendorf's 58th Regiment had been ordered to take the heavily defended ravine lying a kilometer south of Hill 257. The first assault failed, as did the second. Only on the third assault, led by Oberleutnant Deppe at the head of the 3rd Company, were the Russian defenders eliminated. Deppe was wounded but remained with his company. A Russian counterattack to retake the ravine was beaten back.

The failure of the panzer divisions on Grossmann's flanks to advance precluded any further advance of his grenadiers. Early on the evening of July 8, the 6th Grenadier Division was ordered to halt its advance until the panzers were able to catch up. No sooner had the 18th Regiment complied with the order to halt than a Russian attack broke into the northern edge of the village of Kutyrki and was only thrown back after heavy fighting. This episode reflects the reality of the Battle of Kursk. If one was not attacking, then one would most assuredly be attacked.

Understandably, few of Grossmann's grenadiers raised any objections when ordered to halt. Though far from a spent force, after four days of intense combat and having at this point advanced further than any other unit (including the panzers), they could use the brief respite. Grossmann described his losses as having been heavy, "with enlisted men leading squads, Unteroffiziere leading platoons, and Feldwebels at the head of companies." Heavy, perhaps, but not crippling. For example, the 58th Regiment listed for the period July 5–8, fifty-seven dead with total losses in the range of twenty to twenty-five percent, which by Eastern Front standards was not out of the ordinary for any unit at the spearhead of an attack. Certainly the losses were less than those of the Winter and Summer Battles of Rzhev, when companies and battalions had been reduced by 80 percent time and again. In short, the evening of July 8, the 6th Grenadier Division was still very much a potent strike-force in little need of being relieved and replaced by a fresh division.

Concerning the overall course of the battle, Generaloberst Model could hardly be satisfied. Four days of battle and still no breakthrough or breakout, and the Soviet defenses, instead of crumbling, appeared as strong, if not stronger, than before. For most of July 8, rather than advancing, his panzer forces had considered themselves fortunate to have been able to just hold their own and not to have buckled under the waves of Soviet armor and aircraft that had been thrown at them. Even Grossmann's doughty grenadiers, a division Model knew well, had only managed a paltry 1½-km advance that day. Considering the present situation, there was nothing more Model could do but throw in the last of his armored reserves and hope that the Soviet defense would finally break.

It did not break, not the next day nor the days following. Whether the Germans realized it or not, the tide of battle had already shifted to the Russians. The next three days of Model's attack were but repetitions of July 8. He fed in his last reserves, and as his panzers attempted to get the attack rolling again, they were met once more head on with waves of Soviet tanks, such that in many sectors, it was not a matter of advancing but of holding their own ground. Obedient to orders, the 6th Grenadier Division remained in place and attempted no advance. This did not spare them any of the battle's fury. They were the target of repeated Russian assaults, particularly on the left, in the sector of the 58th Regiment, which cost the regiment two more company commanders, Hauptmann Böhland and Oberleutnant Dregger, who both fell out with wounds.

Then suddenly on July 12, the order came from the Führer himself: Operation Zitadelle was to be halted. What had happened to cause this abrupt change? Various reasons were given for the cancellation; least credible among them was Hitler's face-saving excuse that the Anglo-American forces had invaded Sicily (July 10), and divisions in the East would have to be rushed west to shore up the shaky Italo-German alliance.

The reality on the ground was the true reason. After seven days of continuous battle, the Kursk Offensive was going nowhere, neither in the northern nor southern attack sectors. No dramatic breakthrough or breakout had been achieved, and the offensive had degenerated into a World War I style slugfest of attrition with World War I-style results—heavy losses and little gain. With a loss of 22,000 men, killed, wounded, or missing, for a maximum advance of only 15 km, Model could look at his maps, remove the monocle from his eye, and conclude, "Hier schlagen wir nicht." In the southern attack sector, von Manstein and Hoth would soon reach the same conclusion.

The immediate reason for the termination of Operation Zitadelle was that the Soviet commanders, confident that the German attack had shot its bolt, on July 12 unleased their own offensive (Operation Kutuzov), aimed at Orel, 60 km north of Model's attacking force. If successful, the Russians would slice across behind Model and cut off his 9th Army from Army Group Center. Model had no other choice but to halt his attack, withdraw his forces back to the start line of July 5, and employ his panzer divisions to deal with the crisis along the Orel Front.

The withdrawal was not a sprint back north, but a phased operation in which the retreating units utilized the former Russian defenses for which they had paid so dearly over the past several days. The 6th Grenadier Division, which had penetrated the deepest into the Soviet defense zone, was naturally one of the last divisions to be withdrawn. Grossmann was ordered to hold his present positions until July 15. Hitler may have called off the battle, but the Russians most certainly had not. Sensing victory, they were not content with allowing the Germans to withdraw, but were intent on driving the fascists back. In heavy defensive battles between July 9 and 14, the 58th Regiment alone lost thirty-one men killed, including two senior NCOs, Oberfeldwebel Koch and Feldwebel Börger of the 3rd Company. On July 15, just as the division was preparing to take its first step back in the withdrawal, ten Soviet tanks broke into the left flank and stormed toward the command post of the 58th Regiment. The 13th Company engaged them with their short-barreled infantry howitzers at close range, destroying three and driving off the remainder. That evening, the division pulled back 3 km to the Schmetterlingswald.

Determined to destroy the 6th Grenadier Division, which, by now, was essentially acting as rear guard, the Russians attacked the Schmetterlingswald line at dawn July 17. Seventy tanks with infantry rolled against the German positions while fifty Soviet bombers sought to destroy the bridges over the Oka in order to block the German withdrawal. Grossmann's artillery fired for all they were worth to stop the armored onslaught, quickly setting two tanks ablaze. A heavy anti-tank gun destroyed two more. In the sector of the 58th Regiment, Unteroffizier Scherz of the 10th Company revived the spirit of "tank-breaking," which had been so prevalent at Rzhev, and with two volunteers went tank hunting. They climbed out of their holes and crawled forward 400 meters to where a KV-1 tank had taken up a position to shell the German lines. A Russian machine-gun team, blocking Scherz and his tank-hunters' path was taken out with a bundle of grenades. Scherz then bounded forward, swung himself up on the tank and dropped a T-mine into the hatch. A horrendous blast, and the tank and its crew were no more. Unteroffizier Scherz and his companions returned to their own lines, unharmed. There they came across a T-34, which had broken into the German position, and Scherz bagged his second tank of the day with a Hafthohlladung (hollow-charge bomb). For his exploits, Unteroffizier Scherz's name was added to the Wehrmacht Role of Honor.

Around 7 a.m., help arrived for the beleaguered grenadiers in the form of a dozen "Stugs" (Sturmgeschütze) that tackled the Russian tanks head-on, and shot up seven of them. There was more help to come. Major Sauvant's Tigers had returned and none too soon. Although Grossmann's grenadiers had been successful in separating the Russian infantry from their tanks and inflicting heavy losses on them, they were still in danger of being overwhelmed by the Soviet armor. Throughout the battle of Kursk, the Russians had often used the numerous deep ravines in the area to mask their advance so as to close with the enemy. This time, Major Sauvant would use the tactic against them.

Observing a large force of Soviet tanks descend into a deep ravine, Sauvant rolled forward with his 60-ton giants, surrounded the ravine, and from its rim began "shooting fish in a barrel." The Russian infantry who had accompanied their tanks found themselves trapped in the midst of a tank slaughter with nothing but their thin uniforms to protect them. They fled wild-eyed and terrified into the ranks of Grossmann's grenadiers and surrendered, relieved to have escaped the carnage behind them. By the time that Sauvant's Tigers rumbled off, the bottom of the ravine was filled with the twisted, burning remnants of thirty-two T-34s. For this success, Major Sauvant received the Oak Leaves to his Knight's Cross. In all, sixty Soviet tanks had been destroyed that day, and the Schmetterlingswald line had held.

After the battle of the Schmetterlingswald, both sides altered their plans. The Russians left the grenadiers in peace, and the grenadiers decided to dispense with the plan of a phased withdrawal and beat it back to the safety of their original positions along the Oka. After dark on July 17, they abandoned the Schmetterlingswald line and withdrew north. In the early morning hours of July 18, they splashed across the Oka and reoccupied the positions they had left but two weeks before. For the 6th Grenadier Division, Operation Zitadelle had come to a close.

A somber mood hung over the Landsers as they settled in to their old entrenchments and dugouts. Withdrawing from ground won at heavy cost was depressing enough; more depressing yet was the leaving behind of fallen comrades buried in the hastily dug graves at Kutyrki, Karashara, Step, and the Schmetterlingswald. They knew that in time the mounds would sink level with the ground, the Birkenkreuze rot away, and the graves would forever remain unattended and ignored by a foreign people.

# 13

# The Year of Retreat

If 1943 had opened on a grim note for the German war in the east, then it would end on a note far grimmer as the Red Army took control of the war. After the failure of Operation Zitadelle, the German High Command and the commanders in the field no longer made decisions but had decisions forced upon them—decisions involving the choice among unpleasant alternatives.

For Germany, there would be no more grand offensives aimed at either winning or changing the course of the war, only continuous retreats or "tactical withdrawals" in order to avoid military disasters. The Battle of Kursk had not been the "decisive turning point" of the war, but the confirmation that the course of the war had irrevocably turned against Germany. The Soviet Orel Offensive, which had prompted the halt of Zitadelle, was only the beginning of the Red Army's march west that would end two years later in the streets of Berlin.

The Rhinelanders and Westphalians of the 6th Grenadier Division would be swept up and dragged along by the changing tide of the war, their fate and the fate of millions of other Landsers would no longer lie in the hands of their Führer or their officers, but in the hands of Stalin and the ascendant Red Army.

The Russian-held westward projecting Kursk Salient had correspondingly created a German-held eastward projecting salient about Orel with similar dimensions and similar vulnerabilities. Within the Orel Salient were the German 2nd Panzer and 4th Armies with some 600,000 men, 7,000 artillery pieces, 1,000 armored vehicles, and 1,100 aircraft. If the Soviets were able to eliminate the Orel Salient and destroy the forces within, they would achieve a victory even greater than Stalingrad—and they definitely possessed the necessary forces to do so. The three Soviet fronts aligned about the Orel Salient: West Front (Sokolovsky), Brjansk Front (Popov), and Central Front (Rokossovsky) represented a force of nearly 1.3 million men; 21,000 artillery pieces and rocket launchers; 2,400 armored vehicles supported by 2,000 aircraft, which gave them a superiority over their German opponent of two to one in men, armored vehicles, and aircraft and three to one in artillery.[1]

As soon as it had become obvious that Model's northern attack into the Kursk Salient had been halted, the Soviets unleashed their Orel Offensive (code name Operation Kutuzov). Whereas the Germans had sought to cut off the Kursk Salient, the Russians intended to crush the salient about Orel. Having been burned by von Manstein the previous March when they had sought to apply the German Blitzkrieg tactic of deep converging thrusts to encircle the enemy, the Russians opted for a simpler and less risky plan for Operaton Kutuzov (i.e. essentially attacking along the entire front of the salient, fixing the enemy in place, and destroying him in place). Crude perhaps and devoid of brilliant maneuver but, with such a superiority of force, certainly effective. (Such tactics would prove even more effective the next summer.)

Dawn, July 12: after a two-and-a-half-hour bombardment, the heaviest yet of the war, Operation Kutuzov commenced as four Soviet Armies (more would follow) of the West and Brjansk Fronts assaulted the northern and eastern faces of the Orel Salient. Rokossovsky, who was still contending with Model in the south, would join the attack two days later. By the end of July 13, the Russians had pushed forward from 6 to 20 km at various points, and although the German defenders were not overwhelmed, they were being pushed back.

As the Soviet armies were pounding the German divisions along the northern and eastern faces of the Orel Salient, the 6th Grenadier Division was still holding the original front line in the south, from which it had launched its attack during Operation Zitadelle. Here, in the familiar positions along the Oka, the men felt confident that they could hold the line as long as necessary. Had they not held Rzhev for a year and a half?

However, as the Russian commanders threw three more armies into the assault and the German defenses in the north began to buckle, the German divisions along the eastern face of the salient were in danger of being cut off, and Model's forces in the south could well find themselves caught between Soviet forces advancing from the north and Rokossovky's armies facing them in the south. As a result, on July 23, the 6th Grenadier Division was ordered to abandon the Oka Line and withdraw to the northwest.

As with previous withdrawals, the division was to pull back (at night, of course) in short hops of 3–5 km to defensive positions previously prepared by a construction company commanded by Leutnant Berger of the 18th Regiment. Certainly no easy task when one considers the short time between the stages of the withdrawal and the lack of civilian workers. The Russian population had sensed the changing tide in the war. The Germanski were leaving, and soon the Bolsheviks would return. Understandably, fewer and fewer civilians were willing to work for German Komissbrot and the soon-to-be-worthless Reichsmark.

Between July 23 and 26, the division had withdrawn 10–12 km. The Soviets pursued them with what might best be termed "extreme caution." The last time they had ventured to engage the 6th Grenadier Division back on July 17, they had lost sixty tanks to Sauvant's roving Tigers and Grossmann's infernal "Panzerbrechers," and they were in no great hurry to repeat the experience. Not until the morning of July 27 did the Russians attempt an attack. Grossmann had suddenly been directed to pivot his division's left flank 90 degrees back so that now the division faced east instead of south and, most dangerously, was holding a position devoid of prepared defenses. The Russians seized the opportunity and attacked the left flank. At 10 a.m., Soviet tanks broke into the positions of the 18th Regiment. Oberleutnant Weege with a small assault group immediately counterattacked. With tanks swirling about him, he and his men took on the Russian infantry. In desperation, he made the call that all officers dread—he radioed back and ordered the regiment's anti-tank guns and infantry howitzers to bring their fire down on the enemy, irrespective of his assault team. The Russians were driven back with the loss of ten tanks. That evening the division pulled back another 3 km to the more tenable Stiefelwald Stellung, where over the next four days the division fought off numerous Soviet infantry and tank attacks.

During this period, word came through that the Kommandeur of the 18th Regiment, Oberstleutnant Höke, the Landser who had become the "father" of the regiment, had been awarded the Ritterkreuz for his regiment's performance during Operation Zitadelle. He was the second (and also the last) commander of the 18th Regiment to be so honored. The event was celebrated throughout the regiment, but, as with all such Ritterkreuz celebrations, there hung the shadow of Albrecht Schnitger's prophetic words, "Das nächste Kreuz ist das Birkenkreuz."

On the night of July 31, Grossmann pulled his division out of the Stiefelwald Stellung and over the next two days withdrew 20 km and dug in the Kroma River along a 14-km front facing southeast with the 37th Regiment on the right flank at Glinki, Regiment 58 in the center at Kromy, and the 18th Regiment on the left flank at Rassylnaja. Here again, the division was the target of repeated attacks as the enemy attempted to force his way across the Kroma.

On August 4, a serious situation arose in the center of the Kroma Line as Russian assault troops succeeded in getting across the river and breaking into the defenses of the 1st Battalion, 58th Regiment. The crisis was only averted by the rapid response of Oberleutnant Küster, commander of the 1st Company, who led a counterattack and wiped out the Russian lodgment on the north bank. Oberleutnant Küster would later be awarded the Ritterkreuz for this action.

The next day, August 5, the Russians renewed their assault. At 4 a.m., a heavy preparatory barrage of artillery and mortar fire rained down upon the 6th Grenadier Division. With a Soviet attack imminent, Grossmann ordered that the bridge at Blinki, which still stood, be destroyed. Three men and an unteroffizier of the 3rd Engineer Company climbed aboard a Sturmgeschütz with their mines and went rolling towards the bridge 300 meters away. Once there, the engineers were able to place their mines, but before they could set the fuses, they came under heavy fire from machine guns and anti-tank guns, forcing the Stumgeschütz and engineers to beat a hasty retreat, during the course of which the unteroffizier and two of his men were wounded. The task was only half-finished and the bridge still stood. Gefreiter Roos, who had been wounded in the hand and face, collected several mines and a bag of fuses and began crawling the 300 meters back to the bridge. After only 50 meters, he was wounded again, with a shot through the lungs. Determined, he continued on, but because he was short of breath, his progress was painfully slow. Eventually, he reached the bridge and, while still under heavy fire, was able to fuse the mines and place two more on the bridge. On his long crawl back to the German lines, he heard a loud crash behind him. He turned and watched with satisfaction as the wooden timbers of the bridge flew into the air and then splashed into the water. Exhausted, he could go no further. The Sturmgeschütz rolled forward to rescue Roos, and friendly hands hauled him aboard, where he fell into unconsciousness. Gefreiter Roos would survive his wounds and soon received the Ritterkreuz for his remarkable exploit.

The bridge at Glinki was gone, but Roos's heroics did not deter the Russians from launching attack after attack, often in regimental strength with heavy armor support in the effort to break across the Kroma. The 6th Grenadier Division was soon reinforced by a battalion of infantry from the Brandenburg 383rd Division and some Tiger tanks from Sauvant's Heavy Tank Battalion 505. Throughout August 5, the Soviets threw no less than fifteen attacks against the Kroma Line, but the line held. Thirty-seven Soviet tanks were destroyed by Sauvant's Tigers and the Sturmgeschütze. Four more had been hunted down and destroyed by Grossmann's "Panzerbrechers."

Having fought the entire day to hold the Kroma Line, Grossmann received orders that night to change front by swinging his center and left flank sharply back northwest so that his divisional line would again face east. Grossmann was both puzzled and disappointed by the directive. Why had they fought so hard to hold the Kroma Line? However, orders are orders, and the night of 5th August the division began its wheel to the rear.

Unknown to Grossmann, elsewhere on the front the German situation was rapidly deteriorating as the Soviets were gradually achieving their goal of eliminating the Orel Salient. Orel itself had fallen to the Russians on August 5, and despite dogged resistance, the Germans were slowly being squeezed out of the salient—which, perhaps, one might say was preferable to being crushed within it. Far to the south in the sector of von Manstein's southern Kursk attack force, the Soviets had launched Operation Rumiantsev on August 3. Eleven Soviet armies of the Voronezh, Steppe, and Southwest Fronts with 980,000 men—a superiority over the Germans even greater than that of Operation Kutuzov—sought to destroy von Manstein's 4th Panzer Army and Armee Abteilung Kempf. Belgorad fell to the Soviets on the second day of the offensive, and now the German armies in both the north and south, which had launched Operation Zitadelle, were fighting for their lives.

Meanwhile, the 6th Grenadier Division occupied its new position. Although the division had pivoted to face east, its right flank was still anchored at Glinki, which Grossmann promptly reinforced with the 3rd Battalion of the 383rd Division and the newly arrived 8th Jäger Regiment. If August 5 had been a day of heavy combat for his grenadiers, then August 6 would be even worse or, as Grossmann described it, "Ein besonders heisser Tag."

This "especially hot day" began at 4 a.m. when three battalions of Russian infantry with forty tanks attacked the right flank at Leschnja, and two infantry battalions with fifteen tanks stormed Glinki, driving the 8th Jäger Regiment and the 3rd Battalion of the 383rd Division out of both villages. Höke's 18th Regiment, now held in reserve, counterattacked and pushed as far as the middle of Glinki. A single anti-tank gun from the divisional panzerjägers destroyed seven T-34s. The Soviet attack was halted, but only after it had penetrated 1,200 meters into the German defense zone. Further north, seventeen tanks rolled through the lines of the 58th Regiment. They were soon followed by another forty tanks. How do infantrymen fight tanks? They do not; they squeeze themselves down into the bottom of their miserable holes and allow the steel monsters to roll over them while praying that the earthen walls do not collapse under the clanking tracks.

Tanks are not necessarily an anti-personnel weapon. They are mobile firepower that can move about the battlefield in the open with a certain level of survivability. Against entrenched infantry, there is little the tank can do other than roll over them and hope to crush one or two of them. But tanks are also a weapon of fear. If the infantry panics and attempts to flee, then the slaughter can begin. Panic, however, could hardly be said to be a part of the German soldier's psyche. In addition, during his training, the military had gone to considerable lengths to inoculate him against "tank fright." A recruit would be given a certain period of time to dig himself into the ground, after which an armored vehicle would roll over his hole thereby accustoming the recruit to the sound of clanking treads and instilling in him trust in the safety of his Panzerdeckungsloch. With typical Landser humour, troops often remarked that since the Panzerdeckungsloch had the same dimensions as a regulation grave, if the training exercise failed, then only a wooden cross would be needed for completion. Humor aside, to remain in a Panzerdeckungsloch while an enemy tank rolled over it required either nerves equal to the steel of the monster overhead or the paralysis of stark terror.

The grenadiers of the 58th Regiment did not panic. They remained in their holes and let the T-34s roll over them. Here and there, a Soviet tank sought to crush a hole and its occupants by spinning about on top of it—an unwise choice for a Russia tank crew. Remaining too long in one place on the battlefield only increased the chance of falling prey to a well-concealed anti-tank gun or a Panzerbrecher with a bag of magnetic mines. Some tank commanders attempted the tactic of coaxing the grenadiers out of their shelters with calls of "Come out, comrade—you are worker, I am worker, too!" The usual Landser reaction: an unprintable reply followed by a "geballte Ladung" hurled against the tank turret.

The tanks rolled past and the grenadiers rose up in their holes and took on their enemy—the brown waves of Russian infantry following in the wake of their armored brothers. Machine guns hammered away at the advancing Russians, either cutting them down or driving them to ground. The grenadiers had become quite adept at separating infantry from their tanks. As for the tanks themselves, the Tigers, "Stugs," and panzerjägers would take care of them.

After the waves of Soviet tanks had rolled through (or rather over) the lines of the 58th Regiment, Obergefreiter Zöllner struggled to dig his way out of his half-collapsed Panzerdeckungsloch, which had narrowly avoided becoming one of those lacking only a wooden cross for completion. He hastily cleared his "Spritze" of dirt and dust and blazed away at the Russian infantry, who immediately went to ground—obviously experienced troops who had long since learned to respect the devastating firepower of the MG-42. A T-34 returned to the aid of the infantry, determined to finish the job of burying this stubborn German machine-gunner once and for all.

For a second time, Zöllner squeezed down into the bottom of his hole while heavy tank treads clanked overhead. Zöllner decided that he had had enough of this game, and as the tank pulled away, he slid a T-mine onto its tread. A few meters from his hole came an explosion and the tank was minus one tread. Immobile, the tank quickly became the victim of a 7.5-cm anti-tank gun. A German counterattack drove the Russian infantry back, and Zöllner's comrades helped him dig himself out of his hole.

At the end of the day, the German line still held. Nine heavy attacks had been repulsed and twenty-four Soviet tanks destroyed, but at a cost. The 58th Regiment, which had borne the brunt of the Soviet assaults, mourned the loss of Oberleutnant Helmut Kramer, commander of the 2nd Company, and Leutnant Karl Rindfleisch of Stoßtrupp fame. Also killed that day were three indispensable senior NCOs, Feldwebels Kasper, Brandt, and Kelle.

At 9 p.m., the division received the order to abandon its position and withdraw to the "Hagen Stellung," a previously constructed defensive line 150 km long, running north–south across the base of the Orel Salient to which the German armies in the salient were retreating. In the three days of battle in the Kroma Stellung, the 6th Grenadier Division had fought off thirty-two attacks, inflicting heavy losses on the enemy. Eighty-six destroyed Soviet tanks (mostly T-34s) dotted the landscape, proof that the German soldier was as deadly in retreat as he was in the attack.

For the next eight days, the division continued its retreat westward in much the same manner as before: a night march of a few kilometers to a new position and then a day or two of resisting Soviet attacks followed by another night march. The men got little rest, and the unexpected heavy rains only increased their hardships as both motor and horse-drawn transport became stuck along the muddy roads, forcing the already exhausted grenadiers to unload and carry much of the equipment until the vehicles were pulled free.

During the withdrawal to the Hagen Stellung, Oberstleutnant Höke noticed a familiar face among his grenadiers. Leutnant Spieker, the victor of the Eiwald in the Kursk Offensive, who had been taken out of action by a landmine on July 8, was now back with the 18th Regiment after "recovering" from his wounds in only a month. Höke observed a comrade assist the young leutnant in wrenching his right knee back into place. With an audible crunch, Spieker's right leg was returned to serviceable condition. Höke had seen enough. Despite Spieker's protestations, Höke ordered him to get back to the homeland and not to return until his wounds were completely healed.

On August 13, the division suffered a hard blow when its Chief of Operations, Oberstleutnant Gerstung, was killed by a Russian artillery shell that dropped out of the sky and exploded 50 meters from his command trailer. He was struck in the head by an errant shell splinter and died instantly. Sadly, a few days earlier, Gerstung had been ordered to report to Corps Headquarters for other duties, but he had requested to remain with the division until the withdrawal had been completed. In Russia no one was immune to random death, not even a staff officer.

On the night of August 14, as the division was preparing to march off on the last leg of the withdrawal, the 58th Regiment became the target of a sudden, intense artillery barrage, which killed Hauptmann Edgar Leder, commander of the 4th Company, and Feldwebel Placek. The next morning, the 6th Grenadier Division crossed over into the safety of the Hagen Stellung, where they were placed in Corps Reserve at Gladnowo, 20 km behind the front. For the first time in forty-one days, the grenadiers would be able to awaken in the morning and not face an enemy hell-bent on their destruction.

Few grenadiers awakened the next morning to enjoy what Generalleutnant Grossmann described as a "beautiful summer's day." They slept through the morning; they slept through the day. Only with the arrival of evening did a few conscientious feldwebels rouse themselves from their exhaustion-induced, near comatose state and attend to a bare minimum of duty. For the next twelve days, the division remained in Corps Reserve behind the front, but for the men, the hoped-for rest and physical restoration never occurred. A cloud had descended upon their stay in "paradise" when two days after their arrival they received word that they were to maintain a state of combat readiness at all times for at any moment they could be recalled to the front. Aerial reconnaissance had revealed that the Soviets were massing forces all along the Hagen Stellung in preparation for another offensive.

Upon receipt of these orders, the officers and staff groaned. The reaction of the Landsers is best left to the imagination. There would be no rest; instead, the days would be filled with making themselves "abmarsch und einsatzbereit." Equipment needed to be refurbished; the depleted units reorganized; and, most important, the replacements who had begun arriving had to be "worked in" and instructed in eastern warfare. Pray there would be sufficient time for training so as to give the newcomers at least some chance of survival in the battles to come.

Throughout the second half of 1943, the Soviet counterstroke, which began with the Orel Offensive on July 12, would spread across nearly three-quarters of the Eastern Front, from Lake Ilmen in the north to the Crimea in the south. With the continued mobilization of its manpower and war resources, the Soviet Union was now able to field an army of 6 million men against a German force of 2.5 million, and whereas the Soviets could both maintain and increase their numbers, German forces would only decline as the requirements of other fronts deprived the eastern armies of critical resources and manpower.

Not only had the Soviets improved their overall force ratio, but they had also greatly improved their conduct of operation and tactics. Previously, the Soviet generals had pushed their offensives beyond the limit until they had drowned in a sea of their own blood, leaving their armies exhausted and vulnerable to German counterattacks. Now the Russians were more measured (and realistic) in their approach, content with taking bites, albeit quite large bites, out of the German front and then pausing to digest their gains and replenish their forces for the next phase of the offensive.

As for tactics, the German after-action reports reflect a definite improvement in the Russian ability to coordinate and conduct attacks. Earlier, as during the Moscow and Rzhev offensives, the Russians would throw in a company or two at a time and a half-dozen tanks in support with little coordination or chance of success. Now attacks were launched with battalions or even regiments supported by dozens of tanks. From the divisional down to the company level, the Russian commanders were learning their trade.

Over the next four months, this new Soviet Army, confident in its strength, would drive the Germans back hundreds of kilometers along the entire Eastern Front, reclaiming huge tracts of the Russian homeland from the fascist invaders. Pounded by relentless Soviet offensives, the German armies would be forced to retreat from one river to the next, from one "impregnable" Stellung to another, narrowly escaping total destruction and desperately seeking some stretch of ground upon which they could halt the Soviet colossus. Once again, the men of the 6th Grenadier Division would find themselves hounded ever westwards during this year of retreat.

August 27, at 11 p.m. the phone rings at Generalleutnant Grossmann's headquarters at Glednewo. As the Chief of Staff hands the receiver to the general, the two men exchange worried glances. Phone calls to divisional headquarters at this time of the evening seldom portend anything good. The general listens in silence and then returns the receiver to his aide. As he feared, the division has been recalled to the front. Grossmann had hoped for another two weeks to train the replacements, but Ivan, as usual, had declined to oblige.

In a matter of two weeks, the Soviets had reassembled the armies of the Brjansk Front, massed their artillery, and renewed their offensive against the German 2nd Panzer and 4th Armies. The Hagen Stellung, which had been intended to stabilize the front, was not holding. At several points along the 150-km front, Soviet attack divisions had broken through and were pushing west.

When Generalleutnant Grossmann and his Chief of Operations, Oberstleutnant Mittermüller arrived at General Freiherr von Roman's XX Corps Headquarters early on the morning of August 28 to be briefed on the situation, they were warmly received by Generaloberst Weiss, commander of the 2nd Panzer Army of which the 6th Grenadier Division was now a part. Weiss knew the Rhinelanders and Westphalians well from the Rzhev battles. He was confident that Grossmann and his old "Rshewkämpfer" would not let him down.

A crisis was looming 60 km to the south: two Soviet divisions had broken through the Hagen Stellung, captured the town of Ssewsk, and pushed 15 km to the northwest, slicing behind those German forces still holding out along the front line. The mission of the 6th Grenadier Division was direct: move with all haste 60 km south to Lugan, relieve the Brandenburg 8th Panzer Division, and halt the Soviet advance. Transport for equipment and supplies would be provided by the 2nd Panzer Army.

As his regiments made their preparations and awaited the promised transport, Grossmann proceeded to the crisis zone to assess the situation. When he arrived, he found Generalleutnant Schrötter, commander of the 8th Panzer Division, anxious to leave. Model was pulling the panzer divisions out of the line to have them available for swift counterblows. Not until 8 p.m., when Grossmann's first units arrived—the Engineer Battalion with the Heavy Weapons Company of the Reconnaissance Battalion and an infantry battalion from Grenadier Regiment 447, which had been picked up *en route*—was Grossmann able to accede to Schrötter's wish.

Unfortunately, while the engineers were in the process of relieving units of the 8th Panzer Division, the Russians attacked and threatened to overrun the German positions. Hauptmann Wellnitz of the engineers counterattacked and drove the enemy back, but, being unfamiliar with the terrain, the engineers paid heavily for their success. At 12:30 a.m., the 2nd Battalion of Grenadier Regiment 447 began relieving the last units of the 8th Panzer Division. No sooner was the relief completed (3 a.m.) than a Russian assault group attacked and was only driven off after the grenadiers had suffered heavy losses.

At dawn on August 29, Grossmann found himself defending a 15-km front between the Ssow and Ussosha Rivers—but with what? A weakened engineer battalion and a weakened battalion of grenadiers from another division? Where were his Rhinelanders and Westphalians? They were still strung out along the road from Glodnewo. The promised transport from the 2nd Panzer Army had either arrived late or proven to be insufficient. Hours would pass before Grossmann's grenadiers would arrive and they would arrive piecemeal. For Generalleutnant Grossmann, August 29 would be one of the longest days of his career. The Russians had already attacked twice, most probably probing attacks. If the enemy ever realized how weakly held the German line was and launched a serious assault, his two battalions would be crushed. As the sun rose higher in the sky, the general sought to conceal his tension from his staff, all the while glancing to the north hoping to spy the rising dust cloud of a marching column. He was said to have groaned, much as Wellington had done at Waterloo, when in the evening he had found himself praying that either night or Blücher would arrive.

Then came the attack. First, from the air as Soviet fighter-bombers unloaded their bombs and strafed the German positions, followed by the first salvos of the preparatory bombardment that increased in intensity as the morning wore on. Almost a waste of ordnance, considering how thinly held the German line was. Just before noon, the Russia infantry attacked—thank God, no tanks yet. The first wave was repelled, but the German companies were entirely too weak. A second assault burst through the line at the juncture of the engineers and the grenadiers of the 2nd Battalion and succeeded in taking Hill 205. Grossmann's small band was on the verge of being rolled over, rolled up, and crushed.

Suddenly, to the north, there appeared a cloud of dust—Gott sei dank—the regiments had arrived. No, not the regiments, only a single battalion, but Grossmann could still heave a sigh of relief for it was Hauptmann Otto Hellweg and his 2nd Battalion of Regiment 18. Hellweg was one of Grossman's most experienced and aggressive officers, and whenever "Onkel Otto" and his grenadiers struck, "dann blieb kein Auge trocken."

A hasty greeting, a quick briefing, and Hellweg launched into his counterattack. A shout of "Hurra!" and the Russians were thrown off Hill 205. Throughout the afternoon, the Russians attempted to regain Hill 205 without success and with heavy losses. Hellweg's grenadiers suffered heavily as well when an entire enemy mortar battalion deluged the hill. Every single platoon leader had become a casualty. Nine senior NCOs, whose absence would be felt, had either been killed or wounded. Two of those killed, Oberfeldwebels Stürmer and Michel had served with the 18th Regiment since before the war, and both held the German Cross in Gold.

When the 3rd Battalion of von Issendorf's 58th Regiment arrived upon the field, it, likewise, went immediately into the attack. On the far right flank, the Russians had broken through Grossmann's line and had crossed the Ssew River. After initial success, the 3rd Battalion's attack stalled and was forced to dig in without having driven the enemy back across the river.

The 37th Regiment was the last to arrive. In front of them stood the enemy-occupied Hill 216.6. It had to be retaken—and it was, quickly. The Russian force there obviously had not occupied the hill long enough to prepare an adequate defense or to grow too fond of the real estate. Although quickly won, Hill 216.6 was dearly held as the Russians, choosing not to throw lives away in retaking it, opted to attempt to blast the grenadiers off the hill with incessant artillery and fighter-bomber attacks. Regiment 37 clung to the hill but suffered heavily in so doing.

As night approached, the fighting died away along the front. The German line had held; Grossmann's small force had not been crushed, but it had been a damned, close-run affair. Nearly eighteen hours of combat from the time that Grossmann's engineers had first relieved the 8th Panzer Division. Eighteen hours of attack, counterattack, heavy barrages, and heavy losses—and this had only been their first day back at the front.

The next day, August 30, the Totentanz resumed. At 5 a.m., Grossmann's grenadiers were awakened by the pounding of drumfire all along the front. Could they have expected anything different? On the right flank in the sector of the 58th Regiment, a two-battalion attack of Russian infantry tore a 500-meter-wide hole in the thinly held lines of the 1st Battalion. Its commander, Hauptmann, led a counterattack with his staff and whatever troops he could find and drove the enemy back. The Russian response was more drumfire and a second infantry assault, which like the first was successful in breaching the German lines. Again, Hauptmann Markus left his command post and led a counterattack, this time aided by Leutnant Rompzick's 6th Company from Regiment 18. Together, they threw the Russians out and restored the original front line.

Throughout the day, the Russians continued to pound the grenadiers with artillery and mortars. Unlike the Germans, they suffered no shortage of ammunition. In previous battles, the division's artillery had often decisively intervened to smash Soviet attacks. Now the grenadiers would have to stop the Russians on their own. At 1 p.m., a crisis arose when a powerful Soviet attack pierced the lines of the Rhineland 86th Division, Grossmann's immediate neighbor on the left, and then swung around and attacked the 6th Grenadier Division from the rear. With two Soviet regiments attacking him from the front, Grossmann was in danger of having his entire left wing annihilated. The Reconnaissance Battalion rescued the situation. Held in reserve, concealed in a ravine behind the division's left flank, Rittmeister Massmann ordered his battalion forward. Accompanied by a pair of Sturmgeschütze that had wandered upon the scene, the Reconnaissance Battalion smashed into the rear of the Russian force that had flanked the division. Caught between Massmann and the grenadiers still holding the front line, the Russians suffered heavy casualties before fleeing off to the north to escape destruction.

August 30 had been another day of heavy combat and heavy losses. Von Issendorf's 58th Regiment was particularly hard hit, counting thirty-one of its ranks killed, including the 3rd Company commander, Oberleutnant Paul Mayer. Two other officers, Leutnants Fischer and Wobert, fell out with wounds. Despite heavy losses, the 6th Grenadier Division succeeded in staving off the Soviet attacks and holding the line. However, the breakthrough that had occurred in the 86th Division's sector necessitated that Grossmann pull back his left flank 2 km after nightfall to restore contact with his neighbor.

August 31 proved to be no different than the previous two days: incessant drumfire, attacks, counterattacks, then more drumfire, followed by more attacks. On the right flank, the 58th Regiment withstood twenty-two attacks that day, many of which had to be driven back with hand-to-hand combat. In one of the German counterattacks, Hauptmann Friedrich Haarhaus, Commander of the 3rd Battalion, fell at the head of his Stoßtrupp, severely wounded in the stomach. He died soon after in the battalion aid station. Oberleutnant Rohn took over command of the 3rd Battalion. Even after these twenty-two attacks, Regiment 58 still held firm. The day had cost the regiment seven dead, including another invaluable NCO, Feldwebel Deimann of the 15th (panzerjäger) Company, as well as several dozen wounded, among them Oberleutnant Steinert, Commander of the 12th Company,

The 18th Regiment had no easier time than the 58th. The regiment was still in possession of Hill 220, and the Russians were determined to take it from them. This critical height, overlooking the battlefield, was being defended by the regimental Kampfgruppe commanded by Leutnant Bovensiepen. He and his small group of forty men fought off assault after assault, all the while being pounded by heavy mortar and artillery fire. By mid-afternoon, the young leutnant was down to only seven men. All the others had been killed or wounded. But still they held.

In spite of all that, the Russians had thrown at them, at the end of the day Grossmann's grenadiers continued to hold the 15-km sector between the Ssew and Ussosha Rivers, thus denying the Soviets their breakout to the northwest to trap the German forces still fighting further east. But the question remained, how long would they have to hold this line, or more to the point, how long would they be able to hold the line with their weakened units? Up to now they had only had to contend with heavy barrages and infantry. Certainly Ivan would soon be bringing up his tanks. What then?

September 1: Ivan brought up his tanks and threw them into the fray. Again the grenadiers found themselves hugging the bottom of their foxholes (and one another), watching with bulging eyes as the steel beasts rolled over them. Then, quick up and take on the infantry. The Stugs and panzerjägers would have to deal with the tanks.

Drumfire, tanks, mass wave attacks, and hand-to-hand combat; the recent replacements were receiving a post-graduate education in Eastern Combat—that is, if they lived, for the tuition was high. As the casualties mounted, commanders watched their companies melt away—if they themselves had not already added their names to the list of killed or wounded. The newcomers were not the only ones filling the dressing stations and the graves. Far too many of the old hands were finding that they had run out their string of luck.

For the next three days, the battle raged as before, along the front of the 6th Grenadier Division. In this period, the Soviets launched well over thirty attacks with armor support. In a counterattack to reclaim two anti-tank guns overrun by the Russians, the commander of the Reconnaissance Battalion, Rittmeister Massmann, was killed and all his squadron leaders wounded. The guns were retrieved but were hardly worth the cost. Casualties, exhaustion, and the relentless Russian attacks were taking their toll. Gradually the lines of the division were pushed back, but they were not broken.

Not so the Hagen Stellung. Under the avalanche of Soviet tanks, artillery, bombers, and infantry, the German front could neither be restored nor held. The 2nd and 9th Armies began a phased withdrawal to the Desna River. Perhaps there they could make a stand.

At 9 p.m. on September 3, Generalleutnant Grossmann was ordered to abandon the Ssew–Ussosha line and begin the 60-km withdrawal to the Desna. After three nights of marching and the two days of warding off the pursuing enemy, on the morning of September 6, the grenadiers stumbled across the railroad bridge over the Desna, 2 km north of Nowy Wassiljewskiy. The Soviets attempted to interfere with the crossing with a few aerial attacks, but the bombs fell wide and caused no damage or casualties. Once across, the exhausted men took up or, rather, collapsed into their new positions along the west bank of the Desna. With last night's march, they had put a good 18 km between them and the pursuing enemy. Ivan would need a day or two to catch up and even longer to bring up and emplace his artillery, so the feldwebels and officers allowed the men to sleep their fill.

The next morning they were awakened by the sound of the bridge being blown into the heavens by the engineers. The shattered ties and rails raining down upon the waters of the Desna were a welcome sight to the men. Although rivers no longer presented a serious barrier in modern warfare, there was still something comforting about having a body of water, no matter how narrow or shallow, between one and his pursuers.

As the division settled into its new position, a 15-km front along the Desna facing due east, both general and Landser held out hope that they might occupy the Desna Stellung for some time. September was here, and soon the rains would usher in the "Schlammperiode," which would preclude any serious military operation by either side—and after that, the frost. Who knew? With any luck, the division could well spend the winter in the Desna Stellung. Anything was preferable to these endless "tactical withdrawals."

Left in peace for the moment by the enemy, Grossmann and his staff took the opportunity to assess the division's condition. The losses incurred during the period July 1 to September 10 could only be described as "erschreckend"—shocking. A total 132 officers and 4,455 NCOs and men were listed as killed, wounded, or missing. If the officer casualty ratio appeared lower than usual, there was good reason: there had been fewer officers present to become casualties. The platoons of a grenadier company normally led by a leutnant had for some time been commanded by feldwebels and oberfeldwebels.

During this same period, the division had received sixty officers and 2,439 NCOs and men as replacements, but the "burn rate" had been so high that the strengths of the regiments and battalions remained extremely weak. The regiments possessed only a tenth of their mobilization strength. Höke's 18th Regiment was the strongest with 344 officers and men; the 37th Regiment was the weakest, counting only 254 in total manpower. The strengths of the battalions were equally shocking. The weakest battalion, the 3rd of Regiment 58, had a combat strength of a mere 126 officers and men—not even that of a typical company. The 18th Regiment's 1st Battalion was the strongest, with a combat strength of only 216 officers and men. With these paltry numbers, Grossmann's division was expected to defend a 15-km front. In practice, this worked out to a single two-man post for every 90 meters of front. This was not a defensive line; it was little more than an infantry screen, an arrangement typically employed on a non-threatened sector.

With the front so thinly manned, it was not long before the enemy attempted to cross the Desna and establish a bridgehead on its western shore. On the night of September 10, two Russian companies crossed the river and dug in. Units of the 37th Regiment and the Reconnaissance Battalion counterattacked and drove the enemy out. Many drowned and 147 dead were counted along the shore of the Desna. Twenty-five were taken prisoner. Grossmann's grenadier companies may have been weak in numbers, but his grenadiers were as aggressive in spirit as ever. The Russians did not attempt to establish a bridgehead again.

Contrary to the hope of going into winter quarters along the Desna, on September 17, the 6th Grenadier division was ordered to abandon the Desna Stellung. Events to the south had made the position untenable. The persistence, strength, and breadth of the Soviet post-Zitadelle offensives and the relative weakness of the German forces resisting them necessitated that the Germans maintain a contiguous and, as much as possible, even front. The two Germany Army Groups, Center and South, which were the primary target of the Soviet offensives, found that developments on the one front directly affected the deployments and movements of the other. If one or the other army group was forced to withdraw any great distance, then the other would be compelled to follow suit or risk having its flank uncovered or overextended, in either case inviting attack, which could lead to the cutting off of considerable numbers of troops.

The autumn rains had arrived, ushering in the "Schlammperiode," but the Russians continued their offensives unabated. In the area of von Manstein's Army Group South, the Soviet Voronezh, Steppe, and Southwest Fronts had hammered the German armies back to the Donets. With his weakened 4th Panzer and 6th and 8th Armies reeling from the relentless Soviet attacks, von Manstein requested permission to withdraw his forces to the Dnieper, essentially surrendering the eastern Ukraine. Reluctant as ever to yield a single meter of ground to the enemy, Hitler finally assented to von Manstein's request on September 15. This withdrawal of Army Group South forced Model to abandon the Desna Stellung and, likewise, pull his 2nd and 9th Armies back to the Dnieper. For Grossmann's grenadiers, this meant another phased withdrawal of night marches and constant battles with a pursuing enemy.

On September 27, after 150 km and ten days of exhausting marches and incessant combat, the 6th Grenadier division reached the end of the withdrawal and took up its assigned position south of Gomel, not along the Dnieper, but 20 km further east along the Ssosh River, which, at this point, runs essentially parallel to the Dnieper. The past ten days had certainly had their share of hardships and moments of crisis, but, in the main, this withdrawal had proceeded more smoothly than the previous one. In the Russian War, however, all such qualifiers are relative. There had been losses. One in particular struck the division hard. On September 21, at Nowo-Jamskoje, Hauptmann Karl Markus, who had been with the 58th Regiment since before the war and who had so often led crucial counterattacks in the past several weeks, fell at the head of his 1st Battalion while leading a counterattack. By the end of September, both Army Groups Center and South had completed their withdrawal to the Dnieper Stellung. To shield the vital rail center of Gomel, Army Group Center had found it necessary to swing that portion of its front northeastwards and take positions along the Ssosh rather than the Dnieper. The 6th Grenadier Division formed part of the Ssosh-shield and was assigned a 12-km sector 20 km south of Gomel, facing due east. The immediate neighbor to the north was the Hanoverian 216th Grenadier Division while to the south lay the positions of the Braunschweig 31st Grenadiers, a division that could boast equal pedigree with Grossmann's division, having, as it did, two regiments from the old Reichsheer.

For one, the construction battalions had been given sufficient time to construct adequate defenses to receive the withdrawing divisions, but when the 6th Grenadier Division took over its sector along the Ssosh, it discovered that the defenses were—as Grossmans described them—completely wrong. The trenches, dugouts, and bunkers had been built too far back from the river so that its banks were unobservable from the German lines. Worse still, the ground between the river and the division's positions was covered with dense vegetation. The enemy could easily mass a force unseen along the riverbank, steal through the brush and hedges, and, at close range, launch a surprise attack. Grossmann had no choice but to task his men, already weary from ten days of marching and fighting, with constructing a new main battle line closer to the river.

They had to work quickly for Ivan had followed closely upon their heels. In the first few days of October, troublesome Russian patrols were already attempting to slip across the river. They were easily driven off, but then came stronger forces. The Russians had learned well from the Germans. If a retreating enemy sought the safety of a river line, the best course of action was to quickly establish a bridgehead to the far bank—no matter how small. It would pay a great dividend in the future.

In the central sector of the division's line, held by von Issendorf's 58th Regiment, there were two eastward-projecting loops in the river, which, due to the increased frontage created by them, could not be adequately manned by the regiment's weak numbers. In the northern bend, the Russians were able to establish a bridgehead and even reinforce it with tanks. All attempts to reduce it failed as the counterattacking forces could be brought under enemy fire from three directions.

Late on October 4, the Russians launched a company-strength attack out of their bridgehead and succeeded in breaking into the 58th Regiment's defenses. After midnight, Leutnant Albersmann led his 1st Company in a counterattack and, after eight hours of combat in the pitch dark, threw the enemy back with heavy losses. As war booty, Albersmann's company claimed two heavy machine guns, three light machine guns, three machine pistols, and six rifles. Their own losses were ten dead, including Stabsfeldwebel Wiedenhöfer and Oberfeldwebel Houtbrun. Though not heavy, these were not losses that the 58th Regiment could afford in its present condition, particulary the loss of two senior NCOs.

Hardly had Leutnant Albersmann returned to battalion headquarters with his trophies than a heavy artillery and mortar barrage crashed down along the entire front of the 6th Grenadier Division. The earlier action had only been a probing attack. At 10 a.m. came the main assault. Two regiments, the 114th and 118th of the Soviet 37th Guards Division, stormed out of the bridgehead and slammed into the positions of the 58th Regiment's 3rd Battalion. Against such overwhelming numbers, the 3rd Battalion was forced to pull back to the original defense line built by the construction engineers despite its disadvantages. Their withdrawal uncovered the left flank of the 1st Battalion, leaving it no other option but to abandon its defense of the southern Ssosh bend and, likewise, fall back to the original front line. The day cost the regiment ten dead and a dozen wounded. Among the dead were Leutnant Erich Renken of the 9th Company, and Oberfeldwebel Leifeld of the 11th Company.

The 37th Regiment, holding the left flank, was also struck hard that day, both in the front and its right flank as some of the Russian forces that had forced back Regiment 58 swung north into the flank and rear of the regiment. Only with the greatest effort and heavy casualties was the Russian thrust to the northwest brought to a halt, but the attempts to push the enemy back failed. At dawn the next day, under the cover of a dense fog, a battalion of Russian infantry was able to slip through the gap now existing between the 37th and 58th Regiments and seize the village of Krasnaja Dolina 4 km behind the front.

A critical situation had arisen in which the Ssosh Stellung appeared in danger of being lost. For two days, the Russians attempted to break through to the west and northwest, but somehow Grossmann's depleted units were able to prevent any further enemy advance. Then, for some unknown reason, the Russian attack appeared to have run out of steam, allowing Grossmann to scrape up sufficient forces for a counterattack. On October 12, the 58th Regiment's 1st Battalion, now commanded by Oberleutnant Küster, drove the enemy out of Krasnaja Dolina, inflicting heavy losses. As war booty, Küster's battalion brought back six 45-mm anti-tank guns, two anti-tank rifles, four machine guns, thirty-two machine pistols, fifty-three rifles, five semi-automatic rifles, one sniper rifle, a 7.5-cm German infantry howitzer, and seventeen prisoners. Although the counterattack did not push the enemy back across the Ssosh, the Russian thrust to the northwest had been halted, and, at least for the moment, the crisis had passed. The Ssosh Stellung had been held, but, as so often before, events elsewhere would soon change all that.

For the next several days, the sector of the 6th Grenadier Division remained calm. During this period, the division received the first replacements it had seen since mid-August. Grossmann and his officers could hardly believe their eyes when the newcomers arrived. An entire full-strength battalion—700 men! Grossmann's regiments had rarely been able to muster more than that number since the first winter battles. Company commanders rubbed their hands together at the thought of filling out their by-now platoon-size units. But it was not to be. Grossmann was instructed that the four companies of replacements were not to have their men distributed among the division's existing units but were to be deployed as whole companies intact and under command of the officers and NCOs with whom they had trained. In Grossmann's opinion, this deprived the new men of the valuable experience of the old Ostkämpfers and the leadership of battle-proven commanders and led to heavy and unnecessary casualties.

The new replacements could not have arrived at a more fortunate time, for, although the 6th Grenadier Division and the neighboring 31st and 216th Divisions had succeeded in holding the Ssosh Stellung, 30 km to the south, where the Ssosh empties into the Dnieper, the Soviet 61st Army had broken

*Above left:* The Landser. (*Alamy*)

*Above right:* Autumn, 1941. The "Rasputiza." The heavy autumn and spring rains, which turned the primitive Russian roads into quagmires, were always of serious concern for both German and Soviet war-planners. Here a German PzKW I is utilized as a tow vehicle. (*Alamy*)

*Above left:* Summer, 1942. A German Stosstrupp prepares for a counterattack. The photo shows the typical arrangement of a soldier's combat gear. (*Alamy*)

*Above right:* The counterattack. The absence of epaulettes suggests that this is a junior officer leading the assault. Officers on the frontlines often removed their badges of rank so as not to become prime targets for enemy snipers. (*Alamy*)

Russian prisoners of war being marched to the rear. Some of the men are obviously conscripts from the more eastern regions of the Soviet Union. (*Alamy*)

Battle's aftermath. Rzhev, summer, 1942. Here a Landser (perhaps a "Panzerbrecher") views a destroyed Soviet KV-1 tank. (*Alamy*)

*Above left:* Two Landsers avail themselves of refreshment during a lull in the battle. The German soldier seldom lacked for alcohol, even during combat. (*Alamy*)

*Above middle:* A Landser enjoys a meal of "Volga stew." (*Alamy*)

*Above right:* Propaganda Company photograph of German soldiers in the Warka Bridgehead (November 1944). In the foreground, Obergefreiter Reiner Niemann of the 58th Regiment. (*Andersson Archives*)

*Above left:* Typical German trench in the Warka Bridgehead. (*Pawel Wyszomirski, photographer; Andersson Archives*)

*Above right:* A German bunker in the Warka Bridgehead discovered in 2014 near the village of Lezenice. (*Pawel Wyszomirski, photographer; Andersson Archives*)

*Above left:* Lezenice battlefield (Reg. 58) in the Warka Bridgehead as it appears today. In the distance lies the Trzebien Forest from where the Soviets launched their massive offensive on January 14, 1945. (*Pawel Wyszomirski, photographer; Andersson Archives*)

*Above right:* The cemetery at Lezenice, little changed since 1945. (*Pawel Wyszomirski, photographer; Andersson Archives*)

*Below:* The Radomka River at the point where the 58th Regiment (left bank) adjoined the 45th Division (right bank). During the Soviet offensive of January 14, a small group from the 58th Regiment escaped across the river into the 45th Division's sector. What became of them remains unknown. (*Pawel Wyszomirski, photographer; Andersson Archives*)

*Above:* A forest clearing near Grabowa along the line of the 6th Infantry Division's retreat out of the Warka Bridgehead, where in 1997 the remains of 157 German soldiers were discovered in two mass graves. Some of the remains were those of members of the 6th Infantry Division. The remains were afterwards removed to the German military cemetery of Pulawy, Poland. (*Pawel Wyszomirski, photographer; Andersson Archives*)

*Below left:* A typical German battlefield burial site with the traditional Birkenkreuze. Such sites are scattered throughout the former Soviet Union. When discovered, the remains are removed to more centralized military cemeteries by the German Kriegsgräberfürsorge association. (*Alamy*)

*Below right:* The German military cemetery at Pulawy, Poland. (*Andersson Archives*)

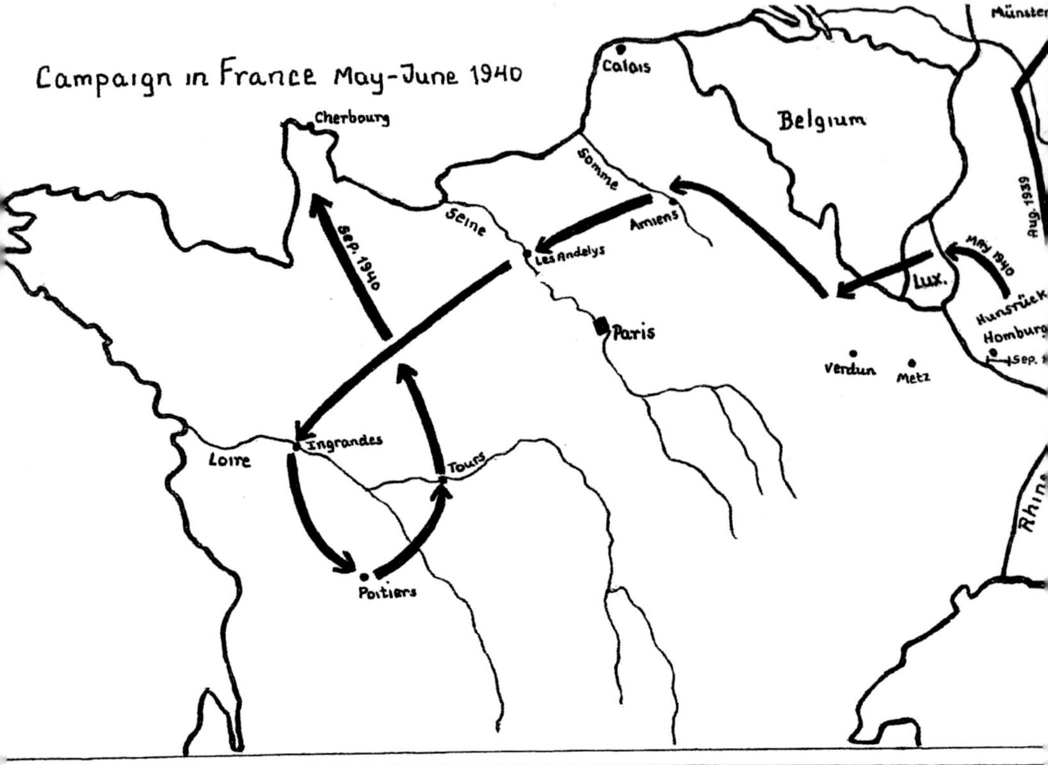


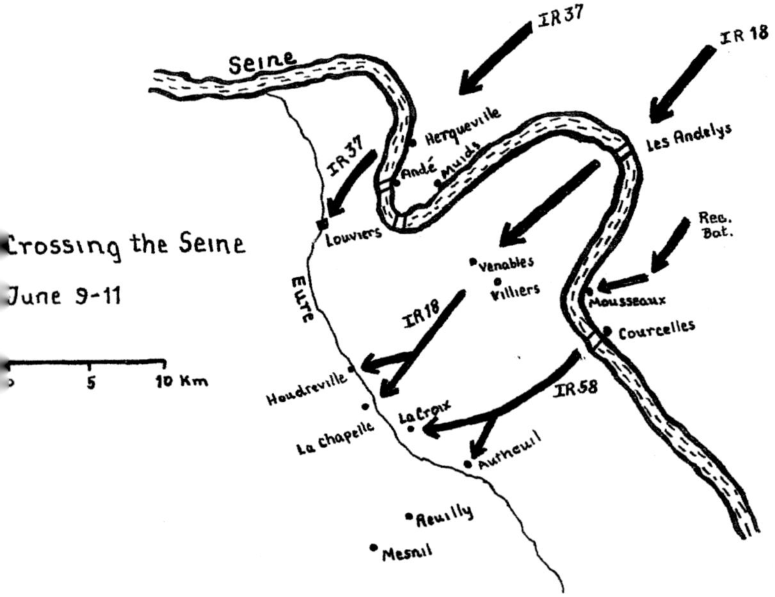


Campaign in France, May-June 1940 and crossing the Seine, June 9–11, 1940. (*Denis Havel*)

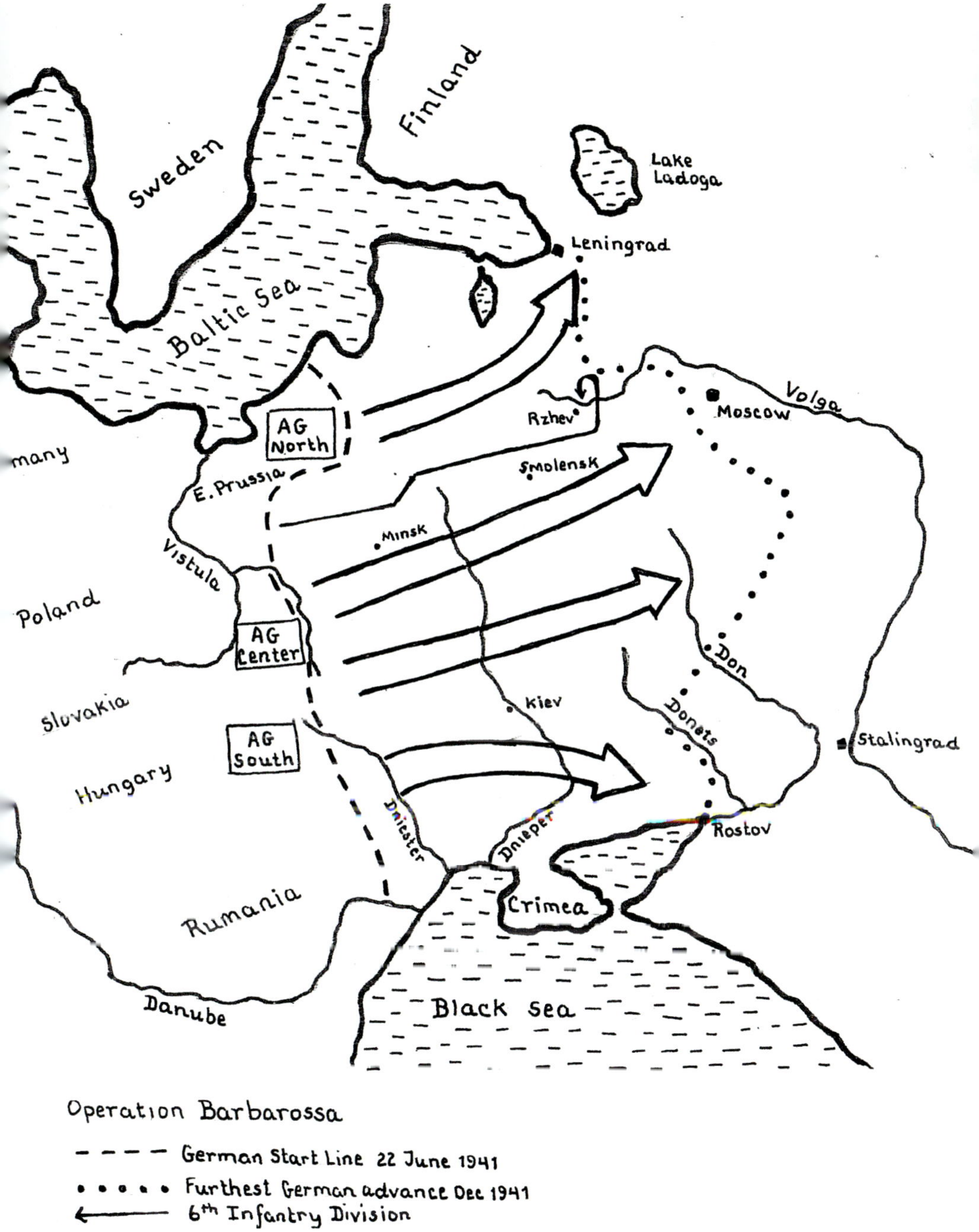


Operation Barbarossa. (*Denis Havel*)

The Eastern War and the Rhineland–Westphalian 6th Infantry Division. (*Denis Havel*)

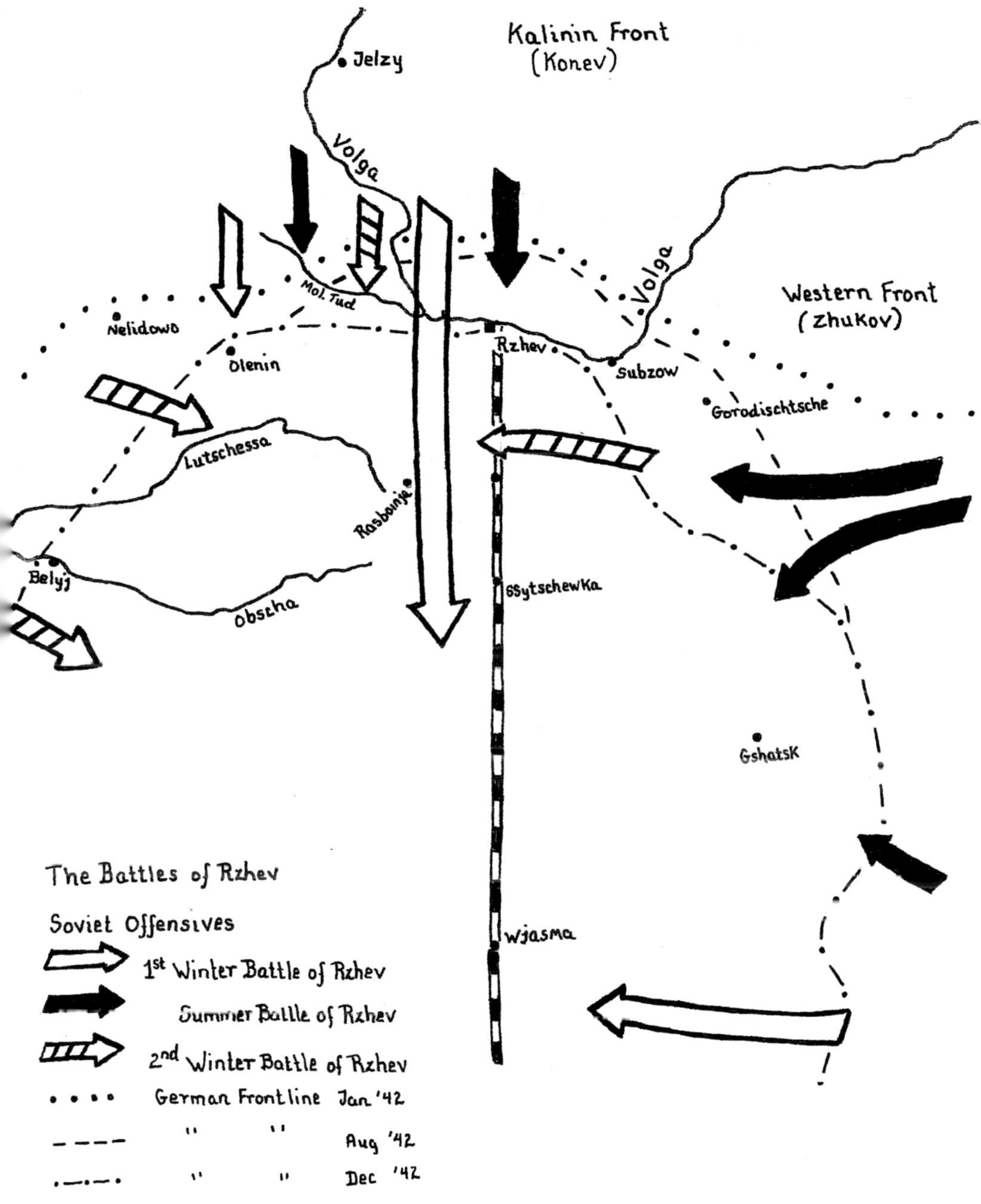


The Battles of Rzhev. (*Denis Havel*)

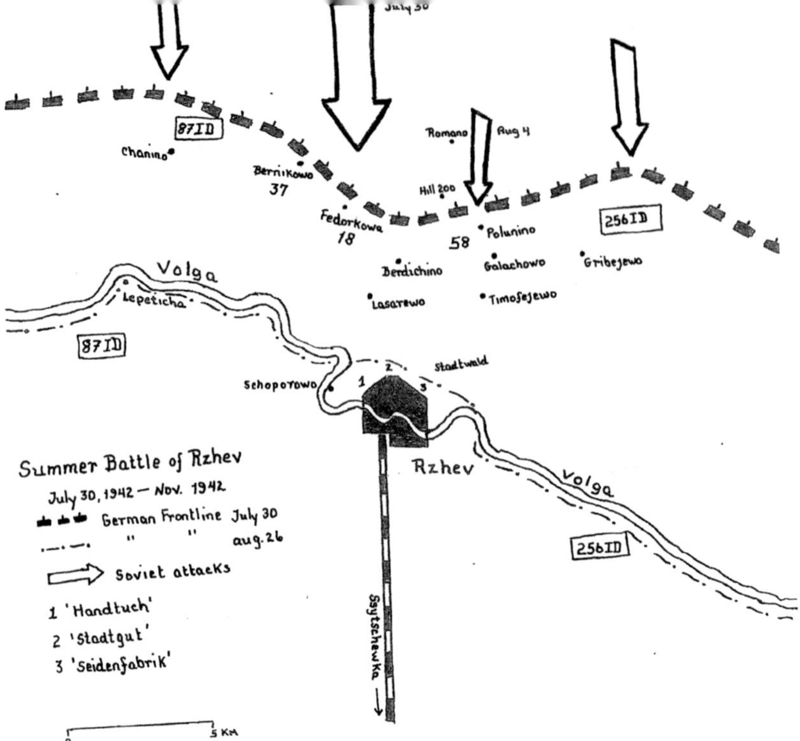


*Above:* Summer Battle of Rzhev. (*Denis Havel*)

*Below:* Operation Büffel. (*Denis Havel*)

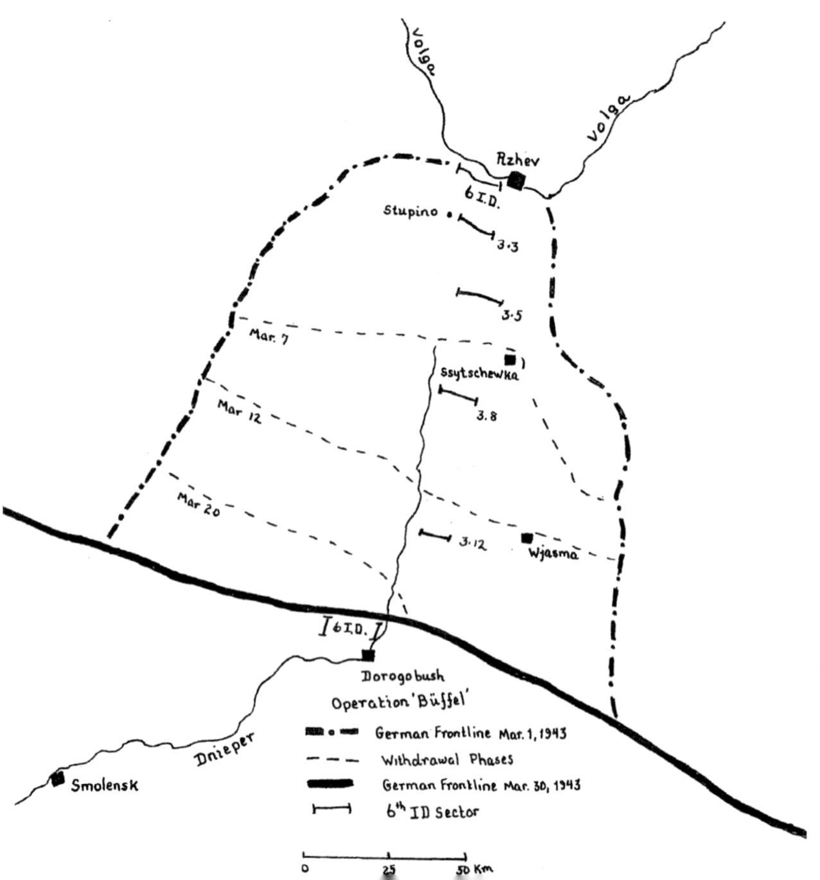

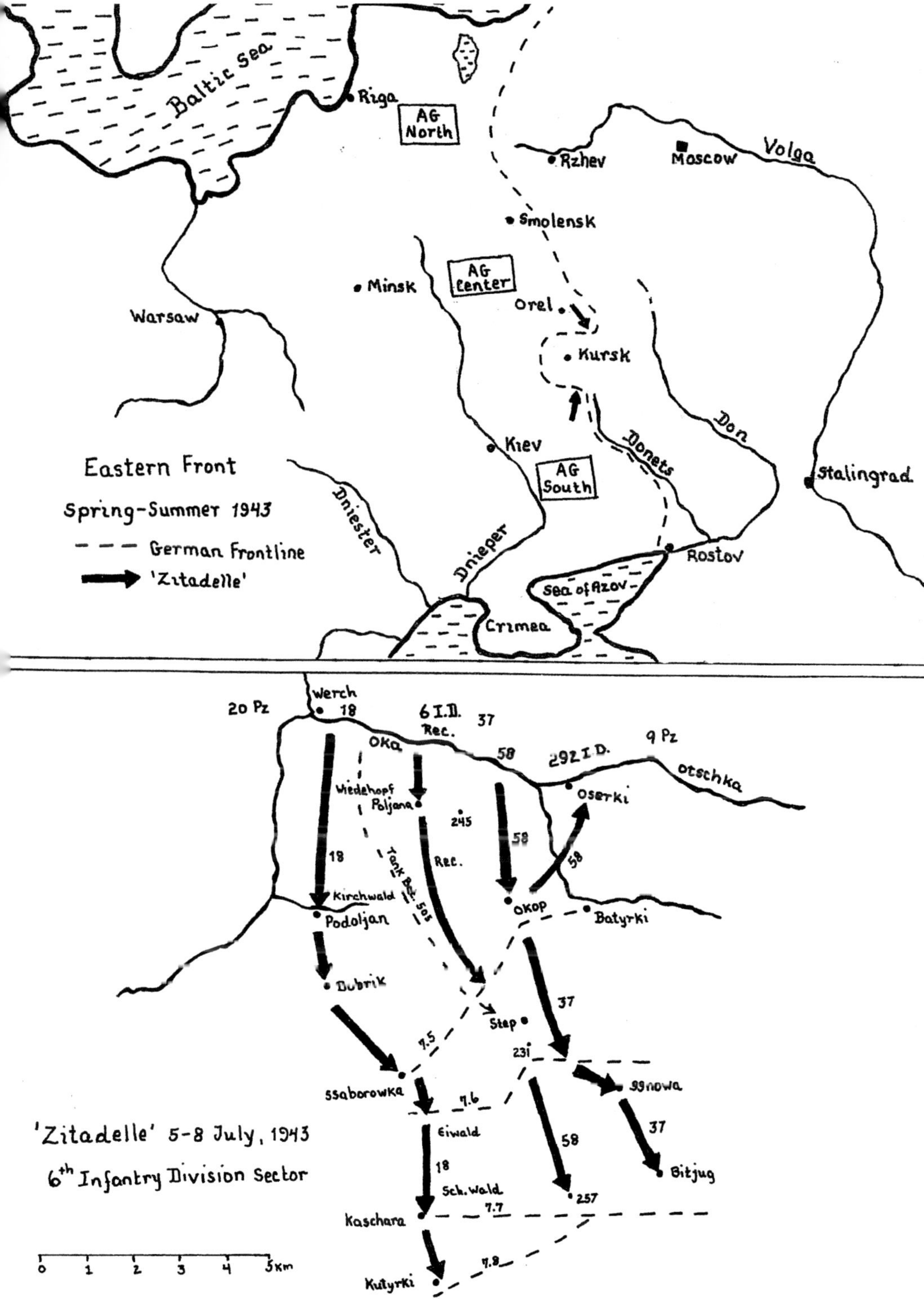


Eastern Front, spring–summer 1943 and "Zitadelle," July 5–8, 1943, 6th Infantry Division Sector. (*Denis Havel*)

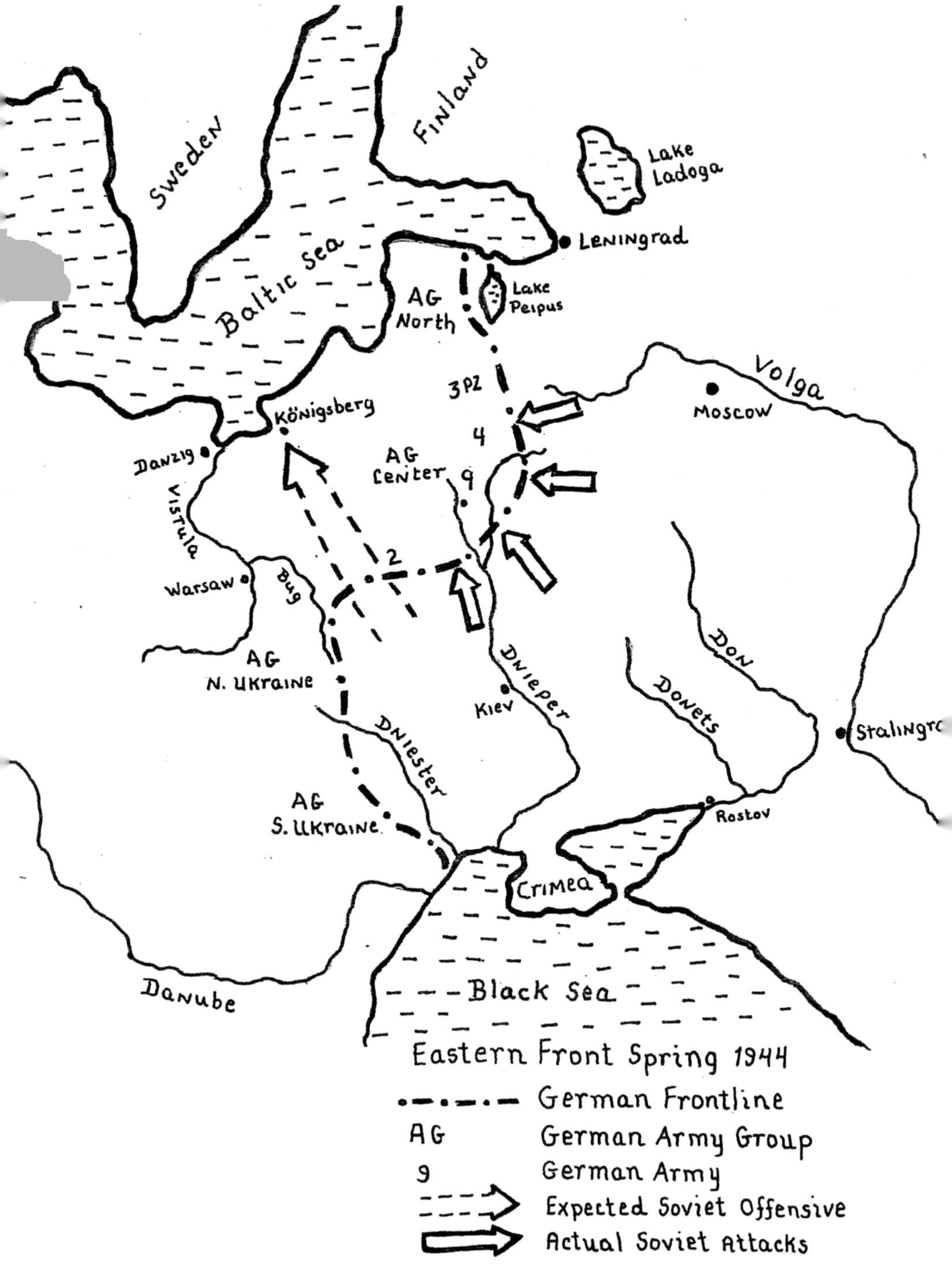


Eastern Front, spring 1944. (*Denis Havel*)

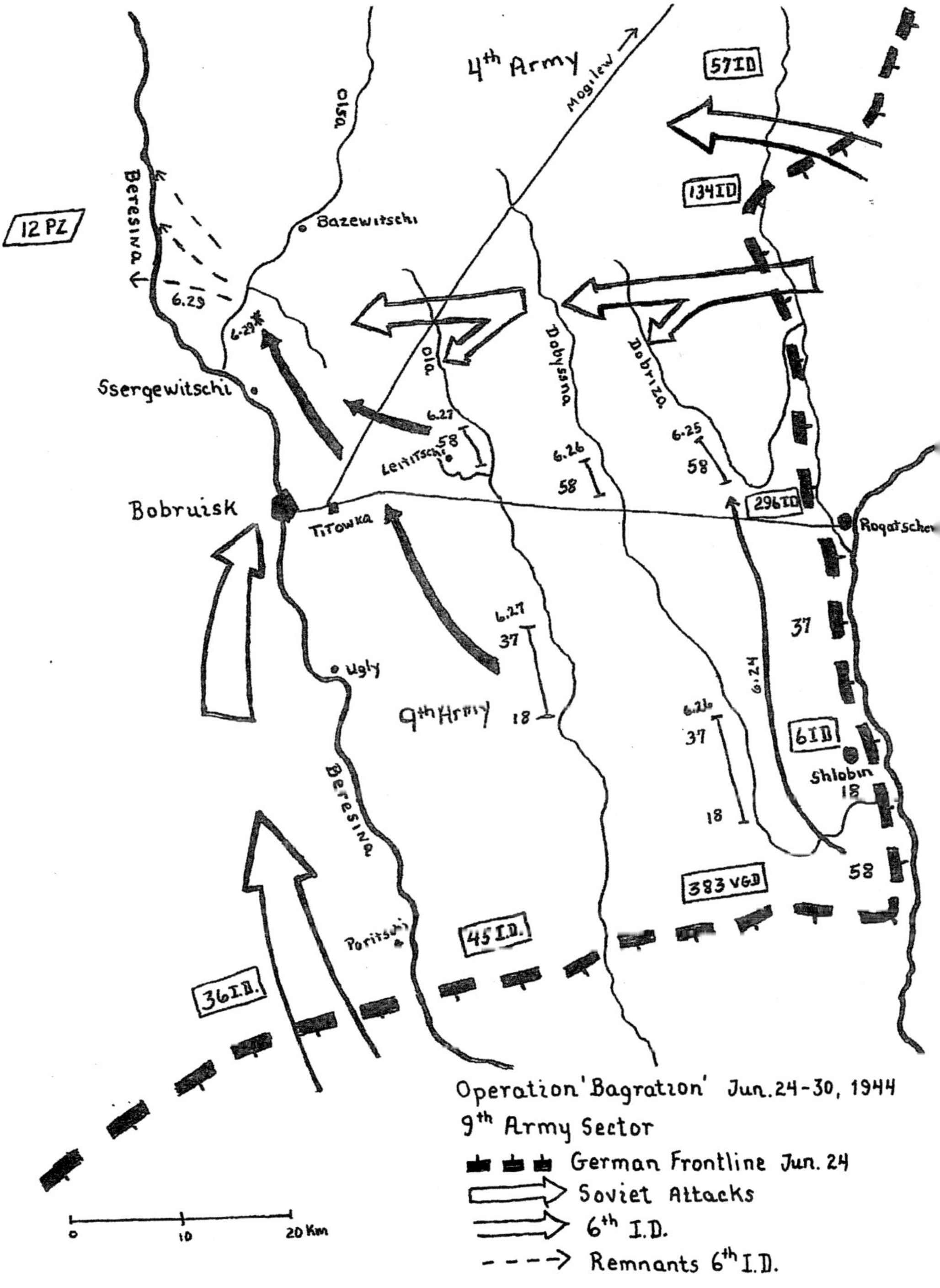


Operation Bagration, June 24–30, 1944. (*Denis Havel*)

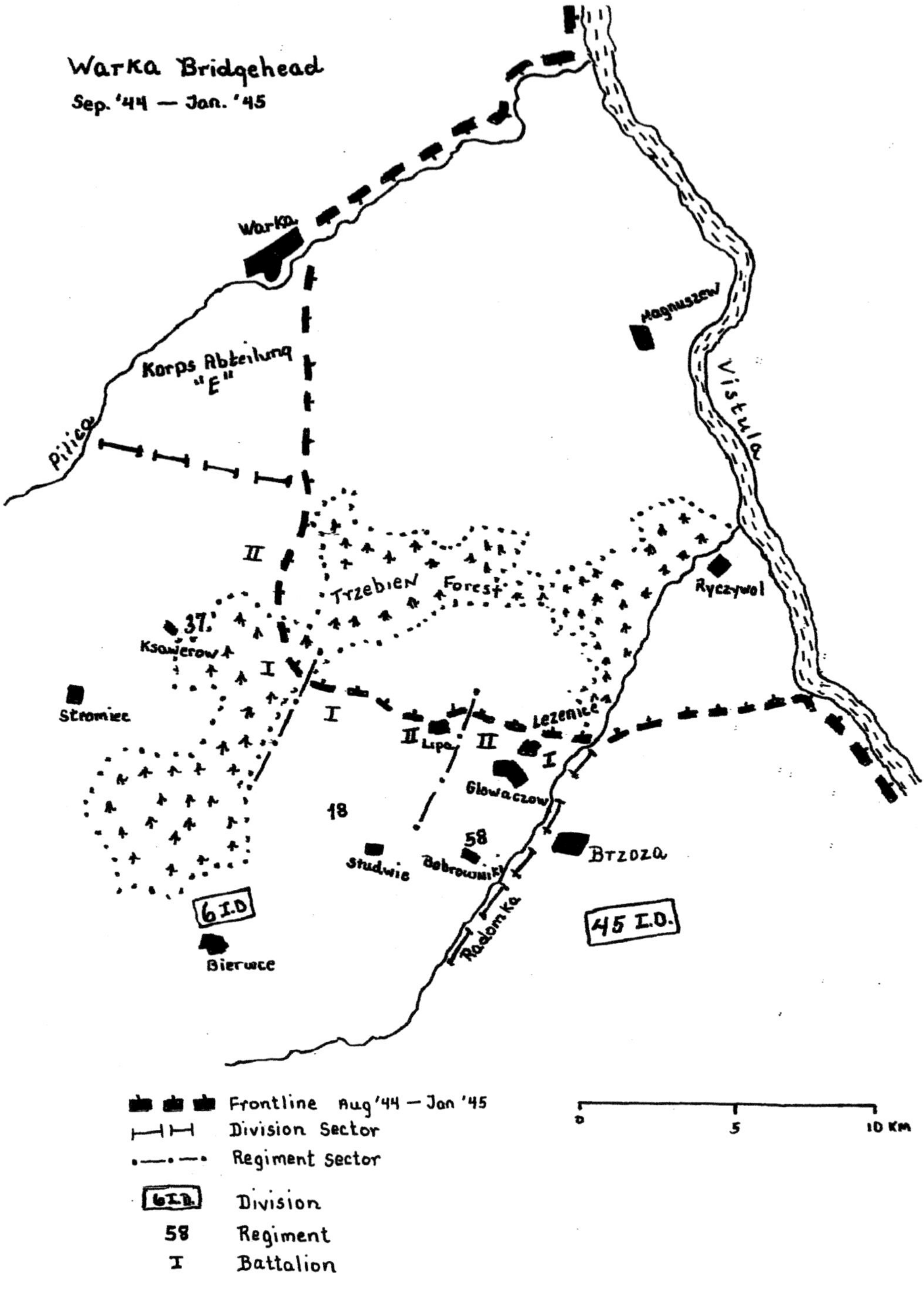


Warka Bridgehead, September 1944 to January 1945. (*Denis Havel*)

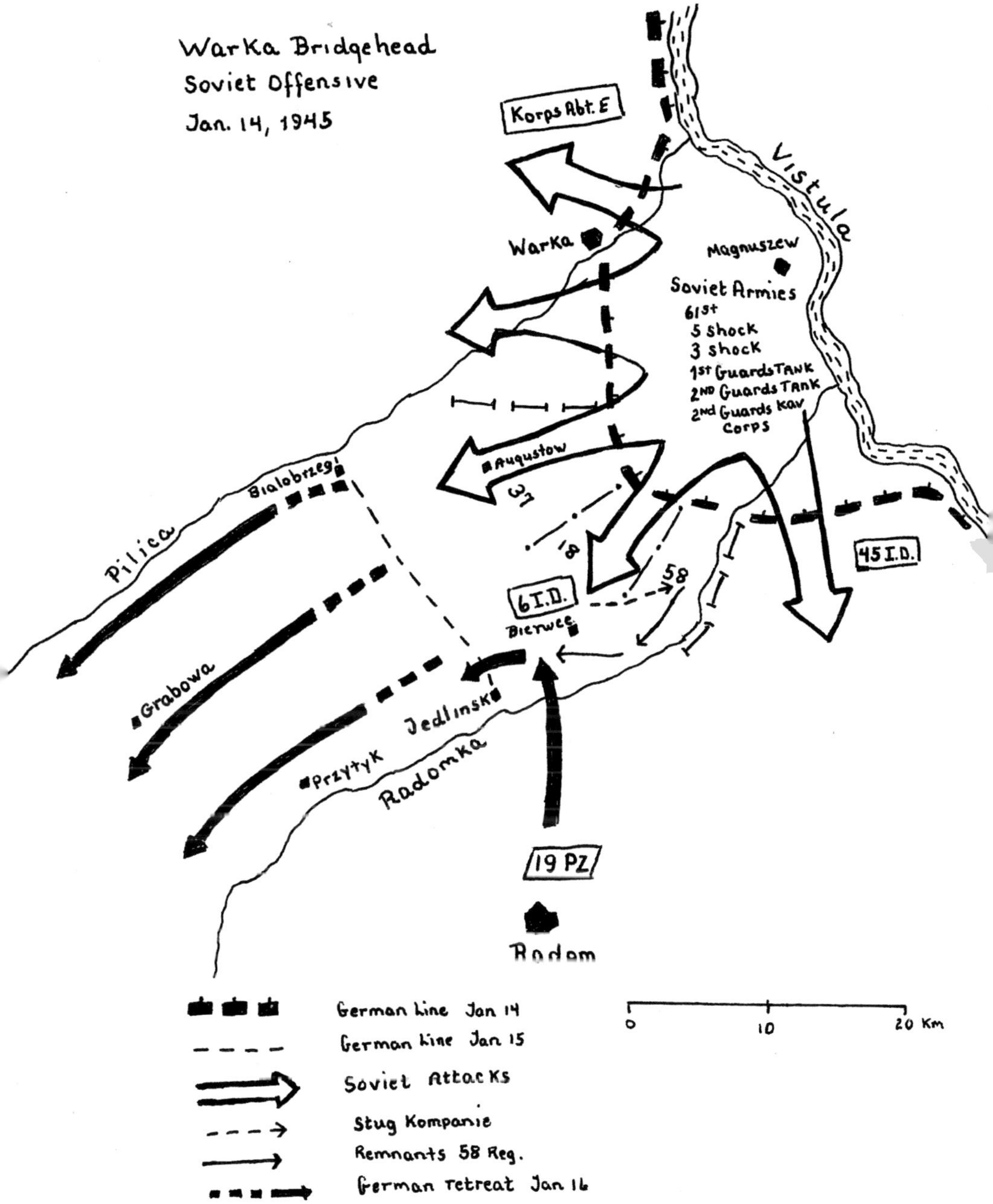


Warka Bridgehead, Soviet Offensive, January 14, 1945. (*Denis Havel*)

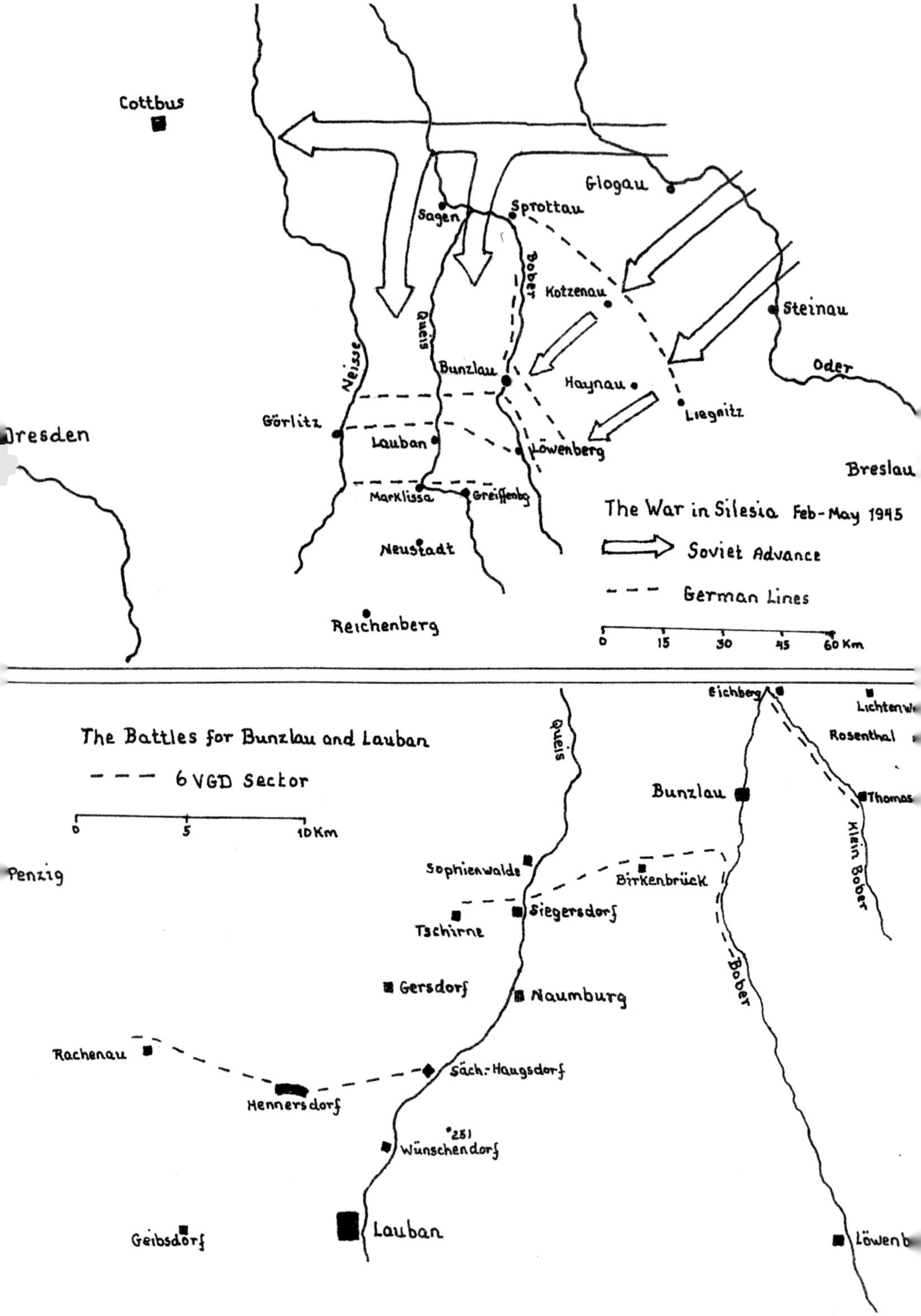


The War in Silesia and the Battles for Bunzlau and Lauban. (*Denis Havel*)

across the Dnieper, swung to the right, and was pushing north along the river's western bank. The objective was the city of Retschiza, which, if taken, would force the Germans to abandon the rail center of Gomel.

With Soviet forces driving hard north, the Ssosh Stellung was in danger of being flanked to the west and cut off. Consequently, the southern half of the Ssosh Stellung had to be abandoned. On October 16, Grossmann's neighbor to the south, the 31st Division, was pulled out of the line and hurried west across the Dnieper to combat the Soviet threat. The 6th Grenadier Division was directed to swing its southern flank back 15 km west to the Dnieper. The division was now holding an 18-km front, stretching between the Ssosh and the Dnieper and facing southeast. No easy task since Grossmann at present had only two of his regiments. The 37th Regiment had been placed under the command of the 216th Division, still battling along the upper Ssosh against Soviet attacks from the east.

On October 21, under the cover of night, a force of approximately 150 Russians had worked their way forward and taken up a position only 100 meters from the front lines of the 58th Regiment's 1st Battalion. Not the wisest course of action in view of the 58th Regiment's aggressive nature. A second mistake on the part of the Russians was to make their presence an annoyance by initiating sniper activity. The next morning at 10 a.m., Oberleutnant "Ferdi" Küster, acting more like a leutnant than a battalion commander, personally led a Stoßtrupp and rolled up the enemy position, killing 110 Russians and collecting five machine guns, five machine pistols, thirty-four rifles, and two anti-tank rifles as war trophies. Unfortunately, the action had cost the 1st Battalion thirteen dead, but the point had been made. The Russians did not attempt to establish a forward position again.

On the west bank of the Dnieper, the crisis was intensifying as the Soviets continued their push north. Instead of being returned to Grossmann, the 37th Regiment, which had suffered heavy casualties while fighting to the north in the sector of the 216th Division, was rushed west of the Dnieper and immediately hurled into the thick of the fighting. Grossmann worried that he might not ever get his 37th Regiment back, and if he did, would there be any grenadiers left in its ranks?

On November 10, three days after arriving on the west bank, the 37th Regiment was the target of a heavy Soviet assault drumfire, fighter bombers, and waves of infantry with armor support. Could the weakened companies hold the line? On that day, the Kommandeur, Oberst Boje, returned from the hospital to resume command of his regiment and the shout went up among the ranks, "Der Alte ist da!" ("The old man is back.") Although not fully recovered from his wounds, he was ever in the front line, limping about, carbine in hand, directing, encouraging, and fighting. To the old hands, this was a definite sign that wounds had not dampened the Kommandeur's pugnacious nature. To the recent replacements and their inexperienced officers, Boje was both an inspiration and an example of how officers—even regimental Kommandeurs—were expected to conduct themselves in the East. For his actions during those desperate November days, Oberst Boje received the long-deserved Ritterkreuz.

Unfortunately, no amount of encouragement or inspiration could much alter the situation on the ground, which was simply a matter of numbers: the Russians had them; the Germans did not. The Soviet advance up the west bank of the Dnieper continued, and the 6th Grenadier Division on the east bank, being constantly outflanked, was directed time and again to abandon its positions and withdraw northwards.

As the grenadiers retreated north under the grey November sky, they often observed dense Russian columns on the far side of the Dnieper marching in the same directions. Neither side bothered to fire upon one another during this footrace north. Grossmann's 58th Regiment and Reconnaissance Battalion were taken from him and sent off to other crisis points of the front. Were this to continue, soon the general would have little more than his driver and a few loyal motorcycle couriers to defend his position. On November 24, Grossmann was ordered back another 15 km north of the Gomel–Retschiza rail line, and Gomel was lost.

For the next nine days, the division continued its retreat north, now and again lashing out at the pursuing enemy if he ventured too close. The 37th and 58th Regiments were returned to Grossmann, which was, at least, something to ameliorate the misery of retreat. Winter was late in coming, but, rather than something to be dreaded, the frost would have been welcomed as a relief from the heavy cold rains that chilled the body and flooded the miserable Russian roads through which the men slogged.

In the first week of December, the pressure of the Soviet advance eased somewhat, and the German front stabilized. The 6th Grenadier Division was directed to take up new positions, still east of the Dnieper, at a place called Shlobin.

The year 1943, which had begun with the disastrous defeat at Stalingrad, ended even worse for the German armies in the East. The brief respite provided by von Manstein in March and the hope of regaining the initiative had all come to nothing at Kursk. Instead, the German armies had found themselves first attempting to withstand the avalanche of Soviet offensives then desperately seeking to escape being buried by them. Retreat had followed on retreat as the Germans sought for a line that could be held. The Donets, the Mius, the Desna, the Dnieper, all had failed to halt the Soviet attackers. Feldmarschalls may have been able to delude themselves that their retrograde movements had all been well-planned, well-executed withdrawals with tactical or strategic value, but in reality, they had been retreats forced upon them by Soviet successes.

The successes of the revitalized Red Army had been considerable; in six months, the Russians had reclaimed nearly one-half of the territory that had taken the Wehrmacht two years to conquer, advancing at various points along the front from 250–600 km. In the south, the Germans had been driven from the eastern Ukraine, the Crimea had been cut off, the Dnieper had been reached, and in many places, the Soviet forces had established sizeable bridgeheads on the western bank. On the central front, the Red Army had pushed all the way to the Pripet Marshes, retaking the cities of Kharkov, Orel, and Gomel. Smolensk, Brjansk, and Kiev, once the symbols of Germany's greatest victories, had all been returned to the motherland.

Although the blows had been hard and the loss of territory great, the German front had not collapsed. The Wehrmacht had retreated, but it had not been routed. The Germans still maintained a continuous front from the Gulf of Finland to the Black Sea. Nor had there been any great military disasters with entire armies annihilated and hundreds of thousands of German soldiers marching off into captivity. However, the cost of surviving the Soviet offensives had been high—nearly a million casualties since July 5, and these losses had been incurred not by great advances and hard-won victories (which in the military culture can always serve as justification for such sacrifices) but through defeats and retreat.

The scales of war had long since tipped in favor of the Soviet Union. As the mobilization of all its resources continued and the amount of British and American aid increased, Russia would only grow stronger and Germany weaker, as the conveyor belt rolling east with replacements could not keep pace with the trains carrying shattered bodies back to the Reich. If the Wehrmacht had been unable to withstand the Soviet hammer blows of 1943, then how, with even fewer resources, could it possibly survive in 1944?

The common Landser did not concern himself with such matters. He left them to the Führer and his feldmarschalls. As for himself, the Landser had been marched all over Russia, rarely knowing where he was or to where he was going. By this point in the war, advancing or retreating were one and the same to him. One Russian village differed little from the next. A mud-swamped road was no easier to struggle through when pursuing the enemy than when being pursued, and in victory or defeat, a comrade's death was a comrade's death.

In spite of the recent setbacks, the morale of the Ostkämpfer for the most part remained high. The men trusted in the Führer, they trusted in their officers, and, most of all, they trusted in themselves. They knew they could take whatever Ivan hurled at them and always best him in combat—at least, in body counts—and this gave them the confidence to continue the struggle. In December 1943, the "End Sieg" was not in doubt.

Heiligabend 1943: the year was coming to a close. A dreadful year of defeat and retreat, but for now all that could be put from the mind as the 6th Grenadier Division prepared to celebrate Christmas—the fifth of the war, the third in Russia. The division's sector southeast of Slobin was strangely quiet, something to which the grenadiers were unaccustomed. The Christmas packages had arrived from home, as well as the "Führerpäckchen" for those without family. The bunkers were well built and warm, and in each stood a makeshift Weihnachtsbaum crafted of spruce branches and imaginatively decorated with strips of foil, empty shell cases, and stubs of the precious bunker candles. There was no shortage of kuchen, stollen, or alcohol.

The divisional chaplains, Bongards and von Schweppenburg, held their respective services, although among the troops, denominational preferences had long since been submerged by the necessities of the front. The officers made the rounds of the bunkers in their sectors, drinking a toast and sharing a carol or two with the men: first, the company chiefs, then the battalion commanders, and finally the regimental Kommandeur, whose night was the longest as he had to visit each bunker of all of his companies.

The regimental Musikmeisters arranged brass quartets to bring Christmas to those men stuck with watch duty in the frontline trenches. Traditional carols echoed into the night, at first arousing unrest in the enemy trenches nearby until the Russian officers explained to their young men that "Fritz" was not up to anything; the fascists were only celebrating their holiest of holidays.

But 1943 refused to go quietly. Not all the grenadiers were able to partake of the joys of the season: 10 km to the northeast, the Russians had taken advantage of Christmas Eve to break into the German positions at Wyssokije-Maiskij. The 3rd and 10th Companies of von Issendorf's 58th Regiment and the 3rd Squadron of the Reconnaissance Battalion were quickly loaded onto trucks and carried off into the night.

Angered at having been robbed of their Weihnachten, when the grenadiers arrived at Wyssokije, they wasted little time. A quick situational briefing, a quick deployment, and then "Los und hinein!" On the holiest of nights, the air was rent by the crump of hand grenades, the rattle of machine guns, cries, and hoarse shouts of "Hurra!" as the grenadiers unleashed their assault. In the pale light of flares, shadowy figures scurried across the landscape, leaping from hole to hole, from trench to trench—grenade first, then bayonet and spade. Ivan was taken totally by surprise. Were the fascists not supposed to be celebrating tonight? The grenadiers made short work of their enemies.

Christmas Day dawned grey, cold, and quiet. The enemy was gone, either dead or fled, and the grenadiers sat in the reoccupied trenches staring blankly at one another in the adrenalin-drained state of post combat. Their own losses had been light; no one counted the Russian dead. For two days, the grenadiers occupied these positions until, on December 27, they were relieved and transported back to their division. With them they brought their war booty: ten heavy machine guns, twenty light machine guns, and eighty rifles—but no prisoners.

# 14

# Death of a Division

New Year's Day 1944: the 6th Grenadier Division rang in the New Year in the traditional manner. At first light, the whistles of the feldwebels trilled, and every piece of weaponry, from howitzer to carbine, blasted away at the opposing Russian positions, but only briefly. Then for the Landsers in the front line, it was a quick dive into a bunker or dugout in case Ivan chose to return the greeting. This time he did not. Ivan remained quiet the remainder of the day and into the evening, which was good, particularly in the sector of the 58th Regiment where the Kommandeur's birthday was being celebrated. Although he had only commanded the regiment since April 1943, Oberstleutnant Georg von Issendorf was an old "58er." He had been with the regiment since before the war—first, as a young leutnant, then as company and battalion commander, and now as "Vater" of the regiment. Naturally, the celebrations were in style: a concert by the regimental band, an officers' "Umtrunk," and an excuse for the Landsers to break into their iron rations of schnapps.

With the celebrations concluded, the war continued. The sector that the division now held was similar to that which they had held the previous September and October—and just as exposed. Near the juncture of the Berezina and Dnieper Rivers, 50 km northwest of Gomel, lay the Slobin sector of Army Group Center. Although to the south, the Soviet offensives had in most places pushed beyond the Dnieper, from Slobin north some 175 km the German Dnieper Line had held. Not only were the Germans still holding the river line, but 6 km south of Slobin, the German front angled off to the northeast, creating a "bridgehead" on the east bank of the Dnieper. This bridgehead is where the 6th Grenadier Division had been positioned since December 4, with its right flank anchored on the Dnieper and holding a 12-km front that ran northeast to the town of Bobowka.

Having been spared any serious enemy attacks over the past weeks, the men had been able to greatly improve their positions. They no longer struggled through snow-filled trenches but had built substantial, well-heated bunkers, reinforced with wooden logs and lined with birch saplings. To the rear, the division had even established an Erholungsheim, where 100 men at a time could be rotated off the front line for a period of forty-eight hours to relax and refresh themselves with plentiful food and alcohol or enjoy a movie or variety show presented by the division's Kabarett-Trupp, "Die Kuriere aus Rshew." In addition, a regular system of home leave had been established. To the men of the 6th Grenadier Division, the conditions in the Slobin Stellung almost resembled those of a "normal" war rather than the accustomed nightmare of the Eastern Front.

In an effort to boost the morale of the German civilian population, which was suffering under the constant Allied terror-bombings, the Propaganda Ministry arranged whirlwind tours of German cities by groups of soldiers fresh from the front. These hardened and bemedaled "Ostkämpfer" were treated as celebrities as they gave stirring and vivid accounts of their experiences at the front. A "Stoßtrupp" of eighteen men from the division, headed by the Knight's Cross holders Hauptmann Deppe and Leutnant Rompzick of the 18th Regiment, were sent on such a tour to the division's garrison towns throughout Westphalia. They were soon followed by another "Stoßtrupp" from the division's engineer battalion, including, of course Gefreiter Roos, who had destroyed the bridge over the Koma back in August '43. With such men as these in the East, could any civilian have doubted the promised "End Sieg?"

Despite Slobin being a "quiet" sector, there were still the occasional trench raids, harassing fire, and snipers. In the East, death was seldom absent. During the month of December, the 58th Regiment alone had lost thirty-two men killed. One of the drawbacks of occupying a "quiet" sector was that units of the 6th Grenadier Division were often "loaned out" to deal with crises arising in other sectors of the front. The most serious of these was to the southwest, where Soviet forces already well west of the Dnieper were pushing hard north along the Berezina in an attempt to cut off those German forces still east of the Dnieper. (This threat eventually forced the Germans to abandon the Slobin "bridgehead" towards the end of February and withdraw back across the Dnieper.)

In mid-January, von Issendorf's Regiment 58 had been taken from Grossmann and placed in 9th Army Reserve, from which it was rushed from one crisis point to another during the heavy fighting to the southwest: Paritschi, Pruschinitschi, Petrowitschi, and a dozen other unpronounceable Russian villages. Eventually, the Russian drive north was stymied, but by the time that Grossmann got his grenadiers back in early March, there were precious few of them left. Eight officers and 119 men had been killed; twelve officers and 402 men wounded, and ninety-one men missing for a total of 632 officers and men removed from the 58th's ranks or nearly 75 percent of its original strength.

Elsewhere on the Eastern Front, the Soviet offensives had continued unabated throughout the winter of '43–'44, and if the German Front had appeared to be holding in one sector or another, that was only because it had not yet been the target of the Soviet onslaught. With an overall superiority of six to one in manpower and without any fear of German counterstrokes, the Red Army essentially owned the Eastern Front. The Russians could choose when and where to concentrate an overwhelming force, crash through the opposing German front and push their gains as far as was deemed prudent and then reconcentrate their forces in a different sector and repeat their success.

In the north, the Red Army had finally broken the 900-day siege of Leningrad, providing Stalin with yet another morale-boosting victory. The greatest gains, however, had been made south of the Pripet Marshes in the sector of German Army Group South. By spring, the Red Army had crossed the Dniester and had reached the Carpathian Mountains and the borders of Rumania, essentially driving the Wehrmacht (at least, in the south) back to its start line of June 22, 1941.

A year ago, the Führer and his General Staff had been huddled over their maps at the Führer's headquarters in Rastenburg, laying out plans of how the eastern armies could regain the initiative and proceed to final victory. But this was 1944, and, instead of planning what they intended to do to the enemy, they were attempting to divine what the enemy intended to do to them.

They knew that in the West, the long-awaited Anglo-American, cross-Channel invasion was coming soon—most likely in June. Unfortunately, this meant that divisions, so desperately needed in the East, would have to be diverted to France to counter the invasion. Hopes were that after the Anglo-Americans had been repelled, these divisions could be rushed back to the East to deal with any crisis that might have arisen. But until then, the Eastern Front would have to manage on its own.

As for the East, the expectation—or rather, hope—that at some point the Red Army would eventually exhaust itself and be forced to grant the German armies a breathing spell had long since been extinguished as the Soviets had launched offensive after offensive, showing no signs of exhaustion. Without doubt, the offensives would continue. As soon as the spring rains ceased and the earth dried out, Stalin would strike—but where? A single glance at a map of the Eastern Front and the answer appeared obvious—at least, to Hitler.

The Soviet advances in the south, which had greatly outstripped those in the Northern and Central sectors essentially created two Eastern Fronts—one north of the Pripet Marshes and one to the south. This served only to further complicate the German efforts to maintain the front with their ever-shrinking resources. The Front Lines of Army Groups North and Center ran in a generally north–south direction for some 800 km from the Gulf of Finland to the Pripet Marshes, but then at Slobin, the German line bent sharply back to the west for

400 km to link up with Army Group South. Not only did this westward bend give the Germans another 400 km to defend, but it also made Army Group Center highly vulnerable to a flanking attack from the south.

That is how the Führer interpreted the situation. He was certain that Stalin's next great offensive would be a massive attack out of the south into the southern flank of Army Group Center, followed by a bold drive north all the way to the Baltic, thus cutting off both Army Groups Center and North. That is what Hitler would do if he were Stalin. Convinced that the Soviet warlord would opt for such a bold, decisive plan, Hitler ordered that all available forces, especially the panzer divisions be concentrated in the southwest near Kowel to counter the expected Soviet attack. This concentration of forces was leaving the Army Group's commander, Feldmarschall Ernst Busch, with thirty-four divisions, of which only one was a panzer division, to defend a nearly 1,000-km front.

The Soviet post-Kusk offensives had achieved remarkable successes. Vast areas of the Russian homeland had been reclaimed, great cities liberated, and, in the south, the fascists had been all but driven from Russian soil. Although Stalin's marshals had given him great advances, they had not given him a singular great victory with armies annihilated and hundreds of thousands of German prisoners. What Stlain wanted was a crushing victory—he wanted the utter destruction of Army Group Center.

Stalin was not Hitler. He had both the numbers and the materiel and need not risk them in some "bold" operation. The Soviet plan for the destruction of Army Group Center called for a frontal assault across the entire eastern face of the army group's front. It would not be outflanked and cut off; it would be carved up, ground up, and destroyed in place. The date of its destruction was set for June 22—the third anniversary of the German invasion of Russia.

Spring 1944 found the 6th Grenadier Division still occupying those positions along the east bank of the Dnieper to which it had withdrawn at the end of February. Here in the southeast corner of Army Group Center, they were manning a front of nearly 50 km around the city of Slobin. Oberstleutnant Boje's 37th Regiment was deployed north of the city, Höke's 18th Regiment at Slobin itself, and the 58th Regiment to the south. The 58th Regiment was actually positioned at that critical point where Army Group Center's front bent back to the west, thus giving the regiment both an eastern and southern front to defend.

Spared of any serious enemy activity and sensing that their stay at Slobin would be for some time, the men set about improving their fortifications and quarters with little reluctance. The area around Slobin is known for its sandy soil—easy to dig out but near impossible to keep out. Trenches and bunkers constantly needed shoring up to prevent their caving in, but the worst was that the sand got into everything: weapons; water; rations; and, with the constant winds, the men's eyes and throats. Eye drops were issued, and for those on sentry duty sand goggles were the normal attire. Red-rimmed eyes and raspy voices soon became the hallmarks of the "Slobin Kämpfer."

Although the division had not changed its positions, changes had come to the division. In April, Oberstleutnant von Issendorf, the "Vater" of Regiment 58, was separated from the men he had led for a year and from the regiment in which he had served since 1937. He had been recalled to Münster to become the IIa of Wehrkreis VI. With a heavy heart, he took his leave of the officers and men, few of whom he would ever see again. His replacement was Oberst Wodtke, a stranger to the regiment, a stranger to the men.

On May 19, Generalleutnant Horst Grossmann bid a sad and final farewell to the men of the Rhineland-Westphalian 6th Grenadier Division. He was leaving to take over command of the VI Army Corps. Theirs had been a mixed marriage of sorts, an East Prussian leading men from the far western regions of Germany—men from a different culture, indeed, men from almost a different world. But the marriage had been a successful union and this son of the East Prussian soil had grown close to his young Rhinelanders and Westphalians. During the dark days of that first winter, the martyrdom at Rzhev, Kursk, and a dozen other battlefields, they had never failed him nor he them. The Ritterkreuz, which hung around his neck, served as a constant reminder of their courage and sacrifice—a bond between Landser and General. He would not share his grenadiers' fate, and when he took leave of them that May morning, he was fortunate that he, like all men, could not see even a single day into the future.

Replacing him was Generalleutnant Hans-Walter Heyne. Hailing from a wealthy estate-owning family and holder of the Ritterkreuz, the fifty-year-old Heyne was regarded as a highly competent officer and personally brave. (He also held the Infantry Assault Badge, a decoration few generals had the opportunity to win.) However, his last command, the Hessian 82nd Grenadier Division, had been disbanded due to heavy casualties—hardly a record to lift the spirits of troops who had just lost a trusted and respected commander.

Leadership changes were not the only changes coming to the division. New replacements had been arriving throughout the spring, and this most recent wave of conscripts revealed the strain that five years of war had put on the German manpower pool. Some were young and fit; others were not. Many of the unteroffiziere were recycled reservists or pencil-pushers dating back to the Reichsheer, and all too many of them were neither Rhinelanders nor Westphalians.

Gefreiter Reiner Niemann, who had recently returned to the 58th Regiment after a thirteen-month recovery from his second wound, described in a letter home the squad in which he had landed:

> Now I have been here for a week, and I am in a squad with an idiot for an unteroffizier. He has no idea of the situation and the men dance circles around

> him. Consequently there is no cohesion in the group and no comraderie. Each guy sneaks off or shirks his duty whenever he can. One is from Luxembourg and is untrustworthy in all respects and does nothing but complain about everything in his poor crude German. Another is from Austria and is both dull and nervous at the same time. The third is quite young and wants to be an officer candidate and opens up his scandal-mongering East Prussian mouth to anyone who will listen. Then we have a street worker from Thuringia, who has a weak character, and a Rhinelander of the indolent, uninteresting type, who hangs back and is just marking time here. And then there is the unteroffizier, a rather dull representation of the Niederlausitz: tall, blustering, clumsy, and at a total loss. He doesn't understand that nothing is going to get done. And by the way, he is a former Landesschütze (home guard) and that says it all. The company commander certainly had a reason for sticking me in this group, and I have often offered the unteroffizier my opinion in private.[1]

There were a few old hands left as well as those like Gefreiter Niemann, who were returning from the division's convalescent companies, but all too often, out of necessity, these men were scattered about the squads and platoons of replacements to be surrounded by strangers and commanded by strangers. As a result, unit cohesion suffered. It was still the Rhineland-Westphalian 6th Grenadier Division, but among many of the old hands, there was an uneasy feeling that somehow the division just was not the same.

In late spring, 1944, Army Group Center's four armies with thirty-eight divisions and 380,000 men were deployed along a 1,000-km front with Generaloberst Reinhardt's 3rd Panzer Army defending the northern (Witebsk) sector, General von Tippelkirch's 4th Army holding the central (Mogilew) sector, while Generaloberst Jordan's 9th Army was protecting the southeast corner of Army Group Center's front where it bent back towards the west. Covering the remainder of the southern flank was General Weiss's 2nd Army.

With such an extensive front to defend, Feldmarschall Busch was able to hold back only five divisions in reserve. His single panzer division, the Hessian 20th Panzer Division, possessed a mere 100 PzKwIV. For air support the army group had the 6th Air Fleet of Generaloberst Ritter von Greim, but with so many aircraft having been sent west to confront the expected Anglo-American invasion of northern France, the 6th Air Fleet was left with only forty aircraft available for operations.

Along the eastern and southeastern faces of Army Group Center's Front—the primary targets of the coming Soviet offensives—there were but twenty-eight divisions to defend the nearly 700-km front, giving each division on average a 25-km sector to hold. Perhaps earlier in the war, tasking a division of 16,000 men with the defense of a 25-km front might not have been too extreme, but what was a German infantry division now after five years of war?

Although the standard infantry division still maintained the three-regiment structure, after the heavy losses of the first winter most regiments had been forced to disband one of their three battalions. However, the actual reduction in manpower was far greater than one-third due to the shrinkage of the subunits. Squads were now generally five to six men instead of ten. Companies were considered "normal size" when they reached a troop strength of eighty. As a result, battalions with their three rifle companies, plus the heavy machine gun company, consisted of no more than 400 men. Proud regiments that had marched across the Russian border in June 1941 with full regulation strength of 3,000 troops could rarely boast of more than 800 in their ranks—little more than the regiments in the time of Friedrich the Great.

Divisions were still shown as having nine battalions for their combat strength, but these three additional battalions included the divisional engineer battalion, the Füsilier Battalion (which was simply the division's reconnaissance battalion renamed), and the division's own training and replacement battalion—no actual increase in combat troop strength. In 1944, veteran divisions of the Eastern Front, even when including the heavy weapon and support units, seldom numbered more than 8,000 men—a reduction of 50 percent from the original regulation strength of 16,000.

Considering the greatly reduced combat strength of a German division (i.e. the infantry battalions and the 25-km front each division had to hold), this left the ridiculously low number of only 100 defenders per kilometer of front. Such a low troop density could not possibly withstand any serious Soviet attack, but the Führer had assured the men of Army Group Center that they would not be attacked.

The weeks went by, summer approached, and the fields and roads dried out, but the expected Soviet offensive out of the south still had not materialized. The army, corps, and divisional commanders of Army Group Center began to wonder if the Führer had gotten it all wrong. Intelligence reports gathered from aerial reconnaissance, patrols, and prisoner interrogations in their own sectors of the front indicated a frontal attack on Army Group Center itself, most probably in the north near Witebsk and in the south along the Berezina. The commanders voiced their concerns to the Führer but to no avail. They were again assured that they would not be attacked. The Soviet offensive would come out of Galicia to the southwest and Stalin was only waiting until the British and Americans launched their invasion of northern France. Such assurances did little to ease their minds as they watched more of their forces being moved to the southwest and their frontlines become thinner and thinner by the week.

Doubting that the weakened defenses would ever hold if attacked, Army Group Center requested of the Führer permission to construct a second or even a third line of defense upon which to withdraw if the front line failed to hold. The request was denied and even worse, Hitler ordered that the cities of Witebsk,

Slutsk, Mogilew, Orsha, Polots, and Bobruisk be declared "Fortress Cities" (Fester Platz) and defended to the last man. This further weakened the front line as divisions were withdrawn to garrison these "fortresses."

The field commanders of Army Group Center regarded their situation with ever increasing apprehension. They were woefully short of men, artillery, and tanks. They were even short of small arms ammunition for the troops. If the Führer and his staff had gotten it wrong, they would be crushed.

Their concerns were well founded. To gain the great victory that Stalin was demanding, the Red Army had amassed the greatest concentration of force yet achieved in the war. Four Soviet fronts—1st Baltic, 1st Belorussian, 2nd Belorussian, and 3rd Belorussian—with 166 infantry, tank, and cavalry divisions numbering 2.2 million men; 5,000 tanks and armored vehicles; 31,000 artillery pieces and rocket launchers, supported by 6,000 aircraft, gave the Soviets a superiority of six to one in men, twenty to one in tanks, twenty to one in artillery, and 100 to one in aircraft.[2]

To mask the extent and intent of the offensive, Operation Bagration, as it was named, was scheduled by the Soviet planners to commence in stages, beginning in the north with the 1st Baltic Front and, over a period of days, spreading across the entire eastern face of Army Group Center's front. Operation Bagration would not descend upon the German defenders like a clap of thunder but rather more like rolling thunder.

As the summer solstice approached, the uneasiness among the field commanders of Army Group Center grew with each passing day. The ground had long since dried out, the British and Americans had landed in northern France, but still there had been no great Soviet offensive out of Galicia, while in their own sectors there were increasing signs that they would be the target of any Soviet attack. This feeling of uneasiness was pervasive throughout the ranks, from general down to Landser. The general had his sheaves of intelligence reports; the Landser had his bones. One could deduce, the other could feel, that Ivan was definitely up to something big. Repeatedly the corps and divisional commanders voiced their concerns and repeatedly their concerns were dismissed.

Down in the southeast corner of Army Group Center, the 6th Grenadier Division was having similar misgivings concerning the Führer's reassurances. Patrols and prisoner interrogations revealed that the enemy units opposite the division were being replaced by second-class troops, a clear indication that an attack was imminent—not against the division directly but rather north and southwest of it, and if successful, the division would find itself hopelessly trapped in a corner. The division could not have been more correct in its assessment.

The first blows of the Soviet offensive were struck the night of June 19 when the 240,000 partisans operating in the forests and swamps deep in the rear areas of Army Group Center launched 14,000 sabotage attacks of which 10,500 were successful. The primary targets were the bridge, railways, and telephone and telegraph lines. When the Soviet assault began two days later, the German transportation and communication system had already been seriously compromised.

Just before dawn on June 22, the "rolling thunder" of Operation Bagration descended upon Army Group Center as the Soviet 1st Baltic and parts of the 3rd Belorussian Fronts unleased their attacks in the northern sector against Reinhardt's 3rd Panzer Army. Although the Soviet tactics employed during Operation Bagration varied along the front, their attacks were generally preceded by an hours-long artillery barrage of incredible fury upon the German Main Battle Zone, after which the fire would be lifted to the rear areas to neutralize, if not utterly destroy, the supporting German artillery. Then came the waves of tanks followed by the masses of infantry, often spearheaded by special assault companies in which every man brandished a submachine gun. Gone were the days of disjointed, repeated, penny-packet attacks with a company here and a company there. Brute mass force is what the Russian understood best, and now, in the third year of the war, he had learned to organize it and apply it to deadly effect.

The Russian tanks and infantry crashed into the thinly held German defensive belt. Incredibly enough, a few Landsers had somehow survived the maelstrom of rocket and artillery fire and in places offered stiff resistance, but not for long. The German lines were rolled over and rolled through, and within twenty-four hours the "Fortress City" of Witebsk had been surrounded and bypassed with its three-division garrison trapped within. The Russian armored columns rushed on by. They had no interest in taking the city. Witebsk would fall soon enough. For the moment, the Russians were only interested in pushing as far west as quickly as possible.

June 23: the second phase of Operation Bagration was launched as the five armies of the 2nd Belorussian Front assaulted the central sector between Orscha and Mogilew, held by General von Tippelkirch's 4th Army. The results were the same as in the northern sector with the thin German defenses being pierced at numerous points along the front. Some German units that had been bypassed were still holding out, but, overall, the 4th Army's front was leaking like a sieve with Russian tanks and infantry pouring through to the west.

Von Tippeskirch threw in one of the few divisions he held in reserve, the West Prussian "Feldherrnhalle" Panzer Grenadier division. When its commander, Generalmajor von Steinkeller, arrived at the headquarters of the XXXIX Army Corps in Mogilew and announced that he had been directed to plug the hole in the German line, the commander of the XXXIX Corps, General Martinek asked, "Just what hole are you to plug? We've got nothing but holes here."

"Nothing but holes," an accurate description of Army Group Center's front after only two days of Soviet attacks. But still the Führer's headquarters insisted that the main Soviet offensive would come out of Galicia. Hitler maintained that the attacks so far on Army Group Center's eastern face were only diversionary attacks.

Twenty-four hours later, reality crashed down upon the Führer's headquarters when the third phase of Operation Bagration was unleashed against the German 9th Army holding the southeast corner of Army Group Center's front. On June 24, Marshal Rokossovsky's 1st Belorussian Front launched a two-pronged attack: one prong against the 9th Army's northern flank near Rogatschew, pushing due west to Bobruisk, and the other prong against the 9th Army's southern flank, driving hard north up the west bank of the Berezina to Bobruisk. This is what the 9th Army had suspected and feared. If the Soviets succeeded in reaching Bobruisk, General Jordan's entire 9th Army would be trapped.

At the Führer's headquarters in Rastenburg, 500 km to the west, staff officers stared in stunned disbelief at the maps and the potential catastrophe unfolding before their eyes. How could they have been so wrong? They had been caught completely wrong-footed. However, once Hitler and his staff had recovered from their shock, frantic demands and directives were sent out to Feldmarschall Busch's headquarters in Minsk—demands and directives that were no longer relevant to the rapidly deteriorating situation of Army Group Center. Likewise, Busch's headquarters sent out orders to the army and divisional commanders, who could only scratch their heads in befuddlement at directives that sent them first here, then there, and betrayed a total ignorance of the local situation.

In the first few days of the Soviet offensive, command and control within Army Group Center had broken down under the weight and rapidity of the Soviet advance. The Red Army of the summer of 1944 was an entirely new beast. The slow advances of the previous offensives, which had proceeded at the ponderous pace of a dinosaur and all too often had allowed the Germans to either counterattack or escape, were a thing of the past. Soviet attacks now were well coordinated and strongly supported by both artillery and air power. Field commanders at both the higher and lower levels no longer hesitated for fear of making a mistake, but, with a new sense of confidence, surged forward to seize any available advantage. This time, the Soviet attacks did not stall or lose momentum. As a result of the massive supply of trucks and other motor vehicles from the United States, the Red Army of 1944 was considerably more mobile than the once swift-striking Wehrmacht, which still relied to a great extent on horse-drawn transport.

Within a week, the fate of Army Group Center and its 380,000 men had been sealed. The front had collapsed under the tidal wave of tanks, men, artillery, and aircraft. The "Fortress Cities" of Witebsk, Orscha, and Mogilew had been surrounded, their garrisons trapped within while powerful Soviet armored columns raced on ever westwards toward the Berezina, leaving behind German divisions trapped in pockets with no other choice but to surrender or attempt to fight their way out. The stage was set for Stalin's great victory—the total destruction of Army Group Center. All that remained was for the tragedy to play itself out.

The final ghastly acts of this play were enacted upon a stage created in hell. Small groups of dazed survivors from the original front line sought desperately to find their way back to whatever remained of their units. The trapped garrisons of the "Fortress Cities" mounted breakout attempts, most of which failed or, if initially successful, resulted in the troops being caught in the open, surrounded by the enemy and annihilated. Pounded continuously by artillery and hounded by ceaseless air attacks, remnants of divisions and columns of *ad hoc* formations of the scattered survivors of battered regiments struggled along the dust-choked, heat-baked roads, littered with abandoned burning vehicles and the corpses of horses and men. All were seeking a way out, trying somehow to reach the new German front line that seemed to recede ever further to the west.

Often when these desperate fugitives approached a position where they hoped to make a stand, they found the Russians already there, well entrenched and blocking their escape. With grim determination, they would raise a shout of "Hurra!" and storm through the enemy line only to discover another enemy barrier further on. Time and again these exhausted survivors raised a shout and fought their way through—until there was no one left to shout "Hurra!"

The Rhineland-Westphalian 6th Grenadier Division soon found itself caught up in this unfolding military disaster. When Operation Bagration rolled down to the 9th Army's front on June 24, the division was still deployed in the Slobin sector, defending perhaps the longest front of any division—50 km. They were not the direct target of the Soviet attack. As the divisional intelligence staff had predicted, the Soviet assaults were to the north at Rogatschew and to the southwest beyond the Berezina.

Twelve hours into the attack, Generalleutnant Heyne lost one of his regiments. On the evening of June 24, the 58th Regiment, now commanded by Major Stampe from the 37th Regiment, was loaded on to trucks and, along with the division's Füsilier Battalion, rushed north to Rogatschew to help shore up the front of the Franconian 296th Grenadier Division. The next morning when Major Stampe arrived at the headquarters of the 296th Division at Koschary, he discovered the staff already destroying the division's records, and was informed that there was no longer a front left for him to shore up. The 58th Regiment was directed to take up a position along the Dobriza River, 5 km to the west, and prepare to receive the retreating remnants of the 296th Division.

When the regiment reached the Dobriza, it found the Russians already entrenched. Without hesitation, the grenadiers launched an assault and quickly drove the enemy out and took over the position. Unfortunately, they were unable to establish contact with the Franconian 134th Grenadier Division, which should have been immediately north of them. Throughout the afternoon the grenadiers of the 58th Regiment watched from their trenches as in the distance the Russians massed their infantry and tanks for an attack.

When the attack came, in early evening, the machine gunners hammered away at the charging Russian infantry while the panzerjägers of the 14th Company and the three Sturmgeschütze operating with the regiment took on the Soviet armor. After two hours and heavy losses, the Russians ceased the attack. Ten T-34s sat smoldering or burning along the banks of the Dobriza. At last, a German line had held fast, but not for long. Taken aback by the unexpected resistance, the Russians began sliding their forces around the grenadiers open left (northern) flank. With the position now compromised, the 58th Regiment was ordered at 11 p.m. to withdraw 10 km west to take up a new position along the Dobyssa River near Parchimkowskaya. After a night march, the regiment reached the Dobyssa near daybreak, but again was unable to establish contact with the 134th Division (for good reason, the Franconian 134th Grenadier Division no longer existed). During the course of the day, the regiment fought off numerous Russian attacks.

The situation was rapidly deteriorating 25 km to the southeast, where the rest of the 6th Grenadier Division was still holding the Slobin sector. Although the division had received no more than light artillery fire, to the north and southwest, the enemy had broken through the German defenses and was threatening to cut off the 6th Grenadier Division—indeed, the entire 9th Army—from the rest of Army Group Center. To avoid entrapment, the division began withdrawing to the northwest on the night of June 25. The next morning, the 37th Regiment became embroiled in heavy combat. During an attempt to retake a village, the regiment's Komandeur, Knight's Cross-holder Oberst Johannes Boje, was killed, shot in the head while leading the attack. The regiment suffered heavy casualties Major von Ribbeck of the divisional staff took over command of the 37th Regiment. He was killed in action the following day.

The 6th Grenadier Division continued its withdrawal to the northwest joined by the scattered remnants of other divisions, all seeking to reach the "Fortress" of Bobruisk on the Berezina before the enveloping jaws of the Soviet offensive snapped shut. Punished by constant air attacks against which they had no protection (the forty aircraft of von Greim's 6th Air Fleet had long since been driven from the skies), the German columns struggled west. They forced their way through one Russian blocking position after another, but it was all for nothing. Unknown to them at the time, Soviet units had rushed ahead and had already taken Titowka, which sat astride the Rogatschew–Bobruisk highway effectively blocking their way to Brobruisk. On June 27, the 6th Grenadier Division reached the Ola River.

Meanwhile, 10 km to the north, the 58th Regiment along the Dobyssa again found itself outflanked. After nightfall on June 26, the grenadiers were ordered to withdraw another 10 km west and entrench themselves along the Ola. When they reached the river early the next morning, they discovered that the Russians had beaten them there. This time the exhausted grenadiers (most had not slept in three days) were unable to dislodge the enemy and were forced to take up an all-around defensive position with an entrenched enemy before them and an enemy rapidly closing in on them from the rear.

At 3 p.m. on June 27, the German divisions of the 9th Army withdrawing west suddenly received puzzling orders: they were to break into the "Fortress" of Bobruisk, unite with the 20th Panzer Division, and organize a further breakout to the west. All heavy equipment was to be destroyed, and the men were to take only their personal weapons—"nur mit dem Karabiner in der Hand." Staff officers exchanged worried glances. Destroy equipment? Break in? Break out? What could all this possibly mean?

These puzzling orders meant that there was no longer any German front east of the Berezina. The Russian jaws had snapped shut west of Bobruisk, and the remnants of the 9th Army were trapped in a pocket east of the city.

The 58th Regiment, operating north of the Rogatschew–Bobruisk highway, had received the same communication. With the way forward blocked and the highway under constant heavy artillery fire, the regiment chose not to attempt to rejoin its division to the south but to swing to the northwest and break out on its own across the Berezina north of Bobruisk. After destroying the heavy equipment, the grenadiers skirted the northern flank of the Russian blocking force, swam across the stream at Leitischi, and reassembled near the village of Dolgorskoye. Here, they awaited the hour of attack. Chaos surrounded them—artillery fire, air attacks, soldiers stumbling about trying to find their units. At 11 p.m., Major Stampe and the grenadiers of the 58th Regiment gathered up their personal equipment and "mit dem Karabiner in der Hand" went forward. It would be their Todesritt—their death ride.

They fought their way past Chimy, crossed the Mogilew–Bobruisk highway near Welitschi, waded through a broad swamp in pitch darkness, and in the morning overran Russian positions along the edge of the forest just south of Morchowitschi. Their goal was to reach the town of Bazewitschi, reportedly still in German hands. (The Russians had already taken the town.) West of Lyubenitschi they came against an enemy position again entrenched along a forest edge. Without waiting for orders, the grenadiers raised a shout of "Hurra!" and stormed forward. They were desperate men, determined to fight their way free. Often in hand-to-hand combat, they smashed through one enemy position after another, but 2 km south of Ssergewitschi, the Russians had established a blocking position that was simply too strong to overcome. It no longer mattered, for by then the 58th Regiment of Grenadiers had ceased to exist as a unit.

South of the Rogatschew–Bobruisk highway, the remaining two regiments of the 6th Grenadier Division set off on their death ride. Documents were burned, equipment destroyed, horses shot. Generalleutnant Heyne conferred with his officers. Like the 58th Regiment, they agreed that a breakout to the northwest was the wiser course of action rather than attempting to break in to Bobruisk. Why exchange one trap for another?

At 11 p.m. on June 27, the division set out into the darkness. The men were able to slip across the Rogatschew–Bobruisk highway undetected and pushed towards the northwest. Throughout the night and all the next day, they fought their way through enemy positions, through forest, swamp, and open fields, all the while taking heavy casualties from artillery, tank, and machine-gun fire that constantly rained down on them from the surrounding heights. Their ranks became thinner and thinner with each kilometer. Oberst Höke, Kommandeur of the 18th Regiment, and Hauptmann Giesel of the engineer battalion were badly wounded. They were carried by loyal hands into a hut for shelter—but what was shelter on this hell ride? An artillery shell soon crashed into the hut, killing them both. During his last visit home in January 1944, "Steppan" Höke had prophetically remarked to his wife: "When the next Christmas rose blooms, I will be no more."[3]

The wounded had been loaded onto carts, but when they crossed over a swamp, the carts sank, and the wounded drowned. Division Surgeon Dr. Lorenz had little time to lament their fate for soon afterwards a shell splinter tore away his lower jaw, and he quickly ended his suffering with a pistol shot to the temple. Staff Surgeon Dr. Schulz did likewise after being wounded in the stomach.

Evening, June 28: as the battered columns approached Baronowitschi, Generalleutnant Heyne organized the survivors for one last breakout attempt, but before the attack could even get started, the Russians struck, tearing great gaps in the ranks of the assembled grenadiers with artillery, mortar, and tank fire. Despite the rain of fire, the grenadiers raised a hoarse shout of "Hurra!" and went forward. In the maze of woods and swamps, units became separated, then rejoined, only to become separated again. Confused and fierce fighting raged throughout the night, but by dawn on 29 June, the Rhineland-Westphalian 6th Grenadier Division had ceased to exist.

The tragedy had played itself out, but the nightmare was just beginning.

As the 6th Grenadier Davison ceased to exist as an organized unit, Army Group Center ceased to exist as an army group. Command and control had broken down entirely. Soviet armored forces had rushed forward, carving up the German front and leaving remnants of German divisions trapped in pockets within which they marched aimlessly about, directed first in one direction and then in another until they eventually ignored higher commands and took it upon themselves to fight their own way out. At this stage of the battle, German military histories often refer to the trapped units as Kampfgruppen—"Kampfgruppe Heyne," "Kampfgruppe Ohms," "Kampfgruppe Windmann," etc. They were nothing of the sort. Kampfgruppen were typically a force tasked with a specific mission. These so-called "Kampfgruppen" of Army Group Center were nothing more than bands of desperate fugitives from scattered units, led by officers whom no one knew and who themselves had no real idea as to where they were leading these fugitive bands. The men were short of food and water, and although most of them had retained their personal weapons, they were dangerously low on ammunition.

Now entered the horror of the "Cauldron of Bobruisk" as the Red Army extracted retribution from the fascist invaders. Confident and secure in his victory, the Soviet soldier was less than magnanimous to his defeated opponent. German wounded, whether found lying on the roads or in field hospitals, were either immediately shot or had their heads bashed in with spade or rifle butt. When the Russians took Bobruisk on June 29, a group of men armed with machine pistols entered the citadel where 700 non-transportable German wounded lay and went from bed to bed, riddling their helpless victims with bullets—nor did the hospital staff fare any better.[4]

German soldiers foolish enough to think that they could surrender to Ivan were generally executed on the spot. Only if there were too many captives (over 200) to dispatch quickly without too much fuss did the Russians take prisoners. In the forests and swamps, bands of partisans hunted down the fugitives like animals and killed them like animals. The fortunate ones were killed outright in combat. Those taken prisoner were often tortured to death in the most bestial manner possible. The partisans had their own version of the "Genickschuss," an empty shell casing hammered into the base of the skull. German soldiers could no longer rely on the aid of the civilian population. With the Germanski obviously defeated and retreating, and the "Red Wolves" returning with their commissars, local villagers quickly betrayed Germans seeking to hide nearby.

One of the many fugitive bands attempting to escape the "Cauldron of Bobruisk" was that of Leutnant Erley of the 18th Regiment. Left behind on the Dnieper the night of June 25 as rearguard when the rest of the regiment began its withddrawal west, he spent the next two days trying to catch up to his regiment. His rearguard unit consisted of a platoon of engineers, a platoon of Reiters (dismounted), and several grenadiers from the 3rd Battalion. Their numbers had been reduced, by constant collisions with the enemy, to a mere twenty men.

Along a forest path they came across the first sign of their regiment, an abandoned "Gulaschkanone" or company cooker. Its vats were still filled with army stew, but Erley and his comrades deemed it inedible. However, they were able to find some bread to fill their empty stomachs. Further on in a forest clearing, they found their regiment—destroyed vehicles, dead horses, dead comrades. They concluded that there was no longer a regiment left to find and that they were entirely on their own. Quickly Erley's men provisioned themselves with food, ammunition, and as many machine pistols as they could, and then plunged deeper into the forest, which was flooded in many places.

Finding refuge on a ridge, they caught the first sleep they had had in days. Beyond the forest they could hear the constant rumble of tanks and other vehicles as the Russian columns continued pushing west. Now there was no doubt; they were cut off. Leutnant Erley explained the situation to the men. If any one of them wished to attempt to make it out on his own, he was free to do so. Unsurprisingly, the men chose to remain together. The leutnant had gotten them this far; he would get them out.

That night they sloshed their way through the swampy woods and reached the forest edge just before dawn. Before them stretched a broad cornfield bisected by a road and beyond it another patch of woods. They decided to risk crossing the cornfield before it grew too light and hide out in the distant woods the remainder of the day. They did not succeed. They were halfway through the cornfield when a Russian truck convoy suddenly appeared on the road. Erley and his men fled deeper into the cornfield and took cover. They lay there, not making a sound, hardly daring to breathe. Had they been spotted? Unfortunately, they had.

Then came the rattle of equipment and loud commands as the Russians dismounted the trucks and plunged into the cornfield. Erley and his men had no intention of surrendering. When the enemy got close, Erley's small band opened fire. For several hours, they succeeded in keeping the Russians at bay, but then they ran out of ammunition. Unteroffizier Christof-Liemke pulled out his pistol. He had saved a last round for himself, but he did not get to use it. Suddenly the Russians leapt upon them. Erley was grabbed from behind and his empty machine pistol wrenched from his hands. He and the few survivors of his group were now prisoners. As they stood on the road, their captors relieved them of their watches, wallets, rings, and canteens. Being an officer, Leutnant Erley was separated from his men. He never saw his comrades again.

A few, but only a few, were more successful in their attempts to escape the "Cauldron of Bobruisk." These were the "Rückkämpfer," those who fought their way back to German lines. After the dissolution of the 58th Regiment on the night of June 27, Gefreiter Reiner Niemann of the 10th Company found himself wandering about in the fields and woods joining first one group of fugitives then another until, by chance, he linked up with a "Kampfgruppe" led by his own battalion commander, Hauptmann Kurt Ohms. This *ad hoc* unit struggled northwards through the forests and swamps, often wading through brackish water a meter deep and constantly fighting off Russian troops and partisans. On the night of June 28, "Kampfgruppe Ohms" reached the Berezina near Sswisslotsch, north of Bobruisk, where the men attempted a night crossing, but in the confusion of the darkness gave up the attempt.

The next morning, they observed that to the southwest, the Russians were preoccupied with a German effort to break out of Bobruisk and decided to risk a crossing in broad daylight. They succeeded only to discover that they had exchanged one cauldron for another. Surrounded, they again fought their way free, but by now their number had been greatly diminished. On the evening of June 30, the remnants of "Kampfgruppe Ohms" were suddenly confronted by tanks, but this time—Gott sei dank—they were the tanks of the Pomeranian 12th Panzer Division. The exhausted survivors climbed aboard the tanks and were transported to Rudensk, where they were quickly loaded onto a train and whisked away to the West. Not all the members of the "Kampfgruppe" were as fortunate. Its commander, Hauptmann Kurt Ohms and Hauptmann Jan Haverkamp were killed when they were trapped by the enemy just west of the Berezina on July 3.

Nor did the division commander escape the cauldron. As Generalleutnant Heyne and his IC, Oberleutnant Ahrens, accompanied by a single gefreiter, slipped along the east bank of the Olsa, seeking a way across, they were surprised by a group of Russian soldiers and taken prisoner. Later during interrogation, Oberleutnant Ahrens was asked by the Russian division commander if he belonged to the "Shestoia Divisia." Ahrens nodded and the Russian remarked, "A good and brave division—we have known you a long time."

As the survivors of this "good and brave division" found their way back to German lines, they were quickly loaded onto trains and rushed away to the West. There seemed to be an attempt to prevent these battered and ragged fugitives from being seen by new German units recently arrived to shore up the front. Their appearance would hardly have been a morale booster.

The 6th Grenadier Division had not been decimated; it had been destroyed. The division's commander was now a prisoner of the Russians, and 90 percent of the men had been killed, wounded, or were missing. As the train carrying the few survivors sped west, a clerk at the OKH Headquarters in Berlin quietly and unceremoniously removed the division from the Wehrmacht's Order of Battle. The Rhineland-Westphalian 6th Grenadier Division—the division that had swept across France, advanced beyond the Volga, this division of "Rshewkämpfer"—was no more.

The Red Army had given Stalin his great victory. An entire German Army Group had been destroyed. Three armies and twenty-eight divisions had been smashed. Over 130,000 German soldiers lay dead among the forests, swamps, and cornfields. Another 170,000 had been wounded or were being marched off to the gulags in Siberia.[5] Ten German generals had been killed or had committed suicide, twenty-one taken prisoner, and the fascist invaders at long last had been driven from the soil of the motherland—and that had only been the beginning. With the central front torn wide open, the Soviet armies continued their drive west.

A state of disbelief reigned over the Führer's Headquarters in Rastenburg. How could this disaster have happened, and so quickly? Feldmarschall Busch was promptly dismissed and forces that had been wrongly placed in Galicia were now rushed north to stabilize the front. Feldmarschall Model was brought in to stabilize the situation, but there were limits to what even the "Führer's Fireman" could accomplish.

Despite Model's efforts, the Soviet advance rolled on. Minsk, the capital of Belorussia, fell on July 3, Baranowitschi was taken by Soviet forces on July 8, and by the end of the month, the Red Army had driven on past Brest-Litovsk and had reached the Vistula in central Poland. Operation Bagration had not only given Stalin a great victory but also an astonishing advance of 700 km. If the German central front appeared to have stabilized at the beginning of August, it was only because the Russians felt that they had achieved quite enough in the center and had turned their attention to the Baltic in the north and the Balkans in the south.

In the summer of 1944, Germany had suffered its greatest defeat yet in the war—far greater than Stalingrad. Stalingrad had cost the Wehrmacht but one army, and afterwards Germany had briefly recovered. After the summer of 1944, there would be no recovery.

# 15

# Resurrection and the Warka

The train carrying the survivors of the 6th Grenadier Division rolled across northern Germany, but it did not take them back to their home bases in Münster or Osnabrück. Instead, they were dropped off at the military training grounds of Sennelager near Paderborn, where they could be better watched and, as if in quarantine, kept separate from other units and particularly from the civilian population. As with other survivors and "Rückkämpfer" of the catastrophe, the few grenadiers on hand were sternly instructed not to discuss what had happened with any other member of the military nor mention the matter to their families. There was yet an effort on the part of the political and military leadership to conceal from the German people the disaster that had befallen the Eastern Front. Soon enough the Geheime Feldpolizei (Military Security Police) descended upon the survivors to debrief them. However, these debriefings had less to do with an attempt to understand why the battle had gone so badly than with an effort to assess and attribute blame.

When the last survivors of the 6th Grenadier division arrived at Sennelager, the division conducted its own assessment, and the results were devastating. The division's commander, Generalleutnant Heyne, was reportedly a prisoner of the Russians. Two regimental Kommandeure, Boje of the 37th and Höke of the 18th, were known to have been killed. No one seemed to know what had become of the 58th Regiment's Kommandeur, Major Stampe. Three other officers of the 58th Regiment, Leutnant Lohmann and Hauptmanns Ohms and Haverkamp, had fallen in battle while another fifteen officers were listed as missing. Of the 1,000 officers and men who had been loaded onto trucks on the night of June 24 and rushed north to Rogatschew, a mere sixty now answered roll call. A total 826 were classified as missing; the other 114 were either known to be dead or in a hospital bed. As for the 18th Regiment, the estimate was that over 400 had been killed in action and an equal number wounded or missing. No longer with the regiment were the two battalion commanders, Denecke and "Onkel Otto" Hellweg, as well as the regimental adjutant, Knight's Cross holder Oberleutnant Johannes Rompzick—whether dead or captured, no one could say. Likewise, the fate of the divisonal chaplain, Freiherr Geyr von Schweppenburg, remained unknown. He was last seen comforting the wounded in Bobruisk. The 37th Regiment had suffered equally as heavy losses as the other two regiments. Of the nearly 8,000 men of the 6th Grenadier Division who had gone into battle on June 24, only 600 had returned to Germany. The question now was what to do with them.

The idea of disbanding the 6th Grenadier Division did not sit well with the military aristocrats. The division was one of the original divisions of the Wehrmacht, and its three regiments were the proud tradition-bearers of historic Prussian regiments. The 18th Regiment dated back to the Reichsheer, and what was more, its titular Kommandeur was none other than Feldmarschall von Rundstedt. Simply writing the Rhineland-Westphalian 6th Grenadier Division out of existence, removing it from the ranks of the Prussian-German Army, was out of the question. The division would have to be resurrected from the grave.

Added to the 600 survivors of Bobruisk were 500 members of the division who had not been with the division during the battle. They had been on leave, detailed off for other duties, or were presently in the division's training or convalescent companies. These 1,100 men would serve as the core of the resurrected division. But where to find the rest of the personnel to fill out the ranks in a manpower-strapped Germany?

From the most recent conscription wave—the twenty-ninth of the war—the Wehrmacht intended to create fifteen to twenty new infantry divisions and eight to ten panzer brigades. One of the new divisions, the 552nd Division was allotted to Wehrkreis VI in Münster, where the decision was made to incorporate the remaining 1,100 men of the old 6th Grenadier Division into it. Although the Wehrmacht Personnel Office intended to designate this new division as a Volksgrenadier division, Wehrkreis VI would hear none of that, pointing out that the division still retained the three-regiment structure rather than the two-regiment structure of the Volksgrenadier-type divisions. Wehrkreis VI prevailed in its argument and so the division would return to the front in the same fashion it had left: the Rhineland-Westphalian 6th Grenadier Division.

The division's new commander was forty-five-year-old Oberst Otto-Hermann Brücker, a stranger to the division and a Brandenburger. With his black-rimmed, civilian-style glasses and his thoughtful unassuming demeanor, he gave more an impression of a high school principal or an accountant than that of a stereotypic Prussian officer. Despite his appearance, he was known to be a competent and brave professional. Born in Berlin in 1899, he had first gone to war as a young officer cadet in the summer of 1918. After the armistice, he had not laid down his arms but chose instead to join in with the Freikorps to battle communists and other revolutionary elements within the Reich. Showing both promise and the correct spirit, he was selected to remain in the Reichsheer and pursue a military career.

In the present conflict, he had for the most part held upper-level staff positions among various army corps. In Poland, he had been awarded the Iron Cross 2nd Class and, in the French campaign, the Iron Cross 1st Class. However, being a staff officer in the German Army, even at corps level, did not shield one from danger. In the early months of Barbarossa, Brücker was wounded but recovered in time to suffer through that first brutal Russian Winter. In May 1942, he was promoted to Oberst, but not until early 1944 did he receive what all staff officers desire: a field command, first as Kommandeur of Infantry Regiment 419 and then as deputy commander of the Franconian 17th Grenadier Division.

Originally appointed to command the newly raised 552nd Volksgrenadier Division, Oberst Otto-Hermann Brücker now found himself leading one of the oldest and most famous divisions of the entire Wehrmacht. This Brandenburger would lead his Rhinelanders and Westphalians back to the Front, and he would lead them to the last day of the war.

In view of the fact that the officer cadre of the old 6th Grenadier Division had been practically wiped out at Bobruisk, division commander was not the only leadership position that needed to be filled. Regimental, battalion, and other sub-unit commanders remained yet to be found. With Oberst von Issendorf, the former Kommandeur of Regiment 58, now heading the Personnel Office of Wehrkreis VI, the new division could rest assured that it would receive the best quality of personnel available at the time.

Oberst Graf took over the 18th Regiment with Hauptmanns Küster and Thiessen as his two battalion commanders. Oberstleutnant Lütkehaus received the 37th Regiment and Hauptmanns Winter and Michahelles to lead its two battalions. Oberstleutnant Müller commanded the 58th Regiment. His battalion commanders were Hauptmanns Wittenbecher and Volkmer. Hauptmann Dregger now headed the Füsilier Battalion while Hauptmann Erpenbach took charge of the division's Training and Replacement Battalion.

With the important leadership positions filled, the time had come for Oberst Brücker to train his new division. Aware that the majority of the men were either experienced soldiers or had been transferred from the Luftwaffe or Kriegsmarine, he correctly assumed that all had received basic standard infantry training and were accustomed to military life—in other words, they were not raw recruits to test the patience and vocal cords of the drill instructors. Spit-and-polish parade ground drill and discipline could be dispensed with, which was fortunate because at any time the precarious war situation could require the division's immediate return to the front.

Brücker did not know how much time he would have to train his troops, but he suspected the period would be short. A veteran of both peace and wartime training, he was aware of some of the problems inherent in the Wehrmacht's training system. Although thorough and comprehensive, it was rigidly carried out one step at a time, beginning with individual training, weapons instruction, and marksmanship, followed by unit exercises. These exercises commenced at the squad level and proceeded in steps through platoon, company, battalion, and regimental levels, culminating in the divisional maneuver. Unfortunately, by the time the troops had completed the divisional exercise, they could well use a refresher course on the earlier phases of their training. In addition to being time consuming, this lengthy process often resulted in troops going to the front who had not fired their weapons in weeks and to whom marksmanship and basic squad tactics were but distant memories.

Well-known for his organizational talents, Oberst Brücker immediately drew up a practical, no-frills combat-oriented training regimen in which one half of each day would be spent in weapons training and practice and the other half devoted to unit exercises. Brücker was adamant that not only were the men to fire their weapons each day but also that each man be proficient with all infantry weapons: pistol, rifle, machine pistol, light machine gun, hand grenade, and the recently issued panzerfaust. His insistence on the daily firing of weapons was based on his appreciation of the repetitive Prussia firing drill in the days of Friedrich the Great. The use of a firearm under combat conditions must be a reflexive, not a deliberate act. Nor were Brücker's firing exercises to take place under the carefully controlled conditions of the firing range but under combat-like conditions—regardless of the safety risks involved.

As for the unit exercises, they would begin the afternoon of day one with squads and platoons and, in the course of three days, proceed through company, battalion, and regimental levels. From the company level up, the exercises would take place in conjunction with artillery, engineers, and Sturmgeschützen. On the evening of the third day, there would be a night maneuver, and the next morning the three-day program would begin again. Brücker realized that his training regimen was demanding of the troops, but the men voiced no objections. Soldiers only complain when they see no purpose in what is asked of them. In Oberst Brücker's training program, the purpose could not have been more clear—effectiveness and survival in combat.

As demanding as the new division commander was, he did not neglect the men's morale. For some of the survivors of Bobruisk, home leaves were granted. Brücker judged that they could be spared the rigorous training—what more could they be taught of war? For the other men of the division, particularly those married with families, he arranged weekend passes for their families to visit them at the camp, providing both transportation from the train station as well as overnight accommodations in an unused barrack located in the older section of Sennelager. For all too many of the men, this would be the last time that they saw their loved ones.

Oberst Brücker had been correct in sensing that the stay at Sennelager would be of short duration. On August 15, the resurrected Rhineland-Westphalian 6th Grenadier Division was ordered back to the front.

In the East, in the West, and even in the air, the summer of 1944 had been a disaster for Germany. After maintaining a stubborn defense for two months against the Anglo-American invasion force in Normandy, the German front in the West collapsed, and the Allied forces began their race across France, reaching the borders of the Reich in early September. Even though the Germans had inflicted heavy losses on the Western Allies, their own losses had been almost as heavy. Over 200,000 men (killed, wounded, and missing) had been removed from the ranks of the Wehrmacht. Added to the 300,000 lost in the East, these were losses that the ever-shrinking Wehrmacht could neither afford nor replace. Tasked with defending the cities and industries of the Reich as well as providing support for German ground forces in East and West, the once dominant Luftwaffe had likewise suffered heavy losses in men and machines and by September had essentially disappeared from the skies.

Not only had Germany lost hundreds of thousands of men and vast tracts of territory, it had lost allies as well. Italy had dropped out of the war the previous year and had joined the Western Allies. As the Red Army approached the borders of Romania and Bulgaria, both countries quickly arranged an armistice and deserted the German cause. In September, Stalin's old enemy, the Finns, were forced to sign an armistice and turn their weapons against their former German comrades-in-arms. Even erstwhile Hungary had engaged in secret negotiations with Stalin, seeking a way out of the war. Only by applying great pressure (and kidnapping the Regent Admiral Horthy's son) was Germany able to persuade Hungary to remain loyal.

Perhaps the most shocking act of disloyalty—as it was perceived at the time—was the attempt in July by a cabal of army officers to assassinate the Führer. These officers had taken to heart Feldmarschall von Rundstedt's advice to the German General Staff shortly after the Allies had landed in Normandy: "Make peace, you fools." They believed that by removing Hitler from power, Germany would somehow be spared from total destruction. But the Führer had survived; the "traitors" were executed and the war continued though now Hitler hated and distrusted the military aristocrats even more than before.

With military disasters in the East and West, disloyalty abroad, and treason at home, a wave of panic swept through the political structure of the Reich in the late summer of 1944. There was first talk of evacuating the cities of the Rhineland, then of surrounding them with trenches and tank traps and defending them to the last man. Propaganda Minister Dr. Goebbels continued his rant of "Total War," and in the spirit of 1813 ("Ein Volk steh'auf und Sturm bräch' los!"), the Volkssturm or people's militia was created. Every male between the ages of sixteen and sixty-five not already in service was called to arms.

However, by mid-September, the fronts in east and west appeared to have stabilized as the opposing armies, exhausted by the summer battles, caught their breath. The enemy may have reached the borders of the Reich, but there he had been stopped. The panic subsided and was replaced by a grim determination and faith in the Führer and his armies.

Six weeks after being destroyed in the cauldron of Bobruisk, the Rhineland-Westphalian 6th Grenadier Division returned to the front. The front was no longer in Russia but now lay in central Poland along the Vistula River. Between August 15 and 20, units of the division began arriving at a place called Warka. Some of the veterans, the old "Ostkämpfer" did not fail to notice that the "trip East" now took but a few days instead of weeks.

During the summer offensive, the Red Army had not only reached the Vistula but also had forced a crossing and established bridgeheads in places on the western bank. The largest of these was at Baranow, 150 km south of Warsaw. A further 80 km north was a smaller bridgehead at Pulawy, and the northernmost bridgehead lay at Warka, 50 km south of Warsaw. In the first half of August, heavy fighting had erupted around Warka as the Soviets attempted to enlarge their bridgehead. They succeeded in taking the village of Glowaczow and pushed beyond the Glowaczow–Warka road, but a counterattack by the Lower Saxon 19th Panzer Division and elements of the "Hermann Goering" Panzer Division threw the Russians back and re-established the original German front line. Unfortunately, the German panzer forces were unable to push the advantage and eliminate the bridgehead entirely for, as so often was the case, they had to rush off and deal with a crisis that had erupted elsewhere on the front (in this case, the Warsaw uprising).

Upon arrival, the 6th Grenadier Division was directed to relieve the "Hermann Goering" Panzer Division and occupy the Main Battle Line, which turned out to be little more than shallow trenches and rifle pits. Brücker's grenadiers would have much work before them to create a viable defensive zone.

The Warka Bridgehead lay in the sector of General der Panzertruppe von Lüttwitz's 9th Army. Assigned to its defense were the three infantry divisions (6th, 45th, and Korpsabteilung E) of General der Panzertruppe Hartmann's VIII Army Corps.[1] The bridgehead formed a westwards-projecting bulge, the base of which ran 25 km along the Vistula, and was 20 km at its deepest. The VIII Army Corps deployed its three divisions along the perimeter of the bulge with Korpsabteilung E in the north, the 6th Grenadier Division in the center, and the Austrian 45th Grenadier Division in the south. The 6th Grenadier's sector was a 15-km stretch of front between the Pilica and Radomka Rivers, which run in a northeastwards direction almost parallel to one another into the Vistula. Brücker placed the 58th Regiment on the right flank, anchored on the Radomka and adjoining the 45th Division. The 18th Regiment held the center while the 37th Regiment occupied the division's left flank, tying in with Korpsabteilung E. The divisional headquarters was based in the village of Bierwce.

Although he had been given only a brief period to train his division, Oberst Brücker was confident it could perform any reasonable task assigned to it. He had good men, good officers—a good division. What concerned him was what he did not have. The artillery regiment of a standard infantry division normally consisted of three twelve-gun Abteilungen of light howitzers (10.5 cm) and one twelve-gun Abteilung of heavy (15.5-cm) howitzers, and cannons (17.0 cm) for a total of forty-eight guns. When Brucker's artillery regiment set off for the front, its four Abteilungen possessed only eight guns each—a one-third reduction in firepower. To compensate for this shortfall, Brücker was soon given twelve 7.5 guns—a fine field piece in its time but hardly possessing the range and throw-weight of a howitzer. To employ them as divisional artillery made no sense. With shorter range and a flatter trajectory, the guns would require being positioned closer to the front, which would only complicate fire control without yielding any appreciable increase in destructive power.

Of equal, if not more, concern to Brücker was the absence of anti-tank guns. Considering the tank masses employed by the enemy, the anti-tank gun was essential to the survival of infantry. His division had no Panzerjäger Abteilung, and the Panzerjäger companies of the regiments, instead of anti-tank guns, had been issued forty-eight of the new Panzerschrecks—an effective anti-tank weapon at close range but certainly no substitute for the high-velocity 5-cm and 7.5-cm guns. As a remedy for his ordnance problems, Brücker elected to deploy the 7.5-cm field guns close behind the front line to be used in an anti-tank role.

The division was also suffering from a shortage of certain personnel. The Füsilier Battalion was actually only a Füsilier company as were the division's engineer and communications battalions. Brücker was assured that all these shortages would be made good when possible, but until then he would have to make do with what he had. The Oberst was confident that he could—unless Ivan attempted something major.

Ivan did not. However, following common military practice—if not doctrine—Ivan did attempt to take advantage of the opportunity always offered when a new division arrives and takes over a sector of the front. The attempt was ill advised. Although Brücker's grenadiers had only the shallow trenches and rifle pits left behind by the "Hermann Goering" Panzer Division and had not yet organized a defensive zone, all efforts by the enemy to seize valuable ground were beaten back with heavy loss. Brücker's insistence on intensive weapons training and constant practice had yielded dividends and a rich harvest of Russian dead. After two weeks of local heavy attacks, Ivan contented himself with the usual activities of an "inactive front": random harassing artillery and mortar fire and, of course, that curse common to all trench warfare—snipers.

Snipers had always been looked upon with distaste by most Western armies, both by the military establishment and the troops themselves. Consequently, there had never been any concerted effort to create, organize, or train a sniper force. Nations that rely on universal conscription for their armies also intend to return the conscripts to the everyday civilian society—as dutiful sons having served their country—not as trained killers. Soldiers are trained to kill, but they kill when necessary and as directed. Killing a man at close range who poses an immediate threat to one's existence is what a soldier has to do. Killing a man at long range while he harmlessly consumes his rations is nothing less than premeditated murder. Nevertheless, in both world wars, Western armies had found it necessary to temporarily resort to sniping and to train and equip troops to carry out the distasteful task.

In contrast, the Soviet Union, born as it was out of a revolution that rejected all norms of bourgeois society, including the Laws and Customary Usages of War (which, after all, had been written by imperialist nations), actively recruited, equipped, trained, and rewarded snipers.

To combat the enemy sniper activity that was taking an increasing toll of his grenadiers, Brücker created his own force of Scharfschützen. There was no lack of excellent marksmen in the division, nor any lack of volunteers for the oberst's new unit. The best marksmen were selected and granted special leave to visit the arsenal in Suhl to personally select their rifles and optics and to test them before returning to the front.

Back at the front Brücker's Scharfschützen were methodical in their technique. They did not, as in World War I, stand in the trenches their eyes glued to their telescopic sights and wait for a target to foolishly expose itself. Instead, they would observe the enemy positions, sometimes for days, carefully noting all activity and troop movement. Only then would they go "hunting" by crawling out beyond the German frontline to a preselected position based on their acquired knowledge of the enemy's behavior. Soon Brücker's Schafrschützen were amassing impressive scores of confirmed "Abschüsse" or kills.

To be confirmed, each "Abschüss" required two independent witnesses. Soon a third witness from an unexpected source became available as German radio intercepts revealed Russian voices speaking of so many "whites" (dead) or so many "reds" (wounded), usually followed by unprintable curses leveled at the fascist snipers. In two months, over 300 Russians had been killed by Brücker's Scharfschützen or, as a Wehrmacht report stated, "Ten snipers have eliminated the equivalent of an entire Soviet battalion."

The ten Scharfschützen were naturally invited to Brücker's headquarters for a "Scharfschützenkaffe," where in addition to being awarded the Iron Cross 1st Class, they enjoyed coffee and cake with Brücker and his staff. Gefreiter Schöne of the 37th Regiment was credited with fifty-three "Abschüsse," while Grenadier Baumann of Regiment 58 was close behind with fifty-one confirmed kills. Soon these two Scharfschützen had raised their respective scores to over 100. Little wonder that by mid-October, Soviet sniper activity had all but ceased.

As Gefreiter Schöne and Grenadier Baumann were adding to their toll of "Abschüsse," the other grenadiers were hard at work constructing defenses rather more permanent than those they inherited. They sensed that their stay in the Warka would be of some duration, which would not be all that bad. The heat of late summer had given way to the cool crispness of autumn and, except for the occasional artillery or mortar round dropping from the sky, the sector was relatively quiet. Nor was there any shortage of food. In August, the war had swept into the Warka region almost without warning, and the local villagers had been forced to flee, leaving the crops unharvested in the fields—and the harvest was good that year for any grenadier willing to risk attracting enemy fire by scavenging about in the fields. Tomatoes, onions, and potatoes were all in abundance and offered a welcome relief from the monotony of Komissbrot and "Gummiwurst."

The troops' notion that their stay in the Warka might be for some time proved correct, for almost before the enormity of the summer's disastrous defeats in the East and West could be fully assessed, Hitler was already planning Germany's next move. At a conference at his headquarters in Rastenburg, Hitler announced to the General staff that in the coming months, Germany would go on the offensive. One can well appreciate the dismay of his generals, who were still reeling from the summer's disasters. Germany take the offensive? Many a general was wondering if the Reich could even last out the year. However, the Führer insisted. New divisions would be raised; the shattered panzer forces would be rebuilt and re-equipped with the latest models of tanks; a strike force of 250,000 men and 1,000 tanks would restore Germany's military fortunes. But where to strike? Although an impressive force, in the enormity of the Eastern Front, a quarter of a million men could achieve little more than a local success.

By contrast, the West offered certain enticing opportunities. The Anglo-American advance had stalled at the German border and at some points had even suffered a setback. Hitler proposed that the newly raised strike force smash through the Allied line in the Ardennes region and then swing north and seize the vital supply port of Antwerp, thereby cutting off the British and Canadian armies in the north and possibly forcing another Dunkirk upon them. This is what he had done in 1940, and he was confident that he could again achieve it in 1944.

On paper and in theory, the plan appeared to have merit, but few German generals shared their Führer's confidence. Outnumbered and outgunned, any major German offensive stood little chance of having any long-lasting effect on the course of the war. Few Generals, however, voiced their concerns to the Führer, for in the wake of the attempted assassination and coup, legitimate disagreement on military matters could all too easily be interpreted as disloyalty.

The matter then was settled—Germany would attack in the West sometime in November or December.

And what of the East? Once more, the weakened eastern armies watched as much-needed men and resources were diverted to the West while their own fronts continued to be over extended. The Führer was convinced that for now the Red Army had shot its bolt. He assured his eastern commanders that Stalin would not be able to launch any major offensive until after the new year, by which time, success would have been achieved in the West, and the forces there could be sent east. Such assurances had been given before—the previous spring—and they did little now to ease the minds of the eastern generals.

In the sector of the 6th Grenadier Division, between the Radomka and Pilica Rivers, the men continued to improve their positions. Bunkers of timber and concrete were constructed to provide the troops shelter from both the elements and the enemy. In the rearward zones, large Wohnbunkers were built, whereas in the battle zone, the bunkers were only large enough to accommodate three or four men in order to minimize casualties in case of a direct artillery hit. Although the men often complained of the cramped conditions of their "Tropfsteinkellers" in the battle zone, they would prove effective in the coming Soviet offensive in reducing casualties from the preparatory barrage.

Far to the rear, a Soldatenheim was erected to which the men could be sent on a rotational basis to rest and relax and enjoy food, entertainment, and drink, but only for twenty-four hours. Due to the brevity of this privilege, many a grenadier chose to forgo the pleasure and remain in their "Tropfsteinkeller" to sleep away their "twenty-four-hour leave."

In October, Oberst Brücker was promoted to Generalmajor and began receiving some of the equipment promised him. The twelve 10.5-cm howitzers his artillery regiment lacked finally arrived, and, in addition, he also received an entire Nebelwerfer (multiple rocket launcher) regiment with sixteen 16-cm and 32-cm rocket launchers and a heavy mortar battery with two 21-cm Mörser.

Other shortages Brücker addressed himself. By purloining men from the grenadier companies, who were then replaced by troops of the division's Training and Replacement Battalion (who in turn were replaced by combing out the service units), he was able to fully man the Füsilier and Engineer Battalions.

Perhaps the greatest and most welcome addition to the division was the arrival of an entire Sturmgeschütz brigade commanded by Major Kapp. With three companies of "Stugs," though some of older design, Brücker now found himself almost as well supplied with armor as some panzer divisions.

Although the Warka sector had been an inactive front since mid-September, in the East, death had never been known to go on leave. Young men of either side died daily, and nightly—a random mortar round, a sniper's prey, patrols colliding violently in the night, and, of course, the brutal trench raids. These trench raids had become, in Brücker's words, "a dangerous sport," in which the grenadier companies competed among themselves for prestige and bragging rights as to damage inflicted, prisoners taken, and war booty brought back. Nor was there any lack of volunteers for this "dangerous sport"—and this in the sixth year of the war, when one might expect a certain degree of risk aversion among the troops.

On the night of October 27, Oberleutnant Willi Stoffels, commander of the 2nd Company of Regiment 18, led one such Stoßtruppunternehmen against the Russian positions opposite the village of Helenow. The conditions could not have been better. Clouds had drifted across the moon, and the wind was blowing from the east—hence, no sound would be carried to the enemy trenches. At 10 p.m., Stoffels, six unteroffiziere, and twenty-six men slid over the edge of their trench and began crawling toward the Russian lines. Meter by meter, they moved silently in the dark, taking nearly three hours to cover 200 meters. Stoffels' Sicherheitstrupp took up position 50 meters from the enemy trench. With its three machine guns it would support the assault team's attack and cover their hasty escape. The three six-man assault teams then made their way forward—Feldwebel Guddorp's team on the left, Feldwebel Steffan's group on the right, and Stoffels, with his six men, in the center. The plan was to hit the enemy trench at three different points and then "roll it up," but as they neared the trench, two Ivans were spotted walking toward Guddorp's team. Just as one of the Russians was about to step on Guddorp, the feldwebel leapt up and quickly rendered the man unconscious, but the other Russian ran off, shouting the alarm. Stoffels fired off a signal flare, and the Sicherheitstrupp began hammering the trench with its MG-42s, concentrating fire on the flanks, thereby sealing off the stretch of trench Stoffels had selected to assault. Eighteen stick grenades spun through the dark and crashed into the Russian trench and then "Los und hinein!" Guddorp's team was first in, quickly followed by the other two, and a vicious, hand-to-hand *mêlée* ensued, in which Feldwebel Steffen was wounded. Two men grabbed the feldwebel and began dragging him back to the German lines while Stoffels and the others "rolled up" the trench with hand grenades and "bunker bombs." Judging they had inflicted sufficient damage, Stoffels fired off another signal flare, and covered by the fire of the Sicherheitstrupp, the raiders hustled back to their own trenches. Behind them came Guddorp and one of his men dragging along a wounded prisoner.

Back in the safety of their own trenches, they were met by their battalion commander, Hauptmann Küster, who first gave Stoffels a dressing down for not having informed him of the trench raid before hand, but then softened and congratulated the young oberleutnant on his success, adding "We were worried about you."

Although these nocturnal raids served no real tactical purpose and risked the lives of some of the best officers and men, they were always encouraged. They served to keep Ivan on edge and wreak havoc upon the enemy, and, most important, they nurtured the aggressive spirit of the troops. By November, the men of the 6th Grenadier Division could boast, "Wir beherrschen nachts das Vorfeld." ("At night, we rule the front.")[2]

Autumn in the Warka had come and gone. Winter had arrived, but here in central Poland, the winter was nothing like the frozen purgatories of Russia. The winter thus far had been quite mild with temperatures remaining mostly above freezing, and on the few occasions that a light snow had fallen during the night, by midday it had melted away.

For almost six months now, the 6th Grenadier Division had occupied the Warka bridgehead, and the Russians had not yet launched a major attack; perhaps this time the Führer had been correct. In mid-December came news of a great battle in the West and reports of German successes, but in the Warka there was no great battle, and the men were preparing to celebrate Christmas, their sixth of the war and, for many, their last.

Heiligabend, 1944: the company cooks and bakers had outdone themselves for the sake of the frontline troops this Christmas. Kuchen, strudel and even stollen were in abundance and certainly no small quantity of alcohol. The men had decorated their cramped bunkers with spruce and juniper, and in each stood a small Weihnachtsbaum. In some companies there were "bunker contests" as regards the inventiveness of the Christmas decorations, the winner receiving a bottle of Steinhäger for the occupants.

For fear that Ivan might attempt an attack on that holiest of nights, the companies were forced to celebrate the evening in shifts, a platoon at a time being rotated out of the trenches. Company commanders made their rounds of the bunkers sharing a toast and a carol with the men. With ten or more bunkers per company to visit, many a company chief returned to his quarters with unsteady gait and spinning head. Later in the evening came the much-anticipated visit of the regimental Kommandeur, who, like Father Christmas, brought cheer and gifts to his grenadiers.

In a letter to his parents, Obergefreiter Reiner Niemann (a survivor of the "Cauldron of Bobruisk") described the Christmas celebrated by Oberstleutnant Müller's 58th Regiment:

> … here we have three Christmas trees, two made from packages and paper from home and one real tree 40 cm tall. This one will only be placed on the table when the officers come by like yesterday when the company commander came by and joined us in an unskilled singing of "Stille Nacht" and "O, Tannenbaum," or tonight when the regimental commander visited our position. As he came through the trench, he was wearing a white fur hat that I honestly thought was part of a Santa Claus outfit, and I couldn't help but laugh when he asked me who from the company would be playing Santa Claus—I mean, I thought he was. He laughed as well and clapped me fatherly on the shoulder and told

> me that the unteroffiziere would be bringing up a chocolate bar for each of us. His adjutant was rather less amused and later explained that the Kommandeur always wore a fur hat in winter ...[3]

However, there was one member of the division who could not fully enjoy the festivities. Generalmajor Brücker had much on his mind that Christmas Eve. Intelligence reports, aerial reconnaissance, and prisoner interrogations all revealed a heavy Soviet build-up of troops and materiel in the Warka bridgehead, indicating a major attack—most probably soon after the new year, when the ground had sufficiently frozen to support heavy tank traffic.

Outside his headquarters in Bierwce, Generalmajor Brücker looked up into the night sky. The night was clear and the stars shone crystal-white in the darkness. Off in the distance, he could hear the traditional carols rising from the trenches and drifting across the fields. A peaceful night. Let the men enjoy it. Brücker sensed that it would not remain peaceful much longer.

January 1, 1945: following tradition, Brücker's grenadiers saluted the New Year by shaking Ivan out of his sleep with a deluge of artillery, mortar, and small arms fire. As Obergefreiter Niemann recounted:

> At the blast of our commander's whistle the game took off. Every machinegun and heavy weapon had received its full allotment of ammunition. The machinegun fired without jamming, as always. Only after 150 rounds did we have to change barrels.[4]

This year Ivan returned the greeting in kind, and the grenadiers had to run for the bunkers and dugouts. Soon though, the front became quiet once more. Over the next two weeks, there were only the usual harassing fire, patrols, and trench raids.

Brücker had been correct in his assessment that the Soviets were massing their forces for a major attack in the Warka sector. By January 1945, the Red Army could field a total force of 6,298,000 men, 15,100 armored vehicles, 91,400 artillery pieces, and 14,500 aircraft along the entire Eastern Front. The upcoming offensive was not restricted to the Vistula bridgeheads but was intended to smash open the entire central front and drive into the Reich itself. To oppose the massive Soviet armies, the Wehrmacht could deploy only 700,000 men.[5] Nor could the German armies in the East expect any help from the Western Front. The divisions diverted west to launch Hitler's offensive in the Ardennes had achieved initial success, but then the attack had stalled, leaving these divisions either struggling to hold their gains or seeking to avoid being cut off and destroyed. The panzer divisions that had spearheaded the attack were but shadows of their former selves and would not be available for the Eastern Front for some time—if, indeed, they ever would be.

German intelligence sources were not far off the mark when they estimated that in the east the Red Army possessed a superiority of eleven to one in men, seven to one in armor, and twenty to one in artillery. Hitler rejected such an assessment, referring to the Soviet build-up as "the greatest bluff since Genghis Khan." His Chief of Staff, Generaloberst Heinz Guderian, was far more realistic in his prediction that when attacked, the Eastern Front would "collapse like a house of cards."

In the Warka bridgehead, the odds facing Brücker and his grenadiers were not better. To break out of the bridgehead, the Soviets had concentrated the forces of five armies of the 1st Belorussian Front with nearly 400,000 men; 8,700 artillery pieces and rocket launchers (250 per kilometer of front); and 1,700 armored vehicles.[6] To oppose this mammoth force assembled to obliterate them, the Germans had only the three infantry divisions of the VIII Army Corps and the recently arrived 19th and 25th Panzer Divisions. Earlier in the war three infantry and two panzer divisions would have represented a force of 80,000 men or more and over 300 tanks, but now, considering the level to which German divisions had shrunk, the defenders of the Warka numbered less than 40,000 men supported by only 200 artillery pieces. The two panzer divisions possessed a mere fifty tanks apiece.[7]

Despite the considerable reduction in the 6th Grenadier Division's manpower (its regiments numbered approximately 700–800 each), at the basic level there had been no corresponding reduction in infantry firepower, perhaps even an increase as pertains automatic weapons. Companies of eighty men still employed ten MG-42 light machine guns, twenty or more MP-40 machine pistols, and recently the division had been issued the revolutionary MP-44 assault rifles at a rate of thirty per company. In the days to come, the grenadiers would need every bit of this firepower.

The German defenders in the Warka sector well understood the odds they were facing and were determined that their defenses would not be a "house of cards." The defense zone that they had constructed did not consist of belts of deep interconnected trenches behind walls of barbed wire—that system belonged to an earlier war. Instead, it was one of strongpoints scattered throughout the 10-km deep battle zone in a checkerboard fashion. These strongpoints were armed with heavy machine guns, mortars, and anti-tank weapons, and were themselves protected by small, flanking machine-gun bunkers, which, after the German fashion, were near invisible from the front and designed to fire to the rear. When the Russian assault troops entered the battle zone, they would find themselves trapped in a "kill box" with fire coming at them from all points of the compass. This checkerboard defense in depth was not designed to necessarily prevent an enemy breakthrough, but to ensure that any advance through the defense zone would be scattered and uneven. Russian troops who had somehow succeeded in fighting their way through the defense zone to emerge on the other side would most likely be isolated groups of men from different units, who, lacking any coordination or unified command, would be highly vulnerable to swift counterattacks.

The three infantry divisions of the VIII Corps defending the Warka were still in the same positions they had occupied at the end of August: the 45th Division south of the Radomka, the 6th Grenadier Division between the Radomka and the Pilica, and Korpsobteilung E north of the Pilica. Likewise, Brücker's regiments lay in their original positions with Müller's 58th Regiment on the right flank anchored on the Radomka, Graf's 18th Regiment in the center, and Lütkehaus' 37th Regiment extending to the Pilica. Each regiment was supported to its rear by one of the artillery regiment's light howitzer Abteilungen (twelve 10.5-cm howitzers per regiment). The heavy howitzer and cannon Abteilung (twelve guns) were slightly further to the rear in the sector of the 18th Regiment.

Also to the rear of the battle zone were the division's reserve units. The Füsilier Battalion and a Sturmgeschütz company were placed near the juncture of the 58th and 18th Regiments; the Engineer Battalion along the seam of the 18th and 37th Regiments, while the Training and Replacement Battalion was held in overall reserve at Zawady just west of the divisional headquarters at Bierwce.

The two panzer divisions of General Heinrici's XXXX Panzer Korps were deployed with Generalleutnant Källner's 19th Panzer Division near Radom, 30 km southwest of the Warka bridgehead, and Generalmajor Audörsch's 25th Panzer division at Bialobrzegi, 15 km to the rear of the 37th Regiment. As the day of battle approached, these two divisions were to move closer to the front to counter any Soviet breakthrough.

Such was the deployment of the German forces in the Warka, but decisions yet remained on how best to employ them to meet the imminent Soviet offensive. At this late stage of the war, much of the Wehrmacht's planning was characterized by compromise and hope. With ever dwindling resources, German military planners had to make compromising choices among unattractive alternatives and then hope that they would be blessed with good luck in battle. Nowhere is this more evident than in the plans to defend the Warka bridgehead.

The first decision concerned the tactical deployment of the infantry in the battle zone. From bitter experience in the past, the Germans had learned to respect their Soviet opponent's ability to amass incredible amounts of artillery for a given offensive. The destructive fire that such a concentration of artillery could bring to bear on a defensive position often eliminated a quarter to a third of the defenders. To avoid this mass slaughter of their infantry, the Germans had often resorted to the tactic of withdrawing their troops the night before the expected attack and moving them back to previously prepared positions beyond the range of Soviet artillery (10–12 km). Raining down upon empty trenches and bunkers, the much-vaunted Russian "hurricane of fire" would be nothing more than an entertaining display of fireworks and a huge waste of ordnance.

The enemy would then need at least two weeks to bring his artillery forward and to resupply and reregister the guns before assaulting the new German frontline.

However, in the Warka, the decision was made not to pull the German infantry back to safety. They would remain in their positions and ride out the storm of steel the best they could. With luck, perhaps enough of them might survive to offer a viable defense. This decision was based on the reasoning that withdrawing the troops would only delay the inevitable Soviet assault for a few weeks. In addition, both officers and men had expressed confidence in the protective qualities of their fortifications and a preference to conduct the battle on ground with which they were intimately familiar.

The next decision involved how best to employ the two panzer divisions with their limited number of tanks. There were two options available to the German planners, either of which would have serious consequences if the option chosen proved wrong for the developing battle conditions. One option was to hold the panzer divisions well back from the battle zone in order to allow them time to assess the direction and threat of a Russian breakthrough and how to best counter it with their meager forces. The danger inherent in this option was that the enemy would also have time to consolidate his breakthrough, gain momentum, and consequently become unstoppable.

The other option was to deploy the panzer forces up close to the battle zone to be immediately available to halt any Soviet advance and then to push forward and restore the original front line. The risk here was the possibility that the panzers could become embroiled in the fighting within the battle zone, lose the ability to maneuver, and thus be unable to counter a more threatening Soviet thrust elsewhere along the front. The second option was selected despite its risks. The panzer divisions would be ordered up close to the front.

The final decision was how to utilize the artillery. Again, the German planners were confronted with limited resources. Not only was there an inadequate number of guns *vis-à-vis* what the enemy possessed, but there was also a critical shortage of ammunition. The normal daily allotment for an artillery piece—termed an Ausstattung—was 225 rounds for a light howitzer and 150 rounds for a heavy howitzer. In view of the Soviet forces facing them, the Germans would have liked to have had two or three Ausstattungen to counter the enemy barrage, but, despite all efforts, the German artillery in the Warka had been unable to stockpile even one Ausstattung. A debate naturally arose over how best to use this limited supply of ammunition. Some argued that the bulk should be fired off in a pre-dawn, pre-emptive bombardment of the densely packed forward trenches of the Soviet assault troops to inflict heavy casualties and to disrupt the attack. Others, particularly the artillery officers, insisted that the limited ammunition should be reserved for direct observable fire during the actual attack. The decision was made to compromise: one-third of the rounds were to be expended in a pre-dawn barrage and the remaining two-thirds held back for direct fire during the assault. This compromise later proved to be disastrous.

With the troops now deployed and the final decisions made, there was nothing more for Generalmajor Brücker and his grenadiers to do but await the coming Soviet onslaught.

Near the Radomka River, a young grenadier of the 58th Regiment stared beyond his trench into the night. He had drawn the short straw that evening and had watch duty until dawn. The weather had been somewhat mild for January, only now and then a light dusting of snow. But tonight there was a sharp wind blowing from the east. No doubt the hard winter was coming soon, and so was Ivan, for the night wind also brought with it the muffled sound of constant tank and truck traffic from beyond the Russian front line. What was it the poet had written decades ago during an earlier war? "Es fährt ein Sturm aus Ost … von allen Gräbern weht's aus Ost…" Ah, yes, the poem "Graves in Poland." How appropriate—and chilling.[8]

In contrast to the Führer and his headquarters, after three and a half years of war in the East, the German commanders in the field had become quite adept at divining the intentions of their Soviet opponent. Based on information gathered from patrols, prisoners, and observation of enemy activity, the German staff officers in the Warka had come to the conclusion that the Soviet offensive would commence at dawn January 14. At noon on January 13, Generalmajor Brücker was informed that the panzer divisions would be moving up that night closer to the battle zone: the 19th Panzer Division behind the 18th Regiment's sector, the 25th Panzer Division to the rear of Regiment 37. Both divisions were expected to be in position by daybreak. During the afternoon, Brücker informed his regimental commanders of the impending Soviet attack.

Winter nights are long in the East, and the night of January 13 seemed particularly long. Throughout the Warka sector, those grenadiers who could sleep, slept. Those who could not tended their weapons, wrote letters home, or stared with blank minds into the glowing embers of the small fireplace built into the walls of each bunker.

At 4 a.m., the pre-dawn darkness was suddenly illuminated by the muzzle flashes of the German artillery as it began the pre-emptive bombardment of the known enemy forward positions. For a half hour, fire rained down on the Russian trenches sending up columns of fire and smoke. Then as quickly as it had begun, the barrage ceased. The rumbling of the explosions echoed away, replaced by the screams and pitiful cries for help of the wounded. Though limited by plan, the pre-emptive barrage had caused heavy casualties in the densely packed Russian trenches. But what were a couple thousand dead and wounded to an attack force that numbered more than a third of a million men? If an assault company was smashed to bits, then it would be quickly replaced by another company—and the Russians had waves and waves of assault companies.

At 6:30 a.m., just as it was growing light, the Soviet barrage erupted like a volcano as the 8,000 guns and rocket launchers of the 1st Belorussian Front unleashed their fury along the entire Warka front. The Soviet fire first pounded the German frontline positions and then raked its way back to the artillery emplacements. With 250 guns per kilometer of front, few meters of the German defense zone remained unscathed. Added to the cacophony of exploding shells was the mournful roar of the rockets as they streaked across the sky. No one in the 6th Grenadier Division, with the exception of its commander, who as a young officer had endured the Trommelfeuer of World War I, had ever experienced such a hurricane of fire. By comparison to this storm of steel, the German pre-emptive barrage had been but summer heat lightning flashing across the sky.

Inside their bunkers the grenadiers hugged the walls, floors, and each other, praying somehow to survive the storm. They could pray all they desired, but the old soldier's maxim, "If your number is up, death will find you," was never truer than in the Warka that day.

Familiar with Soviet tactics, the German defenders expected a one-hour bombardment followed by a mass infantry and tank attack. However, in the Warka, the Soviet commanders opted for the callous and potentially costly tactic of sending the assault companies into their own barrage in hope of catching the German defenders still sheltering in their bunkers. They did not expect their assault troops to suicidally advance into the rain of artillery fire, but to follow along previously delineated "fire-free" paths. Unfortunately, concussive blast waves and flying shards of metal are no great respecters of lines drawn on a map. The Soviet assault troops suffered horribly from their own barrage.

As the day grew light, Brücker and his staff peered out from their shelter and were horror-struck. The entire battle zone was enveloped by a heavy fog that reduced visibility to less than 100 meters. Now there was no possibility of direct, observable artillery fire—better to have fired off the bulk of the ammunition during the pre-emptive barrage. And what of the carefully designed interlocking fields of fire? With such limited visibility they were rendered ineffective. There would be no "kill boxes."

But in a sense, the fog had turned the entire battle zone into one great "kill box" for all the young men, both German and Russian, trapped within. Still huddled in their bunkers waiting for the barrage to lift, German troops were taken by surprise by the Russian assault troops. A kicked-open door and the flash of a grenade were the last things they saw. Russians, lost in the fog, strayed from the "fire-free" paths and were ripped apart by their own artillery or mistakenly fired upon one another. In the chaos of exploding shells and the swirling mist, men stumbled into each other, recognizing in the last instant that they were facing an enemy. Only he with the quickest reflexes would live—at least, for a few minutes more.

In his command bunker near Helenow, Oberleutnant Willi Stoffels, commander of the 2nd Company 18th Regiment, was recovering from his initial shock at the violence of the Russian barrage. He was determined to make his way to the front line to see if there was any front left. Three times he attempted to leave his bunker only to be forced back inside by the fury of the explosions. On his fourth attempt, he succeeded in reaching a communication trench and, accompanied by his runner, Obergefreiter Feiser, the two crawled forward to Feldwebel Rasch's platoon on the right flank. On their way, they encountered Rasch crawling to the rear and dragging a wounded comrade. Rasch informed them that Ivan was already in the trenches and that there was no longer a right flank or a right flank platoon. Stoffels could not believe that the Russians would attack into their own barrage, but when he called to a group of men approaching him, they answered in Russian. Stoffels and Feiser emptied the magazines of their MP-40s into the group, but more Russians appeared and Stoffel's group beat a hasty retreat back to the company command bunker. In the fog, Obergefreiter Feiser collided with a Russian. Both men fired; both men died.

When Stoffels approached his bunker, he saw that the enemy had already occupied it. He came across Unteroffizier Knels and the two of them sought a way out of the chaos. Knels was struck in the chest by a shell splinter and collapsed. Stoffels remained with him for a few minutes until the man died. Mercifully, Knels had been knocked unconscious by the blow and so knew nothing of his own death. With Russians snaking through the communication trenches, Stoffels proceeded above ground. Packs of enemy soldiers sped past him, mistaking him for one of their own. In the nightmarish confusion, Stoffels watched as a shell exploded in the midst of a group of Russians, blowing them to pieces. Another group of enemy troops rushed past them, paying no heed to the carnage. He saw several wounded German soldiers overtaken by the Russians in a communication trench. What became of the wounded men, he was unable to observe. Then Stoffels was struck—a shell splinter in the left knee. He limped his way to the battalion command post only to find the Russians already there. Eventually he was able to reach the artillery positions at the rear of the battle zone, where he informed the gunners that soon they would be firing point blank for Ivan was only minutes away.

Continuing his journey, he came across a tank from the 19th Panzer Division. No, they could not take him with them; they were going into action and had no room for him in the turret. The tank commander arranged for a truck to transport him back to the main dressing station. At last, Oberleutnant Willi Stoffels was out of the Hell of the Warka.

Stoffels may have escaped from the Hell of the Warka, but the Hell continued, and it spread. The German defense zone had not collapsed; it had been pulverized and then swamped by a tidal wave of men and tanks. By mid-morning, Brücker had lost all contact with the 37th Regiment after its last communication, which had reported that the Kommandeur, Oberstleutnant Lütkehaus, had fallen in battle. At noon a frantic message from the 18th Regiment reported that the regimental headquarters was under attack by tanks and infantry and that Oberst Graf had been killed while attacking an enemy tank with a pannzerfaust—then silence.

Where were those damned panzer divisions that had been promised for support? One can understand Brücker's frustration. The day was only half gone and already two of his regiments had been scattered or destroyed.

The two panzer divisions of the XXXX Panzer Korps had been delayed by the fog and had been unable to reach the battle zone at daybreak, as intended. Not until mid-morning did the 19th Panzer Division arrive. Of the whereabouts of the 25th Panzer Division, no one could tell. General Källner had informed Brücker that his division would be ready to counterattack at 11:30 a.m., but then he had postponed his attack to 12:30 p.m., then again to 2 p.m. No reason had been given for the postponements, but most probably Källner, an experienced panzer commander, recognized that there was no longer a defense zone to restore and was little inclined to sacrifice his division in a hopeless mission.

At 2 p.m., still no panzers and Brücker had just received word from the 58th Regiment that its headquarters was under attack and that Oberstleutnant Müller was preparing for all-around defense. Brücker was now in danger of losing his last regiment. Was the 6th Grenadier Division to be destroyed a second time? He could wait no longer for Källner and his panzers. He ordered Major Kapp of the Sturmgeschütz brigade to assemble what Stugs he could, break through to the 58th Regiment, and haul Müller and whatever survivors he had left out of the battle zone. Under the circumstances, a near suicide mission, but like von Bredow at Mars-la-Tour (Koste es was es wolle), he accepted the order stoically, and climbing aboard his Stug, he led his modern-day Kürassiers forward. Joined by Oberleutnant Eyrich and his Stugs and Oberleutnant Kahler with the 2nd Schwadron (company) of the Füsilier Battalion, they rolled into the battle zone to rescue their comrades. Barrels blazing, they stormed through to the 58th Regiment's embattled headquarters at Bobrowniki, loaded Müller and his survivors (a mere 200 men) aboard their Stugs and fought their way back out, destroying or scattering any Soviet tanks they encountered; 3 km outside the battle zone, Müller and his men were unloaded at Kukawa, where they dug in and awaited instructions. Behind them, in the smashed bunkers and trenches, they had left 462 of their comrades—ninety known dead and 372 missing.

The situation in the Warka continued to deteriorate. North of Bobrowniki, Major Specht's Nebelwerfer crews fired off the last rockets, took up their carbines, and went down fighting as infantry. Even though the division's artillery was emplaced to the rear of the battle zone, it had suffered little less than the infantry from the Soviet barrage, and the gunners soon found themselves fighting off Soviet armor that had broken through the defense zone. Twenty-five enemy tanks were destroyed at point-blank range, but of the three light howitzer Abteilungen commanders, one, Hauptmann Schmiedecke, had been killed, and the other two, Hauptmann's Korsten and Lotz badly wounded. Eight of the nine battery commanders were either dead or missing. By early evening, Brücker's artillery regiment was down to seven heavy and two light howitzers.

Elsewhere in the Warka bridgehead, the situation was no better. In the north and south, the fronts of Korpsabteilung E and the 45th Division had collapsed and the Russians were pouring through the battle zone. Brücker had long since lost all contact with the neighboring divisions. With no hope of either holding or restoring the defense zone, VIII Corps directed Brücker to withdraw what was left of his division 5 km west and, in conjunction with the 19th and 25th Panzer Divisions, establish a new defensive line between the Radomka and Pilica Rivers along the Bialobrzegi–Jedlinsk road.

As night fell, the survivors of the 6th Grenadier Division climbed aboard the tank and trucks of the 19th Panzer Division and drove away to the west. A heartrending withdrawal, for behind them, in the battle zone, they could see flares arching into the night sky and hear the sounds of combat as some of their comrades trapped in the "kill boxes" of the Warka were still resisting the enemy.

The new front line could not be held. Throughout the next day, January 15, the battered remnants of the Warka defenders fought back all Soviet attempts to advance further, but to the southeast and northeast, enemy forces were rushing westwards threatening to outflank the Bialobrzegi–Jedlinsk line. Late that evening, the German defenders were ordered to withdraw 150 km west to the town of Schieratz on the Warthe. Brücker's grenadiers once again piled into the trucks provided by the 19th Panzer Division and bid a bitter farewell to the Warka. This was but the beginning of a long retreat that would continue until the last day of the war.

16

# Silesian Requiem: The Last Battles of the Rhineland-Westphalian 6th Infantry

The Russian steamroller that had burst out of the Vistula bridgeheads rolled relentlessly on. Chief of Staff Heinz Guderian had been correct—when attacked, the Eastern Front had collapsed like a house of cards. From the Baltic to the Carpathians, five Soviet fronts with 250 divisions and 4 million men raced ever westwards, driving the shattered remnants of German armies before them. The puny German attempts to counterattack were swamped almost unnoticed by the Soviet tidal wave. Warsaw and Radom fell to the Red Army on January 17, Krakow and Lodz on the 19th. Two German army groups were smashed, and hundreds of thousands of German troops were removed from the Wehrmacht's ranks—killed, wounded, missing, or trapped in pockets far behind the Soviet advance. For the Germans, the Russian Oder-Vistula offensive was an even greater calamity than Operation Bagration the previous summer. By the end of the month, the Soviet steamroller had pushed into East Prussia, driven the Germans out of Poland, and had not only reached the Oder River but had also established bridgeheads on its western bank. The Red Army now stood only 60 km from Berlin.

Caught up in the chaotic retreat was the Rhineland-Westphalian 6th Grenadier Division—or what remained of it. Directed to Schieratz on the Warthe, when it arrived, it discovered that the Russians had already broken across the river 20 km to the north. Brücker's grenadiers were ordered to continue their retreat another 170 km west to the Oder River, where the Wehrmacht hoped to establish a new line of defense and bring the Soviet advance to a halt.

When they reached the Oder at Glogau on the morning of January 27, Generalmajor Brücker was immediately tasked with organizing the defenses—not only of the city but also of the entire 60-km-long Glogau sector. The local population was set to work digging trenches and tank traps, and as the retreating units of the 4th Panzer Army arrived, Brücker quickly organized them and detailed them to take over sectors of the Oder front. In addition to retreating soldiers, he had to deal with the thousands of civilian refugees fleeing the advancing Red Army. The hard winter having arrived, these poor wretches had suffered greatly and were in need of food, medical care, and shelter.

After a week, the defense of the Glogau sector was taken over by the 4th Panzer Army, and the 6th Grenadier Division was pulled back to Sagen 50 km to the west, where Brücker was to receive replacements and rebuild his division. There was not much left to rebuild. For the first time in two weeks, Brücker had the opportunity to take measure of what he still had—and of what he had lost. His 18th and 37th Regiments were gone, their Kommandeure dead, the men killed, wounded, captured, or scattered to the winds. All the artillery and anti-tank guns had either been destroyed or abandoned. The Füsilier Battalion and Eyrich's Sturmgeschütz company had been incorporated into the 19th Panzer Division and were off fighting far away. He would never see them again.

What remained to him were the 200 survivors of Müller's 58th Regiment, 320 artillerymen, who had been organized as an infantry battalion, a battalion comprised of communication and support personnel and the division's Training and Replacement Battalion, now renamed Battalion Erpenbach after its commander.

Four weak battalions—1,200 men—were all that remained of the 8,000 that Brücker had marched into the Warka bridgehead five months ago. A number barely more than the number of those who had escaped the cauldron of Bobruisk, but this time no staff clerk in Berlin would stamp the division extinct. The Wehrmacht no longer had the luxury of disbanding mauled divisions and reassigning the survivors to existing units. With the remnants of the 6th Grenadier Division, the Wehrmacht still possessed a competent general and four battalions of battle-tested men. Weakened though it was, the division would remain in the Wehrmacht's Order of Battle, albeit renamed the 6th Volksgrenadier Division.[1] With these 1,200 "Volksgrenadiers," Generalmajor Brücker would fight the last battles of the Reich.

And they would fight with whatever weapons and whatever troops they could acquire: errant police battalions, old men of the Volkssturm and young boys of the Hitler Youth, Luftwaffe ground crews suddenly become infantry, scattered units from other divisions, captured Russian artillery, and men on bicycles armed with panzerfausts. They would fight to the bitter end; they would fight to the last hour of the war.

But why? Certainly not for the "End Sieg" or final victory. That illusion, or rather delusion, had been shattered long ago. For Führer and Reich? Hardly. Those words now rang hollow. The Reich was rapidly disappearing; its life expectancy could be measured in months. As for the Führer, hiding away in his bunker issuing grandiose orders to armies and divisions that no longer existed or, if existing, were no longer listening—the man had ceased to be relevant.

Why then? Simply stated, they were German soldiers, and, as the sworn protectors of the German people and arising as they had from a generation that still believed that the highest duty of German manhood was to defend the Volk, they had no choice but to continue the struggle, now more than ever. The war, which had progressively revealed ever-greater horrors throughout its course, now that it had reached German soil, was revealing yet a new barbarity—the wholesale murder and rape of the German civilian population by the Red Army, sparing neither the young nor the aged. While in the Warka, the men of the 6th Grenadier Division had certainly heard of the atrocities unleased upon the German population when the Russians had first entered East Prussia back in September. In Silesia they could witness the horror with their own eyes. No longer fighting for Führer and Reich, the German soldier now fought and died to allow the German civilian population a chance to escape the rapacious hands of the Red Army.

After reaching the Oder River along the central front, the Soviets shifted the impetus of their winter offensive to the north, pushing into East and West Prussia. The central front, however, did not remain entirely inactive during this period, as the ten armies of Marshal Konev's 1st Ukrainian Front prepared to breach the Oder defenses and advance into Silesia.

The replacements that had been promised Brücker never arrived. Despite this, on February 5, he and his "Volksgrenadiers" were ordered back into action. At least, this time they were not sent directly to the front line. The commander of the 4th Panzer Army, General der Panzertruppe Gräser, had no great confidence that the hastily erected defenses along the Oder in the Glogau–Steinau sector would be able to withstand the expected Soviet assault. Consequently, he directed Brücker to establish a secondary line of defense 30–50 km to the west between Sprottau and Liegnitz, a sector nearly 60 km in length. And with only 1,200 men barely recovered from the disaster in the Warka? Unmöglich—impossible.

But no, he would also have the local Volkssturm battalions—old men armed with Italian carbines and panzerfausts, most clad in their inadequate civilian clothing with nothing more than a white and black Volkssturm armband to indicate that they were part of the German Armed Forces. Perhaps a few had military experience dating back to the Great War and might prove useful, but for the most part, they were untrained and ill equipped—truly "das letzte Aufgebot." However, as pathetic as they might appear to Brücker and his veterans, they were Silesians and this was their home. They would do their duty, and most would probably die, defending to the end Kinder und Frau.

When Brücker arrived at Kotzenau on February 6, he was unimpressed by the defenses already constructed along the Sprottau–Liegnitz line. They consisted primarily of tank traps with a few strongpoints scattered throughout, most located in the towns and villages. Unfortunately, these tank traps could be circumvented with little difficulty by Soviet armor and infantry, and although Brücker supposedly had twenty-two battalions of Volkssturm at his disposal, he could easily see that their numbers were insufficient to cover the gaps between the tank traps. Even worse, he had no means to communicate with the Volkssturm units. He still had no radios and his communication troops were now serving as infantry. Other than the local postal phone network, he had no way of receiving reports or issuing orders. In the coming battle, he could only hope that his phone calls would be answered by a Volkssturm commander and not a postal clerk. Such was the state of the Führer's Eastern Armies in February 1945.

While pondering the difficulties facing him, Brücker received welcome reinforcements—two Panzerjagdverbände, each with three companies. These Panzerjagdverbände must not be confused with the standard Jagdpanzer Abteilungen of the Wehrmacht, which were equipped with either the Sturmgeschütze III or the recently deployed "Hetzer" tank destroyers.[2] Brücker's Panzerjagdverbände consisted of infantrymen armed only with panzerfausts and nerves of steel to combat Soviet armor, but as he could see, the men were first-class human material and well-armed with panzerfausts, machine pistols, and the new assault rifles—and perhaps more important, they had volunteered for this near-suicidal mission.

Unfortunately, with no mobility other than their legs, Brücker would not be able to employ them in company-strength units held behind the front ready to be rushed here and there to counter a crisis. Instead, he would have to deploy them throughout the front in squads and platoons to provide support to the Volkssturm. In addition to the Panzerjagdverbände, Brücker's division received a new name, the curious and rather dramatic title of "Stab Panzertod" or "Staff Tank Death."

Without reliable communications, in order to have any hope of exercising command and control in the coming battle, Brücker located his headquarters at Kotzenau in the center of the Sprottau–Liegnitz line. He kept with him only his communication—now infantry battalion—and one of the Panzerjagd companies. The battalions of Müller and Brunk (Battalion Erpenbach was still fighting somewhere in the vicinity of Glogau) were pulled back 20 km west to occupy positions along the Bober River at Oberleschen (Brunk) and Kittlitztreben (Müller). After the Warka, Brücker was determined that never again would he allow his grenadiers to be trapped in frontline positions, waiting to be pulverized and crushed by the enemy onslaught.

Did Generalmajor Brücker believe that old men with obsolete carbines and panzerfausts, even with the support of the Panzerjagdverbände, would actually be able to halt the waves of Soviet tanks and infantry that would soon be upon them? In a word, no, but he did hold out hope that they might slow the enemy advance or even channel it, thereby providing him and his regular troops the opportunity to deliver sharp counterattacks to halt the Soviets for a while—at least long enough to evacuate the civilian population of Bunzlau.

General Grässer's pessimism concerning the efficacy of the Glogau–Steinau Oder front was confirmed when, on February 7, Soviet forces of the 4th Tank and 13th Armies breached the German defenses and pushed swiftly west and southwest. The front did not collapse entirely as the Vistula front had done back in January. The "Fortress" of Glogau, although surrounded, held out for several days before its trapped garrison attempted to break out. Only a few of the men succeeded in reaching German lines to the west. The city's Kampfkommandant was not among them.

Early in the morning of February 9, Russian tank and infantry columns were seen approaching the defenses of Brücker's "Stab Panzertod." Would they live up to their name? To an extent, they did. The Silesian Volksturm did their duty; they remained in their shallow pits with their panzerfausts until the T-34s got within range, stood up, and fired their single round, and then were either cut down by the accompanying Russian infantry or crushed by a following tank.

That young men die in war has always been understood—that is what young men do—and the acceptance of their deaths, tragic though they may be, has always been tinged with a certain romanticizing or, at least, a deep appreciation of their sacrifice. Only bronze images of the young and vigorous adorn the monuments of war. But the reality of men well past their prime being sent off to the slaughter to be crushed beneath the treads of a tank or shot down without mercy by an enemy young enough to be their sons can only evoke feelings of revulsion or, at best, a pitiful sadness.

As the Soviet forces made their way into the defensive belt, the battle soon degenerated into small individual conflicts over which Brücker had no control. Toward evening, in order to have any possibility of exercising command, he and his staff moved their command post 15 km west to the high ground at Lichtenwaldau. Despite the move, there was no great increase in command and control. The first that Brücker knew of the Russians having made their way through the defensive belt at various points was when a local forester came rushing past, shouting that the Russians were close behind.

And so they were, but even though some Soviet units had pierced the defenses, the Volkssturm had had an effect. The enemy was advancing slowly and with great caution. The widespread issuance of the panzerfaust in the latter stages of the war (indeed, they were passed out almost like hand grenades to the troops) had changed the tactics of armored warfare. Now that every German soldier potentially had the means to destroy a tank, the hell-for-leather rush into battle was a thing of the past. In every fold of ground, behind every window of a house, under every pile of brush, a panzerfaust-wielding German landser, Volkssturm, or Hitler Jugend might be hiding, waiting to incinerate the crew of a tank. Understandably, the normal aggressive nature of Soviet tank commanders had been considerably dampened.

Eventually, the Russian force emerged from the woods east of Lichtenwaldau and advanced on the airfield near Rosental. Brücker saw his opportunity and launched an attack into their flank with his divisional staff company and a platoon from the Panzerjagdverbände. Taken by surprise, the Russians hastily withdrew back into the forest. Also surprised were the German ground crews still at the airfield, who had been unaware that the enemy was so close. They were even more surprised when Brücker immediately commandeered them and organized them into an infantry battalion under the command of the division's IIa, Hauptmann Buhl.

The earlier Russian advance had obviously been a probing attack, and it was only a matter of time before the enemy launched a serious assault. Around midnight, Brücker withdrew his forces 5 km to take up positions along the Klein Bober (a tributary of the Bober) between Thomaswaldau and Eichberg in order to shield Bunzlau from the northeast. Unfortunately, during the withdrawal, all but thirty of the newly minted infantry from the Luftwaffe ground crews managed to get themselves lost in the dark.

Doubtful that he could hold this line for long—and another twenty-four hours were needed to complete the evacuation of civilians from Bunzlau—Brücker drove back to the city to scout out a possible "fallback" position along the northeast edge of the city. Here he came across a police battalion preparing to withdraw from the city to the west bank of the Bober. Brücker commandeered them and ordered them to remain in place.

In the morning hours of February 10, a Panzerjagerdveband, made up of Luftwaffe ground personnel, arrived at Brücker's headquarters at Gross Krauschen. As with the other Panzerjagdverbände, they were armed only with panzerfausts, but they were well provided with jeeps and were a desperately needed reinforcement since the other tank-hunter units had been decimated in the previous day's fighting.

This was not the only reinforcement that Brücker received that day. Later in the morning, a genuine tank hunting unit arrived: Jagdpanzer Abteilung 1183 commanded by Hauptmann Jaenisch. Brücker and his staff could hardly believe their eyes. An entire company of twenty-two of the new PzJg 38t "Hetzer" tank destroyers. Recently raised and fresh from the training grounds in Bohemia, they had detrained the previous night and made their way to the front, where at their own request they would go into their first action with the insignia of the 6th Infantry division painted on the hulls of their "Hetzers." Jaenisch and his tank-hunters would remain with the division until the end of the war.

Another unexpected reinforcement arrived that morning. Battalion Erpenbach, the division's former Training and Replacement Battalion, had found its way home. Ordered from the Glogau sector to Liegnitz, they had found their way blocked by the rapid Soviet advance, and unable to carry out their orders, they decided on their own initiative to proceed to Bunzlau and rejoin the division.

Throughout the morning of February 10, the Russians had remained quiet, but in the afternoon a strong enemy force moved out of the forest at Lichtenwaldau and advanced towards Brücker's right flank, occupying the village of Thomaswaldau in the early evening. Fearing panzerfausts in the darkness, the Russians halted their advance. Brücker now had the forces and the opportunity. When night fell, Battalion Erpenbach and the "Hetzer" company, commanded by Leutnant Josef Dallmeier, went into the attack. Wild, confused street fighting ensued among the burning houses of Thomaswaldau as Dallmeier's nimble "Hetzers" skidded about the narrow village streets, taking the Russian tanks in flank and rear and setting them alight. Caught totally off guard by the violence of the attack, the Russians were quickly driven from the village, suffering heavy losses including six tanks.

Despite the success, Hauptmann Erpenbach realized that his small group would not be able to hold what was left of Thomaswaldau and withdrew to their jump-off position along the heights west of the village. The attack had made a strong impression on the Russians. Here along the Klein Bober, they were obviously not facing old men armed with obsolete carbines, but hard-bitten, experienced regular troops. The Soviet commanders did not renew their advance later that night nor all the next morning.

The 6th Volksgrenadiers had fulfilled their duty. At 5 a.m. that morning, February 11, the last train carrying civilian refugees departed Bunzlau for the safety of the west.

With the civilian population evacuated and the city empty, there was no longer any reason for Brücker to remain in the exposed and essentially untenable position west of Bunzlau. He pulled his force back to the northeast edge of the city only to discover that the police battalion he had left holding the position had disappeared. Whether they had withdrawn on their own initiative or had been commandeered by another unit, made no difference. They were gone, and with the Russians close upon his heels, Brücker continued his withdrawal west over the Bober, destroying the bridges behind him and abandoning the empty city to the enemy, Bunzlau had not been declared a "Fortress City" by the Führer to be defended to the last man, and Brücker had no intentions of allowing his grenadiers to become entrapped in street fighting and eventually annihilated.

On the west bank of the Bober, Brücker came across—of all things—an entire Luftwaffe Flak regiment. He could have wept with frustration. If only he had known (again, the absence of a communication system). With his forward observers and the Flak regiment's 8.8-cm guns, he could have wreaked havoc upon the advancing enemy the day before.

That evening, Brücker established his command post at a farm 4 km northwest of Bunzlau, where the next morning he was reunited with his other two battalions (Müller and Brunk). For the past two days, they had been holding the northern sector of the Bober line and had beaten back any Soviet attempt to cross the river. Despite the heavy fighting, their casualties had not been too severe. On the night of February 11, they had been relieved by the Latvian 19th SS Division and had proceeded south to rejoin Brücker.

Although in this part of the Silesian front the German defenders had been slowly pushed back and the city of Bunzlau taken, the Soviet forces had not achieved the breakthrough they had sought. However, to the north, the Soviet armies that had broken across the Oder near Glogau and had pushed west now swung south and threatened to outflank the Bober line from the north. To counter this threat, the German defenders found it necessary to pivot their line north of Bunzlau 90 degrees back south to establish an east–west line facing north and giving them now both a northern and eastern front to defend. Brücker's forces were at the juncture of the two fronts with two battalions facing north and two battalions facing east.

Fortunately at this time Brücker began receiving reinforcements. First, an infantry company sent out from Germany by the Home Reserve Army and then a Sturm battalion commanded by a reserve officer, Hauptmann Rommelspacher. A march-battalion appeared as from nowhere, and, whether or not it was actually designated for his division, Brücker did not inquire. Because the battalion was not organized to operate as an independent unit, its personnel were used as replacements to build up the strength of Brücker's other units. Best of all was when six 10.5-cm howitzers were found. Since February 9, Brücker had conducted the defense of the entire sector without a single artillery piece. He wasted no time organizing an artillery Abteilung under the command of Oberleutnant Freiherr von Weichs.

Possessing now five battalions of infantry, howitzers, and a company of "Hetzers," General Brücker felt as though he were in command of a full division again (that is, by 1945 standards)—nearly 3,000 men. He would need every one of them in the coming days, for facing him was an entire Soviet tank corps, determined to eliminate this pocket of stubborn resistance and complete the conquest of Silesia.

For the past few days, the Soviet advances had been characterized by caution. Presumably the absence of their usual mass of artillery had resulted in a reluctance on the part of their forward elements to launch all-out assaults against German positions that had not first been pounded to pieces. All that would now change as the Soviets had been able to bring forward their mobile rocket launchers and were prepared to eliminate Brücker and his "Volksgrenadiers" once and for all.

Over the next three days, February 13–16, battles raged all along the front as the Russians launched attacks against both the northern and eastern faces of the German line. The infantry company from the Home Reserve Army was sent south towards Naumberg (still in German hands) and eventually disappeared in the fighting. Whether overrun by the Russians or commandeered by the

Kampfkommandant of Naumberg, Brücker never learned. On the northern front, the Russians pushed time and again into the village of Siegersdorf, and time and again they were thrown out by the counterattacks of Battalion Erpenbach, during the course of which its erstwhile commander was severely wounded. Leutnant Regel assumed command of what now became Battalion Regel.

During this fighting, Brücker received aid from a most unexpected source. Twelve fourteen-year-old lads from the local militia appeared at his command post in Siegersdorf and requested to be takn into his division. They were provided with uniforms of a sort and were assigned to accompany the various patrols, where their knowledge of the local area rendered the division valuable service. They also rendered valuable service when during one of the battles for Siegersdorf, though only recently acquainted with the panzerfaust, the lads succeeded in destroying several Soviet tanks, including some of the new heavy JS models.[3] In the northern part of the village, a group of these boys defended several houses, fighting off numerous attacks until rescued by one of Battalion Erpenbach's counterattacks. Such was the German youth of 1945. General Brücker thanked the lads for their services, awarded them Iron Crosses, and then sent them home.

On the afternoon of February 16 came word that Generalmajor Kretschmer's 17th Panzer Division had arrived in Gersdorf, a mere 5 km to the southwest. Although Kretschmer possessed at most twenty to twenty-five tanks and a single regiment of panzergrenadiers, if combined with Brücker's forces, there lay the opportunity to end this ceaseless passive defense and wage war the only way the German soldier understood—by attacking.

In a conference with Kretschmer, Brücker proposed that his "Volksgrenadiers" launch a frontal assault north against Sophienwalde while the 17th Panzer Division swing to the west, then north, and take the enemy in the right flank. Kretschmer declined. His panzergrenadier regiment possessed only wheeled—not tracked—transport with cross-country capability. His 3- and 5-ton trucks would never be able to cross the open snow-covered fields. An agreement was reached. Both divisions would attack north against the enemy forces massed between Sophienwalde and Tschirne. Time of attack: dawn.

Just as it grew light the next morning, the attack commenced. On the right, the battalions of Remmelsbacher, Regel, and the Sturm Battalion with Dallmeier's "Heters" in support. On the left, Kretschmer's panzers and panzergrenadiers. German soldiers advanced, attacking as in the old days to the sound of clanking tank treads and commands of "Vorwärts, marsch!"

The Russians attempted a defense, but caught completely off guard—where did these fascist tanks come from?—they were rolled over, rolled through, and rolled back. By noon, Brücker's and Kretschmer's forces had pushed the enemy back to the forest edge and had inflicted heavy losses, but before they could continue their advance, Kretschmer's division was suddenly pulled out of the attack by higher command and sent west to deal with a crisis at another point on the front. Reluctantly, Brücker ordered his men to return to their start lines. Although frustrated, he could be content that Ivan had been rocked back on his heels and that many of his "Volksgrenadiers," who had known only defeat and retreat, had had the experience of advancing and defeating a superior enemy force.

They were given little time to savor their success. Events to the east had brought about a new and even greater threat to the defense of Silesia and would draw Brücker and his "Volksgrenadiers" into what would be their final campaign of the war: the battle for Lauban.

Located on the west bank of the Queis River, the city of Lauban sat astride a high-capacity, east–west rail system, vital to the German defense of Silesia. With it, the Germans were able to quickly shunt divisions back and forth along the front to thwart further Soviet advances into the province. For that reason, the Soviets were as intent on taking Lauban as the Germans were on holding it.

While Brücker and his battalions had been resisting the Soviet advances west of the Queis, by mid-February, Soviet forces east of the river had succeeded in advancing south all the way to the northeastern edge of Lauban, and although the city was still being resolutely defended by the Kampfcommandant, Major Tschuschke, the city was well within the range of Soviet artillery, which had essentially brought all rail traffic to a halt. To complete the capture of the city, the Soviets prepared to renew their efforts west of the Queis, sweep the troublesome 6th Volksgrenadier Division aside, and descend upon the city from the north.

Aware of this threat, Army Corps Friedrich, under which Brücker's forces were now subordinated, directed Brücker to withdraw south 5 km and occupy the 10-km east–west line, Sächsen–Haugsdorf–Hennersdorf–Rachenau. On the night of February 17, Brücker withdrew his units without interference from the enemy. As the men made their way through the forested region north of their new positions, they came across the barriers hastily erected by the local Volkssturm and construction battalions. Although unimpressive, these barriers might slow the enemy pursuit long enough to allow Brücker and his "Volksgrenadiers" time to better prepare the new line of defense.

Before daybreak, they reached the Sächsen–Haugsdorf–Hennersdorf–Rachenau line. Originally, Brücker had been directed to occupy the high ground north of Hennersdorf, but even in the darkness, he clearly recognized the impossibility of such a deployment. Other than Dallmeier's Jagdpanzer company, which was down to only a half dozen "Hetzers," his troops' only defense against Soviet armor was their panzerfausts. That meant tackling the tanks at close quarters, and the barren heights in front of Hennersdorf were devoid of any cover. The men would be simply crushed and wiped out by the Soviet armor. Brücker chose to conceal his troops in the stone buildings along the northern edge of the town, where they would have a far better chance of engaging the enemy tanks at close range.

Throughout the day, Brücker set about deploying his five battalions: right flank—anchored on the Queis at Sächsen Haugsdorf, the recently arrived Sturm battalion; center—Battalion Rommelspacher in Hennersdorf-East, and Battalion Dregger in Hennersdorf-West; and left flank—Battalion Regel at Rachenau.

Held in reserve were Kampfgruppe Müller, the Luftwaffe panzerjagdverband and Jaenisch's Jagdpanzer Abteilung. The divisional command post lay behind the center of the line at Geibsdorf. The artillery (six light howitzers) took up position just east of Geibsdorf on the high ground near Löbenlust.

With his inadequate forces, Brücker realized that his only hope of defending Lauban was to adopt the tactic of "aggressive defense." With the city only 7 km to the rear, any ground lost would have to be immediately retaken by counterattack, and if at any time the opportunity arose to attack the enemy first, Brücker's men were instructed to strike with whatever forces were at hand—and to strike hard.

At dawn on the morning of February 20, three enemy columns of armor and infantry were observed emerging from the forested region to the north and moving south toward Sächen Haugsdorf, Hennersdorf, and Rachenau. Three Soviet tank corps against five German infantry battalions. The Soviet 6th Tank Army against the German 6th Volksgrenadier Division. For Brücker and his small band, the Battle of Lauban had begun.

For the next two weeks, battles raged about Lauban in what can only be described as a chaotic, swirling kaleidoscope of bitter combat and death as German and Russian unceasingly hammered one another. Attack—counterattack; ground yielded—ground regained; villages lost—villages retaken. Brücker likened it to a feverish dream in which minutes seemed as hours and hours as days.

The Soviet attack first struck the center of the line at Hennersdorf. Heavy fighting raged throughout the day as the defenders, hidden in the stone buildings battled against both tanks and infantry. In the end, numbers prevailed, and by early evening Battalion Rommelspacher had been forced out of Hennersdorf-East. Dregger and his battalion somehow still clung to the western half of the town. But instead of pursuing their success, with the fall of darkness the Russians ceased their attacks. Tanks battling panzerfaust-armed troops amid narrow streets were dangerous enough in daylight—at night, suicidal.

The pause in the action was all that Dregger and Rommelspacher needed. They immediately launched a counterattack, the speed and fury of which caught the Russians by surprise, and by dawn Hennersdorf-East was again in German hands.

The next day, Brücker's entire front came under attack. Hennersdorf was again lost, and on the right flank, Soviet tanks broke into Sächsen Haugsdorf, and the Sturm Battalion was pulled back south to Wünschendorf. Over on the left flank, despite heavy pressure, Battalion Regel still held Rachenau.

That night Brücker let loose the "Nahkämpfer" of the Luftwaffe Panzerjagdverband. They had joined the division back on February 10, and in a dozen battles around Bunzlau and Siegersdorf, these former aircraft mechanics and staff clerks had more than proven their worth. Now they went prowling about the darkness with their panzerfausts and hunted down the Soviet tanks that had broken through the lines at Hennersdorf and Sächsen Haugsdorf. Throughout the night, the landscape was illuminated when a T-34 or "Stalin" tank suddenly burst into flame. By morning, almost all the enemy tanks had been destroyed, but so too had the Panzerjagdverband. Their ammunition expended, their ranks decimated, Brücker pulled them out of the battle.

As the Soviet tanks continued to smolder in the early dawn light, Battalion Rommelspacher, supported by Dallmeier's "Hetzers," retook Hennersdorf for a second time.

February 23: the Russians renewed their attacks across the front. On the right flank, the Sturm battalion was pushed out of Wünschendorf and withdrew 1 km west beyond the rail line. The enemy advanced on Lauban but were stopped just short of the city by the stubborn defense of a young oberleutnant (name unknown) and his platoon, sent out from the garrison of Lauban.

The next day, the Russians continued their pressure on the right flank. Fourteen Soviet tanks advanced out of Wünschendorf, determined to break into Lauban from the north. Oberleutnant Dallmeier was detailed off to intercept them. (By now, he was down to his last three "Hetzers.") In a short and sharp fight, seven T-34s were destroyed and the remainder forced to withdraw. Meanwhile, the Sturm battalion attacked from the west and succeeded in regaining the rail line.

On February 25, the Russians shifted their pressure back to the center. Protecting their tanks from the hated panzerfausts with wooden timbers affixed to turret and hull, the Russians took Hennersdorf for a third time. Dallmeier was rushed back from the right flank and with Battalion Rommelspacher recaptured the town, destroying most of the enemy tanks. Wooden tmbers may have reduced the effectiveness of the panzerfausts hollow-charge projectile, but to the "Hetzer's" 7.5-cm gun, they were only so much kindling.

That evening, Brücker received reinforcements for his embattled division—a battalion of infantry commanded by a Hauptmann Schindel and a Fortress battalion sent out from Görlitz. Normally comprised of men from the older age groups, these Fortress battalions were well supplied with both light and heavy machine guns. Though unsuited for offensive operations, Brücker could make good use of them manning strong points along the line, thereby freeing up his other units for counterattacks.

February 26 was a day of crisis. The young oberleutnant from the Lauban garrison, still holding his position north of the city, was badly wounded and without him, the defense collapsed. Ten Soviet tanks pushed into the cemetery at the city's edge, and once again, Dallmeier was sent to rescue the situation.

He quickly turned the cemetery into a tank graveyard, destroying all ten enemy tanks. Unfortunately, his last two "Hetzers" succumbed to mechanical failure. With the exception of panzerfausts, Brücker and his men now found themselves devoid of any anti-tank defenses.

In the center of the German line, Soviet forces again pushed Battalion Rommelspacher out of Hennersdorf, and again, for some inexplicable reason, halted their advance. In the early evening, Brücker received a critical reinforcement—an entire Flak-Sturm regiment commanded by Oberst Lyncker. Quickly the regiment's batteries were deployed across the front. When the Russians finally resumed their advance from Hennersdorf later that night, they were stopped dead in their tracks by the deadly 8.8-cm guns of the former anti-aircraft gunners, but not before two of the guns were destroyed by direct hits and an Abteilung and a battery commander were killed.

For seven days now, Brücker and his men had engaged in this unequal David and Goliath struggle. Stubbornly they had clung to every meter of ground, meeting every attack with counterattack, and if they had given ground, they had given very little and only after extracting a heavy toll from the enemy. The ghosts of the old "Rshew Kämpfer" would have been proud.

More reinforcements arrived. Most welcomed were the Six Tiger and ten PzKwIV tanks commanded by Oberst von Luck. Then came two infantry battalions made up of men previously excused from military duty: a "Stomach Battalion," whose members suffered from digestive ailments and required a special diet, and an "Ear Battalion" comprised of men who were deaf or near deaf. They were immediately thrown into the battle and, despite their physical ailments, performed well even though the WStomach BattalionW had to be pulled out of action after a few days due to total physical exhaustion. But there was no shame in that for von Luck's panzers all had to be pulled out of battle due to total "mechanical exhaustion."

Throughout the battle, Brücker still had to rely on the postal phone network. At one point while he was on the line directing a counterattack, a voice with a heavy Slavic accent broke in and announced, "We know you well, General Brücker—you will all be shot!" Brücker was unfazed; he had never expected any other fate from the enemy.

Although on the left flank and in the center, the 6th Volksgrenadier Division had yielded little ground, the right flank had been forced back to the northwest corner of Lauban. On the last day of February, Soviet forces broke into the city from the north and east. To Brücker, the battle for Lauban appeared lost despite the sacrifices of his men.

True, the Soviets had succeeded in pushing a wedge into the German line and had reached Lauban, but one could also say that they had pushed themselves into a pocket, a pocket that the German 4th Panzer Army intended to crush. Unknown to Brücker, the XXXIX and LVII Panzer Corps had assembled a force of three panzer divisions (8th, 16th, and 17th) and two infantry divisions (Führer Grenadier and Führer Escort), and although none of these divisions were anywhere near full strength in men or tanks, they still represented what to the Wehrmacht at this stage of the war was a considerable strikeforce that would not only eliminate the Lauban pocket but also drive back the Soviet forces along a 45-km front from Penzig to Löwenberg.

On March 2, the Führer Grenadier Division arrived in the sector of the 6th Volksgrenadier Division, and Brücker was informed that in the coming counteroffensive, his division was to join in on the right flank of the Führer Grenadier Division and retake Hennersdorf. The attack was to commence on the night of March 3 at 7 p.m.

The attack went in on schedule. Unfortunately for the Russians, they had realized the predicament in which they had placed themselves and, at the last minute, attempted to withdraw from the Lauban pocket. When the German attack rolled forward, the Russians were caught out in the open, and in the confusion of a night battle, their columns of troop carriers were trapped on the roads and shot to pieces. The Russian casualties were described as 'horrendous'. By 5 March the Soviet 6th Tank Army had been pushed back 10 km along the entire front. Lauban had been saved, and the threat of the Red Army overrunning the remainder of Silesia averted for the moment.

The Battle of Lauban was perhaps the last major victory the Wehrmacht could claim in the war. Propaganda Minister Goebbels wasted no time making the most of it. In a brief visit to the city (cameras rolling of course), he congratulated the defenders and then hurried back to Berlin to broadcast news of the victory to an anxious public.

Generalmajor Brücker could be proud of his "Volksgrenadiers," the older reservists of the Fortress battalion, the men of the "Stomach" and "Ear" units, the former mechanics and clerks of the Luftwaffe Panzerjagdverband, and, especially, the "Hetzers" of Leutnant Dallmeier. With limited and varied resources, they had done all that had been asked of them. Their tenacious defense had to a large extent created the conditions allowing the German counterattack of March 3, and over the two weeks, they had inflicted heavy casualties on the enemy, particularly in armor. In the fields around Sächsen Haugsdorf, Hennersdorf, and Rachenau sat the burned-out hulls of 104 Soviet tanks, the victims of panzerfausts, Flak guns, and "Hetzers."

As war booty, Brücker's men claimed sixteen Soviet 7.62-cm guns, which were used to create the division's Panzerjäger Abteilung; two batteries of 12-cm heavy howitzers; and ten undamaged Soviet tanks. Many of these tanks had been quite literally stolen from under the enemy's noses during the battle when adventuresome grenadiers had crept out at night to the enemy's lines, overpowered the crews sleeping nearby, and driven off with their trophies.

War booty aplenty but very few prisoners. After witnessing the unspeakable atrocities inflicted upon the German civilian population by the Red Army, the German soldier had little interest in taking prisoners—and his officers understood.

With Lauban saved and the Soviet 6th Tank Army mauled, the 50-km front from Löwenberg to Penzig enjoyed a period of relative calm. As the smoke of battle drifted away, Generalmajor Brücker was ordered to assemble his eclectic collection of units and relieve the divisions of the LVII Panzer Corps east of the Queis, who were being sent off to other sectors of the front. Brücker's men packed their gear, and in the spirit of the old soldier's maxim, "Any change is good," they crossed over to the land beyond the Queis to occupy the 20-km stretch of front between the river and Löwenberg.

However, before they settled into their new positions, there remained a matter that required their attention. Hill 251 stood 1½ km northeast of Lauban, on which the enemy still maintained a strongly manned artillery observation post from which the Russians were able to direct their long-range artillery onto the rail center in Lauban. This threat had to be eliminated.

The Sturm battalion, though seriously weakened from the two weeks of desperate fighting at the northwest edge of Lauban, was able to take the hill quickly enough but was driven off it the following night. Battalion Bornemann (mostly comprised of survivors of the Warka) took over the task and in a vicious assault, using panzerfausts and bundled grenades, retook Hill 251. They were not driven off, and the Soviet shelling of Lauban immediately ceased.

Soon after occupying the new position, Brücker began receiving new units—not only to replace losses but also to completely rebuild his division. A newly raised infantry regiment and artillery regiment from Saxony arrived, followed by the remnants of the famous East Prussian 291st "Elk Division," which had been so badly mauled in the Baranow bridgehead back in January. From the hodge-podge collection of units he had been commanding since the beginning of February and the newly arrived reinforcements, Brücker was able to organize a division near full regulation strength (1944–45 levels).

The 18th and 37th Regiments, which had disappeared during the Warka disaster, were recreated from the Saxon regiment and the survivors of the "Elk Division." The original surviving infantry of the 6th Grenadier Division were all placed under the command of Oberstleutnant Müller and became the new 58th Regiment. The former Training and Replacement Battalion (Battalion Rommelspacher) was now the divisional Füsilier Battalion. With the arrival of the Saxon artillery Abteilung and the captured Soviet heavy guns, Brücker had at his disposal a complete regulation-strength artillery regiment. Jaenisch's Jagdpanzer Abteilung 1183 remained with the division, and with a Sturmgeschütz company that Brücker had received in return for the ten captured Soviet tanks he had turned over to Army Group Center, the division was able to restore its Panzerjäger Abteilung. An engineer battalion was created, and the communication troops finally received their full complement of radios.

For a second time, the division had been resurrected. Brücker was promoted to Generalleutnant and awarded the Knight's Cross, and the division got its name back. It would finish the war as it had begun the war: the Rhineland-Westphalian 6th Infantry Division.

And as for the war, it would run its final course, but it would not go quietly. Hundreds of thousands would yet have to die or be maimed in a final orgy of destruction before the beast had slaked its thirst for human misery. In March, the Anglo-American forces crossed the Rhine, the final barrier into Germany. There they encircled the Ruhr region, the industrial heart of the Reich and its 300,000 defenders. Their commander, Feldmarschall Model, did not make the same error of judgement that von Paulus had made at Stalingrad. As befitting a German feldmarschall, he committed suicide rather than surrender.

In the East on April 16, the Red Army launched its long-awaited Berlin offensive as the unleashed armies of Zhukov's 1st Belorussian and Koniev's 1st Ukrainian Fronts raced one another to the capital of Hitler's Reich. By April 25, they had surrounded the city, cutting it off from the rest of the country and trapping the Führer within its ruins. In the last week of April, the eastwards advancing American armies met up with the westwards advancing Soviet armies at Torgau on the Elbe. Very little of the "Thousand-year Reich" still remained in German hands. On April 30, Hitler put a pistol to his head and pulled the trigger. Two days later, the last defenders of Berlin gave up the struggle.

The Führer was dead; his Reich in ruins. There was nothing left for which to fight—there was no country left to defend, and there was no reason left to allow the dying to continue for even one more day. In the early morning hours of May 7 at the Supreme Allied Headquarters in Reims, Generaloberst Alfred Jodl, representing the German High Command, agreed to the total capitulation of Germany. The second Great European War had finally come to an end.

But far away to the southeast in Silesia, the war continued. Here in this forgotten corner of the war along the foothills of the Isergebirge, Brücker and his men knew nothing of the surrender, and so they fought on—"wie das Gesetz es befahl," obedient to the law, loyal to the end.

During the evening of May 7, the division had withdrawn from the Lauban line 10 km south to occupy a 25-km front running from Greiffenberg in the east to Seidenberg in the west. Brücker established his headquarters behind the center of the line in Neustadt at the foot of the Tafelfichte. The division had been able to withdraw without enemy interference, but on the afternoon of May 8, the pursuing Russians launched attacks all along the lines of the new position. Either they too were unaware of the German surrender or were seeking to have a last go at a hated enemy.

Over on the right at Greiffenberg, Oberst Heinlein's 37th Regiment had been forced back while in the center near Marklissa, Russian infantry supported by tanks had broken into Brücker's lines. Yet again, Jaenisch's Jagdpanzer Abteilung came to the rescue. Moving from one crisis point to another, the "Hetzers" and Stugs either shot up the enemy tanks or drove them off. Despite this, heavy infantry fighting continued into the night.

Late in the evening, Brücker received word from Oberst Heinlein that the 37th Regiment had restored the situation at Greiffenberg, but then he received another message: at midnight, the division was to cease hostilities and lay down its arms. Cease hostilities, perhaps? But lay down arms and surrender?

No, Brücker would not deliver his men to such an uncertain fate. The words on the postal phone at Lauban echoed through his mind, "We know you well, General Brücker, you will all be shot!" And even if they were not all rounded up and executed, what then? A slow death in a Siberian Gulag? A quick G'nickschuss would be preferable to that.

Brücker pondered his options. Surrender was out of the question, but to ignore the order and as a division attempt to fight through to the West would place him and his men outside international law. They would be considered partisans and treated accordingly. An agonizing decision lay before him, involving honor, legalities, and what was best for his officers and men. He called his Kommandeure to his headquarters and announced his decision: the division would be disbanded, the regimental flags burned, and the men, now absolved of their oath, were free as individuals to attempt to make their way to the West. He owed them that chance. As for himself, he would resign his command and await his fate alone in his headquarters.

Neustadt, May 8, 1945, 12 a.m.: the door swung open and standing there in the open doorway was not a drunken Ivan brandishing a machine pistol, but his trusted adjutant, Hauptmann Buhl; his personal aide, Unteroffizier Berger; and his driver, Gefreiter Fleig. Unable to bring themselves to leave their general behind, they had returned for him. Brücker protested that at his age, he would be an encumbrance to them. They allowed no argument; the Herr General was coming with them. Both touched and persuaded, he collected his personal gear and stepped out into the street, and there, before him stood a column of vehicles packed with grenadiers—his grenadiers. Generalleutnant Brücker resumed his command of the 6th Infantry Division and prepared to lead his men to the West.

He was still fraught with concerns. They would have to cross over the Isergebirge into Czechoslovakia and then make their way west to Bohemia, where it was rumored that the Americans were. Since May 5, all of Czechoslovakia had been in open revolt and gangs of partisans were roaming the countryside in search of Germans, both civilians and soldiers. They had even erected barricades on the main roads. What if Brücker and his men were forced to shoot their way through? Would that not place them in legal jeopardy?

But hunting down and murdering fleeing German civilians or individual German soldiers seeking to escape was quite different from facing a determined German general at the head of a column of heavily armed grenadiers. Brücker and his men crashed through one barricade after another without once having to fire a shot. The Czech partisans had stepped aside, making no attempt to stop then.

Kilometer after kilometer, past Prague and into Bohemia, the column made its way west. Upon reaching Pisek, they made contact with elements of Patton's 3rd Army and were able to surrender. Brücker was assured by American officers that he and his men were now prisoners of the United States Army. The general could breathe a sigh of relief. He had performed his last duty to his men. He had brought them through and, if not to freedom, then at least to the safety of American captivity.

But then one morning, the Americans were gone, and the Russians arrived. Brücker had no choice but to surrender to the Red Army.[4] Generalleutnant Otto-Hermann Brücker then led the men of the Rhineland-Westphalian 6th Infantry Division into Russian captivity—a brutal captivity that for many of them would last for ten years.

# Epilogue

After six years of war, the Rhineland-Westphalian 6th Infantry Division was no more, its members either scattered to the winds or marching the long trek to Siberia. Those who had availed themselves of the opportunity offered by their general to attempt to escape to the West soon questioned the wisdom of their choice. As they climbed over mountains, swam across rivers, and slithered through forests, they found themselves to be hunted animals—animals with a bounty of 25 Reichsmarks on their heads, dead or alive. Some were captured by Russian soldiers, who had lost some of their lust for German blood now that the war was finally over. Instead of a "G'nickschuss," the captives were promptly relieved of watches, rings, and money, and sent off to join their comrades on the march east. The fate of others, tracked down by Czech partisans, depended on whether the partisans preferred to drag in a dead German for the bounty or march him back to the Soviet authorities under his own power.

Incredibly enough, some of Brücker's men did succeed in evading the Russians and partisans and reached the West where they either surrendered to the Americans or simply cast away their weapons and uniforms, blended in with the thousands of civilian refugees, and returned home. Hauptmann Erpenbach and most of his battalion, Major Pflugfelder and Hauptmann Freiherr von Weichs with part of the artillery regiment, Oberleutnant Eckhard and a few members of the divisional staff, and Leutnant Josef Dollmeier of "Hetzer" fame were among those who avoided Soviet captivity.

But even those who had managed to surrender to the Western Allies could not rest entirely easy. Stalin was demanding that those German soldiers, now in British or American hands, who had fought in the East be immediately turned over to the Red Army. Except for those unfortunate Soviet nationals and those of the Baltic States who had fought alongside the Germans, Stalin's demands were largely ignored. The Western Allies kept their German prisoners, and Stalin kept his.

Although at times rations were sparse, German prisoners in the West were for the most part spared brutal treatment and humiliation. After what many of them had endured during the war, an empty stomach, occasional kick, or insult from an aggravated guard were hardly things about which to complain. Some prisoners were released in months; for others, confinement was longer, but by 1947, the majority of German prisoners had been sent home.

But what was home? Cities and towns reduced to rubble, 3 million dead at the front, 3 million civilian dead, millions of homeless refugees, hunger, humiliation, despair, defeat. Is this what they had fought and died for? Then came the revelations of the horrors of the camps and the crimes of the Nazi regime: Auschwitz, Dachau, Bergen-Belsen, mass deportation, mass extermination—the criminalization of a nation. Is this what they had fought and died for?

There was no answer. So they got on with the daily struggle to survive amid the physical and spiritual ruins of the Reich, and when the times improved, they got on with life—jobs, family, a future. They rebuilt their nation, they rebuilt their lives, and the past was left behind, repressed and forgotten, never to be revived.

Those members of the 56th Infantry Division who had not escaped to the West joined the endless columns of plennis (prisoners) trudging east. Despite the cynical phrase "Auf nach Siberien!" often repeated among the German prisoners, few actually found themselves exiled to that frozen waste. Most were sent off to the hundreds of camps west of the Urals and put to hard labor. Once again, the Eastern War had reverted to a more barbarous age when those of a vanquished tribe who were not slain were marched off by their conquerors into slavery.

The condition of the German prisoners varied with the camp, the day, or the guard. When sent out in the morning to labor, one did not know if one would survive the day. Of the 3.4 million German soldiers in Soviet captivity, 1.5 million died from hunger, disease, overwork, or execution. However, in the main, their deaths were more the result of indifferent neglect rather than intentional cruelty. To the Soviets, with one-third of their nation laid waste and 20 million of their own dead, the life of a single pathetic plenni or for that matter a thousand plennis was of little consequence.

The labor was hard, the climate harsh, the food less than adequate—500 grams of bread per day and a thin barley soup that the captives christened "blauer Heinrich" due to its blueish color. Then there was the "re-education" or rather attempt to brainwash a literally captive audience to the "more just" communist system. Members of the Antifa descended upon the camps and conducted endless lectures, with no great successes. The plennis had seen with their own eyes the "justness" of Bolshevism and wanted no part of it. Besides, starving, exhausted men are hardly receptive to long-winded discussions of political and economic theory. Of course, there were those who, for a bit more bread and a few more grains of barley in their soup, did cooperate with their captors, but they were quickly shunned and ostracized by their comrades and would continue to be so long after their release and return to Germany.

Despite Soviet attempts to sow political discord among the prisoners and drive a wedge between the men and their officers, the captives held solidly together. The "unshakable bond between officer and man," expressed in von Hindenburg's proclamation a decade before, remained firm as the German soldier strove to prove his soldierly superiority even in captivity. Some Soviet camp commanders, particularly those with front-line experience, were wise enough to recognize that a camp with a body of well-disciplined prisoners ran much smoother, and rather than wasting time on indoctrination and creating discord, actually encouraged the prisoners to continue wearing their badges of rank and maintain order and discipline in the well-respected Wehrmacht fashion.

Purgatory, however, was not indended to be forever and so it was with the purgatory of the Soviet labor camps. As early as 1946, nearly a million German prisoners had been released from Soviet captivity, but not for any humanitarian reasons. They had been judged too ill or weak to be of any use as slave laborers. Over the next few years, more prisoners were sent home, sometimes a flood, sometimes a trickle, seemingly without rhyme or reason. Others, mostly officers or prisoners of particular interest, languished on. To provide a façade of legal justification for not repatriating German prisoners of war, the Soviets held mock trials in which the verdict was always "guilty," and the sentence, a uniform twenty-five years hard labor.

But eventually, even those so convicted were released. In 1955, the Chancellor of the new state of West Germany, Konrad Adenauer, travelled to Moscow and secured their freedom. After ten years, the last German soldiers came home from the war.

But what was home? A new Germany. A modern Germany. A democratic Germany. No Führer, no war, no streets filled with rubble and corpses. Instead, the streets bustled with well-dressed and well-fed people—people in a hurry for they had somewhere to go. As the former prisoners or "Spätheimkehrer" shuffled through the noisy and busy streets, they stared around in wide-eyed astonishment as though visitors from another planet. Now and then a passer-by would glance at these pathetic creatures with their ragged uniforms and hollow faces—uniforms of a forgotten past, faces of a forgotten past, a past now suddenly brought back. Embarrassed, the pedestrian would quickly look away and rush by.

Eventually even these "Spätheimkehrer" were able to adjust to this new post-war world, and the Rhineland-Westphalian 6th Infantry Division, which a decade ago had been scattered to the winds by defeat, was now scattered to all corners of Germany by peace as the old "Ostkämpfer" got on with their lives and left the past behind.

In time, though, they found one another again. A chance meeting on the street; a face, though middle-aged, still vaguely familiar; a flash of recognition and the sudden rush of memories. Then an afternoon in a Bierkeller—the office could wait. Then on into the evening, Frau und Kinder could wait. As with veterans of any war, of any nation, there does come a time when enough years have passed to dull the sharp edge of the horror and the pain so that the past, rather than repressed, can be revisited.

And so it was with the Rhinelanders and Westphalians. Contacts increased. Comrades thought long dead were discovered to be alive. Informal get-togethers grew larger and occurred more often until the decision was made to formally establish the regimental Kameradschaftbünde or veteran organizations and hold yearly reunions in the division's old garrison towns throughout the former Wehrkreis VI.

Throughout the '60s and '70s and on into the '80s, the veterans of the 18th, 37th, and 58th Regiments held their reunions, often meeting in the same barracks where they had first put on the "graue Rock" and marched off to war. The beer flowed freely as did the memories. Memories of fallen comrades: Schnitger, Rindfleisch, Küster, Hellweg. Memories of the winter, the victories and retreats of Rzhev, Bobruisk, the Warka, and Lauban. They looked back on all they had endured, on all they had achieved, and shook their greying heads in disbelief—Mein gott, could they have really been that young and reckless of life?

There were also memories of what to them represented "lighter" moments—the impromptu trench raids and the racing back to their trenches dragging along whatever war trophies they had grabbed. Now they could laugh at the insane risks they had taken. Or how on New Year's Day they had always sent Ivan diving for cover with their customary greetings of ordnance. Then there was the time at Lauban when they had stolen Ivan's tanks right out from under his nose.

The high point of these regimental reunions was the occasion when the Kommandeur was able to attend. The shout would go up, "Der Alte ist da!" and as in the old days, the "Vater" of the regiment would review his troops, who stood as upright and stiff as their aging limbs allowed. He would slowly pass them by, one by one, eye to eye, and the bond between officer and man was renewed yet again.

Also renewed at the reunions were the bonds with their fallen comrades, who lay beneath the Birkenkreuzen in graves from the Loire to the Volga. The list of the gefallenen was read out. The list was long. The regiments each counted over 3,000 of their ranks as dead or missing, and now decades after the war the surviving Landsers knew that their missing comrades were never coming home. Their bones lay lost and moldering somewhere in the East. Nor did this reflect the total cost of duty. For the many and varied units that had fought in the ranks of the 6th Infantry Division during the last desperate battles in Silesia, there would be no accounting. Their names and fate would remain forever unknown.

The Kommandeure, the aging veterans, and their fallen comrades were not the only ones present at the reunions. The new German army had revived the custom of "tradition-bearer" with units of the Bundeswehr being entrusted with maintaining the memory of certain regiments of the former Wehrmacht. (In the case of the 18th Regiment, the tradition-bearer was the 213th, later the 214th Panzer Battalion.) The tradition-bearers often attended the reunions and although respectful of these war-hardened veterans surrounding them, there remained a certain uneasiness with the relationship. The old veterans were often asked by the young soldiers, "Why did you continue fighting so long for the criminal Nazi regime? Why didn't you simply desert?"

Though perplexed by such questions, the old warriors tried their best to explain—but in vain. They were speaking across a generational and cultural divide. How could an old "Ostkämpfer" possibly explain a Rzhev, a Kursk, a Warka, or a Silesia to a younger generation—a generation raised in a prosperous, free, and democratic Germany? A generation that had never known war or the iron bonds of comradeship forged in battle? The answers given were as incomprehensible to the young recruits as the questions had been to the old warriors. As German soldiers, they had fulfilled their duty to Volk and Vaterland wie das Gesetz es befahl—obedient to the law. Did that not say it all?

To them, perhaps, but the world would never forgive them. To the world, they were Nazis all and thuggish murderers. Even their own children looked upon them as criminals or, at best, a primitive brutish species, thankfully, on the verge of extinction. With the next generation of Germans, the generational gulf grew wider, the condemnation stronger, the alienation greater. They had become "die verlassenen Söhne" ("Germany's forsaken sons"), who, having been condemned by their parents' generation to fight the Führer's wars, were now condemned by their children's generation for having fought the Führer's wars.

There was nothing more they could say. Their words of duty, sacrifice, obedience, loyalty, fell upon a society whose ears had long since been deafened by the narcissism of prosperity and the illusion of security. So they fell silent and over the years, one by one, joined their fallen comrades, leaving their story to be told by a stranger.

Accusations—explanations; condemnations—justifications still fly back and forth across their graves as accusers and defenders attempt to score their points. Let the debate rage for it touches them no longer. They alone knew who they were, and of that there is no debate. They were, simply put: "Soldaten bis zum letzten Tag." Soldiers to the last day.

# Endnotes

## Chapter 3

1. Freiherr von Biegeleben now lies buried in the German War Cemetery at La Cambe, France.

## Chapter 4

1. Generalleutnant von Hartmann was killed January 24, 1943 while fighting on the front line during the final days of the 6th Army at Stalingrad. Edler von Daniels went on to command the 376th Division. At Stalingrad, he surrendered the remnants of his division to Soviet forces on January 27, 1943. In captivity, he joined the anti-fascist organization the "National Committee for a Free Germany." Branded a traitor by Hitler, he was removed from the Wehrmacht's Officer Role on December 23, 1944.
2. Political youth organization of the Soviet Union.
3. Fortifications along the pre-1939 Soviet border; i.e. before the annexation of Polish territory and the Baltic countries.
4. Soviet border prior to 1939.
5. Soviet secret police.
6. In December 1941, Georg Freiherr von Böselager and his cavalry squadron were detached from the 6th Infantry Division to form Kavallerieregiment Mitte. Promoted to major and then oberstleutnant, he went on to command the 3rd Cavalry Brigade. Sharply critical of Hitler and the Nazis, he joined the circle of officers seeking to assassinate the Führer. Georg von Böselager was killed in action on August 27, 1944 at Lomza, Poland.

## Chapter 5

1. Löhdorf, *Infanterie Regiment 58*, p. 45.

## Chapter 6

1. "Ratsch-bum": German soldier slang for the Soviet 76-mm gun.
2. Three weeks later, Graf von Kageneck's younger brother, sixty-seven-victory fighter ace Erbo von Kageneck, died of wounds suffered in aerial combat over North Africa.

## Chapter 7

1. Mikhalev, *Strategicheskie resheniia*, cited in Gerasimova, *The Rzhev Slaughterhouse*, p. 157.

## Chapter 8

1. The Ballenladung, sometimes called geballteladung, was a deadly creation of German troops consisting of the explosive heads of six stick grenades, with their shafts removed, bound about a central stick grenade with its shaft remaining.
2. Rhein, *Das Infanterie/Grenadier Regiment 18*, p. 167.
3. Havel, *Feldpost, The War Letters of Friedrich Reiner Niemann*, p. 43.
4. *Ibid.*, p. 44.
5. Reichsarbeitsdienst. After completion of high school, German youths were required to perform six months of labor service. As the war progressed, labor units of the RAD were often posted near the front and at times thrown into combat.
6. A PzKw III tank chassis with an armored superstructure but no revolving turret. Originally armed with a short-barreled 7.5-cm gun and designed for infantry support, it was later up-gunned to a high-velocity 7.5-cm gun and became one of the Wehrmacht's most effective tank destroyers.
7. Regiment 18 retained its 1st and 2nd Battalions while Regiments 37 and 58 retained their 1st and 3rd Battalions.

## Chapter 9

1. Gerasimova, *The Rzhev Slaughterhouse*, p. 121.
2. Glantz, *Zhukov's Greatest Defeat*, p. 308, p. 379.

## Chapter 10

1. Oberst Heinz Furbach was promoted to generalmajor and took over Command of the Saxon 331st Infantry Division on March 1, 1944.
2. Rhein, *Das Infanterie/Grenadier Regiment 18*, p. 240.
3. Gerasimova, *The Rzhev Slaughterhouse*, p. 146.

## Chapter 12

1. Carell, *Der Russlandkrieg*, p. 338.
2. Jukes, *Kursk, The Clash of Armour*, p. 78.
3. *Ibid.*, pp. 49-54.

4. Two days later, Spieker was seriously injured when he stepped on a landmine. While being transported back to Germany by hospital train, the train was attacked by Soviet aircraft, and Spieker was wounded twice more, bringing his wound total to twelve.

## Chapter 13

1. Jukes, *Kursk, The Clash of Armour*, p. 110.

## Chapter 14

1. Havel, *Feldpost, the War Letters of Friedrich Reiner Niemann*, p. 108.
2. Hinze, *Der Zusammenbruch der Heeresgruppe Mitte im Osten 1944*, p. 32, 270.
3. Rhein, *Das Infanterie/Grenadier Regiment 18*, p. 318.
4. Hinze, *Ost-Front 1944*, pp. 418-419.
5. Hinze, *Der Zusammenbruch der Heeresgruppe Mitte im Osten 1944*, pp. 274-275.

## Chapter 15

1. Korpsabteilung E consisted of the weakened Hessian 251st Grenadier Division plus the remnants of several other divisions destroyed during the Soviet summer offensive.
2. Stoffels, *Endkampf im Warka-Brückenkopf*, p. 329.
3. Havel, *Feldpost*, p. 204.
4. *Ibid.*, pp. 208-209.
5. Hinze, *Letztes Aufgebot*, p. 84.
6. *Ibid.*, p. 93.
7. Brücker, *Die Division ab Juli 1944 bis Kriegsende*, p. 252.
8. Flex, *Der Wanderer zwischen beiden Welten*, p. 50.

## Chapter 16

1. Brücker and his men cared little for the designation "Volksgrenadier Division."
2. The Jagdpanzer 38(t) "Hetzer" (Baiter) was a highly effective tank destroyer based on the Czech Model 38(t) tank chassis.
3. The JS (Josef Stalin) heavy tank was the Soviet answer to the German Tiger tank. It weighed 50 tons and mounted a 12.2-cm gun.
4. In the last days of the war, some American units had advanced beyond the previously agreed upon demarcation line between the occupation zones of the Western Allies and the Soviet Union. When the Americans withdrew back to the West, those German soldiers who had surrendered to them were left behind to become prisoners of the Red Army. At Pisek, this amounted to some 60,000 members of the Wehrmacht.

APPENDIX I

# Men of the Division

## Generalleutnant Otto Hermann Brücker

Despite their threats, the Soviets did not shoot Generalleutnant Brücker. They did, however, convict him of various "crimes" and sentence him to the standard twenty-five years hard labor, a sentence Brücker regarded as recognition of his division's achievements much like the Ritterkreuz that hung about his collar. He knew that his true crime had been to frustrate the Soviets at every turn during the Silesian battles. Released from Soviet captivity in 1955, he had no desire to return to his home in Soviet-occupied Brandenburg. Like many of his men before him back in May '45, he made his way out to the freedom of the West.

Upon his return, he was asked by General Grossmann to aid in the writing of the history of the 6th Infantry Division, and although still suffering the effects of ten years of Soviet captivity, he readily agreed—he owed his men that much for in his eyes, as he so succinctly stated, "Keine Division war besser!" ("No division was better!") He died in Weinheim (Baden) West Germany in 1964 at the age of sixty-five.

## General der Infanterie Horst Grossmann

After leaving the 6th Infantry Division in May 1944, Grossmann was promoted to General der Infanterie and commanded the VI Army Corps, with which he fought the last desperate battles in his beloved homeland of East Prussia. At the end of the war, he was able to surrender to the Western Allies, who released him in 1947. Unable to return to his native East Prussia, which no longer existed, he settled in West Germany. Although he had commanded numerous units and divisions in the course of the war, he never forgot his Rhinelanders and Westphalians. In 1958, as a tribute to courage, loyalty, and sacrifices of the men he had led, he published the history of this remarkable division, *Die Geschichte der Rheinisch-Westfälischen 6. Infanterie Division.* General der Infanterie Horst Grossmann died at the age of eighty in 1972 in Russelsheim (Hesse), West Germany.

## Oberst Carl "Corle" Becker

The "father" of Regiment 18 from December 1940 until January 1943, Becker was promoted to generalmajor and took over command of the 2nd Luftwaffe Field Division. Promoted to generalleutnant, he commanded the 253rd infantry Division until war's end, when he became a prisoner of the Soviets. The Soviets had not forgotten "Corle" Becker and his 18th Regiment's tenacious defense at Rzhev. As with Generalleutnant Brücker, Becker was convicted of "crimes" and sentenced to twenty-five years imprisonment. Released from captivity on October 12, 1955, he settled in Heidelberg, where he died in 1966, aged seventy-one. In 1987, the Bundeswehr named a barracks of the 213th Panzer Battalion in honor of Generalleutnant "Corle" Becker.

## Oberst Joachim von Tresckow

Kommandeur of Regiment 58, von Tresckow had first come to the regiment in 1938 as commander of the 3rd Battalion, garrisoned in Bückeburg. In June 1942, he was promoted to generalmajor and given command of the 328th Infantry Division. After the division was dissolved in November '43, von Tresckow was promoted to generalleutnant and transferred to the West, where he assumed command of the 18th Luftwaffe Field Division, based in Dunkirk. During the Normandy Campaign in 1944, von Tresckow's division was entrapped in the Mons Pocket by British forces. On September 3, von Tresckow and 300 men were able to fight their way free and reach German lines 260 km away. For this action, von Tresckow was awarded the Knight's Cross. A prisoner of war of the Western Allies at the end of the war, he was released from captivity in 1947. Impossible for him to return to his home in Danzig, he settled in Bückeburg, the old garrison town of the 3rd Battalion, Regiment 58, where he died on November 3, 1958 at the age of sixty-four.

## Oberarzt Dr. Heinrich Haape

After the first winter in Russia, Dr. Haape was transferred to Stuttgart. At the end of the war, he surrendered to the Free French Forces. After his release, he returned to Stuttgart and wrote an account of his experiences in Russia, which oddly enough was first published in Great Britain under the title *Moscow Tramstop*. A German edition did not appear until 1980. In 1952, Haape immigrated to South Africa. He died in 1976. After the war, he never again practiced medicine.

## Hauptmann Ernst-Martin Rhein

After he was severely wounded at Lasarewo on August 25, 1942 during the Summer Battle of Rzhev, Rhein did not return to Regiment 18. Late in 1944, he was assigned to the staff of the 320th Volksgrenadier Division, stationed near Cracow, where, by his account, he first learned of the activities in a place called Auschwitz. Deeply shaken, he questioned the idea of obedience to a criminal regime. When the war ended, he was in Czechoslovakia and, like his former comrades of the 6th Infantry Division, was abandoned by the Americans to the Soviets. After four years of captivity in a work camp near Tiflis, Rhein was released in 1949, settled in West Germany, and got on with his life, leaving the war and the past behind.

Not until 1979, after his retirement from professional life, did Ernst-Martin Rhein return to Regiment 18. He became active in the regiment's Traditionsgemeinschaft and became its chairman in 1981. In the 1990s, Rhein and his old war comrade Max Hunzinger were instrumental in establishing relations with Russian veterans and the city of Rzhev. These two old "Rshewkämpfer" worked tirelessly to promote peace and reconciliation, making numerous trips to Rzhev. As a result of their efforts, in 2002, the Rzhev "Friedenspark," containing a German and Russian war cemetery located side by side, was dedicated. Ernst-Martin Rhein died on April 20, 2016 at the age of ninety-nine.

## Oberleutnant Johannes Rompzick

Knight's Cross holder and regimental adjutant of Regiment 18, Johannes Rompzick did not perish in the "Cauldron of Bobruisk" as feared. He was taken prisoner by the Russians and remained in captivity for five years under the harshest of conditions. Released in 1949, he was unable to return to his native Danzig and settled instead in Hanover, where, as with many of his comrades, he quietly faded into the obscurity of civilian life, becoming the branch manager of a forwarding company. In 1952, Rompzich along with another former adjutant of Regiment 18, Jörg von Kalckreuth organized the first regimental reunion and established the Kameradschaftsbund of the 18th Regiment. Rompzick never fully recovered from the years of Soviet imprisonment and died at the age of fifty in 1970.

## Obergefreiter Friedrich Reiner Niemann

A member of Regiment 58, Niemann first arrived at the front at Rzhev in May 1942. Wounded twice in the course of the war and awarded the Iron Cross 1st and 2nd Division at Bobruisk. He even managed to survive the Soviet onslaught of January 14, 1945, but somewhere along the line of retreat out of the Warka, Niemann went missing. He was never classified as either killed or missing—simply "disappeared." Despite decades-long efforts, his family was unable to find out what had happened to him—a fate shared by the families of the 1.2 million German sons, who "disappeared in the East."

In 1997, two mass graves (Kameradengräber) containing the remains of 157 German soldiers were discovered in a woods near Grabowa. Only thirty-seven of the remains were identified. Friedrich Reiner Niemann was one of them. He now lies buried in the German Military Cemetery in Pulawy, Poland.

APPENDIX II

# Das Ritterkreuz

Knight's Cross Recipients Rhineland-Westphalian 6th Infantry Division

Oberst Carl Becker
Generalleutnant Freiherr von Biegeleben
Oberleutnant Georg Freiherr von Böselager
Oberst Johannes Boje
Generalleutnant Otto-Hermann Brücker
Leutnant Josef Dallmeier
Oberlaeutnant Hans-Werner Deppe
Oberst Heinz Furbach
Generalleutnant Horst Grossmann
Oberstleutnant Hermann Hennicke
Oberst Stefan Höke
Leutnant Günther Kreckow
Oberleutnant Ferdinand Küster
Unteroffizier Hans-Werner Moeller
Oberleutnant Ernst-Martin Rhein
Oberleutnant Johannes Rompzick
Gefreiter Fredinand Roos
Obergefreiter Franz Shmitzer
Oberfeldwebel Albrecht Schnitger

APPENDIX III

# Das Birkenkreuz

Gravesites of the Rhineland-Westphalian 6th Infantry Division

In accordance with German military practice, those killed in action were not returned to the homeland for burial either during the war or after. They were buried close to where they fell among those comrades who had fallen alongside them, in a sense, eternally claiming those small mounds of earth as German soil. As a result, the graves of the Rhinelanders and Westphalians are scattered across the continent from the Loire Valley to the Volga. Here is a partial list of the gravesites of the 6th Infantry Division.

France

Beauvois
Bourdon
Le Cambe
Marigny
Mont de Huisnes
Orglandes
Solers
St. André de l'Eure

Russia

Abakumowo
Galachowo
Iwanowitschi
Kalibowka
Kanat
Katkowo (forest)
Katkowo (town)
Komsky-Most
Konotop

Kromy
Kutyrki
Malachowa
Michalewo
Okop
Paritschi
Polunino
Rudnja
Rzhev
Rzhev North
Rzhev S/W
Rzhev-Stariza
Schoprowo
Shlobin
Spiritschina
Ssytschewka
Step
Stupino
Subzow
Wassiljewka

Poland

Lezenice
Zielenic

Silesia

Alt Lauban
Hennersdorf
Kloster Naumburg
Siegersdorf
Stoltenberg

In the 1990s, after the collapse of communism in Russia and Eastern Europe, the German government sought to consolidate the widely scattered German graves into more centralized locations to facilitate their care and visitation by German families. Through a lengthy process of treaty negotiations with former enemies, Germany was able to establish military cemeteries for its war dead throughout Eastern Europe and the former Soviet Union. Their care and upkeep are the responsibility of the German organization Volksbund Deutsche Kriegsgräberfürsorge e.V. Over the past two decades, the remains of German soldiers have been exhumed from their scattered and lonely graves and moved to these centralized military cemeteries. Even so, they still lie in foreign lands, claiming forever that bit of earth as German soil.

# Bibliography

## German-language Sources


Brücker, O., *Die Division ab Juli 1944 bis Kriegsende* in Grossmann, H., *Die Geschichte der Rheinisch-Westfälischen 6 .Infanterie Division* (Bad Nauheim: Podzun Verlag, 1958)

Carell, P., *Unternehmen Barbarossa* (Frankfurt am Main, Berlin: Verlag Ullstein GmbH., 1963)

*Der Kampf um Ostpreussen* (München: Gräfe und Unzer Verlag, 1960)

*Die 19. Panzer Division 1939–1945* (Eggolsheim: Dörfler im Nebel Verlag GmbH., 2003)

Fellgiebel, W., *Die Träger des Ritterkreuzes des Eisernen Kreuzes* 1939–1945 (Frieberg: Podzun-Pallas, 1986–2000)

Flex, W., *Der Wanderer zwischen beiden Welten* (Paderborn: Antigonos Verlag)

Grossmann, H., *Die Geschichte der Rheinisch-Westfälischen 6. Infanterie Division* (Bad Nauheim: Podzun Verlag, 1958)

Guderian, H., *Erinnerungen eines Soldaten* (Heidelburg: K. Vowinckel, 1951)

Haape, H., *Endstation Moskau 1941–42 Tagebuch eines Frontarztes* (Stuttgart: Motorbuch Verlag, 1980)

Hinze, R., *Der Zusammenbruch der Heeresgruppe Mitte im Osten* (Stuttgart: Motorbuch Verlag, 1980)

Hoth, H., *Panzer-Operationen* (Heidelberg: Scharnhorst Buchkameradschaft, 1956)

*Letztes Aufgebot zur Verteidigung des Reichsgebietes* (Verlag Rolf Hinze, 1995)

Löhdorf, H., *Infanterie Regiment 58* (privately published, 1976)

*Ost-Front 1944* (Stuttgart: Motorbuch Verlag, 2004)

*Plenni dawai, Nachkriegsdrama hinter Stacheldraht* (Verlag K.W.Schütz KG Preussisch Oldendorf, 1974)

Rhein, E., *Das Infanterie/Grenadier Regiment 18* (Bergisch-Gladbach: Eigenverlag Ernst-Martin Rhein, 1993)

*Rshew, Eckpfeiler der Ostfront* (Bad Nauheim: Podzun Verlag, 1962)

Salisbury, H., *Der Unvergessene Krieg 1941 bis 1945* (Wien, München, Zürich, New York: Verlag Fritz Molden, 1981, translated from the English by Johannes Eidlitz)

Stoffels, W., *Endkampf im Warka-Brückenkopf in Rhein, E., Das Infanterie/Grenadier Regiment 18* (Bergisch-Gladbach: Eigenverlag Ernst-Martin Rhein, 1993)

von Ahlfen, H., *Der Kampf um Schlesien 1945* (Stuttgart: Motorbuch Verlag, 1976)

von Hindenburg, P., *Aus Meinem Leben* (Leipzig: S. Hirzel Verlag, 1934)

von Mellenthin, F. W., *Panzerschlachten* (Heidelberg: K. Vowinckel Verlag, 1963)

## Other German-language Sources

Deutsche Dienststelle
Kriegstagebuch Infanterie Regiment 18
Kriegstagebuch Infanterie Regiment 58
Volksbund Deutsche Kriegsgräberfürsorge e.V.

## English-language Sources

Bessel, R., *Germany 1945 From War to Peace* (Simon & Schuster U.K. Ltd., 2009)

Bishop, C., *Order of Battle German Infantry in WWII* (London: Amber Books Ltd., 2008)

Davies, W. J. K., *German Army Handbook 1939–1945* (New York: Arco Publishing Com. Inc., 1973)

Ellis, C., *The German Army 1933–45* (Ian Allen Publishing, 1993)

Fuller, J. F. C., *A Military History of the Western World*, vol. 3 (Funk & Wagnalls Co., Inc., 1956)

Gerasimova, S., *The Rzhev Slaughterhouse, The Red Army's Forgotten 15-month Campaign against Army Group Center 1942–43* (West Midlands, England: Helion & Company Limited, 2013, translated and edited by Stuart Britton)

Glantz, D., *Zhukov's Greatest Defeat, The Red Army's Epic Disaster in Operation Mars 1942* (University Press of Kansas, 1999)

Haskew, M., *The Wehrmacht 1935–1945, The Essential Facts and Figures for Hitler's Germany* (London: Amber Books, 2011)

Havel, D., *Feldpost, The War Letters of Friedrich Reiner Niemann* (United Kingdom: Fonthill Media LLC, 2016)

Healy, M., *Zitadelle, The German Offensive against the Kursk Salient 4–17 July 1943* (Spellmount: The History Press Ltd. UK, 2008, 2010)

Jukes, G., *Kursk, The Clash of Armour* (New York: Ballantine Books, 1968)

Kirchubel, R., *Atlas of the Eastern Front 1941–45* (Oxford, UK: Osprey Publishing, 2016)

Liddell-Hart, B. H., *The German Generals Talk*, (New York, Quill, 1979)

Powaski, R., *Lightning War, Blitzkrieg in the West 1940* (New Jersey, Castle Books, 2006)